AF545169

The Right to Counsel and Privilege against Self-Incrimination

Other Books in America's Freedoms

Donald Grier Stephenson, Jr., Series Editor

Cruel and Unusual Punishment, Joseph A. Melusky and Keith A. Pesto

Equal Protection, Francis Graham Lee

Freedom of Speech, Ken I. Kersch

Freedom of the Press, Nancy Cornwell

Property Rights, Polly J. Price

Religious Freedom, Melvin I. Urofsky

The Right to Bear Arms, Robert J. Spitzer

The Right to Privacy, Richard A. Glenn

The Right to Vote, Donald Grier Stephenson, Jr.

The Right to Counsel and Privilege against Self-Incrimination

Rights and Liberties under the Law

John B. Taylor

ABC CLIO

Santa Barbara, California • Denver, Colorado • Oxford, England

Library of Congress Cataloging-in-Publication Data
Taylor, John B., 1942-
The right to counsel and privilege against self-incrimination : rights and liberties under the law / John B. Taylor.
p. cm. — (America's freedoms)
Includes bibliographical references and index.
ISBN 1-57607-618-0 (hardback : alk. paper) ISBN 1-57607-619-9 (e-book)
1. Right to counsel—United States. 2. Self-incrimination—United States. I. Title. II. Series.

KF9646.T39 2004
345.73'056—dc22

2004019641

07 06 05 04 10 9 8 7 6 5 4 3 2 1

This book is also available on the World Wide Web as an e-book. Visit abc-clio.com for details.

ABC-CLIO, Inc.
130 Cremona Drive, P.O. Box 1911
Santa Barbara, California 93116–1911

This book is printed on acid-free paper.
Manufactured in the United States of America

To Young, Glenn, and Russell

Contents

Series Foreword

America's Freedoms promises a series of books that address the origin, development, meaning, and future of the nation's fundamental liberties, as well as the individuals, circumstances, and events that have shaped them. These freedoms are chiefly enshrined explicitly or implicitly in the Bill of Rights and other amendments to the Constitution of the United States and have much to do with the quality of life Americans enjoy. Without them, America would be a far different place in which to live. Oddly enough, however, the Constitution was drafted and signed in Philadelphia in 1787 without a bill of rights. That was an afterthought, emerging only after a debate among the foremost political minds of the day.

At the time, Thomas Jefferson was in France on a diplomatic mission. Upon receiving a copy of the proposed Constitution from his friend James Madison, who had helped write the document, Jefferson let him know as fast as the slow sailing-ship mails of the day allowed that the new plan of government suffered one major defect—it lacked a bill of rights. This, Jefferson argued, "is what the people are entitled to against every government on earth." Madison should not have been surprised at Jefferson's reaction. The Declaration of Independence of 1776 had largely been Jefferson's handiwork, including its core statement of principle:

> We hold these truths to be self-evident, that all men are created equal, that they are endowed by their Creator with certain unalienable Rights, that among these are Life, Liberty, and the pursuit of Happiness. That to secure these rights, Governments are instituted among Men, deriving their just powers from the consent of the governed.

Jefferson rejected the conclusion of many of the framers that the Constitution's design—a system of both separation of powers among the legislative, executive, and judicial branches, and a federal division of powers between national and state governments—would safeguard liberty. Even when combined with elections, he believed strongly that such structural checks would fall short.

Jefferson and other critics of the proposed Constitution ultimately had their way. In one of the first items of business in the First Congress in 1789, Madison, as a member of the House of Representatives from Virginia, introduced amendments to protect liberty. Ten were ratified by 1791 and have become known as the Bill of Rights.

America's Bill of Rights reflects the founding generation's understanding of the necessary link between personal freedom and representative government, as well as their experience with threats to liberty. The First Amendment protects expression—in speech, press, assembly, petition, and religion—and guards against a union of church and state. The Second Amendment secures liberty against national tyranny by affirming the self-defense of the states. Members of state-authorized local militia—citizens primarily, soldiers occasionally—retained a right to bear arms. The ban in the Third Amendment on forcibly quartering troops in houses reflects the emphasis the framers placed on the integrity and sanctity of the home.

Other provisions in the Fourth, Fifth, Sixth, Seventh, and Eighth amendments safeguard freedom by setting forth standards that government must follow in administering the law, especially regarding persons accused of crimes. The framers knew firsthand the dangers that government-as-prosecutor could pose to liberty. Even today, authoritarian regimes in other lands routinely use the tools of law enforcement—arrests, searches, detentions, as well as trials—to squelch peaceful political opposition. Limits in the Bill of Rights on crime-fighting powers thus help maintain democracy by demanding a high level of legal scrutiny of the government's practices.

In addition, one clause in the Fifth Amendment forbids the taking of private property for public use without paying the owner just compensation and thereby limits the power of eminent domain, the authority to seize a person's property. Along with taxation and conscription, eminent domain is one of the most awesome powers any government can possess.

The Ninth Amendment makes sure that the listing of some rights does not imply that others necessarily have been abandoned. If the Ninth Amendment offered reassurances to the people, the Tenth Amendment was designed to reassure the states that they or the people retained those powers not delegated to the national government. Today, the Tenth Amendment is a reminder of the integral role states play in the federal plan of union that the Constitution ordained.

Despite this legacy of freedom, however, we Americans today sometimes wonder about the origin, development, meaning, and future of our liberties. This concern is entirely understandable, because liberty is central to the idea of what it means *to be American.* In this way, the United States stands apart from virtually every other nation on earth. Other countries typically define their national identities through a common ethnicity, origin, ancestral bond, religion, or history. But none of these accounts for the American identity. In terms of ethnicity, ancestry, and religion, the United States is the most diverse place on earth. From the beginning, America has been a land of immigrants. Neither is there a single historical experience to which all current citizens can directly relate: someone who arrived a decade ago from, say, Southeast Asia and was naturalized as a citizen only last year is just as much an American as someone whose forebears served in General George Washington's army at Valley Forge during the American War of Independence (1776–1783). In religious as in political affairs, the United States has been a beacon to those suffering oppression abroad: "the last, best hope of earth," Abraham Lincoln said. So, the American identity is ideological. It consists of faith in the value and importance of liberty for each individual.

Nonetheless, a longstanding consensus among Americans on the *principle* that individual liberty is essential, highly prized, and widely shared hardly assures agreement about liberty *in practice.* This is because the concept of liberty, as it has developed in the United States, has several dimensions.

First, there is an unavoidable tension between liberty and restraint. Liberty means freedom: we say that a person has a "right" to do this or that. But that *right* is meaningless unless there is a corresponding *duty* on the part of others (such as police officers and elected officials) not to interfere. Thus, protection of the liberty of one person necessarily involves restraints imposed on someone else. This is why we speak of a *civil* right or a *civil* liberty: it is a claim on the behavior of another that is enforceable through the legal process. Moreover, some degree of order (restrictions on the behavior of all) is necessary if everyone's liberties are to be protected. Just as too much order crushes freedom, too little invites social chaos that also threatens freedom. Determining the proper balance between freedom and order, however, is more easily sought than found. "To make a government requires no great prudence," declared English statesman and political philosopher Edmund Burke in 1790. "Settle the seat of power; teach obedience; and the work is done. To give freedom is still more easy. It is not necessary to guide; it only requires to let go the rein. But to form a *free government;*

that is, to temper together these opposite elements of liberty and restraint in one consistent work, requires much thought; deep reflection; a sagacious, powerful, and combining mind."

Second, the Constitution does not define the freedoms that it protects. Chief Justice John Marshall once acknowledged that the Constitution was a document "of enumeration, and not of definition." There are, for example, lists of the powers of Congress in Article I, or the rights of individuals in the Bill of Rights, but those powers and limitations are not explained. What is the "freedom of speech" that the First Amendment guarantees? What are "unreasonable searches and seizures" that are proscribed by the Fourth Amendment? What is the "due process of law" secured by both the Fifth and Fourteenth Amendments? Reasonable people, all of whom favor individual liberty, can arrive at very different answers to these questions.

A third dimension—breadth—is closely related to the second. How widely shared is a particular freedom? Consider voting, for example. One could write a political history of the United States by cataloging the efforts to extend the vote or franchise to groups such as women and nonwhites that had been previously excluded. Or consider the First Amendment's freedom of speech. Does it include the expression of *all* points of view or merely *some?* Does the same amendment's protection of the "free exercise of religion" include all faiths, even obscure ones that may seem weird or even irritating? At different times questions like these have yielded different answers.

Similarly, the historical record contains notorious lapses. Despite all the safeguards that are supposed to shore up freedom's foundations, constitutional protections have sometimes been worth the least when they have been desperately needed. In our history the most frequent and often the most serious threats to freedom have come not from people intent on throwing the Bill of Rights away outright but from well-meaning people who find the

Bill of Rights a temporary bother, standing in the way of some objective they want to reach.

There is also a question that dates to the very beginning of American government under the Constitution. Does the Constitution protect rights not spelled out in, or fairly implied by, the words of the document? The answer to that question largely depends on what a person concludes about the source of rights. One tradition, reflected in the Declaration of Independence, asserts that rights predate government and that government's chief duty is to protect the rights that everyone naturally possesses. Thus, if the Constitution is read as a document designed, among other things, to protect liberty, then protected liberties are not limited to those in the text of the Constitution but may also be derived from experience, for example, or from one's assessment of the requirements of a free society. This tradition places a lot of discretion in the hands of judges, because in the American political system, it is largely the judiciary that decides what the Constitution means. Partly due to this dynamic, a competing tradition looks to the text of the Constitution, as well as to statutes passed consistent with the Constitution, as a *complete* code of law containing *all* the liberties that Americans possess. Judges, therefore, are not free to go outside the text to "discover" rights that the people, through the process of lawmaking and constitutional amendment, have not declared. Doing so is undemocratic because it bypasses "rule by the people." The tension between these two ways of thinking explains the ongoing debate about a right to privacy, itself nowhere mentioned in the words of the Constitution. "I like my privacy as well as the next one," once admitted Justice Hugo Black, "but I am nevertheless compelled to admit that government has a right to invade it unless prohibited by some specific constitutional provision." Otherwise, he said, judges are forced "to determine what is or is not constitutional on the basis of their own appraisal of what laws are unwise or unnecessary." Black thought that was the job of elected legislators who would answer to the people.

It is often forgotten that at the outset, and for many years afterward, the Bill of Rights applied only to the national government, not to the states. Except for a very few restrictions, such as those in section 10 of Article I in the main body of the Constitution, which expressly limited state power, states were restrained only by their individual constitutions and state laws, not by the U.S. Bill of Rights. So, Pennsylvania or any other state, for example, could shut down a newspaper or barricade the doors of a church without violating the First Amendment. For many in the founding generation, the new central government loomed as a colossus that might threaten liberty. Few at that time thought that individual freedom needed *national* protection against *state* invasions of the rights of the people.

The first step in removing this double standard came with ratification of the Fourteenth Amendment after the Civil War in 1868. Section 1 contained majestic, but undefined, checks on states: "*No State* shall make or enforce any law which shall abridge the privileges or immunities of citizens of the United States; nor shall any *State* deprive any person of life, liberty, or property, without due process of law; nor deny to any person within its jurisdiction the equal protections of the laws" (emphasis added). Such vague language begged for interpretation. In a series of cases mainly between 1920 and 1968, the Supreme Court construed the Fourteenth Amendment to include within its meaning almost every provision of the Bill of Rights. This process of "incorporation" (applying the Bill of Rights to the states by way of the Fourteenth Amendment) was the second step in eliminating the double standard of 1791. State and local governments became bound by the same restrictions that had applied all along to the national government. The consequences of this development scarcely can be exaggerated because most governmental action in the United States is the work of state and local governments. For instance, ordinary citizens are far more likely to encounter a local police officer than an agent of the Federal Bureau of Investigation or the Secret Service.

A sixth dimension reflects an irony. A society premised on individual freedom assumes not only the worth of each person but citizens capable of rational thought, considered judgment, and measured actions. Otherwise democratic government would be futile. Yet, we lodge the most important freedoms in the Constitution precisely because we want to give those freedoms extra protection. "The very purpose of a Bill of Rights was to . . . place [certain subjects] beyond the reach of majorities and officials and to establish them as legal principles to be applied by the courts," explained Justice Robert H. Jackson. "One's right to life, liberty, and property, to free speech, a free press, freedom of worship and assembly, and other fundamental rights may not be submitted to vote; they depend on the outcome of no elections." Jackson referred to a hard lesson learned from experience: basic rights require extra protection because they are fragile. On occasion, people have been willing to violate the freedoms of others. That reality demanded a written constitution.

This irony reflects the changing nature of a bill of rights in history. Americans did not invent the idea of a bill of rights in 1791. Instead it drew from and was inspired by colonial documents such as the Pennsylvania colony's Charter of Liberties (1701) and the English Bill of Rights (1689), Petition of Right (1628), and Magna Carta (1215). However, these early and often unsuccessful attempts to limit government power were devices to protect the many (the people) from the few (the English Crown). With the emergence of democratic political systems in the eighteenth century, however, political power shifted from the few to the many. The right to rule belonged to the person who received the most votes in an election, not necessarily to the firstborn, the wealthiest, or the most physically powerful. So the focus of a bill of rights had to shift too. No longer was it designed to shelter the majority from the minority, but to shelter the minority from the majority. "Wherever the real power in a Government lies, there is the danger of oppression," commented Madison in his exchange of letters with Jefferson in 1788. "In our Government, the real power lies in the majority of the Community, and the invasion of private rights is *chiefly* to be apprehended, not from acts of government contrary to the sense of its constituents, but from acts in which the Government is the mere instrument of the major number of the Constituents."

Americans, however, do deserve credit for having discovered a way to enforce a bill of rights. Without an enforcement mechanism, a bill of rights is no more than a list of aspirations: standards to aim for, but with no redress other than violent protest or revolution. Indeed this had been the experience in England with which the framers were thoroughly familiar. Thanks to judicial review—the authority courts in the United States possess to invalidate actions taken by the other branches of government that, in the judges' view, conflict with the Constitution—the provisions in the Bill of Rights and other constitutionally protected liberties became judicially enforceable.

Judicial review was a tradition that was beginning to emerge in the states on a small scale in the 1780s and 1790s and that would blossom in the U.S. Supreme Court in the nineteenth and twentieth centuries. "In the arguments in favor of a declaration of rights," Jefferson presciently told Madison in the late winter of 1789 after the Constitution had been ratified, "you omit one which has great weight with me, the legal check which it puts into the hands of the judiciary." This is the reason why each of the volumes in this series focuses extensively on judicial decisions. Liberties have largely been defined by judges in the context of deciding cases in situations in which individuals thought the power of government extended too far.

Designed to help democracy protect itself, the Constitution ultimately needs the support of those—the majority—who endure its restraints. Without sufficient support among the people, its freedoms rest on a weak foundation. The earnest hope of *America's Freedoms* is that this series will offer Americans a renewed appreciation and understanding of their heritage of liberty.

Yet there would be no series on America's freedoms without the interest and support of Alicia Merritt at ABC-CLIO. The series was her idea. She approached me originally about the series and was very adept at overcoming my initial hesitations as series editor. She not only helped me shape the particular topics that the series would include but also guided me toward prospective authors. As a result, the topic of each book has been matched with the most appropriate person as author. The goal in each instance has been to pair topics with authors who are recognized teachers and scholars in their field. The results have been gratifying. A series editor could hardly wish for authors who have been more cooperative, helpful, and accommodating.

Donald Grier Stephenson, Jr.

Preface and Acknowledgments

The Supreme Court's decision in *Miranda v. Arizona* (1966) brought the due process revolution in the rights of the criminally accused to the attention of the general public, provoked much negative reaction, and engendered continuing political and legal controversy. Although the salience of fear of crime as a political issue abated as crime rates fell in subsequent decades, the events of 11 September 2001 have raised in a new context the problems of maintaining a proper balance between protection of the rights of persons accused of crime—or suspected of terrorism—and protection of society from lawless acts and the persons who do—or might—commit them. The *Miranda* decision forged a new link between the right to counsel and the privilege against self-incrimination, a connection that makes it impossible to understand either right fully without reference to the other. Issues concerning the legal treatment of persons accused of terrorism or designated as enemy combatants are just beginning to emerge, and rights associated with hearings and trial in civilian courts will be prominent. The right to counsel and privilege against self-incrimination will continue to be central, and this is an appropriate moment to take stock of their origins and development.

A comprehensive review of such a broad topic is a challenge to author and reader alike. As all the rights discussed in the *America's Freedoms* series are enshrined in the Bill of Rights or other amendments, and as the United States Supreme Court is, short of constitutional amendment, the ultimate arbiter of the Constitution, the focus of this volume is the elaboration of the meaning of the right to counsel and privilege against self-incrimination by the Supreme Court. That elaboration occurs in a vast and complex tapestry of decisions, precedents, doctrines, and reasoning, which this book seeks to reduce to manageable proportions. The work is intended for serious general readers as well as for students in courses on legal issues, and when the choice had to be made, I have preferred to run the risk of being too thorough rather than the risk of omitting or oversimplifying relevant material. At the same time, I have tried to give some sense of the persons and crimes involved in the cases, and to identify the Supreme Court justices whose positions have been most influential or prominent. In discussing cases, I have often chosen to quote generously rather than to summarize or paraphrase, for Supreme Court opinions are (or were) the law of the land, and it is instructive to see how the justices have stated, defended, and dissented from their formulations of that law.

The first chapter introduces the subject with case studies of blatant denials of the right to counsel and the privilege against self-incrimination, discusses the nature of each right, and summarizes the complex process of the application of the Bill of Rights to the states, where most criminal prosecutions occur. Chapter 2 recounts the background of both rights in England and the American colonies, notes their rather casual inclusion in the Bill of Rights, and explores their interpretation and application by the Supreme Court during the nineteenth century. The third chapter analyzes twentieth-century development of the right to counsel in pretrial proceedings, at trial, and on appeal and explores some of its important contours; the centerpiece here is the celebrated case of *Gideon v. Wainwright* (1963). Chapter 4 then explores the many facets of the privilege against being compelled to incriminate oneself through testimony and traces the contentious evolution of legal protection against coerced pretrial confession. The fifth chapter focuses on the Supreme Court's controversial linking of the right to counsel and the exclusion of coerced confessions in *Miranda v. Arizona* and explores the intricate web of consequences of that revolutionary change for the rights of the accused and for standards of police behavior. Chapter 6 concludes the study with an analysis of key legal issues that are as yet unresolved, discussions of the heated policy debate over the *Miranda* approach and of the realities of the right to counsel for indigent defendants, and an exploration of the emerging issues of right to counsel and privilege against self-incrimination in the context of the war on terror. A variety of reference materials complements the text.

It has been difficult to accomplish that much within the compass of a volume in this series, and thus it is important at the outset to be candid about what has not been attempted. Dissenting opinions have been carefully examined in some cases but ignored in many others. Apart from the two case studies that open the book and the section on terrorism in the final chapter, there is almost no discussion of decision-making in state or lower federal courts, which consider many specific issues not addressed by the Supreme Court and reflect some regional variation. In some cases, state constitutions, laws, or decisions extend broader rights than those protected by the U.S. Constitution. The study is also confined to the context of what might be called standard criminal prosecutions; it does not consider the special issues that may arise in civil cases, juvenile proceedings, military courts, deportation proceedings, prison disciplinary hearings, and similar venues. The evolving contours of the two rights are explored in considerable detail, but not the large body of sophisticated critical analysis of the strengths and weaknesses of the Supreme Court's

Fifth, Sixth, and Fourteenth Amendment jurisprudence, found chiefly in the law reviews. Finally, while this work does consider some policy consequences of Supreme Court decision making and some operating realities of the criminal justice system in the final chapter, it does not delve into empirical studies of the behavior of judges, prosecuting and defense attorneys, or police. All of these topics are worthy of careful examination but are beyond the scope of this volume.

The research and writing of this work have been facilitated by a sabbatical leave and a Faculty Enhancement Grant from Washington College, for which I am grateful. I also wish to express my thanks to *America's Freedoms* series editor Donald Grier Stephenson and to ABC-CLIO senior acquisitions editor Alicia Merritt, senior production editor Melanie Stafford, assistant production editor Laura Stine, and production manager Julie Gunderson for their invaluable assistance in bringing this work to publication. Thanks are due as well to Steven Lubet of Northwestern University School of Law, Lawrence A. Benner of California Western School of Law, Richard A. Nagareda of Vanderbilt University Law School, and Norman Lefstein of Indiana University School of Law for their kind and generous responses to various inquiries. I am in a very different way deeply indebted to my sons Glenn and Russell, who over many years have been a continuing source of inspiration as they have learned from me and I have learned from them. Finally, and most of all, I wish to express my love and gratitude to my wife Young, who has taught me more than anyone else and who deserves not only the customary thanks for cheerfully enduring and supporting my long hours of solitary labor, but also special thanks for helping me to keep the rest of my life in balance at the same time.

John B. Taylor
Washington College
Chestertown, Maryland

1

Introduction

Two Cases of Injustice

More than half of the text of the Bill of Rights—the first ten amendments to the United States Constitution—concerns the rights of persons accused of crime. That emphasis reflects both advances in English law and American colonial experience with techniques of oppression against which free government must guard. In the two centuries and more that have elapsed since the adoption of the Bill of Rights in 1791, many of these criminal provisions have been the subject of both major judicial elaboration and extensive scholarly commentary. The present study selects two of them that are complementary—the right to counsel and the privilege against self-incrimination—and provides a summary and synthesis of the broad sweep of their historical and legal development over several centuries.

Because this study attempts a synthesis of broad scope in brief compass, its focus is on constitutional doctrines as developed in Supreme Court decisions. We should at the outset, however, take time to illustrate just how necessary Supreme Court enforcement of constitutional protections can be to achieve justice for the accused. There is no better way to understand the importance of these two rights than to look closely at their human and political dimension as illustrated by two Supreme Court cases decided within four years in the early 1930s. Let us commence, therefore, by examining the brutal facts and enlightened decisions in *Powell v. Alabama* (1932; see Carter 1969; Goodman 1995; and Geis and Bienen 1998, chap. 3) and *Brown v. Mississippi* (1936; see Cortner 1981).

Powell v. Alabama

On a cool March day in 1931, two groups of young men, one white and one black, hitched rides on a freight train, as so many hard-pressed individuals did in those Depression years. As the train traveled west through northern Alabama, a fight broke out among some of them and, when it was over, the blacks had forced all but one of the whites off the train near the town of Stevenson. The white youths informed authorities that they wished to press charges, and a posse was quickly deputized and assembled at the town of Paint Rock. When the train stopped there, nine black youths, ranging in age from thirteen to twenty, were rounded up and arrested. Two young women, Victoria Price and Ruby Bates, had also been riding that freight, and they now came forward and leveled that most incendiary of charges in the old rural South: the rape of white women by black men. The young men did not learn of that charge until they were in jail in the county seat of Scottsboro, but the whole town soon knew. An angry mob formed, and Sheriff M. L. Wann averted a lynching only with great effort, which included a call to the governor, who dispatched troops of the National Guard.

In an atmosphere of rampant and erroneous prejudicial publicity—including accounts of beatings and victims held at gunpoint and knifepoint on the train, published in local newspapers that called for swift justice for the brutish assailants—Judge Alfred E.

Hawkins convened a grand jury. Hearing only from Victoria Price and Orville Gilley (the only white males who had remained on the train), the jurors returned indictments for rape, a capital offense, just six days after the arrest. The Scottsboro Boys, as they would ever after be known, were arraigned and pleaded not guilty the same day. Six days after that—young, alone, mostly illiterate, and generally despised by a community that did not know them—they were on trial for their lives.

Although Judge Hawkins initially appointed all seven members of the Scottsboro bar as defense counsel, all but Milo C. Moody—elderly and apparently senile—found ways to avoid the responsibility. Moody was joined by Stephen R. Roddy, an incurable alcoholic who had been retained by concerned black citizens of Chattanooga to do what he could. Although Roddy informed the court that he had not prepared for trial and was unfamiliar with Alabama law, he became the primary counsel for the defense. He had had less than half an hour to confer with his nine clients when the first of four trials began for defendants Clarence Norris and Charley Weems.

Huge crowds had gathered and the courthouse was protected by National Guard troops manning machine guns, but Judge Hawkins denied a motion for a change of venue. The principal witness for the prosecution was Victoria Price, who described a gang rape in vivid detail. Two physicians who had examined the women gave testimony that was inconclusive at best. Ruby Bates also testified for the state but her story was inconsistent with Price's. Several white men who claimed to have observed the passing train or who had helped arrest its riders also testified. Defense attorney Roddy's cross-examination consisted largely of efforts to make the jury aware of the fact that the two women were prostitutes, but Judge Hawkins thwarted that line of questioning. The only possible defense witnesses were the Scottsboro Boys themselves. Charley Weems took the stand and denied any involvement in the rape; Clarence Norris did the same, but then accused

Weems and all the others of having committed it. Because the same counsel represented all of the defendants, such testimony created a clear conflict of interest, but Roddy and Moody were left to deal with the situation as best they could. Seeing no hope, they declined to make any closing statement to the jury, which got the case early in the afternoon of the second day. Under the Alabama rape statute, the jury had the power both to determine guilt and to impose a sentence, with the minimum being imprisonment for ten years and the maximum being death.

Haywood Patterson's trial began as soon as the first jury had left to deliberate and was interrupted when it returned a short time later to deliver a verdict of guilty and a sentence of death, which prompted a celebratory demonstration. The prosecution's case was essentially the same, with some of the rough edges smoothed out. Patterson denied guilt but was hopelessly inconsistent about what others had done; some of the others supported him but gave conflicting testimony about the activities of the rest. (It is unclear what sort of threats or inducements may have prompted some of the young men to incriminate others.) The trial concluded the next morning, again with no closing statement from the defense. As soon as that jury retired, the trial of Ozie Powell, Willie Roberson, Andy Wright, Eugene Williams, and Olen Montgomery began. It, too, was soon halted so the court could receive a verdict of guilty and sentence of death from the Patterson jury. This time the state's case was buttressed by testimony from Orville Gilley, the one white who had not been forced off the train by the fight. The five defendants testified that they had been in various locations on the train and had no knowledge of any rape. Again the defense made no final statement, and the final trial began immediately. Because of his age, Roy Wright should have been tried as a juvenile, but he went before the same court and the proceedings took less than an hour. It was the fourth day of trials; two juries were still out. The next day, the Powell jury returned a verdict of guilty and a sentence of death, but the Wright jury had to be polled in open court because it was hopelessly deadlocked. The problem was that although prosecutor H. G. Bailey had in this instance asked only for life imprisonment, seven jurors were holding out for the death penalty. Judge Hawkins reluctantly declared a mistrial in Wright's case but formally sentenced the other eight defendants to death. Many white Southerners were pleased that a mass lynching had been averted and that justice had been served.

Many others felt differently, however, and the case had aroused so much attention that a three-way battle now ensued for control of the defense of the Scottsboro Boys in further proceedings. The National Association for the Advancement of Colored People (NAACP) wished to take over the case for obvious reasons; the International Labor Defense (ILD) wanted to use it to further the political goals of the communist movement; and Stephen Roddy and Milo Moody, who had leverage as the attorneys of record, wished to pursue it for financial gain. The unsophisticated defendants and their parents became pawns in this power struggle. The ILD prevailed, which incited even greater fear and hatred on the part of some white Southerners, even as others began to realize that a great injustice had been done. The trial court denied motions for new trials, so the next step was an appeal to the Alabama Supreme Court, which heard the case in January 1932. Attorneys Joseph Brodsky and George W. Chamlee argued that the exclusion of blacks from Alabama juries, the mob atmosphere and presence of troops, the celebration of the first verdict, the prosecution of a juvenile, and the inadequacy of defense counsel all demonstrated a lack of fundamental fairness in the proceedings. For the state, Attorney General Thomas G. Knight—whose father was an associate justice on the court and participated in the case—rebutted each of the arguments. Two months later, by a vote of 6–1, the court granted Eugene Williams a new trial on the grounds that he might have been a juvenile at the time of the offense, but it upheld the other seven convictions. Adverse publicity had not prejudiced the outcome, speed in punishing crime was salutary, the troops had been present to guarantee a lawful proceeding, and the establishment of qualifications for jury service was the state's prerogative, the court ruled. The lone dissent came from the highly respected Chief Justice John C. Anderson, who concluded that the totality of circumstances had denied the Scottsboro Boys a fair and impartial trial. He cited the uniform sentences for defendants who differed in age, attitude, and alleged degree of participation in the offense as evidence of the indiscriminate influence of passion and prejudice, and he also noted that defense counsel seemed only to be going through the motions of representing their clients.

The United States Supreme Court now agreed to hear the case, and in October a new ILD lawyer, Walter H. Pollak, repeated the arguments for the seven petitioners, as did Attorney General Knight for the state. Only four weeks later, the Court rendered its decision in an opinion by Justice George Sutherland, ordinarily a staunch supporter of states' rights. Setting aside all other issues, Sutherland announced that "we confine ourselves . . . to the inquiry whether the defendants were in substance denied the right of counsel, and if so, whether such denial infringes the due process clause of the Fourteenth Amendment" (*Powell v. Alabama* 52 [1932]). Quoting from the trial transcript and from Chief Justice Anderson's dissent, Sutherland found that the defendants had been denied the opportunity to obtain counsel of their choice and that the appointment of counsel had been so haphazard "that until the very morning of the trial no lawyer had been named or definitely designated to represent the defendants" (*Powell v. Alabama* 56 [1932]). Thus, "during perhaps the most critical period of the proceedings against these defendants, that is to say, from the time of their arraignment until the beginning of their trial, when consultation, thoroughgoing investigation and preparation were vitally important, the defendants did not have the aid of counsel in any real sense, although they were as much entitled to such aid during that period as at the trial itself" (*Powell v. Alabama* 57

[1932]). Quoting Chief Justice Anderson's observation that "the record indicates that the appearance [of counsel] was rather *pro forma* than zealous and active," Sutherland announced that "[u]nder the circumstances disclosed, we hold that defendants were not accorded the right of counsel in any substantial sense" (*Powell v. Alabama* 58 [1932]). The right to a hearing is an essential element of due process, Sutherland continued, and the right to a hearing includes the right to the assistance of counsel.

> In the light of the facts outlined in the forepart of this opinion—the ignorance and illiteracy of the defendants, their youth, the circumstances of public hostility, the imprisonment and the close surveillance of the defendants by the military forces, the fact that their friends and families were all in other states and communication with them necessarily difficult, and above all that they stood in deadly peril of their lives—we think the failure of the trial court to give them reasonable time and opportunity to secure counsel was a clear denial of due process.
>
> But passing that, and assuming their inability, even if opportunity had been given, to employ counsel, as the trial court evidently did assume, we are of opinion that, under the circumstances just stated, the necessity of counsel was so vital and imperative that the failure of the trial court to make an effective appointment of counsel was likewise a denial of due process within the meaning of the Fourteenth Amendment. (*Powell v. Alabama* 71, [1932])

Over a dissent by Justices Pierce Butler and James C. McReynolds, the Supreme Court had ruled, 7–2, that the convictions of the Scottsboro Boys must be overturned because they had been denied the effective assistance of counsel.

That decision was the legal high point of the Scottsboro saga, and it marked a major advance in the evolution of the right to counsel in criminal proceedings. Unfortunately for the defendants, however, the story was far from over. Haywood Patterson was retried and convicted in spite of the fact that Ruby Bates now recanted her entire story and Dr. R. R. Bridges now presented clear medical evidence that the multiple rapes could not have occurred. Judge James Edwin Horton Jr. courageously set aside the verdict as not supported by the facts and delivered a devastating critique of the evidence, surely designed to put a halt to the proceedings. The prosecution persisted, however. Judge Horton was eased out of the case, and new trials of Patterson and Norris before Judge William W. Callahan—who did not disguise his contempt for the defense—again resulted in convictions and death sentences. The Alabama Supreme Court rejected an appeal based in part on the exclusion of blacks from jury service because of their race, even though none had served in that county for sixty years; the United states Supreme Court overturned that judgment in *Norris v. Alabama* (1935) and *Patterson v. Alabama* (1935). A fourth trial of Haywood Patterson, before the biased Judge Callahan, resulted in another guilty verdict. However, because of one juror's threat to hang the jury, a sentence of seventy-five years was imposed rather than death. Once again, the Alabama Supreme Court affirmed, and the United States Supreme Court declined to review the case. Clarence Norris was tried for the third time, convicted, and sentenced to death; second trials for Andy Wright and Charley Weems resulted in convictions and sentences of ninety-nine and seventy-five years, respectively. Ozie Powell was not retried for rape but pleaded guilty to a charge of assaulting one of his prison guards with a knife and was sentenced to twenty years—the only prosecution in the whole affair in which it is clear that a crime was committed. Then, remarkably, the state dropped all charges against the remaining four defendants (the two juveniles and two who had physical ailments that made their participation in the rape unlikely), and they were released after six and one-half years behind bars. The Alabama Supreme Court upheld the Norris, Wright, and Weems convictions; Governor Bibb Graves commuted Norris's sentence to life imprisonment but reneged on a promise to pardon the five still in prison, even though the evidence against them was exactly the same as that against the four who had been released. In 1948, Haywood Patterson escaped from prison; he was captured in Detroit but Governor G. Mennen Williams of Michigan refused to extradite him and Alabama let the matter drop. During the 1940s the other four were released (although two of them violated parole and were returned to prison in Alabama, where one of them remained until 1950). The final act in the drama occurred in 1976, when Clarence Norris, still a fugitive because of another parole violation, was pardoned by—of all people—Governor George C. Wallace.

The Supreme Court's decision in *Powell* made it clear that the assistance of counsel is, at least under difficult circumstances, necessary to achieve justice; subsequent events in the case made it equally clear that the assistance of counsel is not sufficient to achieve justice. Another gruesome case was unfolding at about the same time, one that similarly illustrates the corrosive effect of bias in jurists and jurors but also casts in stark relief the evils of coerced confessions.

Brown v. Mississippi

In March 1934 in Kemper County, Mississippi, Raymond Stuart, a sixty-year-old white man, was brutally beaten to death with an axe or similar implement. In an atmosphere of threatened mob violence by angry white neighbors, Ed Brown, thirty years old, one of Stuart's black tenant farmers, was arrested the same day, and two other young black men, Henry Shields and Arthur Ellington, were arrested shortly thereafter. Within a week, all three men had confessed and had been indicted, tried, found guilty, and sentenced to be hanged. Such prompt action was prominently credited with averting more of the lynchings that had already earned the county the nickname of "Bloody Kemper."

Over defense objections, trial judge J. I. Sturdivant admitted as evidence confessions the three young men had given to two sheriffs. It became clear upon testimony of the defendants and cross-examination of the law officers involved, however, that Brown, Shields, and Ellington had initially admitted guilt to deputies only after being savagely whipped and cut with leather belts with buckles. Prosecutor John C. Stennis—who would later become a United States Senator from Mississippi—argued that no one had told the suspects what to say and that their confessions, however obtained, were truthful. All three defendants testified that their second, "voluntary" confessions to the two sheriffs had been given only out of fear of further beatings, all three denied their guilt at trial, and all of their wives testified and provided them with alibis for the time of the murder. Defense counsel did not renew their motion to exclude the confessions as evidence, and the jury—which was instructed to disregard them if it thought they had been gained by force or intimidation and were not true—apparently had no more problem with them than the judge did, for it convicted all three defendants after deliberating for only half an hour.

The defense attorneys, two of whom had been appointed for the indigent defendants the day before the trial and two the day of the trial, had had virtually no time to confer with their clients or to prepare a case. They were initially under the impression that their clients had confessed voluntarily and were guilty; hence they mounted only a perfunctory defense. Attorney John A. Clark, however, changed his mind as a result of the testimony and the obvious injuries to his clients. Days before the scheduled execution, Clark, without compensation and at the risk of his political career, filed an appeal with the Mississippi Supreme Court on the grounds that the convictions had been based on evidence that, under Mississippi law, should have been inadmissible. That court ruled, however, that under applicable precedents the trial judge had committed no reversible error in not excluding the confessions because the defense had not, at the proper time, renewed its motion requesting him to do so. Clark's error at trial was thus the basis of his defeat on appeal, and a new execution date was set.

When John Clark suffered a physical and nervous breakdown, former Governor Earl Brewer took over the case at the request of Mrs. Clark. At this point no grounds existed for an appeal to the United States Supreme Court because Clark had not raised any federal constitutional issue in his appeal. The one dissenting judge on the Mississippi Supreme Court, William D. Anderson, had nevertheless argued that the proceedings in this case had violated the due process clause of the Fourteenth Amendment as applied in *Powell v. Alabama,* and Brewer corrected Clark's omission in his petition for a rehearing before the state supreme court, a move that once again avoided an execution by a matter of days. In a series of powerful arguments, Brewer contended that use of the coerced confessions violated both the federal constitutional guarantee of due process and a state constitutional prohibition of compulsory self-incrimination, and that, as in *Powell,* due process had also been violated in the denial of the effective assistance of counsel. Although the court effectively conceded that the confessions had been coerced, stating that it could not sanction the method by which they had been obtained, it rejected all of Brewer's arguments on technicalities and found no reversible error. It also refused even to consider a separate motion for arrest of judgment and a new trial, stating that it should have been made to the trial court—even though Judge Sturdivant had adjourned the session of court immediately following the trial, thereby making such a request impossible. This time Judge Virgil Griffith joined Judge Anderson in the minority, suggesting in a stinging dissent that the courts in this matter had served only to lend the trappings of legality to the methods of the lynch mob. The service as defense counsel of a former governor who had now raised a federal question, the open call for reversal by two respected jurists, and the defensiveness of the majority opinion made it clear to all that this case would go on to the United States Supreme Court.

Earl Brewer could not argue directly that the Fifth Amendment privilege against self-incrimination had been violated, as the Supreme Court had declined to apply that provision to the states in *Twining v. New Jersey* (1908). The Court had, however, just held in *Mooney v. Holohan* (1935) that the prosecution's knowing use of perjured testimony was a denial of due process. Brewer therefore maintained that the due process right to a fair trial had been violated by the prosecution's use of confessions that clearly were just as false as the perjured statements in *Mooney* and further tainted by the manner of their acquisition. Brewer also scornfully disparaged the Mississippi Supreme Court's holding that, in a case in which the entire defense rested on an initial objection to the admissibility of confessions, their admission was proper and not reversible error because the objection had not been renewed at the proper moment, under circumstances in which, just as in *Powell v. Alabama*, the effective assistance of counsel had been unconstitutionally denied.

Attorneys for Mississippi noted that under *Twining* there was no Fifth Amendment privilege against compulsory self-incrimination in state court, and they renewed the claim that use of the confessions did not violate either the Fourteenth Amendment or the Mississippi constitutional prohibition of compelled self-incrimination because the defense had failed to make a timely motion to exclude them. They also argued that the confessions actually admitted were the second, "voluntary" ones made to the two sheriffs. The *Mooney* precedent was irrelevant because there had been no use of perjured testimony, they contended, and the issue of right to counsel was not properly before the Court because the Mississippi Supreme Court had not considered it.

The New Deal Court was sharply divided on economic issues but moving toward consensus on matters of criminal procedure, and the questions from the justices during oral argument reflected their hostility to the position of Mississippi. The dramatic high point occurred when the state's assistant attorney general,

William H. Maynard, was asked whether Brown, Shields, and Ellington should die merely because their lawyer had failed to raise an objection. Trapped between a legal rock and a moral hard place, Maynard could not bring himself to answer either yes or no and merely bowed his head in silence. It came as no surprise, therefore, that less than six weeks later the Supreme Court unanimously overturned the convictions, noting that "[a]side from the confessions, there was no evidence sufficient to warrant the submission of the case to the jury" (*Brown v. Mississippi* 279 [1936]).

In his opinion for the Court, Chief Justice Charles Evans Hughes rejected all of Mississippi's arguments. The decision in *Twining* was not conclusive here, for "the question of the right of the State to withdraw the privilege against self-incrimination is not here involved." That privilege relates to "the processes of justice by which the accused may be called as a witness and required to testify. Compulsion by torture to extort a confession is a different matter" (*Brown v. Mississippi* 285 [1936]). On the other hand, the *Mooney* precedent disallowing a state's use of perjured testimony was indeed relevant, for "the trial equally is a mere pretense where the state authorities have contrived a conviction resting solely upon confessions obtained by violence. . . . It would be difficult to conceive of methods more revolting to the sense of justice than those taken to procure the confessions of these petitioners, and the use of the confessions thus obtained as the basis for conviction and sentence was a clear denial of due process" (*Brown v. Mississippi* 286 [1936]). Finally, the state's point that the defense had not objected to admission of the confessions at the proper time was "a contention which proceeds upon a misconception of the nature of petitioners' complaint. That complaint is not of the commission of mere error, but of a wrong so fundamental that it made the whole proceeding a mere pretense of a trial and rendered the conviction and sentence wholly void. . . . [T]he trial court was fully advised by the undisputed evidence of the way in which the confessions had been procured. The trial court knew that there was no other evidence upon which conviction and sentence could be based. Yet it proceeded to permit conviction and to pronounce sentence. The conviction and sentence were void for want of the essential elements of due process, and the proceeding thus vitiated could be challenged in any appropriate manner." The Mississippi Supreme Court had "thus denied a federal right fully established" and its decision had to be reversed (*Brown v. Mississippi* 286–287 [1936]).

Despite the fact that the only evidence against the three defendants had now been declared inadmissible, the Mississippi Supreme Court denied Earl Brewer's motion to order their release and, while reversing their convictions, remanded the case to the trial court for retrial. When Brewer secured an order for release of the trio in a habeas corpus hearing before a county judge, District Attorney Stennis successfully appealed that ruling to the Mississippi Supreme Court. After much negotiation as a new trial loomed, Brown, Shields, and Ellington accepted a plea bargain. Although there was no credible evidence against them, they so feared the processes of justice in Mississippi that they pleaded *nolo contendere* to a charge of manslaughter and accepted sentences that kept them in prison for an additional five years, twenty-six months, and five months, respectively. On that unsatisfactory note, the saga of *Brown v. Mississippi* came to a close.

TWO COMPLEMENTARY RIGHTS

As the *Powell* and *Brown* cases illustrate, the right to counsel and privilege against self-incrimination are linked in important ways. These are the two rights that relate most centrally to the manner in which a criminal defendant presents himself or herself and the case to police, judge, and jury; the rights that affect most directly the defendant's ability to say effectively the things he or she wishes to say and to decline to say the things he or she does not wish to say. These rights are fundamental today, but there was a time in Anglo-American legal history when the problem was not simply that they could be violated, but that they did not exist at all, a time when the accused could be required to answer questions, could not testify under oath on his or her own behalf, and could not enjoy the assistance of counsel. The processes by which these rights evolved are intertwined and should be examined together.

Another compelling reason for joint treatment of these two rights is that the United States Supreme Court forged a new and important link between them in the case of *Miranda v. Arizona* (1966). The *Miranda* decision is, of course, best known for the warnings that it requires police officers to give to suspects upon arrest. However, its underlying rationale is that a trial judge can be most confident that a self-incriminating statement has not been coerced, and is therefore admissible as evidence, when the statement was made by a suspect who was aware of his or her rights to silence and to counsel and who had the opportunity to seek the assistance of counsel before making any statement. Although for Chief Justice Earl Warren and the four justices who joined him this was the common sense of the matter, the resulting legal and political controversy has been voluminous. For the period since 1966, one cannot fully discuss either the right to counsel or the privilege against self-incrimination without reference to the other. Our discussion of both begins with a period several centuries earlier, but we first look more closely at the concept of each of these rights and examine their context in American constitutional law.

Privilege against Self-Incrimination

The self-incrimination clause of the Fifth Amendment to the United States Constitution—"No person . . . shall be compelled in any criminal case to be a witness against himself"—has been termed "an unsolved riddle of vast proportions, a Gordian knot in the middle of our Bill of Rights" (Amar 1997, 46). It is not immediately obvious why persons suspected or accused of crime should not be required to answer truthfully all questions put to them by appropriate officials, even questions bearing on their illegal activity. "Justice . . . would not perish if the accused were subject to a duty to respond to orderly inquiry" wrote the eminent Justice Benjamin Cardozo (*Palko v. Connecticut* 326 [1937]). The system of law enforcement exists to protect the public from harm, and it may be argued that every member of the public has a civic obligation to contribute what information he or she has to the pursuit of truth about criminal activity. The Supreme Court has also, however, more than once cited the comment of Erwin Griswold, respected dean of the Harvard Law School, that "the privilege against self-incrimination is one of the great landmarks in man's struggle to make himself civilized" (Griswold 1955, 7).

Should the obligation to provide information to law enforcement authorities apply to criminals with respect to their own criminal activity? On the one hand, we acknowledge the fundamental principle that accused persons are entitled to be presumed innocent until proved guilty beyond a reasonable doubt and the corollary proposition that the state bears the entire burden of proving such guilt. Accused persons do not have to prove their innocence, so why should they be expected to provide information to help the state prove their guilt? Further, we recoil from the brutal methods of torture that have been used in the past (and are still used in some places) to extract confessions. On the other hand, we are not entirely comfortable with a privilege that seems primarily—if not exclusively—to benefit the guilty, and we do expect some forms of cooperation from the accused, such as submitting to fingerprinting, giving DNA samples, and appearing in lineups. The privilege against self-incrimination is now firmly enshrined in American constitutional law, but arguments about its fundamental purpose and, consequently, its appropriate scope, continue to arouse lively controversy. Problems arise with respect to disagreements about what the purpose of the privilege should be and to inconsistencies in the way the Supreme Court has applied it.

Several plausible justifications for the privilege exist, none of them entirely satisfactory. The Supreme Court listed many of them in a major decision of the reform era under Chief Justice Earl Warren:

> The privilege against self-incrimination "registers an important advance in the development of our liberty—'one of the great landmarks in man's struggle to make himself civilized.'" . . . It reflects many of our fundamental values and most noble aspirations: our unwillingness to subject those suspected of crime to the cruel trilemma of self-accusation, perjury or contempt; our preference for an accusatorial rather than an inquisitorial system of criminal justice; our fear that self-incriminating statements will be elicited by inhumane treatment and abuses; our sense of fair play, which dictates "a fair state-individual balance by requiring the government to leave the individual alone until good cause is shown for disturbing him and by requiring the government in its contest with the individual to shoulder the entire load" . . . ; our respect for the inviolability of the human personality and of the right of each individual "to a private enclave where he may lead a private life" . . . ; our distrust of self-deprecatory statements; and our realization that the privilege, while sometimes "a shelter to the guilty," is often "a protection to the innocent." (*Murphy v. Waterfront Commission* 55 [1964])

"[O]ur unwillingness to subject those suspected of crime to the cruel trilemma of self-accusation, perjury or contempt" reflects the perceived unfairness of the oath *ex officio* of centuries ago (whereby witnesses were bound to answer whatever questions might be asked; see the section on English and Continental origins of the privilege against self-incrimination in Chapter 2), but our legal system nevertheless requires litigants to make damaging admissions in civil cases and compels witnesses to provide damaging information about friends and family (other than spouses) in criminal cases. It also requires witnesses to choose among perjury, contempt, and violent retaliation by criminals against whom they may testify. The trilemma is thus only partially eliminated (and it exists primarily for those with something to hide). The notion of preference for an accusatorial rather than inquisitorial system is also belied by procedures in civil cases, and by the fact that the privilege allows defendants to withhold testimonial but not physical evidence from the authorities. Vigorous judicial enforcement of the privilege surely has helped to eliminate abusive police tactics of interrogation, but it may also have driven some abusive practices underground. The notion that the government should bear the entire burden of proof does not square with the defendant's obligation to provide various kinds of physical evidence, including that taken from his or her body. The concept of "respect for the inviolability of the human personality and of the right of each individual 'to a private enclave where he may lead a private life'" is controverted by civil procedure; by the ability of the state to override the privilege by compelling testimony in return for a grant of immunity; by the power of the state to subpoena private papers; by the fact that the privilege shields information that is incriminating but not that which is merely embarrassing or might lead to civil liability or some other detriment such as loss of employment; and, most generally, by the fact that the forces of prosecution are entitled to invade that sphere of privacy by presenting evidence gained from almost any source other than the defendant himself or herself. The privilege does stand as a safeguard against the attempt to criminalize mere thought and belief, but it hinders the prosecution of sordid and selfish crimes as well. The expressed "distrust of self-deprecatory statements" is more bluntly a recognition that coerced statements may well be unreliable. The goal of excluding unreliable statements was recognized centuries ago and is generally supported, but the privilege prohibits not only the use of compelled statements but also the use of physical evidence gained therefrom—and such physical evidence is not inherently unreliable. The privilege need not protect only the guilty; it may protect the innocent from unfairly damaging consequences of their testimony. On the other hand, innocent defendants who claim the privilege may be hurt by the tendency of the jury—in spite of instructions to the contrary—to draw an inference of guilt from that act. Moreover, the privilege prevents an innocent defendant from compelling a guilty accuser to reveal the truth at trial (Amar 1997, 65–68; Stuntz 1988, 1232–1238; Dolinko 1986, passim).

Each proffered rationale for the privilege thus supports it in part but is also partly inconsistent with the way the privilege and certain other aspects of the law are applied in practice. This confusing state of affairs has led one careful commentator to conclude that the privilege against self-incrimination is best "seen as responding, in part, to the pervasive problem of excusable, self-protective perjury" (Stuntz 1988, 1229). That is, Stuntz maintains, the clearest and most realistic interpretation of the privilege is that because false testimony is so debilitating to the criminal justice process, in circumstances in which the typical citizen would feel an irresistible temptation to commit perjury, the most prudent policy is to give him or her a safe alternative. From this perspective—which is by no means universally accepted (see, for example, Amar 1997, 216 n.153, 217, n.168)—the privilege is best understood not as protection of a fundamental right of the accused but as a mechanism whereby the legal system avoids the problem of perjured testimony (Stuntz 1988, 1293).

Right to Counsel

Far less confusion and controversy attend the counsel clause of the Sixth Amendment: "In all criminal prosecutions, the accused shall enjoy the right . . . to have the assistance of counsel for his defense." There has been disagreement about the obligation of the state to provide an attorney to accused persons who cannot afford one and about the stages of the criminal justice process at which the right to counsel pertains, but the rationale for the right is not in doubt. In the *Powell* case, the Supreme Court noted that the right to a hearing on charges against one is an essential element of due process of law, and it then explained in down-to-earth language why that right includes the right to counsel:

> The right to be heard would be, in many cases, of little avail if it did not comprehend the right to be heard by counsel. Even the intelligent and educated layman has small and sometimes no skill in the science of law. If charged with crime, he is incapable, generally, of determining for himself whether the indictment is good or bad. He is unfamiliar with the rules of evidence. Left without the aid of counsel he may be put on trial without a proper charge, and convicted upon incompetent evidence, or evidence irrelevant to the issue or otherwise inadmissible. He lacks both the skill and knowledge adequately to prepare his defense, even though he had a perfect one. He requires the guiding hand of counsel at every step in the proceedings against him. Without it, though he be not guilty, he faces the danger of conviction because he does not know how to establish his innocence. (*Powell v. Alabama* 68–69 [1932])

Although the essence of the right to counsel is not subject to the sort of fundamental challenge that besets the privilege against self-incrimination, the right has nevertheless been drawn into public and scholarly argument through its convergence with that privilege in the Supreme Court's decision in *Miranda v. Arizona.* When the Court invoked the right to counsel as a means of protecting the exercise of the privilege against self-incrimination, it injected that right into the sort of controversy that even the mandate for state-appointed counsel for the indigent (*Gideon v. Wainwright* [1963]) had not created. The Court's reaffirmation of *Miranda* in *Dickerson v. United States* (2000) makes it clear that these two fundamental protections of the accused will continue to be inextricably linked, but it by no means ensures that the dispute surrounding them will cease.

For that reason alone it is important to examine how these two constitutional protections developed, how they have come to intersect, and how they may evolve. Below the level of disagreements over constitutional principle, moreover, is a more pragmatic level of issues about the proper scope and application of both provisions, and these matters deserve our attention as well. At the most basic level of all is the reality that, even though today little dispute exists in principle about the right to counsel or about the unacceptability of some means of compelling incriminating statements, the process of realizing those protections in actual practice has been uncertain and arduous. The principal reason for that sad fact is that neither the Sixth Amendment right to counsel nor the Fifth Amendment privilege against self-incrimination protected persons accused in *state* criminal proceedings until the mid-twentieth century. Before commencing our examination of these two specific rights, therefore, we must consider the more general question of the applicability of the Bill of Rights to the states.

Incorporation of the Bill of Rights

The U.S. Supreme Court held in *Barron v. Baltimore* (1833) that the provisions of the Bill of Rights were applicable only to the federal government and not to the states. Citing historical and textual evidence, Chief Justice John Marshall concluded that the first ten amendments had been adopted for the sole purpose of safeguarding individual rights against encroachments by the new and more powerful national government that had just been created by the Constitution; the Bill of Rights was never intended as a limitation upon the states. That interpretation held firm until the ratification of the Fourteenth Amendment in 1868 created the opportunity for a constitutional challenge. That amendment contains the strictures "No State shall make or enforce any law which shall abridge the privileges or immunities of citizens of the United States; nor shall any State deprive any person of life, liberty, or property, without due process of law." On the basis of those two clauses, litigants began to urge the Supreme Court to rule that various specific provisions of the Bill of Rights were privileges or immunities of citizens of the United States or—what would become the more important argument—were contained within the concept of due process of law, and thus were now binding on the states as well as the federal government.

Initially, the Court was not persuaded by such arguments. In *Hurtado v. California* (1884), it was asked to apply the Fifth Amendment guarantee of indictment by grand jury to the states by incorporating it into the due process clause of the Fourteenth Amendment. The Court ruled, however, that because the Fifth Amendment also contains a due process clause, the concept of due process must not contain the concept of grand jury indictment, or else separate mention of the latter would be superfluous. By this logic, the remaining provisions of the Fifth Amendment and—by only a slight extension of logic—all the other provisions of the Bill of Rights did not and could not apply to the states through the due process clause of the Fourteenth Amendment because the due process clauses of the two amendments must have the same meaning. For the *Hurtado* majority, then, "any legal proceeding enforced by public authority, whether sanctioned by age and custom, or newly devised in the discretion of the legislative power, in furtherance of the general public good, which regards and preserves . . . principles of liberty and justice, must be held to be due process of law" *(Hurtado v. California* 537 [1884]).

In one of his notable solitary dissents, Justice John Marshall Harlan I took issue with the Court's logic and argued that the concept of due process of law contained all the fundamental rights recognized at common law and that many of them had been listed separately in the Bill of Rights only to make doubly sure that they would not be violated. Harlan found the conclusion that due process did not contain any of the separately enumerated rights preposterous, and it was clear to him why the framers of the Fourteenth Amendment had included a due process clause similar to that of the Fifth Amendment. "That similarity was not accidental, but evinces a purpose to impose upon the States the same restrictions, in respect of proceedings involving life, liberty and property, which had been imposed upon the general government" (*Hurtado v. California* 541 [1884] [dissenting opinion]).

In the long run, Harlan's view would substantially prevail, for while the Court never adopted his position that the Fourteenth Amendment had incorporated the Bill of Rights in its entirety, it did depart from *Hurtado* and gradually incorporated most of the provisions of the Bill of Rights, thereby applying them to the states. (See Cortner 1981 and Mykkeltvedt 1983.) In the short run, however, the Court continued to reject claims for incorporation, particularly from litigants seeking to establish the rights of the criminally accused. For example, in 1887 the Supreme Court refused to consider a self-incrimination claim by holding that "whether a cross-examination [of a defendant] must be confined to matters pertinent to the testimony-in-chief, or may be extended to the matters in issue, is certainly a question of state law as administered in the courts of the State, and not of Federal law" (*Spies v. Illinois* 180 [1887]). No comparable claim of a federal constitutional right to counsel in state criminal trials even reached the Supreme Court in this era (Beaney 1955, 149–150). Because the vast majority of criminal proceedings were (and still are) state rather than federal, for most persons accused of crime the right to counsel, privilege against self-incrimination, and other rights were protected only to the extent that they were guaranteed under state constitutions, statutes, and judicial decisions (or honored in practice at the discretion of state judges and other officials).

The scope of such protection varied considerably from state to state, but the beginning of an important shift occurred with the

Supreme Court's decision in *Moore v. Dempsey* (1923), overturning a federal district judge's denial of a petition for a writ of habeas corpus. Although it appeared clear that in this Arkansas case twelve black defendants had been unfairly convicted of murder and sentenced to death in an atmosphere dominated by the threat of mob violence, the request for a federal review had been denied by the district judge, largely because the state supreme court had considered and denied the appeal. The federal courts should not intervene when the state judicial processes were adequate, Justice Oliver Wendell Holmes held, but they would do so when a trial was demonstrably unjust and the state appellate process, although proper in form, had failed to right the wrong. In a very similar case decided eight years earlier, the Court had shown great deference to state appellate determinations, over a dissent by Holmes in which he asserted that "[t]his is not a matter for polite presumptions; we must look facts in the face" (*Frank v. Mangum* 349 [1915] [dissenting opinion]).

Now Holmes's view had prevailed and the Court was signaling a new willingness to examine the reality of justice in state criminal trials. But what was the constitutional standard of justice? It was the Fourteenth Amendment's requirement that no state shall deprive any person of life, liberty, or property without due process of law, and at this point only the just compensation, free speech, and free press provisions of the Bill of Rights had been applied to the states; none of the criminal justice provisions had been incorporated. In fact, in the *Mangum* case the Court had said that "[a]s to the 'due process of law' that is required by the Fourteenth Amendment, it is perfectly well settled that a criminal prosecution in the courts of a State, based upon a law not in itself repugnant to the Federal Constitution, and conducted according to the settled course of judicial proceedings as established by the law of the State, so long as it includes notice, and a hearing, or an opportunity to be heard, before a court of competent jurisdiction, according to established modes of procedure, is 'due process' in the constitutional sense" (*Frank v. Mangum* 326 [1915]).

Moore v. Dempsey, which led ultimately to the release of the twelve condemned blacks and sixty-seven others unjustly imprisoned (Cortner 1986, 34–35) implied, however, that a more expansive conception of due process was about to be applied. Initially, the Court would move more aggressively in enforcing the standard that the due process clause of the Fourteenth Amendment imposed a requirement of fundamental fairness on the states. In the longer run, the Court would incorporate most of the criminal justice provisions of the Bill of Rights—including the right to counsel priviledge and against self-incrimination—into the due process clause and thus apply them directly to the states. During the 1930s, the Court began to take major steps in its campaign for fundamental fairness in state criminal proceedings. *Powell v. Alabama* and *Brown v. Mississippi* illustrate the depths of injustice associated with the denial of basic rights but also stand as landmarks in an evolution of constitutional interpretation that would come to be known as the due process revolution.

Conclusion

As especially grim examples of racial bigotry in the administration of criminal justice, the *Powell* and *Brown* cases are shocking but not surprising. What might well be surprising, however, is that, as recently as the 1930s, both cases had to ascend all the way to the United States Supreme Court before a just decision was rendered; that in each case the Court had to break new legal ground in order to render that decision; and that, important as they were, the Supreme Court's decisions did not secure a just result for the defendants in either case. Neither the right to counsel nor the privilege against self-incrimination was well established at that point (and other problems are evident as well). The *Powell* and *Brown* decisions were pivotal events, but a tortuous course of legal development lay ahead for each of these rights. In the following chapters we first explore their origins and then examine their further elaboration.

References

Amar, Akhil Reed. 1997. *The Constitution and Criminal Procedure: First Principles.* New Haven, CT: Yale University Press.

Beaney, William M. 1955. *The Right to Counsel in American Courts.* Ann Arbor: University of Michigan Press.

Carter, Dan T. 1969. *Scottsboro: A Tragedy of the American South.* Baton Rouge: Louisiana State University Press.

Cortner, Richard C. 1981. *The Supreme Court and the Second Bill of Rights: The Fourteenth Amendment and the Nationalization of Civil Liberties.* Madison: University of Wisconsin Press.

———. 1986. *A "Scottsboro" Case in Mississippi: The Supreme Court and* Brown v. Mississippi. Jackson: University Press of Mississippi.

Dolinko, David. 1986. "Is There a Rationale for the Privilege against Self-Incrimination?" *U.C.L.A. Law Review* 33:1063–1148.

Geis, Gilbert, and Leigh B. Bienen. 1998. *Crimes of the Century.* Boston: Northeastern University Press.

Goodman, James. 1995. *Stories of Scottsboro.* New York: Vintage Books. Original edition, 1994. New York: Pantheon Books.

Griswold, Erwin N. 1955. *The Fifth Amendment Today.* Cambridge, MA: Harvard University Press.

Mykkeltvedt, Roald Y. 1983. *The Nationalization of the Bill of Rights: Fourteenth Amendment Due Process and Procedural Rights.* Port Washington, NY: Associated Faculty Press.

Stuntz, William J. 1988. "Self-Incrimination and Excuse." *Columbia Law Review* 88:1227–1296.

2

Origins and Early Development

Privilege against Self-Incrimination

English and Continental Origins

At the time of the Norman Conquest (1066), trials in England were very different from what we know today. One party publicly accused another with respect to some ecclesiastical, civil, or criminal matter, and the court determined the form of the trial and decided which party would be put to the proof. Trial could be by compurgation—each side submitting sworn statements supported by sworn oaths of supporters—or by some form of brutal physical ordeal, such as plunging one's hand into boiling water. With the arrival of the Normans, trial by battle between the parties (or their hired champions) became another option. In each case, the point was to seek some sign of divine judgment as to which party was in the right (Levy 1968, 5–10).

This notion of trial was gradually supplanted by the Norman institution of the inquest, in which a royal official convened a body of men from the neighborhood to answer questions under oath. Originally an administrative device to determine such matters as land ownership and tax assessment, the inquest evolved into a means of resolving private lawsuits and investigating criminal accusations as well. In the reign of Henry II (1154–1189), the system of inquests convened by travelling royal commissioners was regularized as a way of bringing charges (thus becoming the forerunner of the modern grand jury), and these officials began to function as judges, taking jurisdiction over serious crimes that threatened the king's peace, although the resolution of disputes by trial jury rather than by some form of oath, ordeal, or battle evolved only very gradually, first in civil cases and later in criminal. The outlines of the modern criminal trial by jury emerged by the middle of the fifteenth century, but full development of essential features did not occur until the nineteenth century (Levy 1968, 7–19; Heller 1969, 4–12).

In contrast to this elaboration of an accusatorial system of justice in English secular courts was the development on the European continent of an inquisitorial system of rooting out heresy in ecclesiastical courts, spearheaded by the initiatives and reforms of Pope Innocent III (1198–1216) and culminating in the Inquisition. As the procedures for heresy trials evolved, accused persons were required to swear an oath to tell the truth in all interrogations that might be administered—the inquisitional oath, or oath *ex officio.* Asked to take the oath without knowing their accusers, the charges, or the evidence, the accused would be condemned as guilty if they refused. Alternatively, if they complied, the accused would face the choice of very likely incriminating themselves (with respect to an unknown charge) or risking punishment as a perjurer. Even if unpunished judicially, perjury courted eternal damnation, so the oath was a powerful incentive for self-incrimination. Because the standards of proof by other means were impossibly high (supposedly a benefit to the accused) but the extirpation of heresy was considered crucial to the preservation of the faith, inquisitors considered confession essential and supplemented the oath *ex officio* with torture in order to obtain it (Levy 1968, 19–28).

During the period after the Norman Conquest in England, a system of ecclesiastical courts grew up alongside the secular courts. They were not initially focused on heresy in the manner of their continental counterparts, but exercised criminal jurisdiction not only in cases involving the clergy but also in cases concerning a wide range of common offenses—perjury, profanity, fornication, adultery, drunkenness, disorderly conduct, and the like. There were inevitable jurisdictional disputes between ecclesiastical and secular courts and various procedural differences as well. The proceedings of the ecclesiastical courts were based on the European *ius commune,* a combination of Roman and canon law that was elaborated in academic treatises and various courts from the twelfth century forward. One of the tenets of the *ius commune* was the maxim *nemo tenetur prodere seipsum* (or *nemo tenetur seipsum accusare*)—no man should be compelled to betray (or accuse) himself. This maxim was taken seriously in the English ecclesiastical courts, but it admitted of significant exceptions and limitations as well, so from the thirteenth century forward the oath *ex officio* was sometimes imposed in these courts. The *nemo tenetur* maxim was not at this time regarded as a substantive right of the accused, but rather—like the modern concept of probable cause—as a means of assuring that officials had a credible basis for bringing a legal action at all, a source of information other than the accused. It thus stood in opposition to the notion of an oath *ex officio*—that is, an obligation to answer questions posed at the discretion of an official.

During the medieval period in England, the *nemo tenetur* maxim and the oath *ex officio* were not major issues. Starting around the middle of the sixteenth century, however, there was a significant increase in the invocation of the *nemo tenetur* principle of the *ius commune* and in refusals to answer specific questions in the ecclesiastical courts, and the issue became more controversial. Religious strife was increasing with the ascendancy of the Church of England in the reign of Henry VIII (1509–1547), the brief return to Catholicism in the reign of Queen Mary (1553–1558), and the continuing opposition of Puritans and other dissenting sects. In addition, the legal stakes were raised with the creation of a new ecclesiastical court, the Court of High Commission, which aimed to suppress heresy and other forms of religious dissent. The High Commission employed the oath *ex officio* but, unlike traditional ecclesiastical courts, could impose civil as well as spiritual penalties. At this point, the *nemo tenetur* principle constituted a protection against compelled self-incrimination in the *ius commune,* but it was narrow, subject to many exceptions, and not a reliable safeguard for most defendants (Levy 1968, 43–46, 75–77; Helmholz et al. 1997, 6–7, 17–35, 40–46).

During the sixteenth and early seventeenth centuries, persons subject to the jurisdiction of ecclesiastical courts sometimes appealed to the common-law courts to issue writs of prohibition or of habeas corpus to prevent ecclesiastical courts—notably the Court of High Commission—from engaging in various practices, including the compulsion of incriminating testimony. These instances raised not only the specific question of whether compelled testimony was, given the circumstances of the case, permissible under the *ius commune,* but also the more general question of the extent to which the common-law courts had supervisory power over the ecclesiastical courts. The common-law judges sometimes intervened to prohibit compelled testimony, but generally only in cases of egregious violation, especially when the action of the ecclesiastical court impinged on the sphere of the common-law court (Helmholz et al. 1997, 7–8, 48–54, 80–81).

The Court of High Commission was complemented by another royal prerogative court (that is, a court that was an instrument of the monarch), the Court of Star Chamber, which was a secular court focusing on political and criminal matters but which used the procedures of the ecclesiastical rather than the common-law courts and thus employed the oath *ex officio.* The Star Chamber became an increasingly important and, by the early seventeenth century, feared instrument of royal control, especially as the events of the English civil war unfolded. It was thus one of the decisive episodes of that conflict when, in 1641, King Charles I (reigned 1625–1649) was forced to convene Parliament and that body abolished the courts of High Commission and Star Chamber and eliminated the oath *ex officio* by prohibiting the ecclesiastical courts from requiring persons to confess to any crime under oath (Levy 1968, 34–35; Helmholz et al. 1997, 66, 101; Perry 1959, 133).

The key venue for the issue of self-incrimination thus became the common-law courts, but until the late eighteenth century the very character of criminal trials militated against the assertion in practice of a right not to be compelled to answer incriminating questions. Defendants could be questioned by judge and prosecutor but were not under oath; their problem was the general expectation that, as the prosecution made its case, the defendant would respond, and that an innocent defendant could do so effectively. In a proceeding in which defense counsel was not permitted, restrictions were imposed on calling defense witnesses, and the prosecution had no clear obligation to prove its case beyond a reasonable doubt, the refusal to speak by a defendant amounted to a forfeiture of the right to mount a defense at all and of the opportunity to influence sentencing in a system in which corporal punishment and the death penalty were common. Under these circumstances, even though the practice of questioning the accused at trial gradually died out, defendants in common-law trials through most of the eighteenth century simply did not claim any privilege against self-incrimination. That could not happen until the nature of trials was transformed. To this point trials had been occasions during which defendants could—had to—refute charges by explaining themselves. Then a new conception gradually emerged. Defense counsel were permitted to speak for the accused, the presumption of innocence obtained, the prosecution bore a high burden of proof, and evidentiary standards were imposed. Only as English trials evolved in this fashion in the late eighteenth and early nineteenth centuries could defendants afford to assert an emerging right not to incriminate themselves (Helmholz et al. 1997, 82–100; Perry 1959, 136).

A closely related issue arose from the fact that defendants were subject to pretrial interrogation by a justice of the peace whose purpose was to bully them into providing information that would aid the prosecution and would be used at trial even if they chose not to speak there. Defendants were expected to answer the magistrate's pretrial questions, and failure to do so would be used against them at trial. Torture, occasionally employed by royal agents, died out after the 1640s, and the system was moving toward an understanding that confessions should not be admitted into evidence unless they were voluntary—if only because involuntary confessions might well be untrue. The right of defendants not to have involuntary confessions used against them in English courts gradually evolved during the eighteenth century but was not fully elaborated until the middle of the nineteenth century, and controversy did not cease even then (Helmholz et al. 1997, 82–100; Levy 1968, 325–329; Stephens 1973, 19–20).

Colonial Experience

Trials in the colonies of British North America were essentially like those in England; defendants were pressured to incriminate themselves in pretrial proceedings and their confessions could be used against them at trial, where they could not afford to remain silent. Indeed, because of the sparseness of population and paucity of trained lawyers, trials—particularly for indigents—were commonly summary proceedings in which a lay justice of the peace would in a swift and informal hearing impose punishment on the basis of his or her examination alone. The acceptability of such procedures can be explained in part by an interpretation of the *nemo tenetur* principle as meaning that no person should be compelled to answer incriminating questions *under oath,* as that would pose a stark choice between courting temporal punishment and courting eternal damnation. At both pretrial examinations and trial, however, defendants were not only not required but not permitted to testify under oath, largely on the grounds that they were self-interested parties. Under these circumstances, it did not seem unreasonable to apply some pressure to the most knowledgeable source for information about what the defendant had done or not done (Helmholz et al. 1997, 114–127). At the close of the seventeenth century, practice differed from one colony to the next, and progress toward establishment of a right against self-incrimination was limited and uneven (Levy 1968, 367).

In the eighteenth century, the American legal establishment gradually became more professionalized and familiarity with the intricacies of English common law increased. The focus of the self-incrimination issue was the preliminary examination of suspects and the admissibility of confessions elicited by various degrees of force, and by midcentury colonial judges were placing limits on the use of pretrial confessions (Levy 1968, 368–369, 375; Stephens 1973, 23). Nevertheless, as threats to public order placed increasing pressure on the judicial system in the decades leading up to the American Revolution, the trend toward summary proceedings intensified, and American trial procedures did not at all seem on the brink of the liberalizing transformation that would soon occur in England. In the revolutionary era, however, onerous British statutes and their enforcement in the courts led Americans to insist on their entitlement to a panoply of traditional common-law rights of Englishmen, focusing on the jury trial and a cluster of associated rights, including the *nemo tenetur* principle. Such rights now seemed threatened by an increase in the resort to prerogative courts such as vice-admiralty and in their use of the oath *ex officio.* The issue had rapidly moved from the level of judicial practice to the level of political theory.

After independence, as a safeguard against abuses government had committed or might commit, states moved quickly to enact constitutional provisions protecting many individual rights. Among those was the right not to be compelled to incriminate oneself, and the leading formulation was that of George Mason in the Virginia Declaration of Rights: "no man could be 'compelled to give evidence against himself'" (Berger 1980, 22). This notion had been in the law of some colonies since the seventeenth century; it was now explicitly stated by all the states that adopted separate bills of rights and was an understood component of a broader statement of a right to trial by jury, or of a recognition of the common law, in the constitutions of the rest (Helmholz et al. 1997, 127–136; Levy 1968, 405–411; Fellman 1976, 305).

Bill of Rights

The Articles of Confederation contained no bill of rights, nor did the Constitution proposed in 1787, but the ratification process for the new charter engendered strong pressure for the addition of such provisions, with the result that amendments were offered in the First Congress by James Madison and quickly adopted. Madison's proposed article on judicial process provided that "no person . . . shall be compelled to be a witness against himself" (Helmholz et al. 1997, 137), but the House of Representatives qualified the right to apply only to persons in criminal cases, and the Senate passed and the states ratified the provision in that form. There is no record of why this restriction was imposed, but it may have been designed to preserve the power of courts of equity to require parties to produce evidence adverse to their interests in civil cases. It was also not clear whether the wording made the clause applicable to all phases of a criminal proceeding or just to the trial, but the right not to be compelled to be a witness against oneself was potentially broader than a right not to be compelled to incriminate oneself (Levy 1968, 425–429; Berger 1980, 49–52).

Congressional action on this provision occurred without controversy or significant debate. The goal was not to reform existing criminal procedures but to conserve what had been achieved, to guard against the oppressive expansion of governmental power by embedding traditional common-law rights in fundamental, constitutional law. "Common law procedure, however dependent in practice on self-incrimination, was not the object of reforming zeal. The goal of even the most enthusiastic advocate was to prevent sovereign authority from overturning the traditional forms of jury trial, instituting 'foreign' or 'innovative' means of coercion that would bypass the jury. The rack in the Tower, not the JP flogging a vagabond, was the emblem of the need for a guarantee against coerced confession" (Helmholz et al. 1997, 137). The new state and federal constitutional provisions on self-incrimination (and other rights) had no immediate impact on criminal procedure, as they were regarded as affirming rather than reforming the common law. The modern conception of the privilege against self-incrimination had yet to emerge; it would begin to do so as newly influential defense counsel moved to reshape the traditional meaning of the English common law in the new American context (Helmholz et al. 1997, 139, 144).

Nineteenth-century Developments

The understanding of the late eighteenth century was that "the Fifth Amendment [and state constitutional] privilege prohibited (1) incriminating interrogation under oath, (2) torture, and (3) probably other forms of coercive interrogation such as threats of future punishments and promises of leniency." It did not confer a right to remain silent; rather, "[i]t focused on improper methods of gaining information from criminal suspects" (Helmholz et al. 1997, 192). Thus understood, the new constitutional right was not initially seen as inconsistent with a judicial process that emphasized pretrial pressure for self-incrimination. Defendants were not under oath at either preliminary examinations or at trial. Although it was of course possible to refuse to answer questions, the serious cost of doing so was the adverse inferences that juries would draw from such an action. By contrast, witnesses—who, unlike defendants, did testify under oath at trial—could invoke a right not to answer incriminating questions, because an oath, with its attendant sanction of punishment for perjury, was regarded as an impermissible technique of compulsion. Over time, however, the protection that sworn witnesses enjoyed would be extended to suspects and defendants as well (Helmholz et al. 1997, 192–193).

Several developments contributed to that process. Especially when defense lawyers were not readily available, defendants spoke at trial to represent themselves, but they were not allowed to testify (give evidence under oath) in any jurisdiction until 1864, as they were presumed not to be disinterested parties. As of that year, states began to abandon the prohibition of sworn testimony by defendants; the federal government did so in 1878 (18 USC §3481 [2000]), and by the end of the nineteenth century so had every state but Georgia. Defendants were not required to testify, however, and the federal and most of the state statutes allowing them to do so provided that a defendant's decision not to testify would not create a presumption against him or her (as might occur if prosecutors or judges were permitted to comment adversely on this choice). As defense counsel became more commonly available to speak on behalf of their clients, defendants not only did not have to answer incriminating questions but did not have to testify at all—in order to avoid cross-examination or for whatever other reason. They thus did acquire a right to silence at trial (Helmholz et al. 1997, 194–199; Fellman 1976, 319–320).

It is important at this point to distinguish between two related strands of the self-incrimination problem. One aspect of the problem is the right of the defendant not to answer incriminating questions at trial, or indeed to answer any questions at all at trial. That right gained protection from the Fifth Amendment and equivalent state constitutional provisions and evolved in practice, as we have seen. The other aspect of the problem is the introduction into evidence at trial of unsworn confessions or other incriminating statements made by defendants in the course of pretrial interrogation. Fairly early in the nineteenth century, magistrates began to caution defendants that they need not respond to pretrial questioning and that if they did, their answers could be used against them at trial (Helmholz et al. 1997, 198). As the century progressed and police departments were established, however, they gradually assumed the responsibility for interrogation of criminal suspects without the direct involvement of magistrates. Because obtaining a confession is often the simplest way to solve a case, police have a continuing incentive to employ methods that will achieve that result. A wide range of such methods is available, from brutal beatings through marathon interrogation sessions, sleep deprivation, psychological intimidation, threats or promises (true or false), and factual misrepresentations, to tough and vigorous questioning, appeals to conscience, and straightforward persuasion on the basis of the reality of the suspect's circumstances. The most important issue that would emerge—related to but initially distinct from the Fifth Amendment protection—was the issue of coerced confessions.

Since colonial times, courts had been refusing to accept confessions elicited by torture and other extreme methods, partly as a reaction against such practices but more importantly as a recognition that confessions gained in such a manner were inherently unreliable. This common-law rule—that is, a rule established by courts rather than by statute or constitutional provision—remained in force in federal and state jurisdictions in the new republic, independent of the Fifth Amendment and similar state constitutional provisions. Until the Supreme Court intervened decisively in this area in the twentieth century, courts determined the admissibility of confessions on the basis of their trustworthiness, a determination that rested in large part on a judgment of whether, under the circumstances of the interrogation, the confession had been made voluntarily (Fellman 1976, 336–338; Stephens 1973, 22–23).

As noted in the previous chapter, the vast majority of criminal cases are state, not federal, and the Fifth Amendment did not apply to the states until 1964. The admissibility of allegedly coerced confessions was thus essentially a matter of state law, and states went their own ways until the Supreme Court began to apply the due process clause to them in the 1930s, starting with *Brown v. Mississippi* (see the case study in Chapter 1 and the discussion of the coerced confession cases in Chapter 4). The long, slow process by which the Supreme Court would address this issue and ultimately create a uniform constitutional standard for state as well as federal courts began tentatively in the case of *Hopt v. Utah Territory* (1884) (a federal case because Utah was not yet a state), in which the Court held that "the presumption . . . that one who is innocent will not imperil his safety or prejudice his interests by an untrue statement, ceases when the confession appears to have been made either in consequence of inducements . . . touching the charge preferred, or because of a threat or promise . . . which, operating upon the fears or hopes of the accused, in reference to the charge, deprives him of that freedom of will or self-control essential to make his confession voluntary within the meaning of the law" (*Hopt v. Utah Territory* 585 [1884]). This formulation is noteworthy because it (1) laid down a general and subjective standard, (2) therefore conferred great discretion on judges, and (3) merely restated the common-law rule, grounded on the need to exclude untrustworthy confessions, without reference to the Fifth Amendment, even though this was a federal case—an approach consistent with a distinction between legal compulsion (such as punishment for contempt for failing to testify) and the sorts of coercion that interrogators might employ.

In 1897, however, the Court took a different tack, casually asserting that in federal trials, the question of the admissibility of a pretrial confession was controlled by the self-incrimination clause of the Fifth Amendment, which it said embodied the common-law standard of voluntariness. "A brief consideration of the reasons which gave rise to the adoption of the Fifth Amendment, of the wrongs which it was intended to prevent and of the safeguards which it was its purpose unalterably to secure," wrote Chief Justice Edward D. White, "will make it clear that the generic language of the Amendment was but a crystallization of the doctrine as to confessions, well settled when the Amendment was adopted, and since expressed in the text writers and expounded by the adjudications, and hence that the statements on the subject by the text writers and adjudications but formulate the conceptions and commands of the Amendment itself" (*Bram v. United States* 543 [1897]). White's historical interpretation is questionable, particularly as the Court had not previously made it in the 106 years since the amendment's ratification, but it nevertheless reflects the close practical connection between the protection against compelled self-incriminating testimony and the protection against coerced confessions. The three dissenting justices did not challenge the majority's interpretation, merely finding the confession to have been voluntary. Thereafter, however, the Court ignored the *Bram* decision, which thus did not significantly modify the assessment of the voluntariness of confessions in subsequent federal cases (U.S. Senate 1992, 1321; Berger 1980, 223). In the twentieth century, the Court would first apply a similar voluntariness standard to the states under the rubric of due process and then resurrect *Bram* and apply a new self-incrimination standard to both the federal government and the states in *Miranda v. Arizona.*

The distinction between compelled testimony at trial and coerced pretrial confessions does not exhaust the possibilities for compulsory self-incrimination, and indeed an early landmark case on that topic arose as a result of a third technique of law enforcement that falls somewhere between the first two. When the United States government suspected the firm of Boyd and Sons of importing merchandise without paying a customs duty, it secured a court order requiring the company to produce a copy of the shipper's invoice, acting under the authority of an 1874 statute that authorized the subpoena of books, invoices, and papers in revenue cases and provided that failure to produce such items without adequate excuse would constitute confession of the allegations the government sought to prove. When Boyd turned over the invoice, was required in a civil proceeding to forfeit the merchandise, and appealed to the Supreme Court (Berger 1980, 163–164), the result was a strong defense of the "indefeasible right of personal security, personal liberty and private property" (*Boyd v. United States* 630 [1886]).

In an opinion by Justice Joseph P. Bradley, the Court held the relevant section of the statute, as applied in such cases, to violate both the search and seizure clause of the Fourth Amendment and the self-incrimination clause of the Fifth Amendment, the object of which was to protect both physical and personal privacy. With respect to self-incrimination, it did not matter that Boyd had not been required to give testimony at trial or that the proceeding was not a criminal prosecution but a civil enforcement action for forfeiture of goods:

> [W]e have been unable to perceive that the seizure of a man's private books and papers to be used in evidence against him is substantially different from compelling him to be a witness against himself. We think it is within the clear intent and meaning of those terms. We are also clearly of opinion that proceedings instituted for the purpose of declaring the forfeiture of a man's property by reason of offences committed by him, though they may be civil in form, are in their nature criminal. . . . If the government prosecutor elects to waive an indictment, and to file a civil information against the claimants—that is, civil in form—can he by this device take from the proceeding its criminal

> aspect and deprive the claimants of their immunities as citizens, and extort from them a production of their private papers, or, as an alternative, a confession of guilt? This cannot be. . . . [A] compulsory production of the private books and papers of the owner of goods sought to be forfeited in such a suit is compelling him to be a witness against himself, within the meaning of the Fifth Amendment. (*Boyd v. United States* 633–635 [1886])

Boyd could have been criminally prosecuted for his actions, and forfeiture of the goods could have been part of a criminal penalty. The Court thus focused on the substance of the evil to be avoided, rather than the nature of the proceeding in which it was to be perpetrated—which it termed "quasi-criminal" (*Boyd v. United States* 635 [1886])—and extended the privilege against self-incrimination. It did not, on the other hand, specify the sense in which Boyd had been compelled to be a witness against himself. A narrow interpretation would be that it was in the act of producing the documents and thus implicitly authenticating them as the ones subpoenaed; a broad interpretation would be that it was in the sense of implicitly testifying to the contents of the documents. This ambiguity did not prevent the *Boyd* decision from being read as a ringing denial of the government's power to compel the production of incriminating private papers, but its scope and authority as a precedent would gradually be reduced in the century that followed (Berger 1980, 53, 165–166).

A final significant self-incrimination case at the end of the nineteenth century, *Counselman v. Hitchcock* (1892), dealt with another aspect of the circumstances in which the privilege could be asserted. Charles Counselman, a grain dealer in Chicago, responded to a subpoena to testify before a federal grand jury investigating kickbacks in the railroad industry in violation of regulations setting freight rates under the authority of the Interstate Commerce Act. He answered various questions but refused to say whether he had obtained cut rates or rebates from any of several railroads serving Chicago, citing his privilege not to incriminate himself. Counselman was thereupon adjudged to be in contempt by the district judge and was taken into custody, fined, and assessed court costs. When his appeal reached the Supreme Court, the principal question was whether, as the government contended, the privilege was available only to someone who was actually being prosecuted, or was available to a witness before a grand jury investigating crimes for which he might be prosecuted. Disagreeing with both the circuit court in Counselman's case and the New York Court of Appeals (the state's highest court) in a comparable case, the Supreme Court asserted that "[i]t is impossible that the meaning of the constitutional provision can only be that a person shall not be compelled to be a witness against himself in a criminal prosecution against himself. It would doubtless cover such cases; but it is not limited to them. The object was to insure that a person should not be compelled, when acting as a witness in any investigation, to give testimony which might tend to show that he himself had committed a crime. The privilege is limited to criminal matters, but it is as broad as the mischief against which it seeks to guard" (*Counselman v. Hitchcock* 562 [1892]). The Court thus found the scope of the Fifth Amendment privilege against self-incrimination "in any criminal case" to be broader than the scope of the Sixth Amendment right to counsel and other trial rights "[i]n all criminal prosecutions."

The mischief the Court was concerned about was the possibility that incriminating testimony could be compelled before a grand jury, in a civil case, or before a legislative committee or other such body, and then be introduced as evidence at a criminal trial, thus circumventing the privilege; aggressive prosecutors might even arrange to have suspects questioned in such forums. An interpretation of the Fifth Amendment that would allow such a result, the Court declared, would "take away entirely its true meaning and its value" (*Counselman v. Hitchcock* 563 [1892]). The government conceded that a witness could invoke the Fifth

Amendment at his trial to prevent such an abuse, but it took the position that Counselman was not entitled to invoke the Fifth Amendment before the grand jury because his situation was governed (and the mischief was precluded) by a federal statute that provided that evidence gained from a witness in a judicial proceeding could not be used against that witness in any federal criminal prosecution or judicial action for enforcement of any penalty or forfeiture. Such immunity statutes, under which witnesses could be punished for contempt for failing to answer questions, had become common in the nineteenth century as a way of allowing law enforcement agencies to compel suspects to provide needed information without violating their state or federal constitutional rights (Amar 1997, 79).

The Supreme Court now ruled, however, that the federal immunity statute was not commensurate with the constitutional protection to which Counselman was entitled. "It could not, and would not, prevent the use of his testimony to search out other testimony to be used in evidence against him or his property, in a criminal proceeding in such court. It could not prevent the obtaining and the use of witnesses and evidence which should be attributable directly to the testimony he might give under compulsion, and on which he might be convicted, when otherwise, and if he had refused to answer, he could not possibly have been convicted." Moreover, the statute provided "no protection against that use of compelled testimony which consists in gaining therefrom a knowledge of the details of a crime, and of sources of information which may supply other means of convicting the witness or party" (*Counselman v. Hitchcock* 564, 586 [1892]).

A proper construction of the self-incrimination clause, the Court announced, was "that the witness is protected 'from being compelled to disclose the circumstances of his offence, the sources from which, or the means by which, evidence of its commission, or of his connection with it, may be obtained, or made effectual for his connection, without using his answers as direct admissions against him'" (*Counselman v. Hitchcock* 585 [1892]). It thus followed that "no statute which leaves the party or witness subject to prosecution after he answers the criminating question put to him, can have the effect of supplanting the privilege conferred by the Constitution of the United States. . . . In view of the constitutional provision, a statutory enactment, to be valid, must afford absolute immunity against future prosecution for the offence to which the question relates" (*Counselman v. Hitchcock* 585–586 [1892]). In the absence of such a statute, a witness was entitled to claim the privilege against self-incrimination in any forum in which his or her testimony could be compelled.

Prior to the *Counselman* decision, the prevalent legislative and judicial understanding had been that the privilege against self-incrimination prohibited the use at trial of any incriminating pretrial testimony that a defendant had been compelled to give, but did not prohibit the use of the fruits of such testimony—that is, information or evidence derived from it—and certainly did not prohibit prosecution entirely. The leading case was a decision of the New York Court of Appeals that asserted that "[i]f a man cannot give evidence upon the trial of another person without disclosing circumstances which will make his own guilt apparent or at least capable of proof, though his account of the transactions should never be used as evidence, it is the misfortune of his condition and not any want of humanity in the law" (*People ex rel. Hackley v. Kelly* 83 [1861]). The Supreme Court now clearly rejected that interpretation.

For Counselman, the decision meant that his assertion of the privilege before the grand jury had been valid and that his contempt conviction was overturned. More generally, first, the decision reaffirmed the understanding that self-incriminating testimony could not be compelled in some other forum and then used in a criminal prosecution, and it confirmed the right to assert the privilege in those other forums.

Second, *Counselman* broke new ground by holding that if the government wished to compel testimony by conferring an immunity equivalent to the protection of the self-incrimination clause, it was not sufficient to bar the use of such testimony, or the use of both the testimony and the fruits thereof; the government would have to forgo prosecution altogether by granting what is known as transactional immunity. Congress responded to this requirement by enacting the Compulsory Testimony Act of 1893, granting transactional immunity to persons compelled to answer incriminating questions before the Interstate Commerce Commission. When this expanded right of immunity was challenged by a witness as still not providing the full measure of protection guaranteed by the Fifth Amendment, the Supreme Court had occasion to address a fundamental question: whether the self-incrimination clause should "be construed literally, as authorizing the witness to refuse to disclose any fact which might tend to incriminate, [or merely] disgrace or expose him to unfavorable comments," or whether "upon the other hand, the object of the provision be [only] to secure the witness against a criminal prosecution, which might be aided directly or indirectly by his disclosure" (*Brown v. Walker* 595 [1896]). The former interpretation would effectively prohibit the government from compelling testimony in return for immunity; the latter would allow it to do so.

There seemed to be a legal consensus, wrote Justice Henry Brown, that the privilege was not available to persons who had been pardoned, or for whose alleged crime the statute of limitations had expired, or who would incur disgrace but not criminal liability by answering, and thus the Court concluded that the second, narrower conception of the privilege was the correct one. Balancing the rights of the individual against the needs of law enforcement (and making clear what the majority saw as the real problem in the case at hand), Justice Brown warned that "[t]he danger of extending the principle announced in *Counselman v.*

Hitchcock is that the privilege may be put forward for a sentimental reason, or for a purely fanciful protection of the witness against an imaginary danger, and for the real purpose of securing immunity to some third person, who is interested in concealing the facts to which he would testify. Every good citizen is bound to aid in the enforcement of the law, and has no right to permit himself, under the pretext of shielding his own good name, to be made the tool of others, who are desirous of seeking shelter behind his privilege" (*Brown v. Walker* 600 [1896]).

Because the Court held that Congress possessed and had exercised the power to grant immunity from prosecution in state as well as federal courts, this witness's rights were fully protected by the statute. The requirement of transactional immunity had greatly expanded the privilege, and a narrow majority of five justices would not further expand it in a manner that would "unduly impede, hinder or obstruct the administration of criminal justice" (*Brown v. Walker* 596 [1896]). Four justices disagreed. Three thought the statute did not provide full protection against prosecution and doubted that any immunity statute could, and one stated flatly that the privilege against self-incrimination was absolute.

At the close of the nineteenth century, the *Boyd* and *Counselman* decisions seemed to erect strong barriers against compulsory self-incrimination in some circumstances—denying governmental access to private papers, guaranteeing the right of any witness to withhold testimony in any governmental forum, and allowing the government to supplant that right and require testimony only with a guarantee of immunity from prosecution for crimes about which answers were required. Recall, however, that at this stage of our constitutional development, it was only the federal government that was so restricted by the Fifth Amendment. The authority of *Barron v. Baltimore* and *Hurtado v. California* still held sway, and an individual's rights in any state judicial system were only such as that state's constitution, statutes, and judicial decisions and practice provided.

Right to Counsel

English Origins

In the era prior to the Glorious Revolution of 1688, it was the anomalous practice in England to grant the right to counsel to persons accused of minor crimes but to deny the right to those accused of major crimes. Persons accused of misdemeanors (as well as parties in civil cases) in common-law courts were entitled to the aid of counsel, and persons accused of lesser political offenses in the Star Chamber were required to have counsel (without whose signature they could not file an answer to the charges against them and would be regarded as having confessed). Persons accused of felonies and of treason, on the other hand, were denied the assistance of counsel. Perhaps the best explanation for this curious situation is that the government was more willing to be liberal when it had less at stake than when it had more. Especially in the revolutionary seventeenth century, the government—monarchy or commonwealth—was far from secure. When stability had been restored (but politicians still felt vulnerable to accusations of political crime), Parliament in 1695 passed a statute not only permitting defendants in treason cases to retain counsel but requiring courts to appoint counsel on request. Parliament did not, however, enact a statutory right to counsel in felony cases until 1836. Especially after 1750, however, judges at their discretion increasingly allowed the appearance of counsel as a matter of trial practice. By this time, the defendant's opponent was more often a public prosecutor than an accusing private party, and English judges had begun to conceive of themselves more as neutral arbiters than as arms of the state, a posture in which they could feel free to be solicitous toward the needs of defendants (but could also conclude that their own impartiality precluded the defendant's need for further assistance). When counsel were permitted, they were sometimes allowed to participate fully in the presentation of a defense but sometimes restricted to arguing points of law. The right to counsel in felony cases was thus problematic until the statute of 1836 (Beaney 1955, 8–11; Heller 1969, 9–10; Tomkovicz 2002, 2–9).

Colonial Experience

As already noted, trial procedures in the American colonies were generally similar to those in England. During the seventeenth century, few trained lawyers were available, and the accused generally defended themselves in court; in some places they were allowed the assistance of others, who could not be compensated. Just as the right to counsel began to evolve in England in the eighteenth century, so it did in America. The Pennsylvania Charter of Privileges of 1701 gave the accused the same right of counsel as the prosecution. A few other colonies moved faster than the mother country, granting counsel more often in practice or by statute conferring a right to court-appointed counsel in capital cases; in other colonies the status of the right was comparable to that in England.

As with the privilege against self-incrimination, however, as political tensions heightened the colonists became increasingly solicitous of the right to counsel as a basic safeguard of liberty. Americans further secured that right in new state constitutions and statutes adopted after 1776. On the eve of the adoption of the Sixth Amendment, the right to counsel was protected by constitutional provision in seven states, by statute in four more, and by common law in one. (Only Georgia held out, until adoption of a constitution in 1798.) As the eighteenth century drew to a close, however, for most offenses most states guaranteed only the right to retain counsel at one's own expense. A few provided for court-appointed counsel in capital cases, but only New Jersey and Connecticut provided counsel to those who could not afford it in all cases. Nevertheless, the states had already sharply diverged from English practice (Beaney 1955, 14–22; Heller 1969, 20–24, 109–110; Perry 1959, 253, 258; Tomkovicz 2002, 9–13).

Bill of Rights

Among the items in the constitutional amendments that James Madison proposed in 1789 was a provision that "[i]n all criminal prosecutions, the accused shall enjoy the right . . . to have the assistance of counsel for his defense" (Heller 1969, 30). Although the placement of this language in the final text evolved through committee and full chamber action in the House and Senate, the provision itself remained unchanged and was not debated; it became part of the Constitution when the Sixth Amendment was ratified in 1791. We can only assume that there was consensus that the right to counsel was fundamental, but as the law and practice on that subject varied from state to state, it would be up to legislators and especially to judges to determine the scope of the right. As the Sixth Amendment did not apply to the states (where most criminal prosecutions occur), that issue remained essentially a matter of state rather than federal law for more than a century, until the Supreme Court began a process of forging a national standard (Beaney 1955, 22–26; Heller 1969, 30–34).

Nineteenth-Century Developments

Few significant developments in the interpretation of the federal—Sixth Amendment—right to counsel occurred in the nineteenth century. Two acts of Congress passed during the period when the Bill of Rights was being proposed and adopted suggest the limited scope of the constitutional right to counsel as then understood. A provision of the Judiciary Act of 1789 stated that parties in federal courts were entitled to the assistance of such attorneys as the rules of the court permitted to practice therein, and the Federal Crimes Act of 1790 established the right of persons accused of treason or some other capital offense to have counsel appointed by the court. It is a fair inference, then, that the Sixth Amendment was not intended to reform existing practice and that it guaranteed only the right to retain counsel, not the right of a needy defendant to have counsel supplied. If the members of the same Congress that framed the Bill of Rights had thought otherwise, the second statute would have been superfluous; it was not, but it met the need of only those indigent defendants who were charged with capital offenses. During the nineteenth and early twentieth centuries federal courts did develop the practice of appointing counsel for needy defendants in other serious felony cases, but there was no constitutional or statutory right to such representation and no system of compensating attorneys for providing it. The appointment of counsel was not automatic; the defendant had to request it, or an attorney had to volunteer. Defendants who did not request counsel and pleaded guilty or were convicted were not considered to have been denied any constitutional right (Beaney 1955, 27–33; Heller 1969, 110). The Sixth Amendment did not apply to the states; the right to counsel in state trials was entirely a matter of state law and practice.

CONCLUSION

As the nineteenth century drew to a close, the federal constitutional right to counsel and privilege against self-incrimination played only a modest role in the administration of criminal justice. Neither provision was binding on the states, where most criminal prosecutions occur, and neither had been the object of extensive judicial elaboration. The Supreme Court had decided no major right-to-counsel cases at all, and its two significant self-incrimination decisions dealt with questions that were important but would have no effect on federal defendants in many cases. *Boyd* prevented the government from compelling the accused to produce incriminating private papers, and *Counselman* held that any witness could claim the privilege against self-incrimination in any forum and that a witness granted immunity in lieu of the privilege could not be prosecuted for the offenses about which he or she was required to testify. Neither of these decisions would survive intact, but the Supreme Court would render others that would make revolutionary advances with respect to both counsel and self-incrimination in the twentieth century, when civil liberties came to the forefront of the judicial agenda. Those developments are the focus of the next three chapters.

References

Amar, Akhil Reed. 1997. *The Constitution and Criminal Procedure: First Principles.* New Haven, CT: Yale University Press.

Beaney, William M. 1955. *The Right to Counsel in American Courts.* Ann Arbor: University of Michigan Press.

Berger, Mark. 1980. *Taking the Fifth: The Supreme Court and the Privilege against Self-Incrimination.* Lexington, MA: Lexington Books.

Fellman, David. 1976. *The Defendant's Rights Today.* Madison: University of Wisconsin Press.

Heller, Francis. 1969. *The Sixth Amendment to the Constitution of the United States.* New York: Greenwood Press. Original edition, 1951. Lawrence: University of Kansas Press.

Helmholz, R. H., Charles M. Gray, John H. Langbein, Eben Moglen, Henry E. Smith, and Albert W. Alschuler. 1997. *The Privilege against Self-Incrimination: Its Origins and Development.* Chicago: University of Chicago Press.

Levy, Leonard W. 1968. *Origins of the Fifth Amendment: The Right against Self-Incrimination.* New York: Oxford University Press.

Perry, Richard L., ed. 1959. *Sources of Our Liberties.* Chicago: American Bar Foundation.

Stephens, Otis H. 1973. *The Supreme Court and Confessions of Guilt.* Knoxville: University of Tennessee Press.

Tomkovicz, James J. 2002. *The Right to the Assistance of Counsel: A Reference Guide to the United States Constitution.* Westport, CT: Greenwood Press.

U.S. Senate. 1992. *The Constitution of the United States of America: Analysis and Interpretation.* 103d Cong., 1st sess. S. Doc. 103–6. Washington, DC: Government Printing Office.

3

The Twentieth Century: Right to Counsel

Right to Counsel at Trial: First Steps

Since the founding of the American constitutional system, the legal right (if not the actual ability) of accused persons to engage their own counsel has been considered secure, a guarantee the Supreme Court reemphasized in the state case of *Chandler v. Fretag* (1954). Chandler, accused of housebreaking and larceny, opted to forgo counsel and plead guilty. On the day of his trial he was informed for the first time that he also faced the charge of being a habitual offender, which carried a mandatory penalty of life imprisonment without possibility of parole. He immediately requested a delay in order to consult an attorney, but that request was denied. Ten minutes later he had pleaded guilty to the charge of housebreaking and larceny, been convicted of being a habitual offender, and consigned to prison for life. The Sixth Amendment right to counsel would not be applied to the states for another decade, but when Chandler's case reached the Supreme Court, the justices unanimously held that he had been denied due process of law. "Regardless of whether petitioner would have been entitled to the appointment of counsel," Chief Justice Earl Warren wrote, "his right to be heard through his own counsel was unqualified. . . . A necessary corollary is that a defendant must be given a reasonable opportunity to employ and consult with counsel; otherwise, the right to be heard by counsel would be of little worth" (*Chandler v. Fretag* 9, 10 [1954]).

Well into the twentieth century, however, it remained true that "[t]here is . . . no general obligation on the part of the government . . . to . . . retain counsel for defendants or prisoners. The object of the constitutional provision was merely to secure those rights which by the ancient rules of the common law had been denied to them; but it was not contemplated that this should be done at the expense of the government" (*United States v. Van Duzee* 173 [1891][dictum]). Although there was thus no *constitutional* right of appointed counsel for indigent federal defendants, Congress had provided a *statutory* right of appointed counsel in capital cases, and federal trial judges had generally gone further, appointing counsel on request in all felony cases and without request in most felony cases (Beaney 1955, 192). In *Powell v. Alabama*, which was a state capital case (see the case study in Chapter 1), the Supreme Court went a step further. Although it did not apply the Sixth Amendment directly to the states by incorporating it into the due process clause of the Fourteenth Amendment, it did hold that "in a capital case, where the defendant is unable to employ counsel, and is incapable adequately of making his own defense because of ignorance, feeble mindedness, illiteracy, or the like, it is the duty of the court, whether requested or not, to assign counsel for him as a necessary requisite of due process of law; and that duty is not discharged by an assignment at such a time or under such circumstances as to preclude the giving of effective aid in the preparation and trial of the case" (*Powell v. Alabama* 71 [1932]). In so interpreting the Fourteenth Amendment, the Court began the process of creating a constitutional right to appointed counsel in state trials.

Federal Trials

Six years later, the Court unequivocally took that step for federal trials when it heard the case of two young and unsophisticated U.S. Marines who, lacking funds for counsel, had been convicted in a civilian court for possessing and passing counterfeit twenty-dollar bills while on leave in Charleston, South Carolina. "The Sixth Amendment," wrote Justice Hugo Black, "withholds from federal courts, in all criminal proceedings, the power and authority to deprive an accused of his life or liberty unless he has or waives the assistance of counsel." Trial judges have a constitutional obligation "to complete the court . . . by providing counsel for an accused who is unable to obtain counsel, [and] who has not intelligently waived this constitutional guaranty" (*Johnson v. Zerbst* 463, 468 [1938]). The Court reiterated its insistence that the waiver of constitutional rights must be intelligent and competent and proclaimed that "[t]he determination of whether there has been an intelligent waiver of the right to counsel must depend, in each case, upon the particular facts and circumstances surrounding that case, including the background, experience, and conduct of the accused" (*Johnson v. Zerbst* 464 [1938]). In announcing this new rule, the Court clearly modified the traditional understanding of the Sixth Amendment, making clear that it confers a right not merely to *retain* counsel but to *have* counsel. This action was not controversial because it simply elevated to constitutional status the policy of the Department of Justice and the general practice of the federal courts (Beaney 1955, 40–44).

State Trials

By ruling that no one could be tried in federal court without an attorney unless he or she had waived that right, the Supreme Court in the *Zerbst* case converted what had been a statutory right to the appointment of counsel in capital cases to a constitutional right to the appointment of counsel in all (or, at least, all serious) criminal prosecutions, a right that is spelled out in Rule 44 of the Federal Rules of Criminal Procedure. It was not long before petitioners started asking the Court to impose the same requirement on the states (where practice varied considerably). It chose to confront such a request in *Betts v. Brady* (1942).

Smith Betts, charged with robbery and unable to afford counsel, asked the judge at his arraignment to appoint one for him. Although the Maryland statute allowed trial judges to appoint counsel at their discretion, Betts was informed that it was the practice in Carroll County to make such appointments only in cases of rape and murder. He thus represented himself at his trial without a jury and was convicted by the judge.

When the case reached the Supreme Court, Justice Owen J. Roberts, writing for the majority, noted that although the *Powell* case and some other decisions contained language suggesting the fundamental character of the right to counsel, the actual decision in *Powell* was that the failure of the court to appoint effective counsel was a denial of due process *under the circumstances.* Betts was asking for a broader ruling: "The question we are now to decide is whether due process of law demands that in every criminal case, whatever the circumstances, a State must furnish counsel to an indigent defendant. Is the furnishing of counsel in all cases whatever dictated by natural, inherent, and fundamental principles of fairness? The answer to the question may be found in the common understanding of those who have lived under the Anglo-American system of law" (*Betts v. Brady* 464 [1942]). An exhaustive review of constitutional and statutory history and judicial practice since colonial times led Roberts to the conclusion that "in the great majority of the States, it has been the considered judgment of the people, their representatives and their courts that appointment of counsel is not a fundamental right, essential to a fair trial. On the contrary, the matter has generally been deemed one of legislative policy. In the light of this evidence, we are unable to say that the concept of due process incorporated in the Fourteenth Amendment obligates the States, whatever may be their own views, to furnish counsel in every such case" (*Betts v. Brady* 471 [1942]).

In *Johnson v. Zerbst,* the Court had decided that the Sixth Amendment obligates the federal government to do precisely that. The explanation for this apparent disparity, said Roberts, lay in the differing character of the constitutional provisions involved:

> The due process clause of the Fourteenth Amendment does not incorporate, as such, the specific guarantees found in the Sixth Amendment. . . . The phrase [due process] formulates a concept less rigid and more fluid than those envisaged in other specific and particular provisions of the Bill of Rights. Its application is less a matter of rule. Asserted denial is to be tested by an appraisal of the totality of facts in a given case. That which may, in one setting, constitute a denial of fundamental fairness, shocking to the universal sense of justice, may, in other circumstances, and in the light of other considerations, fall short of such denial. In the application of such a concept, there is always the danger of falling into the habit of formulating the guarantee into a set of hard and fast rules, the application of which in a given case may be to ignore the qualifying factors therein disclosed. (*Betts v. Brady* 461–462 [1942])

The majority would not consider applying the Sixth Amendment right to counsel directly to the states by incorporating it into the due process clause of the Fourteenth Amendment, so the constitutional standard was the more flexible one of due process itself. In state trials, therefore, there would be no "hard and fast rules" about the appointment of counsel. The absence of counsel would be deemed a violation of due process only when, in the particular circumstances of the case, it made the trial fundamentally unfair. As to Betts, the Court concluded that his case was simple and straightforward; he had conducted his defense reasonably and the outcome had turned on the veracity of prosecution witnesses linking him to the robbery and a defense witness who had provided an alibi. His trial had been fair and his conviction was affirmed.

In a brief dissent joined by Justices William O. Douglas and Frank Murphy, Justice Hugo Black, author of the majority opinion in *Johnson v. Zerbst,* disagreed with every aspect of the majority opinion. Reluctantly setting aside his conviction that the Fourteenth Amendment had applied the entire Bill of Rights to the states as of 1868 and that, therefore, *Johnson v. Zerbst* should be controlling here, Black argued that even by the majority's criterion of the circumstances of the case, Betts, "a farm hand, out of a job and on relief" (*Betts v. Brady* 474 [1942] [dissenting opinion]), had been denied due process of law. He may have been of average intelligence but had little education; the Court in *Powell v. Alabama* had declared that "[e]ven the intelligent and educated layman . . . lacks both the skill and knowledge adequately to prepare his defense, even though he have a perfect one. He requires the guiding hand of counsel in every step in the proceedings against him" (cited in *Betts v. Brady* 475–476 [1942] [dissenting opinion]). The *Powell* decision, Black believed, stood for the proposition that the right to counsel is inherently fundamental and therefore binding on the states in all trials as a matter of due process. Taking a more limited view,

> [t]his Court has just declared that due process of law is denied [only] if a trial is conducted in such manner that it is "shocking to the universal sense of justice" or "offensive to the common and fundamental ideas of fairness and right." . . . A practice cannot be reconciled with "common and fundamental ideas of fairness and right," which subjects innocent men to increased dangers of conviction merely because of their poverty. Whether a man is innocent cannot be determined from a trial in which, as here, denial of counsel has made it impossible to conclude, with any satisfactory degree of certainty, that the defendant's case was adequately presented. (*Betts v. Brady* 475–476 [1942] [dissenting opinion])

The majority considered the appointment of counsel to be a matter of policy rather than a fundamental right, but Black believed that policy decisions reflected the conviction that counsel is a fundamental right, for "most . . . States have . . . constitutional provisions, statutes, or established practice judicially approved, which assure that no man shall be deprived of counsel merely because of his poverty. Any other practice seems to me to defeat the promise of our democratic society to provide equal justice under the law" (*Betts v. Brady* 477 [1942] [dissenting opinion]). Finally, for Black (a jurist who generally preferred the hard and fast rules abjured by the majority), the view that issues of due process should be determined according to the circumstances of each case was "a view which gives this Court such vast supervisory powers that I am not prepared to accept it without grave doubts" (*Betts v. Brady* 475 [1942] [dissenting opinion]).

Justice Black's view that the Fourteenth Amendment had applied the Bill of Rights to the states in its entirety was not the position of the Court, but the doctrine of *Hurtado v. California* (see the section on incorporation of the Bill of Rights in Chapter 1), holding that none of the provisions of the Bill of Rights were or could be a part of that due process applicable to the states, was no longer the position of the Court either. Current doctrine was that due process included some of the Bill of Rights, those provisions that are "of the very essence of a scheme of ordered liberty," the abolition of which would "violate a 'principle of justice so rooted in the traditions and conscience of our people as to be ranked as fundamental'" (*Palko v. Connecticut* 325 [1937]).

Justice Black did not accept this theory of selective incorporation, but he believed that because the *Powell* decision had declared the right to counsel to be fundamental, the majority justices who did accept the theory were obligated to incorporate the Sixth Amendment right to counsel into the Fourteenth Amendment due process clause. That would make the states subject to the same standard as the federal government—the standard of *Johnson v.*

Zerbst. The majority, however, thought that what was fundamental was not the right to counsel per se, but the right to a fair trial, which might or might not require the participation of counsel, depending on the circumstances. *Betts v. Brady* thus engendered the special circumstances rule: due process requires state judges to appoint counsel where failure to do so would result in a "trial [that] is offensive to the common and fundamental ideas of fairness and right" (*Betts v. Brady* 473 [1942]).

Because the majority in *Betts v. Brady* conceded that "[e]xpressions in the opinions of this court lend color to the argument" (*Betts v. Brady* 463 [1942]) that the right to counsel was so fundamental as to require incorporation, and did not specifically repudiate the language of those expressions, the Supreme Court seemed to be sending mixed signals on the constitutional status of the right in state trials. The Court was split, 6–3, and the majority's constitutional standard of "fundamental ideas of fairness and right" was inherently subjective. Conflict on this issue would continue, and the immediate focus of that conflict would be, case by case, the question of whether or not the trial of an indigent defendant without counsel had been fundamentally unfair.

During the two decades following *Betts v. Brady,* the Court decided a series of cases raising this issue. It soon became clear that all the justices believed that the charge of a capital offense was of itself a circumstance sufficient to establish a constitutional right to appointed counsel, and all the states conformed to that standard of their own volition in any event (Fellman 1976, 211, 214). There was no such agreement as to noncapital cases, however, as Justice Stanley F. Reed candidly explained:

> Some members of the Court think that where serious offenses are charged, failure of a court to offer counsel in state criminal trials deprives an accused of rights under the Fourteenth Amendment. They are convinced that the services of counsel to protect the accused are guaranteed by the Constitution in every such instance. . . . Only when

> the accused refuses counsel with an understanding of his rights can the court dispense with counsel. Others of us think that when a crime subject to capital punishment is not involved, each case depends on its own facts. . . . Where the gravity of the crime and other factors—such as the age and education of the defendant, the conduct of the court or the prosecuting officials, and the complicated nature of the offense charged and the possible defenses thereto—render criminal proceedings without counsel so apt to result in injustice as to be fundamentally unfair, the latter group holds that the accused must have legal assistance under the [Fourteenth] Amendment whether he pleads guilty or elects to stand trial, whether he requests counsel or not. (*Uveges v. Pennsylvania,* 440–441 [1948])

The justices who took the latter approach did not necessarily agree with each other in applying it to individual cases, and the result was that the Court produced a confusing and inconsistent line of decisions that engendered growing criticism (Beaney 1955, 164–188; Fellman 1976, 213–215; Lewis 1964, 112–117).

INCORPORATION OF THE RIGHT TO COUNSEL: *GIDEON V. WAINWRIGHT*

Of the justices who had decided *Betts v. Brady,* only Hugo Black and William O. Douglas remained on the Court in 1962, and they still believed it had been wrongly decided and should be overruled. Chief Justice Warren and Justice William J. Brennan had publicly expressed the same view, and the Court now seized an opportunity to reconsider the special circumstances rule when it received a petition for a writ of certiorari from Clarence Earl Gideon. Such a petition is the formal mechanism by which an aggrieved litigant asks the Supreme Court to review his or her case, and the vast majority of such requests are denied. Gideon filed his petition *in forma pauperis*—in the manner of a pauper—which meant that under the Court's rules he was exempted from the normal technical standards and fees for filing the petition. His documents were hand-printed in pencil on prison stationery, but they met the basic requirements for consideration.

Gideon—fifty-one, white, a drifter with a record of intermittent burglaries—was serving a five-year term in the Florida state prison at Raiford for breaking into a pool hall in Panama City with the intent to commit petty larceny. He had asked trial judge Robert L. McCrary Jr. to appoint counsel for him but McCrary had denied the request, telling Gideon that under Florida law such appointments were not allowed in noncapital cases. In fact, the law was that appointments of counsel were not *required* in noncapital cases, but the Florida Supreme Court had rejected Gideon's claim that his rights had been violated. Gideon did not identify special circumstances or present specific evidence of unfairness at his trial; he simply maintained that the due process clause entitled any indigent defendant accused of a felony to appointed counsel. He was wrong about that, but his case, which was factually very similar to *Betts v. Brady,* provided an opportunity for overruling that decision. The Court granted certiorari and directed counsel to address the question of whether the holding in *Betts* should be reconsidered (Lewis 1964, 3–10, 36–38, 97–98).

Gideon's problem, of course, was that he did not have counsel, but the Supreme Court appoints counsel in such circumstances and it chose a high-powered attorney and partner in the respected Washington law firm of Arnold, Fortas, and Porter: Abe Fortas, who would become Justice Fortas upon his appointment to the Supreme Court in 1965. The state of Florida, on the other hand, was represented by Bruce Robert Jacob, a young and inexperienced assistant attorney general.

In his written brief and oral argument, Fortas told the Court that the right to counsel for every defendant was essential to a fair trial—as *Johnson v. Zerbst* and increasing state practice attested—and should therefore be incorporated into the due process clause of the Fourteenth Amendment. The distinction between capital and noncapital cases was without foundation, for due process protects liberty and property just as much as it protects life, and for the more practical reason that legal issues in noncapital cases may be more complicated than in capital cases. Furthermore, the special circumstances rule presented many difficulties in practice: the Court's own decisions under it were confusing, states often failed to appoint counsel when they clearly should, convicted defendants so victimized were unlikely to be able to appeal on the basis of special circumstances without legal assistance, special circumstances were not always evident before trial, and the consequent burden and delay of appeals and retrials were costly for the state and unfair to the defendant. To illustrate the ineffectiveness of the rule, Fortas cited the Pennsylvania Supreme Court's refusal to require counsel for an eighteen-year-old defendant with an IQ of fifty-nine and a mental age of nine (Lewis 1964, 133–138, 169–174). In sum, Fortas urged the Court to abandon the special circumstances rule because it was both unfair and unworkable.

On behalf of Florida, Bruce Jacob argued that the historical record showed that the Sixth Amendment was simply intended to ensure that defendants were free to retain their own counsel, and that the Fourteenth Amendment imposed a flexible rather than uniform standard that left the states free to devise their own systems of criminal justice. Echoing *Betts v. Brady,* he asserted that the fact that states had developed varying standards for provision of counsel demonstrated that the right was not so fundamental as to require incorporation. The special circumstances rule provided a clear and workable standard; some inconsistencies were normal in the development of the common law. A decision requiring appointment of counsel in felony cases would logically apply to misdemeanor and civil cases as well, creating a huge burden for the states. Finally, Jacob warned that if the Court overruled *Betts* and made its decision retroactive, a wholesale release of prisoners might result, more than 5,000 in Florida alone (Lewis 1964, 157–160, 176–178).

Underlying the arguments about the nature and scope of the right to counsel was a more generalized concern about federalism. As we saw in the first chapter, the Supreme Court had left the states essentially free to conduct their criminal justice systems as they saw fit until the 1920s, when it first began to assert closer supervision. The proper balance of state and national power has been a central issue throughout American history and was a principal cause of the Civil War. A century later a strong political sentiment against national dictation to state governments still prevailed, and the jurisprudential counterpart to that sentiment was the view that due process was a flexible standard that allowed for considerable state discretion in its interpretation. By the 1960s, the specter of increasing federal judicial supervision of state affairs was looming not only with respect to criminal procedure but with respect to desegregation, separation of church and state, and legislative apportionment as well, so the *Gideon* case was argued in a climate of considerable controversy about federal-state relations. Bruce Jacob's brief did not claim that no defendants required counsel, but rather that states should be free to determine which ones did, under the due process/special circumstances standard, and it argued that the Court should not impose a heavy burden of providing counsel on the states (a judgment that Justice Roberts had endorsed in *Betts v. Brady*).

Abe Fortas saw this issue as crucial to his case and sought to turn it around: he argued that a straightforward requirement of appointed counsel would be far less of an imposition on the states than continuing federal review of special circumstances, which would result in numerous reversals and retrials (Lewis 1964, 135–136, 171–173). This argument echoed Justice Black's concern in his *Betts* dissent, but it was really aimed at Justice John Marshall Harlan II, the justice most solicitous of the prerogatives of the states.

Because the *Gideon* case raised a constitutional question of concern to every state, Bruce Jacob informed the attorneys general of the other forty-nine states of the litigation and invited them to submit *amicus curiae* (friend of the court) briefs to the Supreme Court in support of his position. The notification was appropriate, but the request backfired. To the surprise of counsel and justices alike, twenty-two states joined in filing a brief in support of Gideon, and only Alabama and North Carolina supported Florida. The twenty-two states agreed that trial without counsel was fundamentally unfair, and one of them, Oregon, also filed a separate brief stating that in its experience it was not only more just but also administratively more efficient to provide counsel in the first place than to correct errors after the fact—not only the error of failure to provide counsel, but other errors that the presence of counsel would have precluded (Lewis 1964, 141–151).

In light of these developments, it was no great surprise that the Supreme Court overturned Clarence Earl Gideon's conviction and overruled *Betts v. Brady.* The vote was unanimous (*Gideon v. Wainwright* [1963]). Chief Justice Warren assigned the opinion to Justice Black, author of the dissent in *Betts v. Brady* and the majority opinion in *Johnson v. Zerbst.* The question, wrote Black, was whether the right to counsel was so fundamental as to be applicable to the states through the due process clause of the Fourteenth Amendment. "While the Court at the close of its *Powell* opinion did by its language, as this Court frequently does, limit its holding to the particular facts and circumstances of that case, its conclusions about the fundamental nature of the right to counsel are unmistakable," and have been reiterated in subsequent cases.

"[I]n deciding as it did—that 'appointment of counsel is not a fundamental right, essential to a fair trial'—the Court in *Betts* v. *Brady* made an abrupt break with its own well-considered precedents. In returning to these old precedents, sounder we believe than the new, we but restore constitutional principles established to achieve a fair system of justice. Not only these precedents but also reason and reflection require us to recognize that in our adversary system of criminal justice, any person haled into court, who is too poor to hire a lawyer, cannot be assured a fair trial unless counsel is provided for him. This seems to us to be an obvious truth" (*Gideon v. Wainwright* 343–344 [1963]).

The states supporting Gideon, Black concluded, argued "that *Betts* was 'an anachronism when handed down' and that it should now be overruled. We agree" (*Gideon v. Wainwright* 345 [1963]).

Three justices wrote concurring opinions. Because he was writing for the Court, Justice Black could not express his personal view that the Fourteenth Amendment incorporated the Bill of Rights in its entirety, so Justice Douglas (who joined the majority opinion) also wrote separately to express that view. Justice Tom C. Clark did not endorse Black's reasoning but stated that he concurred in the result because the due process clause required counsel in capital cases and provided no less protection for those facing loss of liberty than for those facing loss of life. Justice Harlan wrote to express a very different perspective from Justice Black's. "I agree," he said, "that *Betts v. Brady* should be overruled, but consider it entitled to a more respectful burial than has been accorded. . . . I cannot subscribe to the view that *Betts v. Brady* represented 'an abrupt break with its own well-considered precedents'" (*Gideon v. Wainwright* 349 [1963] [concurring opinion]).

The *Powell* decision was based on the particularly unfortunate circumstances of those defendants, Harlan said, and *Betts* built on and extended *Powell* by acknowledging the possibility of special circumstances in noncapital cases as well, while formalizing the requirement that the existence of such circumstances be demonstrated in order to establish a violation of due process. The problem was that the special circumstances rule simply did not work well in practice. In capital cases the Court gradually made clear that the right to counsel was absolute, while "[i]n noncapital cases, the 'special circumstances' rule has continued to exist in form while its substance has been substantially and steadily eroded" (*Gideon v. Wainwright* 350 [1963] [concurring opinion]). When the Court had failed to find special circumstances in cases following *Betts,* it was typically by a very close vote, and it had found special circumstances in every case it had reviewed since 1950. "At the same time, there have been not a few cases in which special circumstances were found in little or nothing more than the 'complexity' of the legal questions presented, although those questions were often of only routine difficulty. The Court has come to recognize, in other words, that the mere existence of a serious criminal charge constituted in itself special circumstances requiring the services of counsel at trial. In truth the *Betts v. Brady* rule is no longer a reality" (*Gideon v. Wainwright* 351[1963] [concurring opinion]). Abe Fortas had argued that the special circumstances rule was both unfair and unworkable; every member of the Court agreed with at least one of those points.

Bruce Jacob had argued to the Court that a requirement to provide counsel to indigents would impose a heavy burden, but in fact that problem was particularly serious only for Florida and four other states—Alabama, North Carolina, South Carolina, and Mississippi—that assured counsel only in capital cases. Thirty-seven states formally guaranteed counsel in all felony cases and eight others did so in practice, at least in the cities. Twenty-four states went further and furnished counsel in misdemeanor cases as well. As a practical matter, counsel for the indigent are either private attorneys appointed by judges on an ad hoc or rotating basis, public defenders employed by the government, attorneys who contract with the government to provide such services, or representatives of legal aid societies organized on a charitable basis.

Promptly after the *Gideon* decision, Florida enacted a public defender system. The other four deficient Southern states made various provisions for counsel, and many other states acted to upgrade their procedures, creating many new public defender offices. For felony cases at least, the results were salutary: disputes over the need for counsel were eliminated; convictions of the truly guilty were less vulnerable to being overturned; the burden on appellate courts was reduced; and most fundamentally, hapless defendants were no longer required to fend for themselves. Congress had taken no such action after *Johnson v. Zerbst,* and indigent federal defendants had typically been represented by young and inexperienced attorneys, randomly appointed and totally uncompensated. Ironically, Congress was just moving to remedy this situation as the *Gideon* case was being argued and decided (Lewis 1964, 132–133, 193–205; Graham 1970, 63–64, 162). The right to appointed counsel does not ensure the quality of appointed counsel, however. (We look further at that issue in Chapter 6.)

The view that every defendant needs a lawyer, regardless of the circumstances, was borne out in Gideon's own case. It seems clear that he was innocent of the charges against him, and when the state retried him, he was acquitted with the aid of an able local attorney. The Supreme Court had, however, left some major questions unanswered. The most immediate one concerned that other worry of Bruce Jacob—that thousands of convicts would have to be released, which might occur if the new right to counsel were applied retroactively. When a group of Florida convicts asked the Court to rule on that question in the fall of 1963, it did not do so but simply overturned their convictions and "remanded [the cases] to the Supreme Court of Florida for further consideration in light of *Gideon v. Wainwright*" (*Pickelsimer v. Wainwright* 3 [1963]). Florida took the hint and applied the decision retroactively, ultimately releasing large numbers of prisoners it was unwilling to retry (Lewis 1964, 205). The Supreme Court never found it necessary to rule formally on retroactivity (although in *Pickelsimer* Justice Harlan argued that it should); it simply affirmed that *Gideon* did apply retroactively (*Burgett v. Texas* [1967]; *Kitchens v. Smith* [1971]).

RIGHT TO COUNSEL FOR LESSER OFFENSES

The degree to which states would have to expand their legal services, and the number of prisoners whose convictions were now subject to challenge, depended in part on another unanswered question. The *Gideon* decision applied to persons accused or convicted of a felony. Were indigents accused of lesser offenses entitled to appointed counsel as well? Many states did not think so, and the Court took up this issue in another case from Florida, *Argersinger v. Hamlin* (1972). Argersinger had been convicted of carrying a concealed weapon. He could have received up to six months in prison and a $1,000 fine but was actually sentenced to ninety days in jail. The Florida Supreme Court ruled in his case that the right to counsel did not include petty offenses and applied only in cases in which the offense carried a prison sentence of more than six months—the standard the U.S. Supreme Court had adopted for the right to a jury trial (*Baldwin v. New York* [1970]).

The Supreme Court found that the right to counsel required a different standard, however, because the legal problems of defending against a charge of a minor offense can be just as difficult as those relating to a more serious charge. Moreover, Justice Douglas wrote for the majority, minor cases are often resolved through a process of assembly-line justice characterized by time pressures, casually arranged bargains for guilty pleas, and insufficient attention to the rights and needs of defendants. "We hold, therefore, that absent a knowing and intelligent waiver, no person may be imprisoned for any offense, whether classified as petty, misdemeanor, or felony, unless he was represented by counsel at his trial" (*Argersinger v. Hamlin* 37 [1972]). As with *Gideon,* the Court summarily decided that the decision in this case would be retroactive (*Berry v. City of Cincinnati* [1973]).

The Court's holding in *Argersinger* made it clear that states may not imprison anyone who was denied counsel, but it masked a disagreement between those justices who thought that for misdemeanors and petty offenses the right to appointed counsel applied *only* to persons actually imprisoned and those justices who would extend it further. To settle this issue and resolve a conflict among state and lower federal courts on the point, the Court heard the case of Aubrey Scott, who could have been sentenced to one year in jail for shoplifting but was fined $50 instead (*Scott v. Illinois* [1979]). A closely divided Court upheld Scott's conviction without counsel, affirming that the constitutional standard was actual imprisonment, not authorized imprisonment. In a sharply worded dissent, Justice William J. Brennan argued that the trial of any offense serious enough to carry a possible prison sentence presented precisely the kind of problems for which the assistance of counsel had been found indispensable, and that an apparent reluctance to impose an economic burden on the states was no basis for the denial of a fundamental right.

The Court's basic problem was to reconcile the Sixth Amendment's guarantee of counsel "in all criminal prosecutions" with the reality that some offenses, such as traffic violations, are so petty that even persons who can afford to retain counsel do not bother to do so. In deciding where to draw the line, the Court not only assessed the need of defendants for legal assistance but was also sensitive to the concerns of federalism and state resentment of excessive federal control. "We do not sit as an ombudsman to direct state courts how to manage their affairs but only to make clear the federal constitutional requirement. How crimes should be classified is largely a state matter," wrote Justice Douglas for the Court (*Argersinger v. Hamlin* 38 [1972]). Douglas would surely have dissented in *Scott v. Illinois* if he had still been on the Court in 1979, but the majority in that case concluded that "the central premise of *Argersinger*—that actual imprisonment is a penalty different in kind from fines or the mere threat of imprisonment—is eminently sound and warrants adoption of actual imprisonment as the line defining the constitutional right to appointment of counsel. *Argersinger* has proved reasonably workable, whereas any extension would create confusion and impose unpredictable, but necessarily substantial, costs on 50 quite diverse States" (*Scott v. Illinois* 373 [1979]). State legislatures have discretion as to whether to make imprisonment a mandatory or possible punishment for criminal offenses, and judges have discretion as to whether to impose imprisonment when it is possible but not mandatory.

Under the *Argersinger/Scott* formula, states are not required to provide counsel for the trial of petty offenses; they are simply prohibited from imposing imprisonment if they do not. For the trial of lesser offenses, states get to draw the line between those defendants for whom they will provide counsel and those for whom they will not. In rejecting a definitive distinction between capital and noncapital cases in the *Betts* era, the Court had refused to interpret due process as providing less protection for liberty than for life. With respect to the right to counsel for minor offenses, however, it now endorsed a distinction between the deprivation of life and liberty on the one hand and property (through fines) on the other.

One further issue on which lower courts divided—suspended sentences—was not resolved for another twenty-three years, when LeReed Shelton, an indigent who was involved in a fistfight after a minor traffic accident, unsuccessfully represented himself in a prosecution for misdemeanor assault. When he was given a suspended sentence of thirty days in jail and placed on probation for two years, Shelton (and his newly acquired counsel) appealed. By the time the case reached the Supreme Court, three positions had emerged. Shelton argued that the suspended sentence could not be imposed because probation could be revoked and he could then be imprisoned as the result of a conviction in the absence of counsel, in violation of *Argersinger* and *Scott.* Alabama had at first argued that the suspended sentence could be both imposed and subsequently implemented, but its position now was that the sentence could be imposed but not implemented (which it thought made sense because it facilitated the use of probation as a means of correction). The Supreme Court therefore appointed former U.S. Solicitor General Charles Fried as amicus curiae (friend of the court) to argue Alabama's original position. A sharply divided Court held that a suspended sentence could not be implemented upon a defendant who neither had nor waived counsel at trial. As to whether a suspended sentence of incarceration could even be imposed, the Court declined to rule that it could in the absence of any indication that under state law it was separable from a sentence of probation. Alabama had not changed its position until after it lost in its own state supreme court, and the Court was now telling the state that it had gotten ahead of itself. As matters stand now, with revocable probation universally tied to suspended sentences, the decision means that such sentences cannot be imposed on indigents who were not afforded the assistance of counsel (*Alabama v. Shelton* [2002]).

Four dissenters thought the Court had decided a case not before it: what would the Constitution require if Alabama *had* sought to revoke Shelton's probation and incarcerate him? They argued that the actual imprisonment standard meant that Shelton's right to counsel had not been violated because he had not been imprisoned. Only if the state should seek to do that, they maintained, would a person like Shelton be entitled to appropriate safeguards, which could be devised. For example, the original case could be reprosecuted with counsel appointed and imprisonment contingent upon a second conviction. Surely, the dissenters reasoned, because probation is revoked in only a minority of cases, states might find it simpler and cheaper to retry a few cases with appointed counsel than to appoint counsel in every case in which they wish to preserve the option of imposing a suspended sentence.

RIGHT TO COUNSEL ON APPEAL

Appeals of Right

A final important question was whether indigent defendants in state cases were entitled to appointed counsel for appeals as well as at trial, and the Court provided a partial answer on the same day it decided *Gideon*, holding in *Douglas v. California* (1963) that counsel must be supplied for an appeal of right (a first appeal that a state chooses to make available to every convicted person as a matter of right). The Court's reasoning in *Douglas* rested not on the Sixth Amendment but on the equal protection clause, as well as the due process clause, of the Fourteenth Amendment, echoing the ruling in *Griffin v. Illinois* (1956) that both clauses are violated when an appeal of right is denied to a person unable to pay for a required transcript. Equal protection requires that people not be treated differently simply because of their poverty. (Both Abe Fortas and Bruce Jacob had argued the equal protection question in *Gideon,* but the Court had chosen not to rest its decision on that ground, as its purpose was to incorporate the right to counsel into the due process clause.)

Discretionary Appeals

In 1974 the Supreme Court, now with a more conservative membership, held that states are not required to appoint counsel for discretionary appeals (that is, requests for further hearings by higher appellate courts) and petitions for certiorari from the U.S. Supreme Court, both of which those courts are free to deny (*Ross v. Moffitt* [1974]). Appellants and petitioners are not being haled into court by the government, the Court noted, the arguments they need have already been prepared by an attorney for their first appeal, and, relative to those who can afford counsel, indigents at this stage are not in such different circumstances that they are denied equal protection. Such arguments did not persuade three dissenters, who thought that wealth still should not matter and pointed out the technical difficulties a layman faces in persuading a court to grant a discretionary hearing.

Other Postconviction Proceedings

When the process of direct appeal of a conviction to higher courts is exhausted, the judgment becomes final. States may, however, adopt statutes providing opportunities for collateral attack on a conviction, and there is also the avenue of a petition to a federal district court for a writ of habeas corpus (a procedure by which a judge considers the legality of the detention of a prisoner). In general, such modes of collateral attack make a claim that the process of conviction involved error that renders the detention unconstitutional. The Court has made it clear that there is no constitutional right to counsel in these kinds of postconviction proceedings (*Pennsylvania v. Finley* [1987]), and it reached the same result in a capital case, although only four justices held that no such right exists regardless of the legal circumstances of a person under sentence of death (*Murray v. Giarratano* [1989]). The Court's reasoning in *Finley* was that there is no obligation to provide these forms of postconviction review in the first place, and that in any event, the right to counsel does not extend beyond a first appeal of right. States may, of course, provide some measure of statutory right to counsel in collateral attacks if they so choose (Tomkovicz 2002, 118–120).

State prisoners do retain some constitutional rights, however. In a case consolidating actions brought by inmates in North Carolina correctional facilities, the Supreme Court held "that the fundamental constitutional right of access to the courts requires prison authorities to assist inmates in the preparation and filing of meaningful legal papers by providing prisoners with adequate law libraries or adequate assistance from persons trained in the law" (*Bounds v. Smith* 828 [1977]). The Supreme Court has not ruled explicitly that there is no constitutional right to counsel in federal habeas corpus proceedings, but many federal courts of appeal have done so. Indigent federal and state prisoners challenging a death sentence in a federal postconviction proceeding do, however, have a statutory right to appointed counsel and certain other services (21 U.S.C. § 848[q][4][B] [2000]).

A statutory right to counsel also exists in postconviction proceedings under certain other specified conditions, and in general, federal judges retain discretion to appoint counsel when they feel the interests of justice require it (Raquet and Stainback 2001, 1870–1871; Leslie 2001, 1893–1894). Inmates do not, however, have a right to retained or appointed counsel in prison disciplinary proceedings (*Wolff v. McDonnel* [1974]), even when the conduct charged could also be prosecuted as a crime (*Baxter v. Palmigiano* [1976]), because such proceedings are not criminal prosecutions.

Right to Counsel in Pretrial Proceedings

In *Powell v. Alabama,* Justice Sutherland characterized the period "from the time of . . . arraignment until the beginning of . . . trial, when consultation, thoroughgoing investigation and preparation were vitally important," as "perhaps the most critical period of the proceedings" and affirmed that a defendant "requires the guiding hand of counsel at every step in the proceedings against him" (*Powell v. Alabama* 57, 69 [1932]). Another important task for the courts, then, has been to determine just *when* an accused person is entitled to the assistance of counsel (or, to put the point in legal terms, just when the right to counsel attaches)—a determination that may affect all suspects, regardless of whether counsel is retained or appointed. The Supreme Court found an opportunity to address this question when it took the case of Billy Joe Wade.

Wade had been indicted for bank robbery and counsel had been appointed, but the FBI had subjected him to a lineup without notifying his attorney, who was therefore absent. While waiting for the proceedings to begin, the two witnesses had been able to look through an open door and see Wade alone with FBI agents before any other prisoners arrived (Graham 1970, 230). In holding that the witnesses' subsequent testimony identifying Wade as the robber could not be used if based solely on observations at a lineup at which defense counsel was not present, the Court set forth its approach to the problem of attachment.

> [T]oday's law enforcement machinery involves critical confrontations of the accused by the prosecution at pretrial proceedings where the results might well settle the accused's fate and reduce the trial itself to a mere formality. In recognition of these realities of modern criminal prosecution, our cases have construed the Sixth Amendment guarantee to apply to "critical" stages of the proceedings. The guarantee reads: "In all criminal prosecutions, the accused shall enjoy the right . . . to have the Assistance of Counsel *for his defence.*" (Emphasis supplied.) The plain wording of this guarantee thus encompasses counsel's assistance whenever necessary to assure a meaningful "defence." . . . [T]he accused is guaranteed that he need not stand alone against the State at any stage of the prosecution, formal or informal, in court or out, where counsel's absence might derogate from the accused's right to a fair trial. . . . [T]he principle of *Powell v. Alabama* and succeeding cases requires that we scrutinize *any* pretrial confrontation of the accused to determine whether the presence of his counsel is necessary to preserve the defendant's basic right to a fair trial as affected by his right meaningfully to cross-examine the witnesses against him and to have effective assistance of counsel at the trial itself. It calls upon us to analyze whether potential substantial prejudice to defendant's rights inheres in the particular confrontation and the ability of counsel to help avoid that prejudice." (*United States v. Wade* 224–225, 226, 227 [1967])

The Court held in *Wade* that a lineup (or a presentation of the suspect alone to the witness) is a critical stage at which the right to counsel is needed, because of the vagaries of eyewitness identifications and the intentional or unintentional employment of lineup procedures that suggest a particular outcome—sources of unfairness from which the accused is hardly capable of protecting himself or herself. The *Wade* decision means that prosecutors at trial may not present testimony identifying the defendant if that identification is based on a lineup at which the assistance of counsel was denied (i.e., the exclusionary rule applies: evidence obtained in violation of a person's legal rights may not be used against that person in court).

A Supreme Court rendered more conservative by three appointees of President Richard Nixon placed a significant qualification on the scope of the right defined in *Wade*, however, in *Kirby v. Illinois* (1972), a pretrial identification case in which the suspect was exhibited to the witness immediately after arrest, before counsel could be retained or appointed. Although they could not muster a majority opinion, five justices did agree that "[i]n a line of constitutional cases in this Court stemming back to the Court's landmark opinion in *Powell v. Alabama*, . . . it has been firmly established that a person's Sixth and Fourteenth Amendment right to counsel attaches only at or after the time that adversary judicial proceedings have been initiated against him. . . . whether by way of formal charge, preliminary hearing, indictment, information, or arraignment. . . . The initiation of judicial criminal proceedings is far from a mere formalism," the Court explained, but is rather the point at which a defendant first experiences the prosecutorial forces arrayed against him or her and the attendant need for legal assistance. "It is this point, therefore, that marks the commencement of the 'criminal prosecutions' to which alone the explicit guarantees of the Sixth Amendment are applicable" (*Kirby v. Illinois* 688–690 [1972] [plurality opinion]). Unlike Wade, who was under indictment, Kirby was not entitled to the presence of counsel at the identification because the formal legal process of prosecution had not yet begun. A lineup is a critical stage of the prosecution only after that point.

In dissent, an incredulous Justice Brennan, author of the opinion of the Court in *Wade*, asserted that:

> [I]t should go without saying . . . that *Wade* did not require the presence of counsel at pretrial confrontations for identification purposes simply on the basis of an abstract consideration of the words "criminal prosecutions" in the Sixth Amendment. Counsel is required at

> those confrontations because [of] "the dangers inherent in eyewitness identification and the suggestibility inherent in the context of the pretrial identification." . . . Hence, "the initiation of adversary judicial criminal proceedings" . . . is completely irrelevant to whether counsel is necessary at a pretrial confrontation for identification in order to safeguard the accused's constitutional rights to confrontation [of witnesses against him] and the effective assistance of counsel at his trial [through meaningful cross-examination of those witnesses]. (*Kirby v. Illinois* 696–697 [1972] [dissenting opinion])

The *Kirby* formula provides that the right to counsel pertains at and after the point at which the formal prosecution begins, and it identifies several events that may mark that point. As early as *Powell v. Alabama*, the Court had affirmed the right to counsel at arraignment (a proceeding in which the accused appears in the trial court to hear the formal charges and enter a plea), and it made the same point to the same state twenty-nine years later, overturning the conviction of a defendant who had been "sentenced to death on a count of an indictment charging breaking and entering a dwelling at night with intent to ravish" (*Hamilton v. Alabama* 52 [1961]). Because practice varies from state to state, an arraignment may not be a critical stage in all jurisdictions, but the holding in *Hamilton* applies at least to "the pretrial type of arraignment where certain rights may be sacrificed or lost" (*Coleman v. Alabama* 7 [1970]). Because one is entitled to be represented by counsel at arraignment, the right to counsel attaches as soon as a formal charge is lodged, by either a grand jury indictment or an information (an alternate charging mechanism used in less serious cases). Under some circumstances, the right may attach even earlier. An information (and sometimes a decision to refer a case to a grand jury) is the product of a preliminary hearing (an adversarial hearing before a magistrate to determine whether sufficient evidence exists to warrant a prosecution). The Supreme Court has held the preliminary hearing to be a critical stage of the prosecution when the accused clearly requires the assistance of counsel, as in entering a plea (*White v. Maryland* [1963]), or when the nature of the proceedings may materially affect the conduct of the trial and the absence of counsel would be prejudicial to the defense (*Coleman v. Alabama* [1970]).

On the other hand, the Supreme Court has not held a grand jury investigation or a suspect's initial appearance before a magistrate (the proceeding in which a suspect, promptly after arrest, is taken before a magistrate to hear the charges, be advised of his or her rights, and have bail determined) to be critical stages at which the right to counsel attaches, and U.S. courts of appeal have held that they are not (even when the suspect is a target of the grand jury investigation, because adversarial judicial proceedings have not yet begun) (Rosenfeld and Klintworth 2001, 1486 n.1462).

Attachment of the right to counsel does not depend upon a request by the defendant; when the right attaches it does so automatically and ceases to apply only if knowingly and intelligently waived (*Brewer v. Williams* [1977], citing *Carnley v. Cochran* [1962]—one of several cases Florida lost under the *Betts* rule just prior to the *Gideon* decision). On the other hand, the timing of the attachment of a defendant's right to counsel depends on the act of initiating formal charges by the prosecution, which may delay to gain a strategic advantage. Moreover, all but the most serious breaches of the right to counsel may constitute harmless error, and therefore not be grounds for application of the exclusionary rule or the overturning of a conviction. On a direct appeal of conviction or sentence, the test is "that before a federal constitutional error can be held harmless, the court must be able to declare a belief that it was harmless beyond a reasonable doubt," that is, that the government has met the burden of demonstrating beyond a reasonable doubt that the error did not contribute to the conviction or sentence (*Chapman v. California* 24 [1967]). For example, the prosecution's use at trial of a postarraignment incriminating statement taken in violation of the right to counsel would be harmless error if other testimony and evidence established guilt beyond a reasonable doubt (Rosenfeld and Klintworth 2001, 1486 n.1465; Tomkovicz 2002, 184–191).

Before the Sixth Amendment right to counsel formally attaches, a suspect may of course retain an attorney, and the government may adopt a more generous policy with respect to the presence of counsel than is required (for example, the federal government allows grand jury witnesses and targets to consult retained counsel, but only outside the grand jury room), but the suspect has no constitutional right to the appointment of counsel or to the presence of counsel at such events as lineups and noncustodial police questioning, and statements or evidence taken in the absence of counsel are not subject to the exclusionary rule for that reason. Two other provisions of the Constitution do, however, provide some protection. The *Kirby* plurality noted that constitutional standards of due process apply to lineups and other pretrial confrontations even when the right to counsel does not, citing an earlier decision in which the Court had stated that a claim of the denial of due process "is a recognized ground of attack upon a conviction independent of any right to counsel claim" (*Stovall v. Denno* 302 [1967] [plurality opinion]).

Due process claims may be difficult to sustain, however. Theodore Stovall was suspected of fatally stabbing a doctor and gravely wounding the man's wife. Before he could obtain counsel, he was exhibited alone to the wife at the hospital, in handcuffs, and required to repeat a few words; at trial, she identified him as the assailant. The Court held that although the "practice of showing suspects singly to persons for the purpose of identification, and not as part of a lineup, has been widely condemned . . ., a claimed violation of due process of law in the conduct of a confrontation depends on the totality of the circumstances surrounding it, and the record in the present case reveals that the showing of Stovall to Mrs. Behrendt [the victim] in an immediate hospital confrontation was imperative," because she was unable to attend a lineup at the jail and was in danger of dying. Because no other procedure was feasible in Stovall's case, the confrontation in the hospital was not "so unnecessarily suggestive and conducive to irreparable mistaken identification that he was denied due process of law" (*Stovall v. Denno* 302 [1967] [plurality opinion]).

Under less exigent circumstances, the due process question may turn on the way in which the confrontation was conducted, rather than on its necessity, and two years after *Stovall* the Supreme Court did find a denial of due process on that basis. In this case, the suspect was positively identified only after he was required to (1) wear a jacket similar to the perpetrator's and to appear in a lineup with other men noticeably shorter than he, (2) meet individually with the identifying witness, and (3) appear several days later in a second lineup where he was the only one who had also appeared in the first. The Court found such police conduct so suggestive of a desired result that it constituted "a compelling example of unfair lineup procedures" (*Foster v. California* 442 [1969]).

Advocates of the right to counsel argue, however, that it is more difficult for an attorney to sustain a due process claim when he or she was not privy to the event and it is the suspect's word against that of the police. More fundamentally, they contend that due process violations are less likely to occur in the presence of defense counsel.

The other constitutional provision that affords suspects some protection before the Sixth Amendment right to counsel attaches is the Fifth Amendment. In *Miranda v. Arizona* (1966), the Court held that a person taken into custody may assert a right to the assistance of counsel in order to safeguard his or her privilege against self-incrimination. The *Kirby* plurality did not challenge that ruling, even though it applies when formal judicial proceedings against the suspect have not been initiated, but rather pronounced *Miranda*, a Fifth Amendment case, irrelevant to the interpretation of the Sixth Amendment right to counsel. (The topic of *Miranda* rights is treated extensively in Chapter 5.)

Even when the right to counsel has attached at some critical stage, a defendant is not entitled to the assistance of counsel in every subsequent context of the prosecution. In *Wade,* the Supreme Court distinguished lineups from forms of evidence gathering such as the scientific analysis of fingerprints, blood samples, clothing, and hair, for which the presence of counsel is not necessary because the defendant's interests can be adequately protected at trial through cross-examination of expert witnesses for the prosecution and presentation of such witnesses for the defense. For the same reason that these activities do not constitute critical stages of a prosecution, the Court concluded in a companion case to *Wade* that there is no right to counsel for the taking of handwriting samples (*Gilbert v. California* [1967]).

Six years later, in holding that a defendant has no right to the presence of counsel at a photographic display of suspects to witnesses, the Court revised its concept of critical stages (U.S. Senate 1992, 1445–1446). According to the new formulation, which builds on the *Kirby* modification of *Wade,* the historical purpose of the right to counsel was to provide needed assistance *at trial,* "when the accused was confronted with both the intricacies of the law and the advocacy of the public prosecutor," and the Court's extension of that right "has resulted from changing patterns of criminal procedure and investigation that have tended to generate pretrial events" at which "the accused was confronted, just as at trial, by the procedural system, or by his expert adversary, or by both." Thus, critical pretrial stages arise "only when new contexts appear presenting the same dangers that gave birth initially to the right itself" (*United States v. Ash* 309, 310, 311 [1973]). The majority agreed that lineups are such confrontations, so the right to counsel pertains, but concluded that because the defendant is not present at photographic displays, they are more like the prosecution's pretrial interviews with its witnesses, which defense counsel has no right to attend. Once the right to counsel has attached, a lineup is a critical stage, but a photographic display is not.

Justice Brennan and two colleagues in dissent found no justification for either the Court's result or its rationale. A critical stage, they argued, had until now been understood as any proceeding at which the presence of counsel is required to preserve the right to a fair trial, not just one at which the accused confronts the forces of the prosecution. Contrary to the majority's assertions, photo-identification sessions are fraught with the same risks of error and manipulation as lineups and very different from events like fingerprinting and the taking of blood samples. To deny that reality, and to deny the assistance of counsel at pretrial events unless the accused faces some sort of adversarial confrontation, was "a wholly unprecedented—and wholly unsupportable—limitation on the Sixth Amendment right" to counsel (*United States v. Ash* 338 [1973] [dissenting opinion]). The majority, Brennan concluded, could not square its decision with his opinion for the Court in *Wade* by reinterpreting that opinion as affirming a right to counsel at lineups because they are adversarial confrontations between the prosecution and the accused.

Justice Brennan could take only small satisfaction from the fact that in narrowing the concept of critical stages by departing from the premise of *Wade*, the majority had avoided overruling that decision. The arguments about the need for counsel to monitor lineups and effectively cross-examine witnesses who identified the defendant at trial still had force—although, as Brennan had lamented in his *Kirby* dissent a year earlier, they no longer applied to lineups held before the initiation of formal judicial proceedings.

The result of *Kirby* and *Ash* is that, prior to trial, a defendant is entitled to the assistance of counsel at those stages of the prosecution that occur after formal judicial proceedings have been initiated against him or her and that involve some form of adversarial confrontation with the prosecution.

Beyond the specific need for counsel at such pretrial events as lineups and preliminary hearings looms the reality that most defendants' cases are resolved before they ever get to trial. Plea bargaining is the normal way of disposing of criminal cases in the United States, and about 90 percent of all felony defendants plead guilty (Cole, Gertz, and Bunger 2002, 197). A plea bargain involves the waiver of constitutional rights (self-incrimination, jury trial) and depends on an informed estimate of the admissibility and strength of the prosecutor's evidence. Justice Douglas succinctly stated the defendant's need for the assistance of counsel in this process when he noted that the guilty plea is "a problem which looms large in misdemeanor as well as in felony cases. Counsel is needed so that the accused may know precisely what he is doing, so that he is fully aware of the prospect of going to jail or prison, and so that he is treated fairly by the prosecution" (*Argersinger v. Hamlin* 34 [1972]). Defendants have an unchallenged right to the assistance of counsel for the process of negotiating a plea in lieu of standing trial (Tomkovicz 2002, 109–110).

RIGHT TO COUNSEL IN OTHER PROCEEDINGS

Sentencing and Revocation Hearings

Long before the right to counsel was applied to the states, the Supreme Court held that when the lack of counsel at a sentencing hearing is prejudicial to a defendant (as when the sentence is based on false information that might have been corrected), due process has been denied (*Townsend v. Burke* [1948]). After incorporation of the right in *Gideon,* the Court made it clear "that appointment of counsel for an indigent is required at every stage of a criminal proceeding where substantial rights of a criminal accused may be affected," and that sentencing is such a critical stage (*Mempa v. Rhay* 134 [1967]).

Indigents on probation or parole and facing hearings to determine whether that status should be revoked do not necessarily have a right to appointed counsel. The Court has observed that such proceedings, in contrast to criminal trials, are not adversarial but informal and focus not only on fact-finding about the conduct of the probationer or parolee but also on the exercise of discretion with respect to the threat he or she poses to the community and his or her rehabilitative needs. Counsel is therefore not normally necessary or desirable, the Court has concluded; thus, although the person faces loss of liberty, the *Argersinger* standard does not apply. In some cases a person facing revocation does, however, require the assistance of counsel to present his or her position, and so, in these proceedings, the constitutional standard is not the Sixth Amendment right to counsel but, as in the pre-*Gideon* era, the due process standard of fundamental fairness, to be determined on a case-by-case basis (*Gagnon v. Scarpelli* [1973]). If, however, a probationer's sentence was not determined at the time of conviction and then suspended, but was rather deferred until such time as the probation might be revoked, "a lawyer must be afforded at this proceeding whether it be labeled a revocation of probation or a deferred sentencing" (*Mempa v. Rhay* 137 [1967]).

Juvenile Cases

Separate systems of juvenile justice for youthful offenders were originally created on paternalistic rather than adversarial premises, but juvenile delinquency can involve serious infractions and lead to confinement in state institutions. As part of a decision revolutionizing the standards of juvenile justice in 1967, the Supreme Court ruled "that the Due Process Clause of the Fourteenth Amendment requires that in respect of proceedings to determine delinquency which may result in commitment to an institution in which the juvenile's freedom is curtailed, the child and his parents must be notified of the child's right to be represented by counsel retained by them, or if they are unable to afford counsel, that counsel will be appointed to represent the child" (*In re Gault* 41 [1967]). A study has found that states took action to comply with the *Gault* requirement, but that they vary considerably in the nature of the protection offered, and that large numbers of juveniles choose to waive their right to counsel (Caeti, Hemmens, and Burton 1996).

Counsel and Client

Attorney of Choice

In its first major decision on the subject, the Supreme Court declared that "a defendant should be afforded a fair opportunity to secure counsel of his own choice" (*Powell v. Alabama* 53 [1932]). That right is not absolute, however, for "the essential aim of the [Sixth] Amendment is to guarantee an effective advocate for each criminal defendant rather than to ensure that a defendant will inexorably be represented by the lawyer whom he prefers" (*Wheat v. United States* 159 [1988]). A defendant's right to an attorney of his or her choice must be weighed against competing interests. The defendant has no right to be represented by an attorney who is not a member of the bar, or who does not wish to take the case, or whom the defendant cannot afford, or who has a previous or current relationship with the opposing party, and trial judges have discretion to disallow representation by an attorney with a potential or actual conflict of interest.

Wheat, a drug distributor who wanted to retain the same attorney as his codefendants, was not permitted to do so because there was a reasonable possibility that the prosecution would arrange for some of the defendants to testify against others. The Supreme Court upheld the trial judge's decision, even though the trials were separate and the defendants had waived their right to conflict-free representation.

The Court's approach is further illustrated in a case in which it upheld a trial judge's refusal to grant a defendant's motion for a continuance because of the hospitalization of his public defender, when a fully qualified replacement had declared himself ready to proceed. "[W]e reject the claim that the Sixth Amendment guarantees a 'meaningful relationship' between an accused and his counsel," declared the Court (*Morris v. Slappy* 14 [1983]).

Self-Representation

Section 35 of the Judiciary Act of 1789 (28 U.S.C. §1654 [2000]), enacted before the Sixth Amendment was proposed, guaranteed the right of an individual to represent himself or herself in federal court. In a case decided four years after *Johnson v. Zerbst* had established the right to appointed counsel in federal courts, the Court affirmed that "the Constitution does not force a lawyer upon a defendant. He may waive his Constitutional right to assistance of counsel if he knows what he is doing and his choice is made with eyes open" (*Adams* v. *United States ex rel. McCann* 279 [1942]). Most states followed that practice as well, and the Supreme Court often suggested that it was required, but after the incorporation of the right to counsel in *Gideon v. Wainwright*, the question of whether a defendant had the constitutional right to self-representation in state court was still technically open.

When the judge in the trial of Anthony Faretta, accused of grand theft, denied his request to represent himself and required that his defense be conducted by a public defender, the issue was joined. In *Faretta v. California* (1975), the Supreme Court noted that in all of British, colonial, and American history prior to the adoption of the Bill of Rights, the only court to impose counsel on a defendant was the notorious Star Chamber (see the discussion of English and continental origins of the privilege against self-incrimination in Chapter 2). Further, it found that the Sixth Amendment was a compilation of *personal* rights—to be tried by jury, to be informed of the charges, to confront witnesses, to have compulsory process (subpoena power), and to have the *assistance* of counsel, and it found no evidence that the latter provision was ever intended to undermine the right to defend oneself in court. "Although not stated in the Amendment in so many words," the Court concluded, "the right to self-representation—to make one's own defense personally—is thus necessarily implied by the structure of the Amendment" (*Faretta v. California* 819 [1975]).

Three dissenters disputed the Court's historical and textual analysis and offered a fundamental criticism. It is not "accurate to suggest," wrote Chief Justice Warren Burger, "that the quality of his representation at trial is a matter with which only the accused is legitimately concerned." It is the responsibility of the state to ensure that justice is done in every criminal trial, and

> [t]hat goal is ill-served, and the integrity of and public confidence in the system are undermined, when an easy conviction is obtained due to the defendant's ill-advised decision to waive counsel. . . . [B]oth the "spirit and the logic" of the Sixth Amendment are that every person accused of crime shall receive the fullest possible defense; in the vast majority of cases this command can be honored only by means of the expressly guaranteed right to counsel, and the trial judge is in the best position to determine whether the accused is capable of conducting his defense. True freedom of choice and society's interest in seeing that justice is achieved can be vindicated only if the trial court retains discretion to reject any attempted waiver of counsel and insist that the accused be tried according to the Constitution. This discretion is as critical an element of basic fairness as a trial judge's discretion to decline to accept a plea of guilty." (*Faretta v. California* 839–840 [1975] [dissenting opinion])

Justice Blackmun summed up his misgivings more caustically: "If there is any truth to the old proverb that 'one who is his own lawyer has a fool for a client,' the Court by its opinion today now bestows a *constitutional* right on one to make a fool of himself" (*Faretta v. California* 852 [1975] [dissenting opinion; emphasis in the original]).

The *Faretta* majority acknowledged that the issue was a thorny one and conceded in a footnote that "[t]he right of self-representation is not a license to abuse the dignity of the courtroom. Neither is it a license not to comply with relevant rules of procedural and substantive law. Thus . . . a defendant who elects to represent himself cannot thereafter complain that the quality of his own defense amounted to a denial of 'effective assistance of counsel'" (*Faretta v. California* 835, n46 [1975]). The Court had already ruled that a defendant representing himself or herself could be removed from the courtroom for repeated obstructionist and disruptive conduct, with his case to be conducted by standby appointed counsel (*Illinois v. Allen* [1970]), and it later held that a trial judge may, even over a defendant's objection, appoint standby counsel to assure compliance with courtroom procedures and protocol (*McKaskle v. Wiggins* [1984]).

A notable example of the potential for abuse of the right to self-representation occurred in the case of Zacarias Moussaoui, accused of conspiracy in the terrorist attacks of 11 September 2001. Federal district judge Leonie M. Brinkema initially allowed Moussaoui to represent himself but ultimately revoked that privilege because of his filing of "'frivolous, scandalous, disrespectful, or repetitive'" court papers containing "'contemptuous language that would never be tolerated from an attorney'" (cited in Shenon 2003, A8).

When confronted with the issue of self-representation on appeal (where arguments relate to issues of law and not of fact), the Supreme Court found that the state's interest in the orderly administration of justice outweighs the individual's interest in autonomy. The language of the Sixth Amendment applies exclusively to criminal prosecutions, and the right to appeal itself is statutory, not constitutional; hence, there is no constitutional right to self-representation on appeal (*Martinez v. Court of Appeal* [2000]).

Attorney-Client Privilege

The attorney-client privilege is a venerable protection of the common law that has been acknowledged by the Supreme Court at least since the late nineteenth century and is honored in federal and state courts. The privilege, which may be waived only by the client, allows clients and requires attorneys to refuse to divulge confidential communications between the two. Because the client also enjoys the privilege against self-incrimination, the confidentiality of the relationship is particularly salient in the context of criminal law. The right to counsel cannot be fully effective unless defense attorneys have full and unfettered access to the information they need, and clients would not be in a position to provide such information if they risked the possibility that it could then be used against them. There is a public as well as a personal interest in the effective assistance of defense counsel, and the privilege does not deprive the government of much evidence because without it, the client would generally not reveal the evidence in the first place. Furthermore, clients may have valid reasons for preserving the confidentiality of information that would not incriminate them.

So fundamental is this principle that the Supreme Court has recently reaffirmed the sanctity of the privilege even after the death of the client. After Vincent Foster, a deputy White House counsel in the Clinton administration, committed suicide during the course of an investigation of the firing of employees of the White House travel office, a federal grand jury issued a subpoena for notes taken by his lawyer during their consultations. The lawyer and his firm resisted, citing their obligation under the privilege, and the Supreme Court agreed, noting that clients may fear posthumous disclosure as much as disclosure during their lifetimes and rejecting the notion "that in criminal proceedings, the interest in determining whether a crime has been committed should trump client confidentiality" (*Swidler and Berlin v. United States* 406 [1998]).

Effective Assistance of Counsel

"It has long been recognized that the right to counsel is the right to the effective assistance of counsel" at trial, observed the Supreme Court in 1970 (*McMann v. Richardson* 771 n.14 [1970]), and fifteen years later it came to the same conclusion with respect to appeals of right. "[T]he promise of *Douglas* [*v. California*] that a criminal defendant has a right to counsel on appeal—like the promise of *Gideon* [*v. Wainwright*] that a criminal defendant has a right to counsel at trial—would be a futile gesture unless it comprehended the right to the effective assistance of counsel" (*Evitts v. Lucey* 397 [1985]). A defendant thus has the opportunity to have a conviction overthrown or an appeal reconsidered on the grounds that the ineffective performance of counsel caused him or her to be deprived of liberty without due process of law, and he or she may make that claim (presumably with a new lawyer) even if his or her original attorney was retained rather than appointed (*Cuyler v. Sullivan* [1980]). One may not, however, gain relief on the basis of ineffective assistance of counsel with respect to any proceeding for which the constitutional right to counsel did not apply in the first place—for example, the performance of retained counsel with respect to a discretionary appeal (*Wainwright v. Torna* [1982]).

The issue of ineffective assistance looms larger at the trial level, where it may involve a claim either that the defense attorney failed to provide adequate assistance or that the state imposed rules or conditions that unduly inhibited the performance of his or her role. In two cases decided on the same day in 1984, the Supreme Court announced a two-prong test for determining when a deprivation of right at trial (or at a capital sentencing hearing) has occurred (and it later made clear that the same general standards govern claims of ineffective assistance on appeals of right). "First, the defendant must show that counsel's performance was deficient. . . . Second, the defendant must show that the deficient performance prejudiced the defense. . . . that counsel's errors were so serious as to deprive the defendant of a fair trial, a trial whose result is reliable" (*Strickland v. Washington* 687 [1984]).

When the claim is that the government impermissibly interfered with the functioning of defense counsel, the question of what counsel was required to do or prevented from doing by the government (the deficiency prong) is sometimes relatively straightforward, and the critical question is whether or not the effect undermined the reliability of the trial (the prejudice prong). Some kinds of interference are so blatant that prejudice will be presumed and need not be shown. For example, the Supreme Court had ruled eight years earlier that a trial judge's order preventing a defense attorney from conferring with his client during a seventeen-hour overnight recess between direct examination and cross-examination of the defendant (issued because of the judge's fear of improper coaching) was on its face a violation of the right to counsel (*Geders v. United States* [1976]). Five years after *Strickland,* the Court cited *Geders* with approval and confirmed that "'[a]ctual or constructive denial of the assistance of counsel altogether' . . . is not subject to the kind of prejudice analysis that is appropriate in determining whether the quality of a lawyer's performance itself has been constitutionally ineffective" (*Perry v. Leeke* 280 [1989]).

If state action inhibits but does not preclude the assistance of counsel, however, the defendant must establish prejudice (and in *Perry,* the Court upheld a prohibition of consultation during a recess of only fifteen minutes, because there is no right to consult with counsel in the midst of one's testimony). In the companion case to *Strickland,* the defendant in an alleged check-kiting scheme faced charges of mail fraud brought after a governmental investigation of more than four years, involving thousands of documents. When retained defense counsel withdrew right before trial, the judge appointed a young and inexperienced real estate attorney who had never conducted a jury trial and gave him only twenty-five days to prepare his case. The Supreme Court found that these facts alone did not support the defendant's claim that his conviction should be overturned; his burden was both to identify specific errors of his counsel and to demonstrate their prejudicial effect (*United States v. Cronic* [1984]).

When the claim is simply that the defense attorney failed to perform adequately, a claim of ineffective assistance is even more difficult to sustain. Under the *Strickland* test, the Constitution requires only that attorneys provide "reasonably effective assistance . . . considering all the circumstances." To satisfy the deficiency prong of the test, a "defendant must show that counsel's representation fell below an objective standard of reasonableness . . . under prevailing professional norms." He or she "must identify the acts or omissions of counsel that are alleged not to have been the result of reasonable professional judgment," and "[t]he court must then determine whether . . . the identified acts or omissions were outside the wide range of professionally competent assistance. . . . Judicial scrutiny of counsel's performance must be highly deferential," and "a court must indulge a strong presumption that counsel's conduct falls within the wide range of reasonable professional assistance" (*Strickland v. Washington* 687–690 passim [1984]).

As for the prejudice prong of the test, the Court said in *Cronic* that in certain rare circumstances, prejudice will be presumed. These include complete denial of the assistance of counsel at a critical stage; governmental interference with counsel of the sort in the *Geders* case; conditions so inimical to the effective performance of counsel as to resemble those encountered in *Powell v. Alabama;* proceedings in which "counsel entirely fails to subject the prosecution's case to meaningful adversarial testing" (*United States v. Cronic* 659 [1984]); and, the Court noted in *Cuyler,* an attorney's conflict of interest if "a defendant shows that his counsel actively represented conflicting interests" in a way that "adversely affected his lawyer's performance" or was denied an opportunity to show that at trial (*Cuyler v. Sullivan* 350, 348 [1980]). In all other cases, the defendant must meet the prejudice prong of the test by demonstrating "a reasonable probability that, but for counsel's unprofessional errors, the result of the proceeding would have been different" (*Strickland v. Washington* 694 [1984])—that is, a reasonable (but not necessarily better-than-even) chance that there would have been reasonable doubt as to guilt or that the sentence in a murder case would not have been death.

The *Strickland* analysis focused on issues of guilt or innocence in general and on sentencing in capital cases; the Court has applied it to sentencing in noncapital cases as well and has ruled that imposition of increased prison time does satisfy the prejudice prong of the test when the court made a classification error against which the attorney raised no argument (*Glover v. United States* [2001]). The two-prong test also applies to claims of ineffective assistance in cases that were plea bargained, when, "in order to satisfy the 'prejudice' requirement, the defendant must show that there is a reasonable probability that, but for counsel's errors, he would not have pleaded guilty and would have insisted on going to trial" (*Hill v. Lockhart* 59 [1985]).

Most claims of ineffective assistance of counsel must meet both the deficiency and prejudice prongs of the *Strickland* test, and such claims are only rarely successful. In the state and lower federal appeals courts there are many examples of claims that have failed in spite of the apparently seriously deficient conduct of defense counsel (Craven and Pitman 2001, 995). Although lower courts sometimes did so after 1984, the Supreme Court did not find that a claim satisfied both prongs of the *Strickland* test until sixteen years later, when it upheld a claim of ineffective assistance when an attorney had failed to present voluminous evidence of mitigating circumstances in the sentencing phase of a capital case (*Williams v. Taylor* [2000]; see Benner et al. 2001, 285–295, 318). Because the Court may have taken this case only to deal with confusion over proper interpretation of a provision of the federal habeas corpus statute in light of one of its other decisions, the *Williams* case did not make clear whether the Court also intended to send a signal that lower courts had allowed the standard of adequate performance of defense counsel to sink too low.

In any event, the standard for establishing ineffective assistance reflects great deference to the presumed competence of defense counsel. Although this approach makes it difficult for individual defendants to prevail in their claims of inadequate representation, the Court has apparently concluded that it is essential to maintain the integrity of the defense function overall. It averred in *Strickland* that "[t]he availability of intrusive post-trial inquiry into attorney performance or of detailed guidelines for its evaluation would encourage the proliferation of ineffectiveness challenges. Criminal trials resolved unfavorably to the defendant would increasingly come to be followed by a second trial, this one of counsel's unsuccessful defense. Counsel's performance and even willingness to serve could be adversely affected. Intensive scrutiny of counsel and rigid requirements for acceptable assistance could dampen the ardor and impair the independence of defense counsel, discourage the acceptance of assigned cases, and undermine the trust between attorney and client" (*Strickland v. Washington* 690 [1984]).

Conclusion

In the middle decades of the twentieth century, the Supreme Court revolutionized law and practice with respect to the right to counsel. The transformation was gradual rather than abrupt; after the horrors of *Powell v. Alabama* the Court soon mandated counsel in federal cases but moved slowly (too slowly, some would say) with respect to the states, experimenting with a special circumstances rule that proved inadequate. By the time the Court mandated counsel in state cases as well, however, consensus on the correctness of that position had largely formed and compliance was prompt. Serious issues of the quality of representation remain, but criminal defendants since *Gideon* have routinely had the assistance of counsel.

One major issue remains to be considered—the role of counsel in the interrogation of suspects. The issue of interrogation involves not only the suspect's right to counsel but also his or her right not to have involuntary confessions used against him or her. We therefore first explore the modern development of the privilege against self-incrimination in Chapter 4, and then examine the convergence of these two rights in Chapter 5.

REFERENCES

Beaney, William M. 1955. *The Right to Counsel in American Courts.* Ann Arbor: University of Michigan Press.

Benner, Laurence A., Marshall J. Hartman, Shelvin R. Singer, and Andrea D. Lyon. 2001. "Criminal Justice in the Supreme Court: A Review of United States Supreme Court Criminal and Habeas Corpus Decisions (October 4, 1999–October 1, 2000)." *California Western Law Review* 37:239–319.

Caeti, Tory J., Craig Hemmens, and Velmer S. Burton Jr. 1996. "Juvenile Right to Counsel: A National Comparison of State Legal Codes." *American Journal of Criminal Law* 23:611–632.

Cole, George F., Marc G. Gertz, and Amy Bunger. 2002. *The Criminal Justice System: Politics and Policies.* Belmont, CA: Wadsworth.

Craven, Michelle, and Michael Pitman. 2001. "To the Best of One's Ability: A Guide to Effective Lawyering." *Georgetown Journal of Legal Ethics* 14:983–999.

Fellman, David. 1976. *The Defendant's Rights Today.* Madison: University of Wisconsin Press.

Graham, Fred P. 1970. *The Due Process Revolution: The Warren Court's Impact on Criminal Law.* Rochelle Park, NJ: Hayden Book Company,

Inc. Original edition, 1970. *The Self-Inflicted Wound.* New York: Macmillan.

Leslie, Felix S. 2001. "Thirtieth Annual Review of Criminal Procedure: Introduction and Guide for Users: V. Review Proceedings: Habeas Relief for Federal Prisoners." *Georgetown Law Journal* 89:1877–1896.

Lewis, Anthony. 1964. *Gideon's Trumpet.* New York: Random House.

Raquet, Rebecca C., and Sara Stainback. 2001. "Thirtieth Annual Review of Criminal Procedure: Introduction and Guide for Users: V. Review Proceedings: Habeas Relief for State Prisoners." *Georgetown Law Journal* 89:1870–1876.

Rosenfeld, Jeffrey M., and Sheri Klintworth. 2001. "Thirtieth Annual Review of Criminal Procedure: Introduction and Guide for Users: III. Trial: Right to Counsel." *Georgetown Law Journal* 89:1485–1514.

Shenon, Philip. 2003. "Judge Bars 9/11 Suspect from Being Own Lawyer." *New York Times* (15 November, A8, late edition).

Tomkovicz, James J. 2002. *The Right to the Assistance of Counsel: A Reference Guide to the United States Constitution.* Westport, CT: Greenwood Press.

U.S. Senate. 1992. *The Constitution of the United States of America: Analysis and Interpretation.* 103d Cong., 1st sess. S. Doc. 103–6. Washington, DC: Government Printing Office.

4

The Twentieth Century: Privilege against Self-Incrimination

As we saw in Chapter 2, it was not until late in the nineteenth century that the Supreme Court began the process of elaborating the meaning of the self-incrimination clause in *Boyd, Counselman,* and related cases. That process continued slowly for a time, but in the middle third of the twentieth century it became entwined with a parallel process of amplification of the due process clause in state cases involving confessions, and the pace accelerated. In those state cases the Court's view of the due process standard became less and less distinguishable from the self-incrimination standard for federal cases, and in 1964 the privilege joined the list of many other provisions of the Bill of Rights incorporated into the Fourteenth Amendment and applied to the states by the Warren Court. In many respects the Court expanded the scope of personal protection, but with regard to private papers and immunity from prosecution, it contracted it. In this chapter we explore the contours of the privilege against self-incrimination as shaped by the Supreme Court.

THE TESTIMONIAL PRIVILEGE

Forum

The privilege against self-incrimination originally and most fundamentally concerned compelled testimony under oath. In *Counselman v. Hitchcock* (see the discussion of nineteenth-century developments in the section on privilege against self-incrimination in Chapter 2), the Court ruled that the privilege may be asserted in any forum in which testimony can be compelled, and it has held consistently to that position. Thus, when the government argued in a case involving a federal bankruptcy hearing "that the constitutional privilege against self-incrimination does not apply in any civil proceeding," Justice Louis D. Brandeis responded for a unanimous Court that "[t]he contrary must be accepted as settled. The privilege is not ordinarily dependent upon the nature of the proceeding in which the testimony is sought or is to be used. It applies alike to civil and criminal proceedings, wherever the answer might tend to subject to criminal responsibility him who gives it" (*McCarthy v. Arndstein* 40 [1924]).

Similarly, in a case involving the rights of a witness before a congressional investigating committee, the Court remarked that as a matter of course, "[t]he Bill of Rights is applicable to investigations as to all forms of governmental action. Witnesses cannot be compelled to give evidence against themselves" (*Watkins v. United States* 188 [1957]). The privilege applies not just to defendants at their own trials, but to all witnesses in all official proceedings. Persons called to testify at civil trials or before grand juries, legislative committees, or administrative bodies thus have the same privilege as witnesses in a criminal trial, because they run the same risk—that their words (or information derived from their words) may be used against them in a criminal prosecution.

Personal Privilege

The privilege may be asserted only by the person from whom the information is sought, and who will be incriminated by it. Further, the privilege shields the person, not the information. "[T]he Fifth Amendment privilege is a *personal* privilege: it adheres basically to the person, not to information that may incriminate him. As Mr. Justice Holmes put it: 'A party is privileged from producing the evidence but not from its production.' . . . The Constitution explicitly prohibits compelling an accused to bear witness 'against himself'; it necessarily does not proscribe incriminating statements elicited from another. . . . It is extortion of information from the accused himself that offends our sense of justice" (*Couch v. United States* 328 [1973] [emphasis in the original]). Lillian Couch was a restaurateur whose tax returns were prepared by an accountant who was an independent contractor, not her employee. When the Internal Revenue Service, suspecting Couch of tax fraud, issued a summons to the accountant for her records in his possession, she claimed the privilege against self-incrimination. The Court denied her claim because, although the records were her property, no compulsion to produce them had been directed against her (and because she had no reasonable expectation of privacy with respect to documents shared with her accountant).

Consider also the example of a defendant who has discussed his or her crime with a friend. The defendant has not been compelled to incriminate himself or herself in this manner, but the friend may be compelled to testify against the defendant because "[t]he Court has held repeatedly that the Fifth Amendment is limited to prohibiting the use of 'physical or moral compulsion' exerted *on the person asserting the privilege*" (*Fisher v. United States* 397 [1976] [emphasis supplied]). The defendant cannot assert the privilege to prevent compulsion of the friend, and the friend cannot assert the privilege to avoid incriminating the defendant. In this example, the friend can assert the privilege only if by his or her testimony he will incriminate himself or herself.

Natural Persons

The privilege, moreover, applies only to natural persons. Although legally sanctioned associations have some rights under the law and can be subpoenaed and prosecuted, the Supreme Court has adopted the view that allowing them to withhold incriminating information would thwart the ability of the government to regulate the entities that it has authorized and to enforce its laws, especially those against white-collar crime, because organizational records are often the only good evidence of wrongdoing.

Early in the twentieth century the Court ruled that corporations have no privilege against self-incrimination (*Hale v. Henkel* [1906]; *Wilson v. United States* [1911]), and it has reached the same result for unincorporated labor unions (*United States v. White* [1944]) and small business partnerships (*Bellis v. United States* [1974]). The occasion for compelled incrimination commonly comes in the form of a subpoena for records and other documents of the association, and the Court has not deviated from its collective entity doctrine. This holds that the organization has no privilege and that the custodian of organizational documents acts in a representative rather than a personal capacity as an agent of the organization, and, therefore, that the custodian has no privilege to withhold organizational documents, even if he or she wrote them and even if they incriminate him or her personally. If the custodian could assert his or her personal privilege under these circumstances, the organization would effectively enjoy the privilege as well, as it can act only through its officers. On the other hand, the Court has made clear that the custodian retains the personal privilege not to answer questions about the documents he or she has been ordered to produce (*Curcio v. United States* [1957]).

The Court has enforced the collective entity rule even when the claim was made by the president of a corporation who was its sole shareholder, and even if incrimination would result from the mere act of producing the documents (as opposed to the revelation of their contents). In that case, the contents of the documents can be used against both the collective entity and the individual who acted as custodian, and so can the *collective entity's* act of production. The fact that the individual was the custodian who produced the documents can not be used against him or her, but four dissenters strenuously objected to denial of the privilege to the custodian when the very act of producing the documents would nevertheless assist the government in prosecuting him or her (*Braswell v. United States* [1988]).

When the collective entity doctrine does not apply, the Court has held that individuals may not claim the privilege with respect to the contents of their business papers but may do so when the act of producing the papers would itself be incriminating, and the *Braswell* dissenters thought that the same rules should be applied to the custodians of collective entities. (See the discussion of incrimination through the act of production in the section on private papers below).

Claim and Waiver

In a series of cases on the Sixth Amendment (as opposed to the *Miranda*) right to counsel, the Supreme Court made clear that circumstances determine when that right attaches; no action is required to invoke it and the accused retains it unless he or she executes an intelligent and competent waiver (see the section on the right to counsel in pretrial proceedings in Chapter 3). For the privilege against self-incrimination, however, the situation is essentially the reverse. A witness subject to contempt or some other sanction has no right to refuse to answer questions unless he or she formally invokes the privilege and establishes a reasonable basis for doing so. "The [Fifth] Amendment speaks of compulsion. It does not preclude a witness from testifying voluntarily in matters which may incriminate him. If, therefore, he desires the protection of the privilege, he must claim it or he will not be considered to have been 'compelled' within the meaning of the Amendment" (*United States v. Monia* 427 [1943]).

A criminal defendant or other witness who testifies voluntarily may not invoke the privilege with respect to relevant cross-examination. Because cross-examination is properly confined to matters raised on direct examination, such a witness, especially a party to the case, controls the topics that can be discussed and, having raised issues himself or herself, cannot then prevent further exploration of those issues by the opposing party. A witness who testifies under compulsion, however, can invoke the privilege at any point that presents a risk of incrimination, even if that means his or her testimony will be one-sided (*Brown v. United States* [1958]).

Once a witness has made incriminating admissions, she may not assert the privilege as to additional questions that will not further incriminate her. That was the decision in the case of Jane Rogers, who, testifying under subpoena, admitted to a federal grand jury that she had been the treasurer of the Communist Party of Denver but then refused to name the person to whom she had turned over the books. Upholding her contempt conviction, the Court reaffirmed the rule that "petitioner cannot invoke the privilege where response to the specific question in issue here would not further incriminate her. Disclosure of a fact waives the privilege as to details" (*Rogers v. United States* 373 [1951]). A further problem in this case was that Rogers had initially indicated that she wished to save her successor from the ordeal she was going through and only belatedly asserted that by answering she would incriminate herself. The Court was brusque in reminding her that the privilege is a purely personal one. "[A] refusal to answer cannot be justified by a desire to protect others from punishment, much less to protect another from interrogation by a grand jury. Petitioner's claim of the privilege against self-incrimination was pure afterthought" (*Rogers v. United States* 371 [1951]).

In a strong dissent, Justice Black argued that answering the question would have further incriminated Rogers, if only by identifying witnesses who could be called to testify against her in a prosecution under the Smith Act. More fundamentally, Black objected to

> the Court's holding . . . that at some uncertain point in petitioner's testimony, regardless of her intention, admission of associations with the Communist Party automatically effected a "waiver" of her constitutional protection as to all related questions. To adopt such a rule for the privilege against self-incrimination, when other constitutional safeguards must be knowingly waived, relegates the Fifth Amendment's privilege to a second-rate position. Moreover, today's holding creates this dilemma for witnesses: On the one hand, they risk imprisonment for contempt by asserting the privilege prematurely [with respect to requests for information they think would be incriminating but the court or other authority does not]; on the other, they might lose the privilege if they answer a single question. The Court's view makes the protection depend on timing so refined that lawyers, let alone laymen, will have difficulty in knowing when to claim it. (*Rogers v. United States* 377–378 [1951] [dissenting opinion])

Clearly concerned by the threat to liberty posed by governmental practices that reflected the climate of anticommunism that came to be known as McCarthyism, Black lamented the fact that "[s]ome people are hostile to the Fifth Amendment's provision unequivocally commanding that no United States official shall compel a person to be a witness against himself. They consider the provision as an outmoded relic of past fears generated by ancient inquisitorial practices that could not possibly happen here. For this reason the privilege to be silent is sometimes accepted as being more or less of a constitutional nuisance which the courts should abate whenever and however possible" (*Rogers v. United States* 375–376 [1951] [dissenting opinion]). The Court's venerable tradition of broad construction of the scope of the privilege, Black argued, was undercut by its equally broad interpretation of circumstances under which the privilege was waived, even unintentionally.

The Court now wishes to reserve the term "waiver" for those instances when a witness formally declines to invoke the protection of the privilege, but it has not abandoned the concept that a witness may by his or her answers to some questions inadvertently forfeit his or her right to assert the privilege as to other questions, the answers to which may be used against him or her. This concept is in tension with the concept that compelled admissions may not be used as evidence against the person who made them, which is discussed in the following section (U.S. Senate 1992, 1312 n. 205).

Compulsion

As we have noted, there is no right not to have one's own incriminating words used against one; there is only a right not to be *compelled* to utter words that can be so used. The routine form of compulsion occurs when a witness is called upon to answer questions in an official forum, under subpoena, and is convicted of contempt and imprisoned when he or she does not. Such measures are perfectly legal as long as the answers would not incriminate the witness, but if they would then the sanction of conviction and punishment is the sort of compulsion against which the privilege protects, and it may be invoked.

Other kinds of sanctions also amount to unconstitutional compulsion. For example, the Supreme Court has ruled that the government may not give public employees the choice of answering incriminating questions or being fired. Statements made under such circumstances are involuntary and may not be used against the employee in a criminal prosecution (*Garrity v. New Jersey* [1967]). Public employees may not be fired for asserting the privilege and refusing to sign a waiver of immunity (but, with immunity, may be fired for refusing to answer relevant questions about their performance of official duties) (*Gardner v. Broderick* [1968]).

Similarly, a person's privilege of entering into business contracts with the government may not be suspended for asserting the privilege against self-incrimination rather than answering questions about such business before a grand jury, unless immunity has been granted (*Lefkowitz v. Turley* [1973]); a lawyer may not be disbarred for asserting the privilege in a disciplinary hearing (*Spevack v. Klein* [1967]); and a political party official may not be stripped of his or her party office and temporarily barred from holding any party or public office for refusing to answer questions or waive immunity from prosecution (*Lefkowitz v. Cunningham* [1977]). All of these forbidden sanctions threaten the ability to earn a livelihood, and the last seriously impinges on First Amendment rights of political participation as well.

The dilemma posed by plea bargaining, however, does not constitute compulsion. A defendant facing the choice between the certain or probable consequences of a plea agreement offered by the prosecutor and the more severe consequences (perhaps even death) probable upon conviction at trial has a strong incentive to plead guilty. Although threats or inducements to confess may be unconstitutionally coercive when presented to a suspect under interrogation, the Court views a plea bargain in a different light. A defendant who, with the assistance of counsel, knowingly and intelligently enters a plea of guilty under such circumstances is acting voluntarily, simply making a rational choice among available alternatives—and the opportunity to make that choice is a concession by the state, because it could simply have taken the defendant to trial without offering any deal. Further, as the Court acknowledges, the criminal justice system would grind to a halt if plea bargaining were held to violate the privilege against self-incrimination (or the right to jury trial), as the vast majority of cases are disposed of in that fashion (*Brady v. United States* [1970]).

Other kinds of dilemmas imposed by government do not amount to compulsion, either. For example, young men who have failed to register for the draft are ineligible for federal financial aid to attend college; they can qualify for aid by registering late but must thereby inform the Selective Service System that they have violated the law. The Supreme Court decided on narrow grounds that this requirement did not violate the privilege, noting also that such men were under no compulsion to apply for federal financial aid (*Selective Service System v. Minnesota Public Interest Research Group* [1984]).

The Court had explained its approach more broadly the year before when it addressed the common state practice of requiring motorists stopped on suspicion of drunk driving to choose whether or not to take a blood-alcohol test. If they take the test the results can be used against them in court, and if they do not their refusal can be used against them (and, typically, their driving privileges are revoked). It can thus be argued that such motorists are compelled to incriminate themselves, one way or the other. In a case contesting the state's use of a refusal as evidence, however, the Court concluded that the refusal had not been compelled. "We recognize, of course," wrote Justice Sandra Day O'Connor, "that the choice to submit or refuse to take a blood-alcohol test will not be an easy or pleasant one for a suspect to make. But the criminal process often requires suspects and defendants to make difficult choices. . . . We hold, therefore, that a refusal to take a blood-alcohol test, after a police officer has lawfully requested it, is not an act coerced by the officer, and thus is not protected by the privilege against self-incrimination" (*South Dakota v. Neville* 564 [1983]). The Court further reasoned that the state could have simply required the test and not allowed any choice. (For an explanation of why the use of the results of compulsory blood tests does not violate the privilege, see the discussion of testimonial evidence below.)

An arguably clearer form of compulsion was upheld by a narrowly divided Court in *McKune v. Lile* (2002). The Kansas prison system's sexual abuse treatment program requires offenders to take responsibility for the sex crimes for which they have been convicted and to disclose any other sexual offenses they may have committed; they are subject to prosecution for the latter and to prosecution for perjury if they denied the former at trial. When Robert G. Lile declined to participate, citing the privilege against self-incrimination, he was transferred from medium-security to maximum-security status and lost various privileges concerning such matters as visitation, prison earnings and expenditures, and television viewing. The Court was unable to forge a standard for applying the self-incrimination clause in a prison setting, but five justices found that the consequences of Lile's nonparticipation were not comparable to the loss of livelihood in the cases noted above, were within the realm of normal administrative discretion of prison authorities, and therefore did not amount to compulsion. Vigorously disagreeing, four dissenters argued that voluntary programs or grants of immunity would serve the rehabilitative goals of the program and decried the sanctioning of punishment for the exercise of a constitutional right.

The Court's approach to these questions has been essentially pragmatic; no clear doctrinal principle distinguishes permissible and impermissible forms of pressure applied to suspects (U.S. Senate 1992, 1308). The issue of confessions made under interrogation has raised the most difficult problems of compulsion; it is discussed in the section on coerced confessions below.

Incrimination

In *Rock v. Arkansas* (1987), the Supreme Court held that the right to testify in one's own defense is a fundamental aspect of due process and of the Sixth Amendment rights to conduct a personal defense and summon witnesses in one's own behalf, and is a necessary corollary of the Fifth Amendment right not to be compelled to testify. "Every criminal defendant is privileged to testify in his own defense, or to refuse to do so" (*Harris v. New York* 225 [1971]), but a witness under any other circumstance can assert the privilege against self-incrimination only when his or her answer to a question would in fact be incriminating. The determination of when that is so is not an exact science but rather the product of a reasonable judgment. The Court has distilled the elements of the problem this way:

> The privilege afforded not only extends to answers that would in themselves support a conviction under a federal [or state] criminal statute but likewise embraces those which would furnish a link in the chain of evidence needed to prosecute the claimant for a federal [or state] crime. . . . But this protection must be confined to instances where the witness has reasonable cause to apprehend danger from a direct answer. . . . The witness is not exonerated from answering merely because he declares that in so doing he would incriminate himself—his say-so does not of itself establish the hazard of incrimination. It is for the court to say whether his silence is justified . . . and to require him to answer if "it clearly appears to the court that he is mistaken." . . . However, if the witness, upon interposing his claim, were required to prove the hazard in the sense in which a claim is usually required to be established in court, he would be compelled to surrender the very protection which the privilege is designed to guarantee. To sustain the privilege, it need only be evident from the implications of the question, in the setting in which it is asked, that a responsive answer to the question or an explanation of why it cannot be answered might be dangerous because injurious disclosure could result. (*Hoffman v. United States* 486–487 [1951])

The privilege does not protect against merely speculative risks. The witness thus must have a realistic fear of prosecution, but he cannot be required to demonstrate that fear if the explanation itself could incriminate him. Witnesses are therefore entitled to some benefit of the doubt. As the Court wryly remarked in overturning Hoffman's contempt conviction for refusing to answer questions before a grand jury, "[t]he court should have considered . . . that the chief occupation of some persons involves evasion of federal criminal laws, and that truthful answers by petitioner . . . might have disclosed that he was engaged in such proscribed activity" (*Hoffman v. United States* 487–488 [1951]).

The privilege protects not only those answers that would clearly show guilt, but those that could be used against the witness, as evidence or leads to evidence or links in a chain of evidence. The standard formula, therefore, is that a witness can refuse to answer if doing so would tend to incriminate him or her. The formula leaves a gray area in which it may be possible to claim the privilege successfully for an illegitimate purpose, such as to avoid adverse consequences other than criminal punishment or to prevent the incrimination of someone else.

Paradoxically, a witness may assert the privilege even if his or her answers would deny all involvement in criminal activity, for "one of the basic functions of the privilege is to protect *innocent* men" (*Grunewald v. United States* 421 [1957] [emphasis in the original]), and "[t]he privilege serves to protect the innocent who otherwise might be ensnared by ambiguous circumstances" (*Slochower v. Board of Higher Education* 557–558 [1956]). That possibility was well illustrated in a case in which the father of a child who had died of shaken-baby syndrome was tried for involuntary manslaughter. When Susan Batt, the infant's babysitter, was called as a witness and indicated her intention to claim the privilege against self-incrimination, she was given transactional immunity and testified for the prosecution, denying any knowledge of or responsibility for the child's injuries. The father was convicted but that verdict was overturned by the Ohio Supreme Court on the grounds that because the babysitter had claimed complete innocence, she was not entitled to claim the privilege against self-incrimination and therefore should not have been granted immunity in order to serve as a prosecution witness. A unanimous Supreme Court ruled that Ms. Batt could indeed invoke the privilege. She had spent much time alone with the victim in the weeks preceding his death, including some of the time period within which medical evidence established that the trauma had been inflicted, and the defendant's theory of the case was that she had fatally shaken the child. Even if she was completely innocent, the Court pointed out, she had a reasonable fear that her truthful answers to some questions could be used in a prosecution against her (*Ohio v. Reiner* [2001]).

Even if answers would provide information about criminal activity under U.S. law, "if the testimony sought cannot possibly be used as a basis for, or in aid of, a criminal prosecution against the witness, the rule ceases to apply" (*Brown v. Walker* 597 [1896]); that is the case when the witness has been pardoned for the crime or the statute of limitations has expired. Moreover, a witness may not invoke the privilege to prevent use of information in noncriminal proceedings. Thus, compelled statements may be used in a civil proceeding for involuntary commitment of a sexually dangerous person (*Allen v. Illinois* [1986]), and a witness may not claim the privilege simply because the information sought could be used in a proceeding for revocation of probation (*Minnesota v. Murphy* [1984]). In the latter example, as long as the government cannot use the information in an additional criminal prosecution, the convicted person faces no criminal liability beyond that which he or she has already incurred. The government may use either answers or refusal to answer to justify revoking probation. (It may not, however, threaten to revoke an individual's probation unless he or she incriminates himself or herself with respect to some other offense; that would be impermissible compulsion.)

Criminal liability does not cease at the point of conviction, however; the privilege also applies to the sentencing phase of a trial (*Estelle v. Smith* [1981]), even if the defendant has pleaded guilty to the offense (*Mitchell v. United States* [1999]). The risk of adverse consequences is not removed until sentence has been determined and final judgment has been entered, and a plea of guilty to the offense does not constitute a waiver of the right to assert the privilege at a sentencing hearing. In the *Mitchell* case, in which sentencing for the distribution of cocaine depended on resolution of a dispute about the quantity of the drug involved, the Court pointed to the danger of an opposite result. "Were we to accept the Government's position, prosecutors could indict without specifying the quantity of drugs involved, obtain a guilty plea, and then put the defendant on the stand at sentencing to fill in the drug quantity. The result would be to enlist the defendant as an instrument in his or her own condemnation, undermining the long tradition and vital principle that criminal proceedings rely on accusations proved by the Government, not on inquisitions conducted to enhance its own prosecutorial power" (*Mitchell v. United States* 325 [1999]).

That particular risk was reduced a year later when the Court ruled that due process requires that factors that could extend a sentence beyond the statutory maximum must be charged in the indictment and proved beyond a reasonable doubt (*Apprendi v. New Jersey* [2000]). If a case does not go to trial, those elements will play a role in the plea bargain. The *Apprendi* case concerned the enhancement of sentences for offenses committed as hate crimes, but its relevance for sentencing in drug crimes was apparent, and the federal government immediately started to specify in its indictments the amounts of drugs involved (Greenhouse 2002, A14). The privilege against self-incrimination nevertheless continues to apply in sentencing hearings and to be an important protection for convicted persons.

Testimonial Evidence

Early in the twentieth century, the Supreme Court considered the contention of a convicted murderer who argued that his privilege against self-incrimination had been violated when he was forced to try on a blouse to see if it fit him. Calling this claim "an extravagant extension of the Fifth Amendment," Justice Oliver Wendell Holmes proclaimed that "the prohibition of compelling a man in a criminal court to be witness against himself is a prohibition of the use of physical or moral compulsion to extort communications from him, not an exclusion of his body as evidence when it may be material. The objection in principle would forbid a jury to look at a prisoner and compare his features with a photograph in proof. Moreover, we need not consider how far a court would go in compelling a man to exhibit himself" (*Holt v. United States* 252–253 [1910]).

A half century later, when modern science had greatly expanded the ways in which the government might compel a person to exhibit himself or herself, and when the application of the privilege against self-incrimination to the states brought many more cases to the Supreme Court, the Court took up this issue again and elaborated the rationale for its position. The key decision grew out of an accident in which one Schmerber smashed his car into a tree and was taken to a hospital. A policeman with probable cause to believe Schmerber was intoxicated directed a doctor to draw a blood sample, which was done in spite of Schmerber's refusal to consent. When blood-test results were used to convict him of driving under the influence of alcohol, Schmerber appealed on several grounds, including violation of the privilege against self-incrimination. Readily conceding that "in requiring petitioner to submit to the withdrawal and chemical analysis of his blood the State compelled him to submit to an attempt to discover evidence that might be used to prosecute him for a criminal offense," the Supreme Court declared that "[t]he critical question . . . is whether petitioner was thus compelled 'to be a witness against himself'" (*Schmerber v. California* 761 [1966]).

Although it promotes the sanctity of the human person and the obligation of the government to establish guilt through its own independent efforts, the Court noted, "the privilege has never been given the full scope which the values it helps to protect suggest. History and a long line of authorities in lower courts have consistently limited its protection to situations in which the State seeks to submerge those values by obtaining the evidence against an accused through 'the cruel, simple expedient of compelling it from his own mouth.' . . . [T]he privilege protects an accused only from being compelled to testify against himself, or otherwise provide the State with evidence of a testimonial or communicative nature"; in this case "[n]ot even a shadow of testimonial compulsion upon or enforced communication by the accused was involved either in the extraction or in the chemical analysis. . . . Since the blood test evidence, although an incriminating product of compulsion, was neither petitioner's testimony nor evidence relating to some communicative act or writing by the petitioner, it was not inadmissible on privilege grounds" (*Schmerber v. California* 761–765 passim [1966]).

The privilege thus protects persons from being compelled to incriminate themselves by communicating in some way—orally, in writing, or by a communicative act such as a nod of the head—but it does not protect them from being required to yield physical evidence from their bodies. The Court noted that "both federal and state courts have usually held that [the privilege] offers no protection against compulsion to submit to fingerprinting, photographing, or measurements, to write or speak for identification, to appear in court, to stand, to assume a stance, to walk, or to make a particular gesture." On the other hand, "[s]ome tests seemingly directed to obtain 'physical evidence,' for example, lie detector tests measuring changes in body function during interrogation, may actually be directed to eliciting responses which are essentially testimonial. To compel a person to submit to testing in which an effort will be made to determine his guilt or innocence on the basis of physiological responses, whether willed or not, is to evoke the spirit and history of the Fifth Amendment" (*Schmerber v. California* 764 [1966]).

In distinguishing between testimonial and nontestimonial evidence, just as in distinguishing between the person and incriminating information about the person (see the discussion of personal privilege above), the Court focused on the concept of being a witness and harked back to the origins of the privilege as a protection against being forced to answer questions at the risk of incrimination, a protection against being forced to speak of one's own guilt. For the Court, the answer to the question of whether someone in a situation like Schmerber's has been compelled to be a witness against himself or herself is that he or she has not, because of not being compelled to communicate in a narrow and literal sense of the term.

The *Schmerber* decision was 5–4, however, with three justices rejecting such an interpretation of self-incrimination. "To reach the conclusion that compelling a person to give his blood to help the State convict him is not equivalent to compelling him to be a witness against himself strikes me as quite an extraordinary feat," wrote Justice Black. "How can it reasonably be doubted that the blood test evidence was not in all respects the actual equivalent of 'testimony' taken from petitioner when the result of the test was offered as testimony, was considered by the jury as testimony, and the jury's verdict of guilt rests in part on that testimony?" To Black it did not matter that the testimony that communicated evidence of Schmerber's guilt was actually offered not by the defendant but by a prosecution witness responsible for the chemical analysis of his blood; Schmerber had been compelled to do something without which an incriminating communication to the jury could not have occurred.

Drawing on a different strand of tradition from the majority, Black pointed out that "[i]t concedes, as it must so long as *Boyd v. United States* . . . stands, that the Fifth Amendment bars a State from compelling a person to produce papers he has that might tend to incriminate him. It is a strange hierarchy of values that allows the State to extract a human being's blood to convict him of a crime because of the blood's content but proscribes compelled production of his lifeless papers." Characterizing *Boyd* (see the discussion of nineteenth-century developments in the section on privilege against self-incrimination in Chapter 2) as "among the greatest constitutional decisions of this Court," Black feared that the "refined, subtle reasoning and balancing process used here to narrow the scope of the Bill of Rights' safeguard against self-incrimination provides a handy instrument for further narrowing of that constitutional protection, as well as others, in the future" (*Schmerber v. California* 773–778 passim [1966] [dissenting opinion]). Within a decade, *Boyd* would meet that fate (see the discussions of required records and private papers below).

As already noted, the *Schmerber* decision cited several kinds of bodily evidence besides blood that were not considered testimonial, and in a series of other cases the Court quickly extended the doctrine and the list. Suspects may be compelled to appear in lineups and to speak words spoken by the perpetrator, which the majority said is to "use the voice as an identifying physical characteristic, not to speak . . . guilt" (*United States v. Wade* 222–223 [1967]; see also the section on right to counsel in pretrial proceedings in Chapter 3).

The Court was still sharply divided, however, particularly over the required speaking, which Justice Abe Fortas declared "is more than passive, mute assistance to the eyes of the victim or of witnesses. It is the kind of volitional act—the kind of forced cooperation by the accused—which is within the historical perimeter of the privilege against compelled self-incrimination. . . . To permit *Schmerber*['s] . . . insidious doctrine to extend beyond the invasion of the body, which it permits, to compulsion of the will of a man, is to deny and defy a precious part of our historical faith and to discard one of the most profoundly cherished instruments by which we have established the freedom and dignity of the individual" (*United States v. Wade* 260, 261–262 [dissenting opinion]).

In a companion case, the Court held that a handwriting exemplar, as opposed to its content, is likewise an identifying physical characteristic, not a communication (*Gilbert v. California* [1967]). Six years later the Court reached the same result for voice exemplars (*United States v. Dionisio* [1973]), and later, in the case of a defendant charged with driving while intoxicated, it held that a videotaped presentation of his slurred speech and lack of muscular coordination was not testimonial (*Pennsylvania v. Muniz* [1990]).

Furthermore, even acts that are nominally communicative, such as the signing of a document, are not necessarily protected by the privilege. When the government insisted that the target of an investigation sign a document authorizing disclosure of records of his foreign bank accounts—phrased so as not to acknowledge identity of, control over, or even existence of any such accounts—the Court held that the target could be compelled to sign the document because it communicated no information to the government (*Doe v. United States* [1988]). If Justice Black had still been on the Court, he might well have argued that this was no different, and no more acceptable, than compelling a person to give a blood sample.

The *Schmerber* doctrine thus remains good law. It rests on a conception of the traditional scope of the privilege, but the Court is not unmindful of its practical consequences. If the position of the dissenters had prevailed, the effectiveness of many techniques of criminal investigation would have been significantly curtailed.

Reporting and Disclosure

Tax and regulatory laws that compel the provision of information may pose problems of self-incrimination for some persons. An early case of this sort arose during Prohibition when a bootlegger failed to file an income tax return on the grounds that to do so would incriminate him. In upholding his conviction for failing to file and pay the tax, the Court held that he had no privilege not to file the return but on the return could (subject to adjudication) assert the privilege with respect to specific requests for information (*United States v. Sullivan* [1927]). A half century later, Roy Garner took the opposite tack, listing his occupation on his income tax return as professional gambler and reporting income from gambling and wagering. When the government used that information in gaining a conviction for being part of a conspiracy to place bets on horse races that had been fixed, Garner claimed that his disclosures had been compelled because he could have been prosecuted under the tax laws for withholding the information. Because a valid assertion of the privilege could not be the basis of a conviction of that sort, and the government conceded that a good-faith but erroneous assertion should not be, either, the Court reaffirmed the rule that a witness who reveals information rather than assert the privilege has not been compelled (see the discussion of claim and waiver above). "Unless a witness objects, a government ordinarily may assume that its compulsory processes are not eliciting testimony that he deems to be incriminating. Only the witness knows whether the apparently innocent disclosure sought may incriminate him, and the burden appropriately lies with him to make a timely assertion of the privilege. If, instead, he discloses the information sought, any incriminations properly are viewed as not compelled" and thus may be used against him (*Garner v. United States* 655 [1976]).

In the meantime, Congress had launched a much more targeted attack on gamblers by enacting legislation requiring them to register and provide information about their business operations and to pay occupational and excise taxes. When this scheme was challenged by gamblers who refused to comply, on the grounds that to do so would violate their privilege against self-incrimination, the Court found otherwise in two cases (*United States v. Kahriger* [1953]; *Lewis v. United States* [1955]). The *Sullivan* doctrine applied; there was no privilege not to file at all, only to withhold specific information. Further, since the requirements applied only prospectively, no one was compelled to reveal any past or present criminal behavior, and the privilege did not apply to criminal behavior contemplated for the future. Self-incrimination would be required by the statute only if a person chose to be a gambler from that point forward, and that choice was entirely voluntary. "The only compulsion under the Act is that requiring the decision which would-be gamblers must make at the threshold. They may have to give up gambling, but there is no constitutional right to gamble" (*Lewis v. United States* 422–423 [1955]).

The Court saw matters in a different light in *Albertson v. Subversive Activities Control Board* (1965), in which it considered the validity of a federal statute requiring members of the Communist Party and other communist organizations to register as such and submit a form providing other information, such as aliases used, offices held, and duties thereof. Because membership in the party was a crime, the Court held 8–0 (Justice White did not participate) that the information required would provide evidence that could be used in a prosecution and leads that could be used in further criminal investigation, and that the registration and reporting requirement therefore violated the privilege against self-incrimination. The government had argued that, under the doctrine of the *Sullivan* case, Albertson could have claimed the privilege as to specific items but was not entitled to refuse to file the forms altogether. However, the Court distinguished that precedent on the grounds that the situation here was different. "In *Sullivan* the questions in the income tax return were neutral on their face and directed at the public at large, but here they are directed at a highly selective group inherently suspect of criminal activities. Petitioners' claims are not asserted in an essentially noncriminal and regulatory area of inquiry, but against an inquiry in an area permeated with criminal statutes, where response to any of the form's questions in context might involve the petitioners in the admission of a crucial element of a crime" (*Albertson v. Subversive Activities Control Board* 79 [1965]).

Because this characterization applied with equal force to the federal gambling laws, the *Kahriger* and *Lewis* decisions were now in limbo, and the Court quickly accepted two new gambling cases and requested the parties to present arguments on the continuing validity of the two earlier decisions. In *Marchetti v. United States* (1968) and *Grosso v. United States* (1968), argued and decided together, the Court found that because gambling was illegal under a pervasive network of federal and state laws, and because the statute required the Internal Revenue Service to share information with law enforcement authorities, who regularly used it to pursue criminal prosecutions, gamblers faced a genuine risk of self-incrimination. The Court could no longer accept the factual assumption that compliance with the statute posed no risk of prosecution for past or present crimes.

Moreover, there was a second, and more fundamental, deficiency in the reasoning of *Kahriger* and *Lewis:*

> Its linchpin is plainly the premise that the privilege is entirely inapplicable to prospective acts. . . . We see no warrant for so rigorous a constraint upon the constitutional privilege. . . . The central standard for the privilege's application has been whether the claimant is confronted by substantial and "real," and not merely trifling or imaginary, hazards of incrimination. . . . This principle does not permit the rigid chronological distinction adopted in *Kahriger* and *Lewis.* We see no reason to suppose that the force of the constitutional prohibition is diminished merely because confession of a guilty purpose precedes the act which it is subsequently employed to evidence. . . . [A]lthough prospective acts will doubtless ordinarily involve only speculative and insubstantial risks of incrimination, this will scarcely always prove true. [I]t is not true here. (*Marchetti v. United States* 53–54 [1968])

Lewis argued that the statutes compelled only a decision about whether or not to be a gambler in the future, and that there is no constitutional right to gamble, but "[w]e find this reasoning no longer persuasive. The question is not whether petitioner holds a 'right' to violate state law, but whether, having done so, he may be compelled to give evidence against himself." The *Sullivan* rule that the privilege is lost if the form is not filed and the privilege asserted thereon is fraught with all the problems of implied and uninformed waivers of privilege. "We cannot agree that the constitutional privilege is meaningfully waived merely because those 'inherently suspect of criminal activities' have been commanded either to cease wagering or to provide information incriminating to themselves, and have ultimately elected to do neither." At trial, Marchetti asserted the privilege in arguing that the statute he was charged with violating was unconstitutional, and that is all that can be expected; "to have required him to present his claim to Treasury officers would have obliged him 'to prove guilt to avoid admitting it.'" Thus, "[w]e conclude that nothing in the Court's opinions in *Kahriger* and *Lewis* now suffices to preclude petitioner's assertion of the constitutional privilege as a defense to the indictments under which he was convicted. To this extent *Kahriger* and *Lewis* are overruled." The statute imposing registration and tax requirements was not unconstitutional, but "those who properly assert the constitutional privilege as to these provisions may not be criminally punished for failure to comply with their requirements." Because Marchetti faced a real hazard of incrimination, and because the doctrine of required records (see the following section) did not apply to him, he "properly asserted the privilege against self-incrimination, and . . . his assertion should have provided a complete defense to this prosecution" (*Marchetti v. United States* 50–61 passim [1968]).

The Court did not strike down the statute because the government is entitled to tax illegally gained income. If the government can establish a gambler's business activities through its own independent efforts, it can take action to collect the taxes due or prosecute for nonpayment (as well as prosecute for engaging in those forms of gambling that are crimes). Although the Court discreetly observed that the "principal interest of the United States must be assumed to be the collection of revenue, and not the prosecution of gamblers" (*Grosso v. United States* 68 [1968]), it placed heavy emphasis on use of the statute to accomplish the latter. In defense of constitutional rights, it made both more difficult.

The rationale of *Albertson, Marchetti,* and *Grosso* applies to other kinds of reporting requirements when the intent is to enhance criminal law enforcement, such as the registration of illegal firearms (*Haynes v. United States* [1968]), but the situation is less clear when the government is pursuing other objectives (U.S. Senate 1992, 1319). For example, a fractured Court upheld a hit-and-run statute (common to all the states) that required drivers involved in accidents with property damage to stop and inform other parties of their names and addresses (*California v. Byers* [1971]). Four justices emphasized that the statute, like the income tax, was directed to the public at large rather than to a select group likely to be engaged in criminal activity. Moreover, its purpose was not to enforce criminal law but to facilitate the adjudication of liability for damages in civil proceedings, and the justices pointed out that being involved in an automobile accident does not normally lead to criminal charges. These justices thus concluded that compliance with the law entailed no significant risk of self-incrimination—and even if it did, they added, the acts of stopping and providing name and address are not testimonial.

Four dissenting justices found these conclusions incredible, pointing out that Byers had been prosecuted not only for failing to stop and notify but also for committing a traffic violation that had caused the accident. By identifying himself as being involved, they argued, he would surely have provided a testimonial link in the chain of evidence for the latter prosecution. Further, the situation here resembled that in *Albertson,* not *Sullivan,* because the statute was directed not to the public at large but to drivers involved in accidents, a group surely under suspicion for having committed one of the many crimes contained in the motor vehicle code.

The deciding vote in the case (and a more convincing explanation of the result) came from Justice John Marshall Harlan II, who upheld the validity of the statute even though he conceded that it *did* compel self-incrimination. Accepting but wishing to limit the approach of the *Albertson* line of cases, Harlan argued that, in the context of a requirement for information genuinely needed for regulatory purposes, a realistic fear of self-incrimination should not necessarily trigger the protection of the privilege. The interests of the state should be balanced against those of the individual. Striking the balance here, Harlan concluded that the interests of protecting personal privacy and preserving an accusatorial rather than inquisitorial system of criminal justice were outweighed by the state's need for self-reported information to maintain a system of personal liability for property damage. The information demanded was not nearly as conclusive of guilt as was that in cases like *Marchetti*, and in an increasingly technological society, Harlan maintained, the government's need for such information was ever growing (which is precisely what the dissenters feared).

Two decades later, without choosing between the plurality and Harlan positions in *Byers*, a clear majority of the justices endorsed its overall thrust, proclaiming that "*California v. Byers* . . . confirms that the ability to invoke the privilege may be greatly diminished when invocation would interfere with the effective operation of a generally applicable, civil regulatory requirement" (*Baltimore City Department of Social Services v. Bouknight* 557 [1990]).

The Court here applied *Byers* to a context other than a reporting requirement, ruling that a juvenile court's order to produce a child under its supervision did not violate the mother's privilege against self-incrimination. Even though Jacqueline Bouknight was suspected of having further abused or perhaps murdered her son Maurice, the Court held that the government's overriding objective was to protect the welfare of the child and that the order had therefore been issued "for compelling reasons unrelated to criminal law enforcement and as part of a broadly applied regulatory regime" (*Baltimore City Department of Social Services v. Bouknight* 561 [1990]).

The decision in *Bouknight* also rested in part on the mother's status as the publicly appointed and supervised custodian of her child, analogous to the status of a custodian of organizational records, who has no privilege to withhold them. (The dissenters argued, however, that while organizations have no privilege that custodians can assert, individual parents have a privilege that official supervision of their custody should not remove). The question of whether or not Bouknight was entitled to claim the privilege against self-incrimination would not, of course, have arisen at all if the act of producing Maurice could not have incriminated her in some way. She "cannot claim the privilege based upon anything that examination of Maurice might reveal," the Court announced, because the examination would not involve any testimonial communication on her part, but "her implicit communication of control over Maurice at the moment of production might aid the State in prosecuting Bouknight" (*Baltimore City Department of Social Services v. Bouknight* 555 [1990]).

Because of the *Byers* doctrine, the privilege did not shield Bouknight from producing her child, but it might prevent the state from using her act of production against her if it brought criminal charges. (For further discussion of the act of production as incriminating, see the discussion of private papers below.)

Required Records

In 1886, *Boyd v. United States* had characterized business records as private papers and held that a government order to produce them violated the privilege against self-incrimination. The Court soon began to undercut that interpretation, however, holding that the records of corporations, business partnerships, labor unions, and similar organizations are not protected by the privilege and that their custodians may be compelled to produce them, even at the risk of personal incrimination (see the discussion of natural persons above). In addition to distinguishing between the rights of organizations and of individuals, and between the rights of private owners and of organizational custodians of documents, the Court announced that by their very nature documents such as the records of public offices and records required to be kept by law do not enjoy the same privilege as private papers because of the legitimate need for public inspection and regulation (*Wilson v. United States* [1911]).

This view of required records is commonly referred to as the *Shapiro* doctrine because of the Court's elaboration and application of it in *Shapiro v. United States* (1948). The Court there repeated earlier assertions that "the privilege which exists as to private papers cannot be maintained in relation to 'records required by law to be kept in order that there may be suitable information of transactions which are the appropriate subjects of governmental regulation and the enforcement of restrictions validly established'" (*Shapiro v. United States* 33 [1948]). As a practical matter, business records may be the only effective evidence against some kinds of offenses. The Court, which found the seeds of the required records doctrine in *Boyd* itself, characterized required records as those of the sort customarily kept by the enterprise in question, concerning what is legitimately public information, and mandated by a general regulatory statute, as opposed to one targeting a group suspected of criminal behavior. (Because the forms required by the gambling tax statutes discussed in the section on reporting and disclosure above did not meet these criteria, they did not qualify as required records, so Marchetti and Grosso were entitled to assert the privilege against self-incrimination rather than to file them.)

Shapiro, a wholesaler of fruits and vegetables, was served with a subpoena to provide records he was required to keep by the Emergency Price Control Act of 1942, a wartime measure designed to prohibit price gouging and other harmful selling practices. Claiming the privilege against self-incrimination, he complied in reliance upon a provision of the statute incorporating the transactional immunity provisions of the Compulsory Testimony Act of 1893 (see the discussion of nineteenth-century developments in the section on privilege against self-incrimination in chapter 2), but information gained from his records was thereupon used to convict him of violations of the Price Control Act. A five-justice majority of the Court affirmed the conviction, arguing that in enacting the Price Control Act Congress knew of the *Wilson* decision and of the Court's ruling, in another context, that the immunity provision "should be construed, so far as its words fairly allow the construction, as coterminous with what otherwise would have been the privilege of the person concerned" (*Heike v. United States* 142 [1913]). Thus, because the constitutional privilege provided no protection at all for required records, even those kept by private individuals, Congress must not have intended the immunity provision of the statute to do so, either.

The language of the provision stated simply that "no person [compelled to provide information] shall be prosecuted or subject to any penalty or forfeiture for or on account of any transaction, matter or thing, concerning which he may testify, or produce evidence" (*Shapiro v. United States,* 3 n.2 [1948]), and four dissenting justices thought it meant just what it said. "There is of course nothing in this [immunity] provision to support the finespun exegesis which the Court puts upon" it, wrote Justice Felix Frankfurter. As for the majority's restrictive view of the scope of the constitutional privilege against self-incrimination, while public records such as those of governmental offices should not be protected, "[i]f records merely because required to be kept by law *ipso facto* become public records, we are indeed living in glass houses" (*Shapiro v. United States* 43, 51 [1948] [dissenting opinion]), because there is a vast quantity of federal, state, and local legislation and administrative regulations requiring record keeping. Almost every federal regulatory statute contained record-keeping requirements and employed the same language on immunity. *Shapiro* turned on the Court's interpretation of congressional intent in the statute, and Congress was free to correct that interpretation if it wished, but unless it passed legislation to extend immunity to required records, there would be no such immunity. The *Shapiro* result was ominous for another reason, Frankfurter warned. The document Boyd had been compelled to produce was much more clearly a required record than the documents Shapiro surrendered. By the logic of the *Shapiro* decision, the landmark *Boyd* decision was wrong.

Private Papers: The Demise of Boyd v. United States

In trying to shield her business records, in the possession of her accountant, from government inspection, Lillian Couch relied on the *Boyd* decision's prohibition of the extortion of private papers as evidence (see the discussion of *Boyd* among the nineteenth-century developments in the section on privilege against self-incrimination in Chapter 2, and the discussion of personal privilege above). Because Boyd's papers had been in his possession, the Court had not distinguished between ownership and possession in that case, but in the *Couch* case it made clear that it is not ownership of papers but possession that is the key to eligibility to assert the privilege against self-incrimination, for it is only possession that renders one susceptible to compulsion. This de-emphasis of ownership subtly undermined the philosophy of *Boyd,* as did other decisions more directly—denial of the privilege to corporations and other organizations (even partnerships like Boyd's) and the custodians of their records, and exclusion from protection of required records, even those of natural persons (see the discussions of natural persons and required records above).

The Court took a decisive step further in *Fisher v. United States* (1976), in which, on the same reasoning it had employed in *Couch,* it held that a taxpayer could not assert the privilege against self-incrimination to shield papers he had turned over to his attorney (because it was the attorney, not the taxpayer, who would be compelled to produce them). The attorney-client privilege (see the discussion of this topic in the section on counsel and client in Chapter 3) would, however, protect the papers, the Court went on—but only if they would have been protected by the privilege against self-incrimination if they had remained in the possession of the taxpayer (i.e., the taxpayer could not lose the ability to shield his papers by consulting an attorney, but could not gain it that way, either). The question, then, was whether the taxpayer could have asserted the privilege to defeat the government's subpoena for his papers (in this case, documents prepared by an accountant) if they had been in his possession, and the Court proceeded to rule on that question.

"The proposition that the Fifth Amendment prevents compelled production of documents over objection that such production might incriminate stems from *Boyd v. United States*," the Court noted, but

> [s]everal of *Boyd's* express or implicit declarations have not stood the test of time. . . . To the extent . . . that the rule against compelling production of private papers rested on the proposition that seizures of or subpoenas for "mere evidence," including documents, violated the Fourth Amendment and therefore also transgressed the Fifth . . . the foundations for the rule have been washed away [in various Fourth Amendment cases]. In consequence, the prohibition against forcing the production of private papers has long been a rule searching for a rationale consistent with the proscriptions of the Fifth Amendment against compelling a person to give "testimony" that incriminates him. Accordingly, we turn to the question of what, if any, incriminating testimony within the Fifth Amendment's protection, is compelled by a documentary summons. (*Fisher v. United States* 405, 407, 409 [1976])

Drawing on its doctrine of testimonial evidence elaborated in *Schmerber* and other cases, the Court declared that although a subpoena compels a taxpayer or other possessor of documents to turn them over, it "does not compel oral testimony; nor would it ordinarily compel the taxpayer to restate, repeat, or affirm the truth of the contents of the documents sought. Therefore, the Fifth Amendment would not be violated by the fact alone that the papers on their face might incriminate the taxpayer, for the privilege protects a person only against being incriminated by his own compelled testimonial communications" (*Fisher v. United States* 409 [1976]). If such taxpayer had been compelled to create as well as to produce the incriminating documents, and they were not in the category of required records, then—as in *Marchetti* and *Grosso* (see the discussion of reporting and disclosure above)—the privilege against self-incrimination would have been violated. In the situation posed by the Court, however, the taxpayer was being compelled to produce the documents and could be incriminated, but he had not written the documents, so they contained no testimonial communication from him. They did contain testimonial communication from the accountant, but he was being neither compelled nor incriminated. The taxpayer may have considered the documents to be his private papers, but the privilege against self-incrimination did not prevent the government from compelling him to surrender them.

Even when the only thing compelled is the act of producing the documents, the Court conceded, that act "has communicative aspects of its own, wholly aside from the contents of the papers produced. Compliance with the subpoena tacitly concedes the existence of the papers demanded and their possession or control by the taxpayer. It also would indicate the taxpayer's belief that the papers are those described in the subpoena" (*Fisher v. United States* 410 [1976]). That final point—commonly referred to as the issue of authentication—was the principal reason the privilege against self-incrimination had been interpreted as applying to subpoenas for documents, the Court concluded, but while the act of production was compelled it was not clear that it necessarily involved testimonial acts that were incriminating. Declining to lay down a general rule, the Court stated that this question was better resolved on a case-by-case basis. In this case, it was "confident that however incriminating the contents of the accountant's workpapers might be, the act of producing them—the only thing which the taxpayer is compelled to do—would not itself involve testimonial self-incrimination" (*Fisher v. United States* 410–411 [1976]).

Justice William J. Brennan concurred in the result because of the involvement of the accountant with the papers and because they were business rather than personal documents, but he was extremely critical of the majority's approach, which he characterized as "fundamentally at odds with the settled principle that the scope of the privilege is not constrained by the limits of the wording of the Fifth Amendment but has the reach necessary to protect the cherished value of privacy which it safeguards" (*Fisher v. United States* 416–417 [1976] [concurring opinion]). From *Boyd* until this day, he argued, personal papers as well as utterances had been considered testimonial and the Fifth Amendment had protected persons from being compelled to reveal them when they would be self-incriminating.

> An individual's books and papers are generally little more than an extension of his person. They reveal no less than he could reveal upon being questioned directly. Many of the matters within an individual's knowledge may as easily be retained within his head as set down on a scrap of paper. I perceive no principle which does not permit compelling one to disclose the contents of one's mind but does permit compelling the disclosure of the contents of that scrap of paper by compelling its production. Under a contrary view, the constitutional protection would turn on fortuity, and persons would, at their peril, record their thoughts and the events of their lives. (*Fisher v. United States* 420 [1976] [concurring opinion])

Although the majority made clear that it did not regard the papers in this case (prepared by the accountant) as private papers in the *Boyd* sense, Justice Brennan saw that concept as threatened. Because the Fifth Amendment does not provide absolute protection for privacy, the question for him was what papers are protected and what are not. That would depend, he thought, on such factors as the nature of the papers and the degree to which they had been voluntarily exposed to others. He was particularly alarmed, however, by the majority's intimation that personal tax records (as opposed to those prepared by or shared with an accountant) and even personal diaries might not be protected. In general, Justice Brennan found the majority's approach "most inadequate. The gaping hole is in the omission of any reference to the taxpayer's privacy interests and to whether the subpoenas impermissibly invade those interests" (*Fisher v. United States* 427 [1976] [concurring opinion]).

A few weeks later, the Court upheld the government's use of incriminating business records acquired through a lawful search and seizure rather than by subpoena (*Andresen v. Maryland* [1976]). Attorney Peter C. Andresen was a sole practitioner, so the collective entity doctrine did not eliminate the privilege, but he had created the documents voluntarily and had not been compelled to produce or authenticate them (the latter was done by a handwriting expert). The Court cited *Fisher* as meaning that compulsory incrimination could result not from the contents of the documents, but only from their production and therefore authentication, which had not occurred here. Nothing in the nature of the papers protected them, and they were in fact the kind of evidence that is needed and commonly used to prosecute crimes such as fraud (as in this case) and gambling. The Court thus relied on the familiar principle that an individual is privileged from having to produce incriminating testimonial evidence, but not from its production (see the discussion of personal privilege above).

Justice Brennan termed this decision an "assault on the Fifth Amendment" because it retreated from the Court's earlier determination that the records of a sole practitioner (as opposed to a corporation or partnership) were within the zone of privacy protected by the amendment (see the discussion of natural persons above). "The Court," he continued, "also sanctions circumvention of the Amendment by indulging an unjustified distinction between production compelled by subpoena and production secured against the will of the petitioner through warrant. . . . Search and seizure is as rife with elements of compulsion as subpoena" (*Andresen v. Maryland* 486–487 [1976] [dissenting opinion]). It was becoming clearer that the category of papers that were private and, as such, were protected by the privilege against self-incrimination was fast disappearing.

Fisher had held that the person under compulsion was not protected from producing his accountant's papers in his possession, but it did not reach the question of whether he would have been protected from producing his own records. A few years later, however, the Court extended the *Fisher* rationale to hold that the privilege did not apply in that circumstance, either. In another case involving subpoenas for business records, the Court reaffirmed *Fisher* in two respects. First, "[r]espondent does not contend that he prepared the documents involuntarily or that the subpoena would force him to restate, repeat, or affirm the truth of their contents. . . . We therefore hold that the *contents* of those records are not privileged" (*United States v. Doe* 611–612 [1984] [emphasis supplied]).

Second, *Fisher* had said that a compelled *act of production* of papers can itself be testimonially self-incriminating, because in some circumstances it can provide information about the existence, possession or control, or authenticity of documents that the government would otherwise be unable to establish. That had not been so in *Fisher*, but the Court deferred to the judgment of two lower courts that it was so in this case. Doe could thus be compelled to produce the documents only if he was given immunity from use of his act of production against him (but immunity from use of the contents of the documents against him was not required). In the *Bellis* case (see the discussion of natural persons above), the Court, citing *Boyd,* had said as dictum that "[t]he privilege applies to the business records of the sole proprietor or sole practitioner as well as to personal documents containing more intimate information about the individual's private life" (*Bellis v. United States* 87–88 [1974]). Now, however, the fact that Doe operated his businesses as sole proprietorships rather than as collective entities did not preserve his privilege as to the contents of his business papers. Under the rule of *Fisher,* decided two years after *Bellis,* he could, as an individual, claim the privilege against self-incrimination only as to the act of production—and not as to the contents—of his voluntarily prepared business records.

The justices could not agree among themselves as to the significance of what they had done in this case. Justice O'Connor fully agreed with the majority opinion but felt it necessary to write separately "just to make explicit what is implicit in the analysis of that opinion: that the Fifth Amendment provides absolutely no protection for the contents of private papers of any kind. The notion that the Fifth Amendment protects the privacy of papers originated in *Boyd v. United States* . . . but our decision in *Fisher v. United States* . . . sounded the death knell for *Boyd,* declaring that its privacy of papers concept '[had] long been a rule searching for a rationale. . . .' Today's decision puts a long overdue end to that fruitless search" (*United States v. Doe* 618 [1984] [concurring opinion]).

Justice Thurgood Marshall, however, joined by Justice Brennan in partially concurring and partially dissenting, declared that

> [c]ontrary to what Justice O' Connor contends, . . . I do not view the Court's opinion in this case as having reconsidered whether the Fifth Amendment provides protection for the contents of "private papers of any kind." This case presented nothing remotely close to the question that Justice O'Connor eagerly poses and answers. . . . [T]he documents at stake here are business records which implicate a lesser de-

> gree of concern for privacy interests than, for example, personal diaries. . . . I continue to believe that under the Fifth Amendment "there are certain documents no person ought to be compelled to produce at the Government's request." (*United States v. Doe* 619 [1984] [dissenting opinion])

Justice Marshall's belief seems to have been in vain, however. It was already clear that personal business records of the sort shielded in *Boyd* (and not subject to the collective entity doctrine) were no longer protected, even if they had been written by the person compelled to produce them. The Supreme Court has not ruled in a case involving personal papers such as a diary, but as of this writing lower federal courts in six of eight circuits have refused to extend the privilege to such documents, most notably in the case of Senator Robert Packwood (R-OR), whose diaries were subpoenaed by the Senate Select Committee on Ethics in the course of its investigation of allegations of sexual harassment against the senator, which led to his resignation (O'Malley 2001, 1601; Nagareda 1999, 1642 n.254). The Supreme Court refused to review the decision in Packwood's case, creating the legal climate in which, during the investigation of President Clinton, Independent Counsel Kenneth W. Starr was free to subpoena Monica Lewinsky's computer and the electronic writings it contained (Rosen 2000, A31). It thus appears that *Boyd's* protection for voluntarily created private papers no longer exists.

Immunity: The Constriction of **Counselman v. Hitchcock**

In the last decade of the nineteenth century, the Court in *Counselman v. Hitchcock* and *Brown v. Walker* set transactional immunity from criminal prosecution as the degree of protection that must be provided before self-incriminating testimony can be compelled without violating the Fifth Amendment (see the discussion of nineteenth-century developments in the section on privilege against self-incrimination in Chapter 2), and that became the standard for federal immunity statutes. (States continued to set their own immunity standards until the privilege against self-incrimination was incorporated and applied to them in 1964; see the discussion of incorporation below.) In a Cold War climate of intense concern about national security in the 1950s, William Ludwig Ullmann challenged the federal standard as inadequate. Called before a grand jury investigating espionage, Ullmann refused to testify in spite of a grant of immunity and was convicted of contempt. When his case reached the Supreme Court, Ullmann argued that, unlike the situation faced by the railroad auditor in *Brown,* "the impact [on a communist] of the disabilities imposed by federal and state authorities and the public in general—such as loss of job, expulsion from labor unions, state registration and investigation statutes, passport eligibility, and general public opprobrium—is so oppressive that the statute does not give him true immunity" (*Ullmann v. United States* 430 [1956]). Seven justices, however, reiterated that the privilege protects only against the danger of criminal liability. "Immunity displaces the danger. Once the reason for the privilege ceases, the privilege ceases. We reaffirm *Brown v. Walker*" (*Ullmann v. United States* 439 [1956]).

Justice Douglas, joined by Justice Black, totally disagreed. Boyd had faced only forfeiture of the goods he had imported and the Fifth Amendment had protected him; by the same token, it should protect Ullmann from the danger of the forfeitures he faced. More fundamentally, these justices believed, the protection of the privilege is not contingent upon the danger of criminal prosecution, or any other danger, and therefore cannot be overridden by a grant of immunity. "The guarantee is that no person 'shall be compelled in any criminal case to be a witness against himself.' . . . Wisely or not, the Fifth Amendment protects against the compulsory self-accusation of crime without exception or qualification" (*Ullmann v. United States* 443 [1956] [dissenting opinion]).

The argument about whether the Fifth Amendment should protect against more than literal incrimination was particularly salient at this time because of the freewheeling investigations conducted by such congressional committees as the House Committee on Un-American Activities, the Senate Subcommittee on Internal Security, and the Senate Permanent Subcommittee on Investigations under Senator Joseph R. McCarthy (R-WI). It is widely believed that the public hearings and reports of these bodies often served little purpose beyond unfairly sullying the reputations of their targets, whether they were communists, radicals, or merely liberals. The "general public opprobrium" of which Ullmann complained led to the ruin of many public and private careers. For persons with unpopular views and associations, a grant of immunity and its concurrent obligation to answer questions (or be punished for contempt) could mean a move out of the frying pan and into the fire. Alleged communists like Ullmann were entitled to claim the privilege (*Blau v. United States* [1950]), but even if they were allowed to remain silent, they often paid a heavy price. Juries are not supposed to draw adverse inferences from a claim of privilege, but no such strictures can be imposed in the court of public opinion. It is hard to see how even Justices Douglas and Black's preferred interpretation of the Fifth Amendment could protect against the evils they decried.

Until 1970, federal immunity statutes regularly provided for the transactional immunity called for in *Counselman v. Hitchcock* and upheld in *Brown v. Walker* (see the discussion of *Shapiro v. United States* in the section on required records above). In that year, however, following a recommendation from the National Commission on Reform of Federal Criminal Laws, Congress enacted a new statute based upon a reconsideration of the meaning of *Counselman.* Although the Court had said there that "no statute which leaves the party or witness subject to prosecution after he answers the criminating question put to him, can have the effect of supplanting the privilege conferred by the Constitution of the United States," the defect that it had found in the immunity statute under consideration was that "[i]t could not prevent the obtaining and the use of witnesses and evidence which should be attributable directly to the testimony he might give under compulsion," and that it provided "no protection against that use of compelled testimony which consists in gaining therefrom a knowledge of the details of a crime, and of sources of information which may supply other means of convicting the witness or party" (*Counselman v. Hitchcock* 564, 586 [1892]). To correct this problem, the Commission and Congress reasoned, the remedy of complete exemption from prosecution for offenses about which testimony was compelled—transactional immunity—was overkill. Immunity from prosecutorial use of the compelled testimony and of any information derived from it—use and derivative use immunity—should suffice. Accordingly, that is what Congress enacted in a provision of the Organized Crime Control Act of 1970 that superseded all other federal immunity statutes (U.S. Senate 1992, 1314). Whenever a witness in a federal forum asserts the privilege against self-incrimination and receives a grant of immunity, "the witness may not refuse to comply with the order on the basis of his privilege against self-incrimination; but no testimony or other information compelled under the order (or any information directly or indirectly derived from such testimony or other information) may be used against the witness in any criminal case, except a prosecution for perjury, giving a false statement, or otherwise failing to comply with the order" (18 USC § 6002 [2000]).

This provision was immediately challenged by Charles Kastigar and Michael Stewart, who had been convicted of contempt for refusing to testify before a grand jury under a grant of immunity. Reaffirming the long and widely held view that "many offenses [such as gambling, bribery, extortion, and various forms of white-collar crime] are of such a character that the only persons capable of giving useful testimony are those implicated in the crime" (*Kastigar v. United States* 446 [1972]), the Supreme Court rejected the petitioners' request to adopt the dissenting position in *Ullmann* and took up again the question of how much immunity was required to secure their testimony.

> The constitutional inquiry, rooted in logic and history, as well as in the decisions of this Court [including *Counselman*], is whether the immunity granted under this statute is coextensive with the scope of the privilege. . . . While a grant of immunity must afford protection commensurate with that afforded by the privilege, it need not be broader. Transactional immunity, which accords full immunity from prosecution for the offense to which the compelled testimony relates, affords the witness considerably broader protection than does the Fifth Amendment privilege. The privilege has never been construed to mean that one who invokes it cannot subsequently be prosecuted. Its sole concern is to afford protection against being "forced to give testimony leading to the infliction of 'penalties affixed to . . . criminal acts.'" Immunity from the use of compelled testimony, as well as evidence derived directly and indirectly therefrom, affords this protection. (*Kastigar v. United States* 449, 453 [1972])

When persons assert the privilege against self-incrimination, the government cannot use anything they have said, or anything derived from what they have said, against them—because they have not said anything—but it remains free to prosecute them on the basis of other evidence. The situation is exactly the same when persons are compelled to testify under a grant of use and derivative use immunity, the Court held, because if they are prosecuted, such a grant "imposes on the prosecution the affirmative duty to prove that the evidence it proposes to use is derived from a legitimate source wholly independent of the compelled testimony." Use and derivative use immunity (now often referred to simply as use immunity) thus provides just as much protection as the privilege it supplants (and the same protection as is afforded the victim of a coerced confession). "Our holding is consistent with the conceptual basis of *Counselman,*" the majority declared, even though its conclusion was different (*Kastigar v. United States* 460, 453 [1972]).

Two justices dissented (and two did not participate). Justice Douglas reiterated his view that the privilege against self-incrimination is absolute, while Justice Marshall maintained that use and derivative use immunity does not guarantee that the defendant will be in the same position as if he or she had not testified at all. The prosecution's burden of proof as to the independent sources of its evidence is not a sufficient protection against derivative use of compelled testimony, Marshall argued, because it is not hard for a prosecutor acting in bad faith to invent a plausible alternate source, and because it is inevitable that prosecutors acting in good faith will, especially in large offices handling complex cases, occasionally simply lose track of the actual sources of some of their leads. "The Court today sets out a loose net to trap tainted evidence and prevent its use against the witness, but it accepts an intolerably great risk that tainted evidence will in fact slip through that net." Moreover, "the Court turns reason on its head when it compares a statutory grant of immunity to the 'immunity' that is inadvertently conferred by an unconstitutional interrogation" through application of the exclusionary rule, which merely provides "a partial and inadequate remedy to some victims of illegal police conduct" (*Kastigar v. United States* 469, 470 [1972] [dissenting opinion]). For Marshall and Douglas, nothing less than transactional immunity would do.

If a defendant chooses to testify, any prior immunized testimony he may have given (as before a grand jury) may not be used to impeach his testimony at trial (*New Jersey v. Portash* [1979]). There is one exception, however, to the prohibition of the use of immunized testimony in a prosecution against the witness. If he or she lies under oath while testifying under a grant of immunity, both the false and true portions of his testimony may be used against him or her in a prosecution for perjury without violation of the federal immunity statute or the Fifth Amendment (*United States v. Apfelbaum* [1980]).

The net that Justice Marshall mistrusted did prevent the government from using tainted evidence in a major prosecution that grew out of Independent Counsel Kenneth W. Starr's Whitewater investigations of President Clinton and his associates. Webster L. Hubbell, a partner of Hillary Rodham Clinton at the Rose Law Firm in Little Rock, Arkansas, was appointed associate attorney general by President Clinton but was forced to resign and ultimately pleaded guilty to charges of mail fraud and tax evasion in connection with his billing procedures while at the Rose Law Firm. His plea bargain called for him to provide further information to the Office of Independent Counsel, which issued a subpoena for such material in 1996. After asserting his privilege against self-incrimination and receiving a grant of use and derivative use immunity, Hubbell delivered to a grand jury in Little Rock 13,120 pages of documents, classified according to the eleven broadly worded categories specified in the subpoena. On the basis of information gained from the documents, a different grand jury in the District of Columbia indicted Hubbell in 1998 for various tax offenses and mail and wire fraud, and he challenged the indictment on the grounds that it violated his grant of immunity.

Under the doctrine of *Fisher* and *Doe,* that immunity related only to the act of production. However, when the case reached the Supreme Court, eight justices agreed that the indictment had to be dismissed (*United States v. Hubbell* [2000]). It was clear, Justice John Paul Stevens wrote, that the government had made derivative use of the testimonial aspects of Hubbell's act of production, for "[i]t is apparent from the text of the subpoena itself that the prosecutor needed respondent's assistance both to identify potential sources of information and to produce those sources. . . . Entirely apart from the contents of the 13,120 pages of materials that respondent produced in this case, it is undeniable that providing a catalog of existing documents fitting within any of the 11 broadly worded subpoena categories could provide a prosecutor with a 'lead to incriminating evidence,' or 'a link in the chain of evidence needed to prosecute.' Indeed, the record makes it clear that that is what happened in this case." Clearly disdainful of "[t]he Government's anemic view of respondent's act of production as a mere physical act that is principally nontestimonial in character and can be entirely divorced from its 'implicit' testimonial aspect so as to constitute a 'legitimate, wholly independent source' (as required by *Kastigar*) for the documents produced," Stevens resorted to metaphor to express a contrary judgment. "What the District Court characterized as a 'fishing expedition' did produce a fish, but not the one that the Independent Counsel expected to hook [i.e., the Independent Counsel expected to find evidence against, and to prosecute, the Clintons, an enterprise that would be unrestrained by the grant of immunity to Hubbell]. It is abundantly clear that the testimonial aspect of respondent's act of producing subpoenaed documents was the first step in a chain of evidence that led to this prosecution [the prosecution of Hubbell instead]. . . . The assembly of those documents was like telling an inquisitor the combination to a wall safe, not like being forced to surrender the key to a strongbox" (*United States v. Hubbell* 41–43 passim [2000]). The government may require production of incriminating sources of evidence of which it is aware, Stevens acknowledged, but it may not require the target of a grand jury investigation to answer questions designed to reveal the existence of such sources.

By the same token, the government may not rely upon the testimonial component of the response to a subpoena designed to discover sources of which it is unaware. To put the matter another way, the privilege against self-incrimination does not protect a person from being compelled to surrender evidence the government has identified through its own efforts, but it does protect a person from having to help the government identify the evidence it needs. Hubbell's indictment had to be dismissed because the government had obtained that indictment on the basis of leads it had derived from information contained in his very act of complying with a subpoena under a grant of immunity.

Concurring, Justices Clarence Thomas and Antonin Scalia announced that they were prepared to go further and reconsider the denial of protection of private papers in cases such as *Fisher* and *Doe* because "[a] substantial body of evidence suggests that the Fifth Amendment privilege protects against the compelled production not just of incriminating testimony, but of any incriminating evidence" (*United States v. Hubbell* 49 [2000] [concurring opinion]). Confounding the ideological interpretation of decision making, the Court's two most conservative members thus echoed the position of the two most liberal members at the time of those restrictive decisions, Justices Brennan and Marshall.

Incorporation Debated: The Adverse Comment Cases

As we saw in Chapter 2, the Supreme Court began to consider issues of self-incrimination toward the end of the nineteenth century, but all of those cases involved assertions of the right in federal prosecutions. State constitutions contained self-incrimination clauses comparable to that in the Fifth Amendment, but they varied in language and were also subject to differing interpretations in various state supreme courts (Berger 1980, 46). As with other provisions of the Bill of Rights, persons who received less protection in state courts than they would have in federal courts sought to have the self-incrimination clause of the Fifth Amendment incorporated into the due process clause of the Fourteenth Amendment and thus applied to the states; the first attempt to be considered by the Supreme Court came in the case of two bank officers who had been convicted of showing falsified documents to a bank examiner. At the trial of Albert C. Twining and David C. Cornell, the judge had instructed the jury that, under state law, it could if it saw fit draw adverse inferences from the fact that the defendants had chosen not to testify in their own defense and had therefore not denied the testimony against them. A federal statute and the statutes of other states prohibited the drawing of such inferences from, and comment by the judge or prosecutor on, a decision to exercise the right not to testify, but New Jersey law did not, and so the defendants sought to invoke three clauses of the Constitution in arguing that the judge's instructions to the jury had turned their silence into an involuntary admission of guilt (or would have compelled their testimony, had they chosen to give it).

In *Twining v. New Jersey* (1908), the Court (over the vigorous dissent of Justice John Marshall Harlan I) refused to reconsider the conclusion of *Hurtado v. California,* that the due process clause did not incorporate provisions of the Bill of Rights (see the section on incorporation of the Bill of Rights in Chapter 1), and it took only a little more time to explain why the privileges and immunities clause did not apply the privilege against self-incrimination to the states, either. Those conclusions did not dispose of the issue, however, for the Court did retreat from the *Hurtado* implication that the protections of the Bill of Rights not only *were not* but *could not* be applied to the states. "[I]t is possible," conceded Justice William H. Moody for the majority, "that some of the personal rights safeguarded by the first eight Amendments against National action may also be safeguarded against state action, because a denial of them would be a denial of due process of law. . . . If this is so, it is not because those rights are enumerated in the first eight Amendments, but because they are of such a nature that they are included in the conception of due process of law" (*Twining v. New Jersey* 99 [1908]).

As we saw in Chapter 1, however, it would be another fifteen years before the Court would begin to enforce substantive standards of due process in state criminal courts. In *Twining,* it engaged in a lengthy survey of Anglo-American legal history to demonstrate that the privilege against self-incrimination might be a prudent rule of evidence but was not "an immutable principle of justice which is the inalienable possession of every citizen of a free government" (*Twining v. New Jersey* 113 [1908]), and it reiterated its deference to the right of the people of each state to govern themselves as they saw fit. Defendants had no federal constitutional privilege against self-incrimination in state court; that meant not only that the state could comment on the defendant's silence but that "[t]he privilege against self-incrimination may be withdrawn and the accused put upon the stand as a witness for the state" (*Snyder v. Massachusetts* 105 [1934]), although, under their own constitutions, laws, or judicial practice, states generally did accord defendants the privilege of not testifying.

Ten years after formulating its approach to incorporation in the *Palko* case (see the discussion of state trials in the section on right to counsel at trial in Chapter 3), the Court revisited the *Twining* issue in the case of *Adamson v. California* (1947). Adamson, under sentence of death for murder, had had the misfortune of being tried in California, one of only six states that still allowed adverse commentary on, and inferences drawn from, a defendant's failure to testify (or, in California, his or her failure to explain or deny evidence against him or her, whether he or she testified or not). Because the alternative had been to have his prior convictions revealed to the jury on cross-examination, he had not taken the witness stand. The district attorney in his arguments and the judge in his instructions to the jury had alluded to Adamson's failure to refute the evidence against him, and Adamson now challenged the constitutionality of California procedure. The Court, however, quickly reaffirmed the *Twining* conclusion that neither the privileges and immunities nor the due process clause applied the privilege against self-incrimination to the states, and it then concluded that Adamson's treatment had not violated due process, either. "The due process clause forbids compulsion to testify by fear of hurt, torture or exhaustion [citing *Brown v. Mississippi*]," but such tactics had not been used here. "It forbids any other type of coercion that falls within the scope of due process," but comment on Adamson's failure to testify was not such coercion because "we see no reason why comment should not be made upon his silence. It seems quite natural that when a defendant has opportunity to deny or explain facts and determines not to do so, the prosecution should bring out the strength of the evidence by commenting upon defendant's failure to explain or deny it." Finally, the requirement that Adamson make a difficult choice did not violate due process because "it does not seem unfair to require him to choose between leaving the adverse evidence unexplained and subjecting himself to impeachment through disclosure of former crimes" (*Adamson v. California* 54, 56, 57 [1947]).

The *Twining* decision had been 8–1; *Adamson* was 5–4. In a majority opinion, a concurrence, and two dissents, the members of the Court used this case for an extended intramural debate about the applicability of the Bill of Rights to the states. Justices Stanley F. Reed and Felix Frankfurter championed the *Twining/Palko* approach, while Justices Hugo Black and Frank Murphy argued that the due process clause incorporated the self-incrimination clause and indeed all of the first eight amendments (and, for Murphy, even more). Ironically, as this great debate over constitutional philosophy unfolded, a major constitutional question remained unresolved.

One of the quirks of the *Twining* and *Adamson* cases is that the practice complained of by both defendants—adverse comment about a decision not to testify—was found not to violate due process, but its status under the self-incrimination clause of the Fifth Amendment remained in limbo because that provision was held to be inapplicable in these state cases. The Court had not had occasion to decide that issue in a federal case, either, because the federal statute of 1878 that first authorized testimony by defendants also provided that a defendant's decision not to testify did not create a presumption against him or her. The Court had ruled that the *statute* prohibited adverse comment (*Wilson v. United States* [1893]), and that a defendant has a right under the statute to have the judge instruct the jury that his or her silence does *not* create a presumption against him or her (*Bruno v. United States* [1939]). In the state cases of *Twining* and *Adamson,* therefore, the Court simply assumed that adverse comment did violate the self-incrimination clause and then went on to decide whether or not that clause applied to the states. (The principal dissenters in the two cases, Justices Harlan I and Black, respectively, both maintained that that approach put the cart before the horse, arguing that there was no occasion to determine whether the self-incrimination clause applied to the states in the absence of any determination that what the states had done violated the clause in the first place. Justice Black went further, suggesting that the *Adamson* majority—or at least four of the five—really believed that the self-incrimination clause did *not* bar adverse comment. In any event, in *Adamson* only Justices Frankfurter, Murphy, and Rutledge stated an opinion that it did.)

This issue was finally settled in 1965, when another murderer under sentence of death in California again challenged that state's constitutional provision allowing comment on his failure to testify. Having applied the self-incrimination clause to the states the year before (in a case to be discussed below), the Court was thus presented with both the opportunity and the necessity of deciding whether adverse comment violated that clause. The majority ruled that it did, holding that, as applied to both the federal government and the states, the self-incrimination clause "forbids either comment by the prosecution on the accused's silence or instructions by the court that such silence is evidence of guilt," because either is "a penalty imposed by courts for exercising a constitutional privilege" (*Griffin v. California* 615, 614 [1965]).

Noting that a jury would take cognizance of a failure to testify even without comment, two dissenters concluded "that the Court in this case stretches the concept of compulsion beyond all reasonable bounds, and that whatever compulsion may exist derives from the defendant's choice not to testify, not from any comment by court or counsel" (*Griffin v. California* 620 [1965] [dissenting opinion]).The Court has agreed that such comment may be harmless error, and therefore not grounds for reversal of a conviction, if the government can show beyond a reasonable doubt that it did not contribute to the verdict (*Chapman v. California* [1967]), and it has also held that when defense counsel at trial complains that the government has given his or her client no opportunity to tell his or her side of the story, the prosecutor may point out that he or she could have testified (*United States v. Robinson* [1988]).

On the other hand, the right to a cautionary instruction to the jury not to draw adverse inferences from exercise of the right not to testify, established for federal defendants in the *Bruno* case, was extended to state defendants in *Carter v. Kentucky* (1981). A trial judge is required to issue such an instruction only upon a defendant's request, but he or she may at his or her discretion issue one over the objection of a defendant who does not want any kind of mention of his or her failure to testify. "Such an instruction cannot provide the pressure on a defendant found impermissible in *Griffin.* On the contrary, its very purpose is to remove from the jury's deliberations any influence of unspoken adverse inferences. It would be strange indeed to conclude that this cautionary instruction violates the very constitutional provision it is intended to protect" (*Lakeside v. Oregon* 339 [1978]).

Another ironic twist on this theme is that if a defendant *does* testify on his or her own behalf, the prosecution may use his or her pretrial silence (as long as it occurs prior to *Miranda* warnings and thus is in no way induced by the government) to impeach the credibility of that testimony—by asking, for example, why, if a defendant's testimony is the true story and he or she is really innocent, he or she did not tell that story during the initial investigation (*Jenkins v. Anderson* [1980]). Once a suspect has been arrested and assured of his or her right to silence through *Miranda* warnings, however, his or her subsequent silence may not be used for impeachment purposes (*United States v. Hale* [1975]; *Doyle v. Ohio* [1976]; *Fletcher v. Weir* [1982]). Finally, the Court has explicitly declined to extend the *Griffin* ruling to prison disciplinary proceedings, in which officials are free to draw adverse inferences from an inmate's decision not to testify on his or her own behalf (*Baxter v. Palmigiano* [1976]).

A Parallel Track: The Coerced Confession Cases

The Progeny of Brown v. Mississippi

The *Twining* precedent remained good law for more than half a century, but the Supreme Court's comments about due process in *Adamson* reflect the fact that in cases involving coerced confessions, the Court had in the meantime begun moving on a parallel and more progressive track. In the early 1930s, several books and the report of the National Commission on Law Observance and Enforcement (the Wickersham Commission) revealed widespread use of third-degree tactics by police seeking confessions (Berger 1980, 105). The Court had recently held in a federal case that compulsion was not only a matter of the inducements, threats, and promises mentioned in *Hopt v. Utah Territory* (see the discussion of nineteenth-century developments in the section on privilege against self-incrimination in Chapter 2), but that a confession could also be rendered inadmissible by the treatment of the suspect during detention and interrogation (*Wan v. United States* [1924]).

Then, just as with the denial of counsel in *Powell v. Alabama,* the outrageous methods used by a state to extort confessions in

Brown v. Mississippi (see the case study in Chapter 1) motivated the Court to invoke the standard of due process of law. It had stated in *Bram v. United States* that in federal trials, the question of the voluntariness of a pretrial confession was controlled by the self-incrimination clause of the Fifth Amendment (see the discussion of nineteenth-century developments in the section on privilege against self-incrimination in Chapter 2), but when Mississippi argued in *Brown* that the Fifth Amendment did not apply to the states, citing *Twining*, the Court responded that "the question of the right of the State to withdraw the privilege against self-incrimination is not here involved." That privilege relates to "the processes of justice by which the accused may be called as a witness and required to testify. Compulsion by torture to extort a confession is a different matter. . . . [T]he use of the confessions thus obtained as the basis for conviction and sentence was a clear denial of due process" (*Brown v. Mississippi* 285, 286 [1936]).

Brown v. Mississippi was the first of a series of important state confession cases decided on due process grounds. Four years later, in an impassioned opinion by Justice Black, the Court overturned murder convictions based on confessions secured in a marathon, week-long interrogation in an atmosphere of possible mob violence. Although the jury had found the confessions to be free and voluntary, the Court asserted its right to make an independent determination on that point: "the record develops a sharp conflict upon the issue of physical violence and mistreatment, but shows, without conflict, the dragnet methods of arrest on suspicion without warrant, and the protracted questioning and cross questioning of these ignorant young colored tenant farmers by state officers and other white citizens, in a fourth floor jail room, where as prisoners they were without friends, advisers or counselors, and under circumstances calculated to break the strongest nerves and the stoutest resistance." Avowing that "[t]he determination to preserve an accused's right to procedural due process sprang in large part from knowledge of the historical truth that the rights and liberties of people accused of crime could not be safely entrusted to secret inquisitorial processes," and that "they who have suffered most from secret and dictatorial proceedings have almost always been the poor, the ignorant, the numerically weak, the friendless, and the powerless," a unanimous Court concluded that "[d]ue process of law, preserved for all by our Constitution, commands that no such practice as that disclosed by this record shall send any accused to his death" (*Chambers v. Florida* 237–241 passim [1940]).

The *Chambers* decision reflected the *Brown* decision's abhorrence of methods of obtaining confessions that were "revolting to the sense of justice" (*Brown v. Mississippi* 286 [1936]), but a year later the Court began the process of making the standard of admissibility in state cases under the due process clause the same as the standard in federal cases under the self-incrimination clause. In *Lisenba v. California,* it noted that whereas state rules of evidence excluded involuntary confessions in order "to exclude false evidence[,] . . . [t]he aim of the requirement of due process is not to exclude presumptively false evidence, but to prevent fundamental unfairness in the use of evidence, whether true or false. The criteria for decision of that question may differ from those appertaining to the State's rule as to the admissibility of a confession." In short, due process required that even a truthful confession be excluded if it had not been given voluntarily. Psychological as well as physical coercion violated due process. Methods of interrogation did not have to be revolting to be coercive; they simply had to accomplish "the deprivation of . . . free choice to admit, to deny, or to refuse to answer" (*Lisenba v. California* 236, 241 [1941]). On the other hand, protracted interrogation was not (as in this case) necessarily coercive. The Court would thus face a long string of cases in which it had to determine whether confessions had in fact been compelled, and the difficulties of that process soon became apparent.

Another notable decision occurred in 1944, when the Court reviewed murder convictions based on nonstop questioning by relays of officers under bright lights over a thirty-six hour period. Again attempting an independent examination of the nature of the interrogation, the Court found that "the testimony follows the usual pattern and is in hopeless conflict," and, remarkably, that "[a]s to whether Ashcraft actually confessed, there is a similar conflict of testimony" (*Ashcraft v. Tennessee* 149–150, 151 [1944]). Noting that "such disputes . . . are an inescapable consequence of secret inquisitorial practices," Justice Black announced that "[o]ur conclusion is that if Ashcraft made a confession it was not voluntary but compelled," because "a situation such as that here shown by uncontradicted evidence is so inherently coercive that its very existence is irreconcilable with the possession of mental freedom by a lone suspect against whom its full coercive force is brought to bear" (*Ashcraft v. Tennessee* 152, 153, 154 [1944]). Such a procedure would never be allowed on cross-examination of a defendant in open court; it was no less unacceptable in secret.

For Justice Robert H. Jackson and two other dissenters, however, the majority had misconceived the constitutional test and failed to give proper deference to the state courts. The test of voluntariness, Jackson argued, required a determination that the suspect's confession "was obtained by pressures so strong that it was *in fact* involuntarily made, that the individual will of the particular confessor had been overcome." The Tennessee courts had made a finding of fact that Ashcraft's confession was voluntary, but the Court "substitutes for determination on conflicting evidence the question whether this confession was actually produced by coercion, a presumption that it was, on a new doctrine that examination in custody of this duration is 'inherently coercive'" and "makes that presumption irrebuttable" (*Ashcraft v. Tennessee* 157 [1944] [dissenting opinion, emphasis in the original]).

Jackson emphasized the distinction between police brutality, which is unconstitutional per se, and intensive interrogation, which is not. "The Court bases its decision on the premise that custody and examination of a prisoner for thirty-six hours is 'inherently coercive.' Of course it is. And so is custody and examination for one hour. Arrest itself is inherently coercive, and so is detention. . . . Of course such acts put pressure upon the prisoner to answer questions, to answer them truthfully, and to confess if guilty." The Court now "hold[s] this confession inadmissible because of the time taken in getting it. The duration and intensity of an examination or inquisition always have been regarded as one of the relevant and important considerations in estimating its effect on the will of the individual involved," but should not replace that assessment as the determinative factor. In *Chambers,* Justice Black had decried the effects of secret inquisitions of weak and powerless suspects; Justice Jackson would weigh the disabilities of the accused in the judgment of voluntariness, but in assessing conflicting testimony about the nature of an interrogation he was "not ready to believe that the democratic process brings to office men generally less believable than the average of those accused of crime" (*Ashcraft v. Tennessee* 161, 167–168 [1944] [dissenting opinion]).

Justice Jackson and others who agreed with him thus raised a double-barreled complaint. First, they rejected the notion that a confession could be excluded simply because the method of obtaining it was deemed inherently coercive. The Court should overturn convictions only when it found *in fact* that the confession of a particular suspect had not been given of his or her own free will. "Even where there was excess and abuse of power on the part of officers, the State still was entitled to use the confession" if a review of all the evidence showed that it had been made as a product of free choice. Second, however, the Court should not casually or routinely undertake such a review of the evidence, for "[h]eretofore the State has had the benefit of a presumption of regularity and legality. . . . In determining these issues of fact, respect for the sovereign character of the several States always has constrained this Court to give great weight to findings of fact of state courts" (*Ashcraft v. Tennessee* 156, 157 [1944] [dissenting opinion]). Justices of this persuasion would thus show far more deference to state court findings than would Justice Black and those who agreed with him. Justices in the Jackson camp did acknowledge that even state supreme courts sometimes approved the use of confessions as blatantly coerced as those in *Brown v. Mississippi* and *Chambers v. Florida.* The Court did not, however, have the same supervisory power over application of rules of evidence in state cases that it did in federal cases. Therefore, in the words of Chief Justice Stone, "[t]he rightful independence of the states in the administration of their own criminal laws in their own courts requires that in such cases we scrupulously avoid retrying the facts which have been submitted to the jury, except on a clear showing of error substantially affecting the constitutional rights of the accused (*Malinski v. New York* 438 [1945] [separate opinion]).

With the Court divided over judgments about the degree of error and the degree of its effect on constitutional rights, the stage was set for continuing tension between the goal of ensuring compliance with due process of law on the one hand, and the goals of fostering effective law enforcement and showing appropriate deference to the fact-finding of state trial courts on the other. In ensuing cases, the Court focused on the question of whether individual confessions had in fact been freely given and for the time being did not pursue the *Ashcraft* concept of inherently coercive practices. Thus, for the majority, lack of counsel during an interrogation and violation of state law requiring an appearance of the suspect before a magistrate were factors to be considered in determining the voluntariness of a confession, but neither was per se grounds for holding a confession to be inadmissible. With respect to counsel, it did not matter whether the suspect was denied a request to consult his or her own attorney (*Crooker v. California* [1958]) or, as an indigent, qualified under the *Betts* rule for appointed counsel at trial (*Brown v. Allen* [1953]). The decision upholding the admissibility of confessions made during a detention rendered illegal by failure to take the suspect before a magistrate (*Gallegos v. Nebraska* [1951]) stood in contrast to the Court's ruling on that point in federal cases.

In *McNabb v. United States* (1943), a case involving three members of a Tennessee mountain family convicted for murdering a federal revenue agent attempting to apprehend them for selling moonshine whiskey, the Court had overturned the convictions because the arresting officers had ignored their statutory obligation to take the suspects for an initial appearance before a magistrate and therefore lacked judicial sanction for detention of the suspects at the time their confessions were made. Shortly thereafter, it had made clear that failure to afford a federal suspect in custody a timely appearance before a judicial officer (where, among other things, the suspect will be informed of his or her constitutional rights to have an attorney and to remain silent) was not just a factor to be considered but rather an error rendering any resulting confession inadmissible (*Upshaw v. United States* [1948]).

Nine years later, relying on the restatement of the statutory requirement in Rule 5(a) of the Federal Rules of Criminal Procedure, the Court reaffirmed *McNabb* and articulated the rationale for the rule: "Presumably, whomever the police arrest they must arrest on 'probable cause.' It is not the function of the police to arrest, as it were, at large and to use an interrogating process at police headquarters in order to determine whom they should charge before a committing magistrate on 'probable cause'" (*Mallory v. United States* 456 [1957]). The confessions in these cases were not found to be involuntary or lacking in credibility, but the manner in which they had been obtained was held to be unjust. The decisions, however, were not based on constitutional grounds but rather mandated under the Court's administrative power to make rules of evidence for the federal system. The Court has no such supervisory authority over state procedures and practices and it held to the view that the constitutional requirement of due process is not necessarily grounds for correction of illegal acts by the states. If a suspect being illegally detained nevertheless confessed of his or her own free will, admission of that confession into evidence in state court did not violate due process. The *Mallory* decision with respect to federal courts, however, embodying what came to be known as the *McNabb-Mallory* rule, provoked a storm of criticism—the conviction of a brutal rapist had been overturned on a technicality—and narrowly escaped being overturned by Congress, which ultimately set the standard of reasonable delay at six hours (18 U.S.C. § 3501[c] [2000]). The reaction against *Mallory* stemmed in part from fear that the decision would be extended to the states, even though just five months earlier the Court had reaffirmed the position that an illegal detention is just one of the factors to be considered in determining the admissibility of confessions in state cases (*Fikes v. Alabama* [1957]; Murphy 1962, passim).

In the two decades after *Ashcraft,* the Court initially adopted Justice Jackson's approach. Eschewing the concept of inherently coercive practices and focusing on the circumstances of individual interrogations, it sometimes concluded that a confession had been coerced and sometimes did not. "The limits [of interrogation] in any case," wrote Justice Jackson in upholding one conviction, "depend upon a weighing of the circumstances of pressure against the power of resistance of the person confessing. What would be overpowering to the weak of will or mind might be utterly ineffective against an experienced criminal" (*Stein v. New York* 185 [1953]). The justices were often closely divided and could not always agree on a majority opinion, but they were unanimous in the last major decision in this series, which came in 1959 when the Court took up the case of Vincent Joseph Spano, who was under sentence of death for murder.

Spano, a twenty-five-year-old, emotionally unstable immigrant with a junior high school education, had been badly beaten in a barroom fight. He went home for a gun, located his assailant, and shot him to death. Within two weeks, Spano was indicted, discussed the matter with a childhood friend who was a police academy cadet, and voluntarily surrendered to authorities on the advice of counsel, who also instructed him not to answer any questions. The interrogation began five minutes later, however, and went on almost continuously for about eight hours. Spano's requests to consult his attorney were denied, and in the face of his continued refusal to talk to any of a large number of questioners, the cadet was brought in to say falsely that he was in a lot of trouble with his superiors because of Spano's phone call and that only Spano's confession could get him out of it. After the fourth such appeal, at around 3:30 A.M., Spano finally gave a statement in the form of answers to a series of questions from an assistant district attorney, and he was then driven around the city until he could identify the bridge from which he said he had thrown the murder weapon.

A decade earlier, Justice Felix Frankfurter had stated the Court's view of such a process:

> A confession by which life becomes forfeit must be the expression of free choice. A statement to be voluntary of course need not be volunteered. But if it is the product of sustained pressure by the police it does not issue from a free choice. When a suspect speaks because he is overborne, it is immaterial whether he has been subjected to a physical or a mental ordeal. Eventual yielding to questioning under such circumstances is plainly the product of the suction process of interrogation and therefore the reverse of voluntary. . . . To turn the detention of an accused into a process of wrenching from him evidence which could not be extorted in open court with all its safeguards, is so grave an abuse of the power of arrest as to offend the procedural standards of due process. (*Watts v. Indiana* 53–54 [1949])

Writing now for the Court, Chief Justice Earl Warren patiently explained again why the confession was invalid.

> We conclude that petitioner's will was overborne by official pressure, fatigue and sympathy falsely aroused, after considering all the facts in

> their post-indictment setting. Here a grand jury had already found sufficient cause to require petitioner to face trial on a charge of first-degree murder, and the police had an eyewitness to the shooting. The police were not therefore merely trying to solve a crime, or even to absolve a suspect. . . . They were rather concerned primarily with securing a statement from defendant on which they could convict him. The undeviating intent of the officers to extract a confession from petitioner is therefore patent. When such an intent is shown, this Court has held that the confession obtained must be examined with the most careful scrutiny, and has reversed a conviction on facts less compelling than these. . . . Accordingly, we hold that petitioner's conviction cannot stand under the Fourteenth Amendment. (*Spano v. New York* 323–324 [1959])

The Court had not always found that persistent interrogation violated due process, in part because, as Justice Jackson had pointed out, it played a role in protecting society from criminal activity. Here, however, it was confronted with the reality that the police would employ that tactic even when it was unnecessary to solve a crime. The result would probably have been the same even if that had not been so, but on a scale balancing public welfare against private right, the former came up short in the *Spano* case.

In its line of state confession cases from the 1940s to the 1960s, the Court commonly determined the voluntariness of confessions by examining the totality of the circumstances of the interrogations that had produced them. In assessing the effect of police tactics on individual suspects, it looked to such factors as the age, intelligence, experience, and emotional stability of suspects and considered whether police had arrested and detained them legally, held them incommunicado, denied requests for counsel and access to friends, conducted extensive interrogation, resorted to intimidation, or employed trickery. No one factor was decisive (as, for example, illegal detention was in federal cases), but the Court gradually placed more emphasis on police tactics (particularly prolonged interrogation) and less on the vulnerability of the suspect (U.S. Senate 1992, 1326–1327). By 1963, it could (by a vote of 5–4) overturn the conviction of an experienced criminal whose treatment consisted only of being held incommunicado for about sixteen hours, being questioned intermittently, and being refused permission to telephone his attorney or his wife until he confessed, on the grounds that, "given the unfair and inherently coercive context in which made, that choice [to confess] cannot be said to be the voluntary product of a free and unconstrained will" (*Haynes v. Washington* 514 [1963]). The Court here seemed to be reverting to the *Ashcraft* concept of an inherently coercive environment—characterized by tactics far less oppressive than in the earlier case—and paying relatively little attention to what Justice Jackson had always insisted upon and the Court had previously considered more carefully: the assessment of whether the will of a particular suspect not to confess had in fact been overborne.

Some years later, however, the Court would make it clear that a constitutional violation occurs only when the compulsion to confess is the product of police behavior. When the compulsion stems from a factor such as mental illness, and police have engaged in no coercion, the confession is voluntary and admissible (*Colorado v. Connelly* [1986]).

In the same year as *Haynes*, enforcing the exclusionary rule of the Fourth Amendment, the Court made clear that confessions that are the product of an illegal arrest (*Wong Sun v. United States* [1963]) or of an unlawful search and seizure (*Fahy v. Connecticut* [1963]) are inadmissible. A dozen years later, it held that a confession that is the product of an illegal arrest is not saved by the fact that *Miranda* warnings were given (*Brown v. Illinois* [1975]).

Competing Claims of Voluntariness and Truthfulness

The confessions in *Brown v. Mississippi* were surely inadmissible both because they were inherently untrustworthy and because the police had employed totally indefensible methods to obtain them. In the *Lisenba* case five years later, however, the Court emphasized to the states that, contrary to what their rules of evidence might be designed to achieve, the standard of due process mandated the exclusion of involuntary confessions not to preclude the use of false evidence but to preclude the use of unfairly acquired evidence. These two considerations are nevertheless related in practice, as confessions obtained by coercive methods are, in general, more likely to be untrustworthy, and in the line of decisions on voluntariness that followed *Lisenba,* changing majorities placed varying emphasis on the rationales of both untrustworthiness and unfairness (U.S. Senate 1992, 1323, 1328 and n.295). One byproduct of the Court's ambiguity on this point was its zigzag course on the related questions of whether judgments about the reliability of confessions could taint judgments about their voluntariness, and whether verdicts of guilty had to be overturned when the jury was aware of an involuntary confession.

Three different methods of determining voluntariness were widely employed, and the degree to which these questions posed problems depended on the method a jurisdiction used when the defense sought to have a confession excluded. The problems were minimized under the orthodox system, in which the trial judge makes an independent decision on admissibility and allows the confession to be presented to the jury only if he or she deems it voluntary, and under the so-called Massachusetts system, in which the judge does the same thing but in which the jury may nevertheless find the confession to have been involuntary and therefore discount or disregard it. Under both of these systems, juries hear only those confessions that have been found voluntary by a trained and impartial judicial official, and problems arise only if the judge's decision to admit a confession is subsequently overruled on appeal. Under the so-called New York system, however, the judge's role was limited to excluding those confessions that were clearly involuntary. Whenever there was a fair question of voluntariness, the confession and evidence concerning the circumstances in which it had been made were presented to the jury for resolution of that question. The jury was instructed to disregard the confession if it found it to be involuntary; if it found the confession to be voluntary, it was to assess its credibility and give it appropriate weight. The two questions we have noted were much more prominent under this system, and the Court dealt with them in four murder cases, three of them from New York.

A year after the *Ashcraft* decision, the Court reviewed the circumstances of a confession that had been accepted in this manner and, 5–4, found that it should have been deemed involuntary and ruled that a conviction based in part on an involuntary confession must be overturned, even if other evidence might have been sufficient to establish guilt (*Malinski v. New York* [1945]).

Eight years later, however, the Court reviewed another New York conviction and reached a contradictory result. The jury had returned a general verdict of guilty, so it could not be determined whether it had found the confession voluntary and relied on it or found it involuntary, disregarded it, and convicted on the basis of other evidence. (The majority recognized but set aside the further unsettling possibilities that some jurors had done the former and some the latter, or that some or all jurors had not resolved the question of voluntariness but had possibly relied on the confession, anyway.) By a vote of 6–3, the Court concluded that "it was not error if the jury admitted and relied on the confession and was not error if they rejected it and convicted on other evidence"; therefore it did not matter which course the jury had followed and the conviction was valid. As to the latter course, it declared that "[w]e could hold that such provisional and contingent presentation of the confessions precludes a verdict on the other sufficient evidence after they are rejected only if we deemed the Fourteenth Amendment to enact a rigid exclusionary rule of evidence rather than a guarantee against conviction on inherently untrustworthy evidence" (*Stein v. New York,* 193–194, 192 [1953]).

The dissenters pointed out that that rationale for excluding a confession contradicted the teaching of the *Lisenba* case and, believing that this confession had been involuntary, argued that the decision upholding the conviction flouted the rule of the *Malinski* case. "The Court now holds," Justice Frankfurter complained, "that it is not enough for a defendant to establish in this Court that he was deprived of a protection which the Constitution of the United States affords him; he must also prove that if the evidence unconstitutionally admitted were excised there would not be enough left to authorize the jury to find guilt" (*Stein v. New York* 201 [1953] [dissenting opinion]).

Another eight years later, the Court heard a case from Connecticut, in which a problem had arisen even though the state used the orthodox system. Acting alone, the trial judge had admitted a confession but had not confined his inquiry to the question of whether the suspect's will to resist had been overborne and had considered as well the probable effect of police conduct on the truth or falsity of the confession. Writing now for a majority, Justice Frankfurter (the principal dissenter in *Stein*) ruled that "this is not a permissible standard under the Due Process Clause of the Fourteenth Amendment. The attention of the trial judge should have been focused, for purposes of the Federal Constitution, on the question whether the behavior of the State's law enforcement officials was such as to overbear petitioner's will to resist and bring about confessions not freely self-determined—a question to be answered with complete disregard of whether or not petitioner in fact spoke the truth." The conviction therefore had to be overturned (even if the trial judge had been correct in finding no reason to question its reliability, as that was irrelevant to the proper inquiry). To the suggestion that the verdict should stand unless the Supreme Court found the confession in fact to have been involuntary, Frankfurter responded that "[s]uch a view ignores both the volatile and amorphous character of 'fact' as fact is found by courts," because the facts available to the Court on the record had already been influenced by an erroneous process of fact-finding. "[I]t would be manifestly unfair, and afford niggardly protection for federal constitutional rights, were we to sustain a state conviction in which the trial judge or trial jury—whichever is charged by state law with the duty of finding fact pertinent to a claim of coercion—passes upon that claim under an erroneous standard of constitutional law" (*Rogers v. Richmond* 543–544, 546 [1961]). The proper course was for the state to retry the case, using the correct standard.

Frankfurter's mention of the jury as well as the judge, and the ruling that a standard including considerations of truthfulness was an unacceptable basis for determining voluntariness, set the stage for the final act in this drama, which came three years later when the Court overruled the *Stein* decision in *Jackson v. Denno,* declaring that "the New York procedure employed in this case did not afford a reliable determination of the voluntariness of the confession offered in evidence at the trial, did not adequately protect Jackson's right to be free of a conviction based upon a coerced confession and therefore cannot withstand constitutional attack under the Due Process Clause of the Fourteenth Amendment" (*Jackson v. Denno* 377 [1964]). *Stein* had maintained that it did not matter whether a jury had accepted a confession and relied on it or rejected it and disregarded it, but the Court now found that a defendant's rights were jeopardized either way.

A jury that accepted a confession also had all the other evidence of the defendant's guilt and, believing him guilty, might not have given proper credence to his testimony about how the confession was obtained—often the only testimony available to counter that of the police. "That a trustworthy confession must also be voluntary if it is to be used at all, generates natural and potent pressure to find it voluntary. Otherwise the guilty defendant goes free [if other evidence is insufficient to convict]. Objective consideration of the conflicting evidence concerning the circumstances of the confession becomes difficult and the implicit findings become suspect." The *Stein* majority's failure to inquire into the validity of the jury's determination of voluntariness had been based on its premise that due process required only that a conviction not be based on untrustworthy evidence, and that considerations of reliability were therefore relevant to a determination of admissibility, the Court now said, but that interpretation "was unequivocally put to rest in *Rogers v. Richmond.* . . . Under the New York procedure, the evidence given the jury inevitably injects irrelevant and impermissible considerations of truthfulness of the confession into the assessment of voluntariness. . . . [W]e cannot determine how the jury resolved these issues and will not assume that they were reliably and properly resolved against the accused" (*Jackson v. Denno* 382–387 passim [1964]).

The Court found the other possibility—that the jury had found the confession involuntary and convicted on the basis of other evidence—equally problematic. "Under the New York procedure, the fact of a defendant's confession is solidly implanted in the jury's mind, for it has not only heard the confession, but it has been instructed to consider and judge its voluntariness and is in position to assess whether it is true or false. If it finds the confession involuntary, does the jury—indeed, can it—then disregard the confession in accordance with its instructions? If there are lingering doubts about the sufficiency of the other evidence, does the jury unconsciously lay them to rest by resort to the confession? Will uncertainty about the sufficiency of the other evidence to prove guilt beyond a reasonable doubt actually result in acquittal when the jury knows the defendant has given a truthful confession" (*Jackson v. Denno* 388 [1964])? These were risks the Court was now unwilling to run.

Whichever course a jury took under the *Stein* dichotomy, therefore, a majority of five concluded that the procedures of the New York system were inadequate to ensure that a defendant would not be convicted on the basis of a coerced confession. A reliable and unambiguous determination of voluntariness was required before a confession could be submitted to the jury that would determine guilt or innocence, which meant that the orthodox and Massachusetts systems were constitutionally acceptable but that the New York system was not. The majority also returned to *Lisenba* and *Malinski* by rejecting *Stein's* tolerance of verdicts in which a jury had (presumably) ignored an involuntary confession but convicted on the basis of other evidence: "It is now clear that reversal follows if the confession admitted in evidence is found to be involuntary in this Court regardless of the possibility that the jury correctly followed instructions and determined the confession to be involuntary" (*Jackson v. Denno* 387 n.14 [1964]).

Four dissenters decried what they saw as the denigration of the jury system that is at the heart of the criminal justice process. The decision, they pointed out, was based not on inherent flaws in that system, but rather on the *possibility* that jurors might not perform as the system required—an acceptable risk, they believed, that applies equally to the determination of guilt beyond a reasonable doubt and is inherent in the very concept of jury trial. Nevertheless, the rule now is that a defendant who challenges the admissibility of a confession is entitled to a pretrial hearing on that issue before the judge, out of the presence of the jury (Seigal and Warren 2001, 1215). Submission to the jury of a confession subsequently determined to be involuntary is no longer always fatal, however, for the Court later held that it may constitute harmless error. Four dissenters, citing *Lisenba, Malinski, Jackson,* and many other decisions, complained that this ruling "without any justification . . . overrules this vast body of precedent without a word and in so doing dislodges one of the fundamental tenets of our criminal justice system" (*Arizona v. Fulminante* 289 [1991] [dissenting opinion]).

Incorporation and Immunity

Incorporation

In its modern decisions on the right to counsel, the Supreme Court had at first mandated the right in federal cases but made it obligatory in state cases only under special circumstances (see the discussion of state trials in the section on right to counsel at trial in Chapter 3). As Justice Harlan pointed out in his concurring opinion in the *Gideon* case, however, when the Court reached the point at which, in practice, the state (due process) standard was virtually indistinguishable from the federal (Sixth Amendment) standard, it took the final step and applied the Sixth Amendment right to counsel to the states. Although the pivotal case did not concern a coerced confession, the Court announced that it was doing essentially the same thing with respect to the privilege against self-incrimination, and only a year later. The case was *Malloy v. Hogan* (1964).

Malloy had been convicted of contempt and imprisoned for refusing to answer questions posed by a court-appointed referee who was investigating gambling and other criminal activity in Hartford, Connecticut. He claimed that the Fifth Amendment privilege against self-incrimination should be available to him in a state proceeding and the Court, in a 7–2 decision, agreed (although only five justices thought that his answers would have posed a realistic risk of incrimination and that the privilege had therefore been violated in his case).

Reviewing the coerced confession cases, Justice Brennan for the majority noted that the "Court in *Brown* [*v. Mississippi*] felt impelled, in light of *Twining* [*v. New Jersey*], to say that its conclusion did not involve the privilege against self-incrimination. . . . But this distinction was soon abandoned, and today the admissibility of a confession in a state criminal prosecution is tested by the same standard applied in federal prosecutions since 1897, when, in *Bram v. United States,*" the Court held that the privilege against self-incrimination is violated by the use of confessions that were not made freely and voluntarily (see the discussion of nineteenth-century developments in the section on privilege against self-incrimination in Chapter 2). "The shift reflects recognition that the American system of criminal prosecution is accusatorial, not inquisitorial, and that the Fifth Amendment privilege is its essential mainstay" (*Malloy v. Hogan* 6–7 [1964]). The Court, Brennan continued, was thus repudiating the assertion of *Twining* that the privilege is merely an expedient rule of evidence, and reaffirming the declaration of *Boyd v. United States* that it is a fundamental principle of justice under a free government.

Making the link between coerced confessions and compelled testimony, Brennan reasoned that "[s]ince the Fourteenth Amendment prohibits the States from inducing a person to confess through 'sympathy falsely aroused,' *Spano v. New York,* . . . or other like inducement far short of 'compulsion by torture,' . . . it follows *a fortiori* that it also forbids the States to resort to imprisonment, as here, to compel him to answer questions that might incriminate him. The Fourteenth Amendment secures against state invasion the same privilege that the Fifth Amendment guarantees against federal infringement—the right of a person to remain silent unless he chooses to speak in the unfettered exercise of his own will, and to suffer no penalty, as held in *Twining,* for such silence." Further, "[i]t would be incongruous to have different standards determine the validity of a claim of privilege based on the same feared prosecution, depending on whether the claim was asserted in a state or federal court. Therefore, the same standards must determine whether an accused's silence in either a federal or state proceeding is justified" (*Malloy v. Hogan* 8, 11 [1964]). The concept of exacting no penalty for silence was about the only part of *Twining* that the Court approved; *Malloy* overruled both *Twining* and *Adamson v. California* and incorporated the self-incrimination clause of the Fifth

Amendment into the due process clause of the Fourteenth Amendment.

Justice Harlan's dissent on the issue of incorporation reflected the fact that his view of federalism was no longer dominant on the Court. Neither compelled testimony nor coerced confessions were acceptable to him, but he adhered to the view that the constitutional standard in state cases was the due process clause, not the self-incrimination clause, and he was perfectly prepared to see the state and federal standards differ: "The Court concludes, almost without discussion, that 'the same standards must determine whether an accused's silence in either a federal or state proceeding is justified.' . . . About all that the Court offers in explanation of this conclusion is the observation that it would be 'incongruous' if different standards governed the assertion of a privilege to remain silent in state and federal tribunals. Such 'incongruity,' however, is at the heart of our federal system. The powers and responsibilities of the state and federal governments are not congruent; under our Constitution, they are not intended to be" (*Malloy v. Hogan* 27 [1964] [dissenting opinion]). The standards for admitting confessions in state cases had been made stricter, Harlan acknowledged, but through expansion of the meaning of due process, not substitution of the federal standard of self-incrimination; there had been a parallel tightening of federal standards for admissibility because the requirements of due process applied there as well. The notion that the *Brown* Court's distinction between self-incrimination (the Fifth Amendment standard) and due process (the Fourteenth Amendment standard) had been soon abandoned was "simply wrong," Harlan said, and Justice Brennan's characterization of the subsequent line of state confession cases was "*post facto* reasoning at best. Certainly there has been no intimation until now that *Twining* has been tacitly overruled," Harlan concluded, and the Court was wrong to overrule it here (*Malloy v. Hogan* 18, 17 [1964] [dissenting opinion]).

Immunity

Application of the privilege to the states required the Court to reconsider two basic questions: can a witness claim the privilege in one jurisdiction to shield information that could be used to prosecute him or her in another jurisdiction, and can information a witness is compelled to reveal under a grant of immunity in one jurisdiction be used to prosecute him or her in another jurisdiction?

Anticipating the possible outcome in *Malloy*, the Court heard arguments in and decided *Murphy v. Waterfront Commission* (1964) as a companion case. William Murphy and John Moody were union officials who had refused to answer questions posed by the commission—a bistate agency—about a work stoppage by longshoremen. Although they had been granted immunity under the laws of New York and New Jersey, the commission had not—and could not have—conferred immunity from federal prosecution. When they had continued to refuse to answer because of that threat, Murphy and Moody had been held in contempt by the courts of New Jersey. This dispute about interjurisdictional immunity provided the occasion for reexamination of three earlier cases.

As early as *Brown v. Walker* in 1896 (see the discussion of nineteenth-century developments in the section on privilege against self-incrimination in Chapter 2), the Supreme Court had stated that Congress could grant immunity from state as well as federal prosecution, and it so held in *Adams v. Maryland* (1954). Congress often did so, but in 1931, in a case in which a witness in a federal forum had sought to claim the privilege out of fear of state prosecution, the Court had held (with virtually no discussion) that all the Constitution requires for self-incriminating testimony to be compelled is immunity from prosecution by the jurisdiction doing the compelling (*United States v. Murdock* [1931]).

The Court now found this decision to be based on a faulty understanding of English and American precedent.

Second, in *Feldman v. United States* (1944), the Court had held that self-incriminating testimony compelled by state officials under a state grant of immunity could be used against the witness in a federal prosecution. Justice Felix Frankfurter's majority opinion had emphasized the proposition that under American federalism a state could not, by granting immunity, impair federal power to investigate and prosecute, but it had reinforced its reasoning by noting that the federal government was also free to use evidence gained by state searches and seizures that would have been unconstitutional if conducted by federal officials. Because the latter rule had been overturned in the meantime, the *Murphy* majority pronounced the *Feldman* question to be open once again because that decision was based on an analogy that was no longer valid.

Finally, the Court dealt with *Knapp v. Schweitzer* (1958), a case arising out of the contempt conviction of a witness who had received state immunity for testimony before a grand jury but who had nevertheless refused to answer questions out of fear of federal prosecution. Knapp had argued that the Fifth Amendment meant that neither the federal nor a state government could compel him to incriminate himself under federal law, but Justice Frankfurter, again writing for the majority, had announced that "such a claim carries dangerous implications" because the ever-broadening scope of federal legislation might therefore work a serious disruption of the states' ability to investigate and prosecute criminal activity, for which they have primary responsibility. The Fifth Amendment is not, Frankfurter had concluded, "a general declaration of policy against compelling testimony. . . . The sole—although deeply valuable—purpose of the Fifth Amendment privilege against self-incrimination is the security of the individual against the exertion of the power of the Federal Government to compel incriminating testimony with a view to enabling that same Government to convict a man out of his own mouth" (*Knapp v.*

Schweitzer 374, 380 [1958]). Now, however, *Malloy* had applied the privilege against self-incrimination to the states, so someone in Knapp's position was entitled to assert it.

This review of earlier cases, wrote Justice Arthur J. Goldberg for the *Murphy* majority, "makes it clear that there is no continuing legal vitality to, or historical justification for, the rule that one jurisdiction within our federal structure may compel a witness to give testimony which could be used to convict him of a crime in another jurisdiction. . . . We hold that the constitutional privilege against self-incrimination protects a state witness against incrimination under federal as well as state law and a federal witness against incrimination under state as well as federal law." Thus, a state authority cannot compel self-incriminating testimony under a grant of immunity unless the federal government is also prevented from using it, and vice versa. A grant of immunity must be as broad as the privilege it displaces, and with the *Malloy* decision, that privilege embraced state as well as federal witnesses.

The Court wished to vindicate the rights of state witnesses like Murphy and Moody without undermining state (or bistate) ability to gain essential information through grants of immunity. It therefore established a rule prohibiting the federal government "from making any . . . use of [state-] compelled testimony and its fruits. This exclusionary rule," Justice Goldberg declared, "leaves the witness and the Federal Government in substantially the same position as if the witness had claimed his privilege in the absence of a state grant of immunity" (*Murphy v. Waterfront Commission* 77–78, 79). *Murphy* clearly means (but did not explicitly hold) that a state, in turn, may not make use of testimony compelled in a federal or other state forum. In any event, the federal immunity statute applies to state as well as federal prosecutions (18 U.S.C. §§6001–6005 [2000]). The privilege does stop at the water's edge, however. Principally because foreign governments—unlike states—are not also bound by the privilege, the Court held many years later that a witness is not entitled to assert the privilege for fear of prosecution in a foreign jurisdiction (*United States v. Balsys* [1998]).

Justice Goldberg spoke for only five justices in *Murphy,* but the other four concurred. Justices John Marshall Harlan II and Tom C. Clark rejected the majority's interpretation of precedents and constitutional analysis but agreed that the exclusionary rule should be imposed on the federal government through the Court's supervisory authority over the administration of criminal justice in federal courts. Justices Byron R. White and Potter Stewart briefly noted their concurrence but wrote at length to emphasize that the majority's rule prohibiting federal use of state-compelled testimony and its fruits was not a rule of interjurisdictional *transactional* immunity, which they believed would cripple state law enforcement efforts. *Counselman* notwithstanding, they argued, the Constitution does not require transactional immunity even within a jurisdiction, for "[i]mmunity must be as broad as, but not harmfully and wastefully broader than, the privilege against self-incrimination" (*Murphy v. Waterfront Commission* 107 [1964] [concurring opinion]). Congress took the same position when it passed a new immunity statute in 1970, and the Court adopted it two years later in *Kastigar,* in which it used *Murphy* to support its decision (see the discussion of immunity above).

CONCLUSION

The elaboration of the scope of the privilege against self-incrimination has required the Supreme Court to tackle many difficult questions of definition that lurk in the Fifth Amendment's deceptively simple language about not being compelled to be a witness against oneself. Although disputes about the right to counsel are, for the most part, not about what the right is but rather about who is entitled to it and when, the Court's treatment of the testimonial privilege reflects continuing philosophical and policy debates about the nature of the right itself, both among the justices and those who comment on their work. The Court's retreat from its one major pronouncement of the nineteenth century—*Boyd's* protection of private papers—has been controversial, and its limitation of the privilege to evidence of a testimonial or communicative nature is criticized as both too broad and too narrow. We return briefly to these issues in the final chapter.

The Court's far clearer expansion of the privilege with respect to coerced confessions has been even more controversial. Prevention of abuses in obtaining and employing pretrial confessions may not have been the point of the privilege against self-incrimination as it evolved prior to the twentieth century, but it has become the most prominent public concern, partly because abuses are more likely to occur in the police station than in the courtroom, and partly because it is conflicting views about confessions, not compelled testimony, that are at the heart of continuing political arguments about the fairness and efficacy of the criminal justice system. By the 1960s, the Court had elaborated standards for confessions that were far stricter than those that had prevailed at the time of *Brown v. Mississippi* a generation earlier, and it had made those standards the same for federal and state prosecutions. A fundamental problem remained, however, and that was the difficulty a trial judge—and, subsequently, appellate judges—inevitably faced in discovering exactly what had happened during a police interrogation and determining whether a suspect had in fact been coerced into confessing.

The year 1964 would have been highly significant just for *Malloy v. Hogan, Murphy v. Waterfront Commission,* and *Jackson v. Denno,* but as the Court grappled with the continuing problem of the admissibility of confessions and other incriminating statements, it made two more decisions in that year tl at set the stage for the *Miranda* revolution two years later. We take up that story in the following chapter.

REFERENCES

Berger, Mark. 1980. *Taking the Fifth: The Supreme Court and the Privilege against Self-Incrimination.* Lexington, MA: Lexington Books.

Greenhouse, Linda. 2002. "Supreme Court Roundup: Laws on Sex Offender Lists to Get Further Look." *New York Times* (21 May, A14, late edition).

Murphy, Walter. F. 1962. *Congress and the Court.* Chicago: University of Chicago Press.

Nagareda, Richard A. 1999. "Compulsion 'To Be a Witness' and the Resurrection of *Boyd.*" *New York University Law Review* 74:1575–1659.

O'Malley, Eric Steven. 2001. "Thirtieth Annual Review of Criminal Procedure: Introduction and Guide for Users: III. Trial: Fifth Amendment at Trial." *Georgetown Law Journal* 89:1598–1614.

Rosen, Jeffrey. 2000. "My Child, Mine to Protect." *New York Times* (7 June, A31, late edition).

Seigal, Robert S., and Matthew J. Warren. 2001. "Thirtieth Annual Review of Criminal Procedure: Introduction and Guide for Users: I. Investigation and Police Practices: Custodial Interrogations." *Georgetown Law Journal* 89:1193–1215.

U.S. Senate. 1992. *The Constitution of the United States of America: Analysis and Interpretation.* 103d Cong., 1st sess. S. Doc. 103–6. Washington, DC: Government Printing Office.

5

Convergence of Rights: The *Miranda* Revolution

Prelude to *Miranda*

Massiah v. United States

In the spring of 1958, Winston Massiah, a merchant seaman, and several associates were arrested on various federal charges related to the importation of cocaine from Chile. Massiah was indicted, retained counsel, and was released on bail but not immediately tried, as the prosecution worked to unravel the conspiracy of which he was a part. About a year and a half later, Jesse Colson, one of the other conspirators, agreed to cooperate with the government by allowing a transmitter to be hidden in his car and engaging Massiah in conversation that was overheard by a government agent named Finbarr Murphy. At trial, Murphy testified as to various incriminating statements made by Massiah, who was convicted of several offenses. When the Supreme Court took up the case, it focused on Massiah's contention that the government's tactics had violated both his right to counsel and his privilege against self-incrimination (*Massiah v. United States* [1964]).

In his opinion for the Court, Justice Potter Stewart noted that in *Spano v. New York* (see the discussion of the coerced confession cases in Chapter 4), four justices would have overturned the conviction solely because the confession of an indicted defendant had been elicited in the absence of counsel. A majority of six now took that step, holding that, because Colson had been acting on behalf of the government, Massiah "was denied the basic protections of [the Sixth Amendment] when there was used against him at his trial evidence of his own incriminating words, which federal agents had deliberately elicited from him after he had been indicted and in the absence of his counsel." The right to counsel had attached, counsel had been retained, Massiah had in effect been interrogated by an agent of the state, and he was entitled to the assistance of counsel at what was deemed a critical stage of the prosecution. Solicitor General Archibald Cox (later to be the Watergate special prosecutor fired by President Richard Nixon) had argued that the government was entirely justified in using Colson to continue the investigation of already-indicted defendants, in order to penetrate a large and well-organized criminal conspiracy. The Court fully agreed that this was an appropriate way to gather evidence against other suspects but made it clear that "the defendant's own incriminating statements, obtained by federal agents under the circumstances here disclosed, could not constitutionally be used by the prosecution as evidence against *him* at his trial" (*Massiah v. United States* 206, 207 [1964] [emphasis in the original]).

The dissent of Justice Byron R. White, joined by Justices Tom C. Clark and John Marshall Harlan II, reflected, in terms of both jurisprudence and public policy, the growing dissatisfaction with the liberalization of the rights of criminal defendants then under way in the Warren Court. "The current incidence of serious violations of the law," wrote Justice White,

> represents not only an appalling waste of the potentially happy and useful lives of those who engage in such conduct but also an over-

> hanging, dangerous threat to those unidentified and innocent people who will be the victims of crime today and tomorrow. This is a festering problem for which no adequate cures have yet been devised. . . . It will just not do to sweep these disagreeable matters under the rug or to pretend they are not there at all.
>
> It is therefore a rather portentous occasion when a constitutional rule is established barring the use of evidence which is relevant, reliable and highly probative of the issue which the trial court has before it—whether the accused committed the act with which he is charged. Without the evidence, the quest for truth may be seriously impeded and in many cases the trial court, although aware of proof showing defendant's guilt, must nevertheless release him because the crucial evidence is deemed inadmissible. This result is entirely justified in some circumstances because exclusion serves other policies of overriding importance, as where evidence seized in an illegal search is excluded. . . . But this only emphasizes that the soundest of reasons is necessary to warrant the exclusion of evidence otherwise admissible and the creation of another area of privileged testimony. With all due deference, I am not at all convinced that the additional barriers to the pursuit of truth which the Court today erects rest on anything like the solid foundations which decisions of this gravity should require. (*Massiah v. United States* 207–208 [1964] [dissenting opinion])

The police tactics, White argued, did not violate the right to counsel because they in no way impeded Massiah's ability to have the full assistance of his attorney in preparing for trial and in no way invaded the privacy of the attorney-client relationship. Surely it was unreasonable to prevent the prosecution from using anything Massiah said without the knowledge and consent of counsel. Moreover,

> the Court's newly fashioned exclusionary principle goes far beyond the constitutional privilege against self-incrimination, which neither requires nor suggests the barring of voluntary pretrial admissions. . . . The defendant. . . . may not be compelled or coerced into saying anything before trial; but until today he could if he wished to, and if he

> did, it could be used against him. Whether as a matter of self-incrimination or of due process, the proscription is against compulsion—coerced incrimination.... [U]ntil now the Court has expressly rejected the argument that admissions are to be deemed involuntary if made outside the presence of counsel (*Massiah v. United States* 209–210 [1964] [dissenting opinion]).

At bottom, Justice White believed the majority had incorrectly weighed the conflicting demands of protecting individual rights and promoting law enforcement. Police should not be allowed to benefit from the sort of oppressive practices of interrogation discussed in the previous chapter, he agreed, but no such coercive tactics had been employed here. "Massiah and those like him receive ample protection from the long line of precedents in this Court holding that confessions may not be introduced unless they are voluntary" (*Massiah v. United States* 213 [1964] [dissenting opinion]). Massiah's surely was, the absence of counsel notwithstanding, White concluded, and a trial jury charged with finding the facts should not be denied such clear evidence of his guilt. For the majority, however, the crucial point was that Colson had functioned as an agent of the government, so that Massiah had been denied the opportunity to consult his attorney during the interrogation (or to waive his right to do so) for the simple reason that he had not known that he was being interrogated. Massiah had a right to counsel at that point, and the government could no more deprive him of it by deception than it could deprive him of it by force. Because it had, it was not entitled to use the incriminating statements it had gained as a result. One year later, the Court applied the same rule to the states (*McLeod v. Ohio* [1965]).

Escobedo v. Illinois

While Winston Massiah's case was moving slowly through the federal criminal justice system in New York, Danny Escobedo, a twenty-two-year-old of Mexican descent, was arrested in Chicago for the murder of his brother-in-law. During his interrogation, Escobedo made several requests to confer with his attorney, and the lawyer made several requests to confer with his client, but the police did not allow them to meet. The police did not advise Escobedo of his right to remain silent or of any other right and urged him to make a statement; eventually, he made incriminating admissions. Told that the police had strong evidence against him and that an accomplice had identified him as the one who had fired the fatal shots, Escobedo asserted that the accomplice was the shooter. What his lawyer could have told him was that "under Illinois law an admission of 'mere' complicity in the murder plot was legally as damaging as an admission of firing of the fatal shots" (*Escobedo v. Illinois* 486 [1964]). Escobedo's statements implicating himself in the plot were used against him and he was convicted of murder. The Supreme Court took the case to determine whether the police had violated Escobedo's right to counsel, thereby rendering his incriminating statements inadmissible at trial.

Unlike Massiah, Escobedo was not being deceived about what was happening to him, but also unlike Massiah, Escobedo had not yet been indicted and thus his right to counsel had not yet attached. For a majority of five, Justice Arthur J. Goldberg concluded that "in the context of this case, that fact should make no difference. When petitioner requested, and was denied, an opportunity to consult with his lawyer, the investigation had ceased to be a general investigation of 'an unsolved crime.' . . . Petitioner had become the accused, and the purpose of the interrogation was to 'get him' to confess his guilt despite his constitutional right not to do so." Escobedo was thus at a critical stage of the proceedings against him, when the outcome might well be determined. "It would exalt form over substance to make the right to counsel, under these circumstances, depend on whether at the time of the interrogation, the authorities had secured a formal indictment. Petitioner had, for all practical purposes, already been charged with murder. . . . [W]hen the process shifts from investigatory to accusatory—when its focus is on the accused and its purpose is to elicit a confession—our adversary system begins to operate, and, under the circumstances here, the accused must be permitted to consult with his lawyer" (*Escobedo v. Illinois* 485, 486, 492 [1964]); if he is not, any statements elicited by the police may not be used against him at trial.

Responding to the assertion that the decision would handicap police in gaining confessions during the period when they were most likely to occur (a consideration that had apparently been persuasive when the Court reached an opposite result in *Crooker v. California* just six years earlier—see the discussion of the coerced confession cases in Chapter 4), Justice Goldberg pointed out that

> [t]here is necessarily a direct relationship between the importance of a stage to the police in their quest for a confession and the criticalness of that stage to the accused in his need for legal advice. Our Constitution, unlike some others, strikes the balance in favor of the right of the accused to be advised by his lawyer of his privilege against self-incrimination. . . . [N]o system of criminal justice can, or should, survive if it comes to depend for its continued effectiveness on the citizens' abdication through unawareness of their constitutional rights. No system worth preserving should have to *fear* that if an accused is permitted to consult with a lawyer, he will become aware of, and exercise, these rights. If the exercise of constitutional rights will thwart the effectiveness of a system of law enforcement, then there is something very wrong with that system (*Escobedo v. Illinois* 488, 490 [1964] [emphasis in the original]).

When, eight years later, the Court held in *Kirby v. Illinois* that the right to counsel does not attach until adversarial judicial proceedings have been initiated (see the discussion of the right to counsel in pretrial proceedings in Chapter 3), it did not overrule *Escobedo* but declared that its application was limited to its facts, in circumstances in which the right to counsel was necessary to safeguard the privilege against self-incrimination. Dissenting in *Escobedo,* Justice Potter Stewart anticipated the *Kirby* rule and would have made no exception with respect to self-incrimination. Escobedo had not been indicted, the right to counsel had therefore not attached, and the statements had been voluntary; there was thus no reason to exclude them from trial. Yes, the police tactics had affected the trial to the detriment of the murderer; that is precisely what an investigation is supposed to do. No, the police had not advised Escobedo of his constitutional rights; the Court had never held that they had any obligation to do so. Stewart made it clear that he thought *Escobedo* was a wrongheaded decision that "frustrates the vital interests of society in preserving the legitimate and proper function of honest and purposeful police investigation" (*Escobedo v. Illinois* 494 [1964] [dissenting opinion]). Three of his colleagues felt the same way, with Justice White lamenting "the amorphous and wholly unworkable principle that counsel is constitutionally required whenever he would or could be helpful" and noting that previous cases granting a right to counsel at various pretrial stages "dealt with the requirement of counsel at proceedings in which definable rights could be won or lost, not with stages where probative evidence might be obtained." The majority, of course, thought that Escobedo's privilege against self-incrimination was at risk, but White argued that the Fifth Amendment protects only against compulsion. As for the failure of police to inform Escobedo of his rights, a suspect's ignorance of his rights is an important factor in determining whether compulsion has occurred, "[b]ut in this case Danny Escobedo knew full well that he did not have to answer and knew full well that his lawyer had advised him not to answer" (*Escobedo v. Illinois* 496, 497, 499 [1964] [dissenting opinion]).

Intersection of Two Rights

The *Massiah* and *Escobedo* cases were both decided on the basis of the right to counsel, but in each case the disadvantage suffered by the accused stemmed from an act of self-incrimination. A narrow majority of the Court saw unfairness to defendants in law enforcement procedures operating in a marginal area between the bounds of the two rights, while a vehement minority saw responsible police work that did not violate either right—not the right to counsel because that was limited to the unimpeded functioning of attorneys in assisting defendants to confront the prosecution in the judicial process, and not the privilege against self-incrimination (or the due process protection against involuntary confession) because that was limited to protecting defendants from those forms of self-incrimination that were the product of compulsion. The Court needed to clarify this ill-defined region of the law, and it faced two other problems as well. One was the continuing dilemma, noted at the end of the previous chapter, of making fair and accurate determinations of whether confessions had been coerced. The second problem was one it had just created in *Escobedo,* by suggesting but not specifying a police obligation to inform suspects of their constitutional rights and to honor requests for counsel at interrogations prior to the initiation of formal judicial proceedings. State and lower federal courts were soon arriving at conflicting interpretations of *Escobedo,* and prosecutors, defense attorneys, police, and judges were all in need of clarification and guidance from the Court. The response came in *Miranda v. Arizona* (1966).

THE *MIRANDA* DECISION

In the spring of 1963, Ernesto Miranda, a young schizophrenic who suffered from sexual fantasies, had dropped out of school in the ninth grade, and had been imprisoned several times, was arrested for forcing a young woman into his car in Phoenix, tying her hands and feet, driving her to a desert area at the edge of town, and raping her. After she tentatively identified him in a lineup, police questioned Miranda and he soon confessed. At trial, he made no claim that the confession had been involuntary and offered no evidence in his defense; the confession was entered into evidence and he was convicted of kidnapping and rape. Three years later, the Supreme Court used Miranda's case (and three others combined with it) to determine the significance of the fact that at the interrogation, the police had not clearly warned Miranda of his rights to have counsel and to remain silent. Its conclusion was that that omission rendered the confessions inadmissible, and that the convictions in *Miranda* and the other three cases had to be overturned.

At the outset of his opinion for a majority of five, Chief Justice Earl Warren candidly acknowledged that the *Escobedo* decision had been the object of considerable speculation, uncertainty, disagreement, praise, and criticism among courts, legal scholars, prosecutors, and police. The Court, he said, had taken the *Miranda* case "in order further to explore some facets of the problems, thus exposed, of applying the privilege against self-incrimination to in-custody interrogation [as opposed to interrogation in forums such as courtrooms, where the compulsion to speak is a *legal* one (U. S. Senate 1992, 1306)], and to give concrete constitutional guidelines for law enforcement agencies and courts to follow." It was not, however, backing down, for "[w]e start here, as we did in *Escobedo,* with the premise that our holding is not an innovation in our jurisprudence, but is an application of principles long recognized and applied in other settings. We have undertaken a thorough re-examination of the *Escobedo* decision and the principles it announced, and we reaffirm it. That case was but an explication of basic rights that are enshrined in our Constitution . . . which were put in jeopardy in that case through official overbearing." Invoking the transcendent evolution of the *nemo tenetur* maxim into constitutional principle (see the discussion of English and continental origins in the section on the privilege against self-incrimination in Chapter 2), Warren announced that the purpose of both the *Escobedo* and *Miranda* decisions was to spell out, "in meaningful language, the manner in which the constitutional rights of the individual could be enforced against overzealous police practices" (*Miranda v. Arizona* 442, 444 [1966]).

The threat to suspects and the challenge for courts, Warren emphasized, was the reality of "incommunicado interrogation of individuals in a police-dominated atmosphere, resulting in self-incriminating statements." Methods of physical coercion—the third degree—had been largely though not completely abandoned by the police, but methods of psychological coercion, as illustrated in police manuals that Warren quoted at length, were pervasive. Even in the absence of such tactics, "the very fact of custodial interrogation exacts a heavy toll on individual liberty and trades on the weakness of individuals," causing suspects to surrender rights that they might have exercised in a different setting. The challenge for courts was that, as sophisticated as judges might be about police practices, "[i]nterrogation still takes place in privacy. Privacy results in secrecy and this in turn results in a gap in our knowledge as to what in fact goes on in the interrogation rooms" (*Miranda v. Arizona* 445, 455, 448 [1966]). What the Court sought was a mechanism to increase the likelihood that rights would not be violated in secret and to enhance the ability of judges to determine which confessions are truly voluntary and therefore properly admissible at trial.

The *Miranda* majority was clearly reacting against the atmosphere of interrogation in general, for it conceded that in the cases before it, "we might not find the defendants' statements to have been involuntary in traditional terms" because "the records do not evince overt physical coercion or patent psychological ploys." Nevertheless, "[i]n each of the cases, the defendant was thrust into an unfamiliar atmosphere and run through menacing police interrogation procedures" and "in none of these cases did the officers undertake to afford appropriate safeguards at the outset of the interrogation to insure that the statements were truly the product of free choice." In the *Ashcraft* case (see the discussion of the coerced confession cases in Chapter 4), Justice Black had suggested that certain tactics of interrogation are inherently coercive; now Chief Justice Warren was going further, concluding that the process of custodial interrogation per se is inherently coercive. Thus, "[u]nless adequate protective devices are employed to dispel the compulsion inherent in custodial surroundings, no statement obtained from the defendant can truly be the product of his free choice" (*Miranda v. Arizona* 457, 458 [1966]).

The appropriate remedy, Warren announced, was the presence of counsel, which would ensure that any statements made by the suspect were the product of his or her own free will and not the result of governmental coercion. To ensure that this remedy was available to the suspect, it was essential that upon arrest he or she be informed of his or her constitutional rights and allowed to exercise them; evidence that the suspect was already aware of those rights would not suffice. From this formulation, the requirement for the well-known *Miranda* warnings for suspects in custody was born: "unless other fully effective means are adopted to notify the person of his right of silence and to assure that the exercise of the right will be scrupulously honored, the following measures are required. He must be warned prior to any questioning that he has the right to remain silent, that anything he says can be used against him in a court of law, that he has the right to the presence of an attorney, and that if he cannot afford an attorney one will be appointed for him prior to any questioning if he so desires" (*Miranda v. Arizona* 479 [1966]). The Court imposed some rules of interrogation as well: suspects may not be questioned in the absence of counsel if they have requested it, and questioning must cease whenever a suspect communicates a desire not to be interrogated.

The suspect's *right* to counsel during custodial interrogation, the Court declared, does not depend on a request (although, as a practical matter, actually *having* the assistance of counsel does), and failure to request counsel does not constitute a waiver of the right. Similarly, the fact that a suspect eventually confesses does not constitute a waiver of the privilege against self-incrimination, nor does his or her failure to respond to the warning. Valid waivers of either right occur only when a suspect, after being warned, voluntarily takes an affirmative step to forgo it. Before it can use any statement—inculpatory or exculpatory—that is the product of custodial interrogation, the government must establish that proper warnings were given, and if the statement was made in the absence of counsel, "a heavy burden rests on the government to demonstrate that the defendant knowingly and intelligently waived his privilege against self-incrimination and his right to retained or appointed counsel" (*Miranda v. Arizona* 475 [1966]). With certain exceptions to be discussed later, statements that do not meet these conditions are inadmissible at trial.

Chief Justice Warren emphasized that the *Miranda* rules apply only in the context of "custodial interrogation, [by which] we mean questioning initiated by law enforcement officers after a person has been taken into custody or otherwise deprived of his freedom of action in any significant way" (*Miranda v. Arizona* 444 [1966]). Thus the rules do not apply, for example, to a person who walks into a police station and volunteers a confession. The questions of when custody begins and what police actions constitute interrogation are, however, subject to interpretation, as we shall see, so police must be careful not to go too far before initiating *Miranda* procedures.

For the *Miranda* majority, the point was to provide a remedy for the inability of many suspects, in the face of significant pressure from the police, to exercise their constitutional privilege against self-incrimination—which the Court for the first time now formally applied to the stage of pretrial interrogation in state proceedings—intelligently and effectively. As Chief Justice Warren later wrote in his memoirs, "[t]there was really nothing new in this except to require police and prosecutors to advise the poor, the ignorant, and the unwary of a basic constitutional right in a manner which had been followed by Federal Bureau of Investigation procedures for many years. It was of no assistance to hardened underworld types because they already know what their rights are and demand them. And it is so with all sophisticated criminals and affluent prisoners who had ready access to their lawyers. However, because so many people who are arrested are poor and illiterate, short-cut methods and often cruelties are perpetrated to obtain convictions" (Warren 1977, 316–317).

The majority also believed the reforms would assist the courts in making proper decisions about the admissibility and credibility of confessions. The presence of counsel at interrogations would help to ensure the accuracy of the defendant's statements and of the reporting of those statements by the prosecution. It would also reduce the likelihood of the use of coercive tactics by the interrogators, and provide the judge with a witness to the proceedings if the issue of tactics should be disputed. (The provision of *Miranda* warnings does not exempt interrogators from the standards for voluntariness laid down in the long line of coerced confession cases discussed in Chapter 4.) Finally, even if suspects decline the assistance of counsel, the fact that they have been clearly informed of their rights and given the opportunity to exercise them gives greater confidence that any statement they do make is the product of their own free will.

None of these arguments were at all convincing to the four dissenters, who thought that the police were being maligned and found the decision to be both bad law and bad policy. Their principal spokesmen were Justices Harlan and White, who argued that neither the right to counsel nor the privilege against self-incrimination, properly understood, could support the decision. Harlan observed that such right-to-counsel decisions as *Johnson v.*

Zerbst, *Gideon v. Wainwright*, *Douglas v. California*, and *Carnley v. Cochran* (see Chapter 3) "turn out to be linchpins of the confession rules announced today." All those decisions found a need for counsel because of the intricacies of trial or appellate procedure, he continued, and "[w]hile the Court finds no pertinent difference between judicial proceedings and police interrogation, I believe the differences are so vast as to disqualify wholly the Sixth Amendment precedents as suitable analogies in the present cases" (*Miranda v. Arizona* 513, 513–514 [1966] [dissenting opinion]). The decisions were analogies rather than precedents because, as White pointed out, the *Miranda* majority did not ground its decision in the Sixth Amendment right to counsel—applied to the states three years earlier—but rather "created a limited Fifth Amendment right to counsel—or, as the Court expresses it, a 'need for counsel to protect the Fifth Amendment privilege.' . . ." The question in self-incrimination cases had been whether the will of the suspect not to confess had been overborne, but now the "focus . . . is not on the will of the accused but on the will of counsel and how much influence he can have on the accused. Obviously there is no warrant in the Fifth Amendment for thus installing counsel as the arbiter of the privilege" (*Miranda v. Arizona* 537 [1966] [dissenting opinion]).

"To reach the result announced on the grounds it does," White argued, "the Court must stay within the confines of the Fifth Amendment, which forbids self-incrimination only if *compelled.* Hence the core of the Court's opinion is that because of the 'compulsion inherent in custodial surroundings, no statement obtained from [a] defendant [in custody] can truly be the product of his free choice,' . . . absent the use of adequate protective devices as described by the Court," but the Court had been holding to the contrary since the late nineteenth century, and the majority could not point to any hard evidence to support its new conclusion. It was seeking a remedy for trial judges' inability to know for sure what had happened during an interrogation, but White turned that argument around: there was no evidence that the *Miranda* regulations were needed precisely because "the Court concedes that it cannot truly know what occurs during custodial questioning, because of the innate secrecy of such proceedings." All the majority could do was to assume that the tactics described in manuals were routinely employed, White maintained, and that surely did not establish that confessions were involuntary in every case, including the four decided here. "Even if one were to postulate that the Court's concern is not that all confessions induced by police interrogation are coerced but rather that some such confessions are coerced and present judicial procedures are believed to be inadequate to identify the confessions that are coerced and those that are not, it would still not be essential to impose the rule that the Court has now fashioned"; less sweeping measures could accomplish that (*Miranda v. Arizona* 532, 535 [1966][dissenting opinion; emphasis in the original]).

"The Fifth Amendment," Harlan argued, "has never been thought to forbid *all* pressure to incriminate one's self in the situations covered by it. . . . Until today, the role of the Constitution has been only to sift out *undue* pressure. . . . [W]ith over 25 years of precedent the Court has developed an elaborate, sophisticated, and sensitive approach to admissibility of confessions" that assesses the totality of the circumstances (which include the conditions of custody and the presence or absence of warnings about rights); that flexible approach was preferable to the rigid rules now being imposed (*Miranda v. Arizona* 512, 515, 508 [1966] [dissenting opinion; emphasis in the original]). The new approach, which was likely to deter confessions, placed too much emphasis on the rights of the accused and too little emphasis on the ability of law enforcement to secure the safety and well-being of society. The ever-judicious Harlan termed the new rules a "hazardous experimentation," warning that the defense attorney in the police station "may become an obstacle to truthfinding" (*Miranda v. Arizona* 517, 514 [1966] [dissenting opinion]); the blunter White was sure "that a good many criminal defendants who otherwise would have been convicted on what this Court has previously thought to be the most satisfactory kind of evidence will now, under this new version of the Fifth Amendment, either not be tried at all or will be acquitted if the State's evidence, minus the confession, is put to the test of litigation" (*Miranda v. Arizona* 542 [1966] [dissenting opinion]). (The majority, of course, believed there was no basis for confidence that convictions based on confessions obtained under such circumstances would be justified.)

Like Chief Justice Warren for the majority, the dissenters focused mostly on general issues of law and policy, but Justice Harlan gave concrete form to his disagreement with a pungent assessment of the disposition of the principal case before the Court:

> Miranda's oral and written confessions are now held inadmissible under the Court's new rules. One is entitled to feel astonished that the Constitution can be read to produce this result. These confessions were obtained during brief, daytime questioning conducted by two officers and unmarked by any of the traditional indicia of coercion. They assured a conviction for a brutal and unsettling crime, for which the police had and quite possibly could obtain little evidence other than the victim's identifications, evidence which is frequently unreliable. There was, in sum, a legitimate purpose, no perceptible unfairness, and certainly little risk of injustice in the interrogation. Yet the resulting confessions, and the responsible course of police practice they represent, are to be sacrificed to the Court's own finespun conception of fairness which I seriously doubt is shared by many thinking citizens in this country. (*Miranda v. Arizona* 518–519 [1966] [dissenting opinion])

Harlan was certainly correct in believing that the decision would engender great opposition, and the majority must have known that as well. For the Chief Justice and his four colleagues, however, the more important consideration was that the Court had taken a major step to ensure that the rights of suspects were not being violated in secret, had given trial judges a more reliable basis for the admission of incriminating statements into evidence, and had provided a clear set of rules defining the obligations of police and prosecutors.

It is reasonable to believe that a further—albeit unarticulated—goal of the majority was to compensate for perceived errors and inadequacies of state (and, to a lesser extent, federal) trial and appellate judges and, ultimately, of its own articulation of the voluntariness test itself. Over the previous three decades, in *Brown v. Mississippi, Chambers v. Florida, Ashcraft v. Tennessee, Spano v. New York,* and other cases (see the discussion of the coerced confession cases in Chapter 4), the Court had found it necessary to overturn convictions because they were based on confessions that state supreme courts had held to be admissible. Trial courts normally resolved disputes over the admissibility of confessions in favor of the prosecution, and appellate courts seemed inclined to affirm those rulings. The Supreme Court could not possibly monitor all of those decisions on a case-by-case basis; it had taken an average of only one state confession case per year since *Brown.* "Given the volume of cases and the vagueness of the test, similarly situated defendants inevitably were treated differently" (Dripps 2001, 22). Because the inherent subjectivity of the voluntariness standard allowed lower court judges to tilt in favor of police and prosecution, it is not surprising that the *Miranda* majority saw the need for some more objective mechanism to level the playing field (Kamisar et al. 2002, 443–445). The minority, of course, disagreed because they were inclined to believe that police generally stayed within proper bounds and that most confessions were therefore properly admissible. What all the justices could agree on was that the Court would soon face a great many questions about the application of the new rules in practice.

IMPLEMENTATION OF *Miranda*

The opinions in *Miranda* were couched primarily in terms of contrasting constitutional philosophies and their implications for public policy. Chief Justice Warren's statement of the Court's new position was very specific about the rules police must follow in conducting custodial interrogations, but it did not (and could not) address all the inevitable issues of implementation of those rules in practice. In the ensuing years, the Court grappled with those problems and adjusted its course as its membership changed. (Three members of the *Miranda* majority and two dissenters left the Court during the next five years.) The Court quickly decided that *Miranda* (and *Escobedo*) would not be applied retroactively (*Johnson v. New Jersey* [1966]), but several other issues also required its attention.

Custody

In the application of *Miranda,* definition of the concept of custody evolved as a process of resolving competing considerations of the degree of official control of the suspect, the location of the encounter, and the perceptions and intentions of the participants. The *Miranda* opinion stated in one place that the new rules applied "after a person has been taken into custody or otherwise deprived of his freedom of action in any significant way," and in another place that they applied to a suspect "while in custody at the station or otherwise deprived of his freedom of action in any significant way" (*Miranda v. Arizona* 444, 477 [1966]). This ambiguity about the significance of being in a police station led to disagreement in subsequent cases. In an early decision, the Court held that a person who is questioned by police while in prison (of a different jurisdiction, for a separate offense) is in custody and must be given *Miranda* warnings. The majority maintained that the fact that the suspect was not in the custody of the interrogator for the offense under investigation did not affect his need for protection, while the dissenters argued that Mathis was not in unfamiliar surroundings, that the "rationale of *Miranda* has no relevance to inquiries conducted outside the allegedly hostile and forbidding atmosphere surrounding police station interrogation" (*Mathis v. United States* 8 [1968] [dissenting opinion]), and that warnings should not be required in what was a civil investigation of a tax matter (which subsequently led to a criminal prosecution). The following year, the Court went a step further, holding that a suspect who was neither in the police station nor in prison but rather under arrest in his bedroom in a boardinghouse was deprived of his freedom in a significant way and therefore clearly entitled to *Miranda* warnings. In dissent, Justice White pointedly disagreed, asserting that "[t]his decision carries the rule of *Miranda v. Arizona* . . . to a new and unwarranted extreme" because there was no reason "for believing that practices outside the station house are normally prolonged, carried out in isolation, or often productive of the physical or psychological coercion made so much of in *Miranda*" (*Orozco v. Texas* 328, 329 [1969] [dissenting opinion]).

A few years later, the Court considered the opposite situation—that of a suspect who was in a police station but had come voluntarily, was not under arrest, and was able to leave freely at the end of the interview, even though he had confessed—and it decided summarily that warnings were not required because he was not in custody (*Oregon v. Mathiason* [1977]). Dissenters argued that there were nevertheless coercive elements in the atmosphere and that the suspect might well have perceived restraints on his freedom. The Court ultimately decided that, by itself, the fact of being in a police station is neither necessary nor sufficient to require *Miranda* warnings, for "the ultimate inquiry is simply whether there is a 'formal arrest or restraint on freedom of movement' of the degree associated with a formal arrest" (*California v. Beheler* 1125 [1983]).

The *Mathiason* decision reflected the fact that the degree of subjection to control by police interrogators, rather than location of the encounter or perceptions or intentions of police, was emerging as the key factor. A year earlier, in another case involving questions posed by an agent of the Internal Revenue Service, the Court had rejected the argument that because the police had made the suspect the focus of the investigation, he had experienced some deprivation of freedom of action and was therefore entitled to warnings prior to noncustodial questioning in his home and office (*Beckwith v. United States* [1976]).

All three factors were considered in *Berkemer v. McCarty* (1984), a case that involved a roadside traffic stop and was important for holding that *Miranda* applies to misdemeanors as well as to felonies. After being pulled over by Trooper Williams of the Ohio State Highway Patrol, McCarty was questioned outside his car at roadside, arrested and taken to jail, and questioned again. He received no warnings at any point, incriminated himself in both sessions, and was convicted of driving under the influence of alcohol and/or drugs. The Court held that although an initial traffic stop does curtail a motorist's freedom of action, such stops are normally brief and temporary and, being public, present little danger of police coercion or abuse. The evils that *Miranda* was designed to prevent are not present at roadside stops, and warnings are therefore not required. Although Trooper Williams had immediately perceived McCarty as intoxicated and determined at the outset to arrest him, he had not initially communicated that fact to him. The trooper's intentions were therefore irrelevant because McCarty had at first had no reason to perceive that he would not be allowed to go on his way. McCarty was not in custody at that point and his roadside statements were properly admissible. Once a motorist is placed under arrest, however, he is in custody for *Miranda* purposes and must be warned. The Court therefore held that McCarty's jailhouse statements were inadmissible.

Probation interviews are comparable to roadside stops. Even though a probationer is required to meet with his or her supervising agent and answer questions, and is not free to leave until the interview is over, he or she is not in custody for *Miranda* purposes and is not entitled to warnings, even though the agent is seeking incriminating information (*Minnesota v. Murphy* [1984]). Similarly, even though witnesses before grand juries, including targets of the investigation, are in an unfamiliar setting, are not free to leave, and are required to answer questions that do not incriminate them, they are not entitled to *Miranda* warnings (although it is the policy of the U.S. Department of Justice to provide similar warnings in federal cases) (Bowles 2002, 1321, n.785).

The fact of custody is necessary but not always sufficient. Lloyd Perkins was in prison on unrelated charges when he was questioned about a murder by an undercover agent posing as a fellow inmate. He was not entitled to warnings, the Court held, because, although clearly in custody, he was not in a police-dominated atmosphere and perceived no pressure at all from what he thought was a casual conversation with other prisoners. As in *Berkemer,* the dangers *Miranda* sought to avert were not present (and, as a practical matter, a requirement that warnings be given would make the use of undercover agents impossible). The situation was different from that in *Mathis,* for there the prisoner had known that he was being questioned by the police. Beyond the *Miranda* question, although the deception in *Perkins* was similar to that in *Massiah,* Perkins's Sixth Amendment right to counsel had not been violated because formal charges for the murder had not been filed and thus, unlike *Massiah,* the right to counsel had not yet attached. In dissent, Justice Thurgood Marshall argued that *Miranda* clearly required warnings for persons who are interrogated by the police while in custody, and that no exception was warranted here because "*Miranda* was not . . . concerned solely with police *coercion.* It dealt with *any* police tactics that may operate to compel a suspect in custody to make incriminating statements without full awareness of his constitutional rights" (*Illinois v. Perkins* 306 [1990] [dissenting opinion, emphasis in the original]). The majority, however, determined that "[p]loys to mislead a suspect or lull him into a false sense of security that do not rise to the level of compulsion or coercion to speak are not within *Miranda's* concerns" (*Illinois v. Perkins* 297 [1990]).

The net result of the Court's custody rulings is that, to be entitled to *Miranda* warnings, a suspect must be under arrest or some comparable restriction of his or her freedom of action by the police, regardless of location. Prior to formal arrest, a police officer's suspicions and intentions are relevant only if communicated to the suspect, and then only to the extent that they affect the way a reasonable person in the suspect's position would objectively perceive restriction of his or her freedom of action. Moreover, even in prison, where the fact of custody is clear, the government can elicit information without warnings as long as the suspect does not perceive himself or herself to be under the immediate control of government agents seeking information. Warnings are required only when the suspect is not only in custody but perceives himself or herself to be under interrogation by an agent of the state in a police-dominated atmosphere.

Warnings

The *Miranda* decision mandated its prescribed warnings "unless other fully effective means are adopted to notify the person of his right of silence" and to counsel (*Miranda v. Arizona* 479 [1966]), and the Court has held that variations on the form of the warnings are acceptable as long as the language used "fully convey[s] to [the suspect] his rights as required by *Miranda*" (*California v. Prysock* 361 [1981]). The Court held that requirement had been met when a suspect was told that he had a right to appointed counsel prior to and during interrogation but also told that the police could not provide a lawyer but that one would be appointed if and when he went to court (*Duckworth v. Eagan* [1989]).

Assertion and Waiver of Rights

When suspects whom the police wish to subject to custodial interrogation clearly assert the right to silence or to an attorney, police must honor those rights. Once a request for counsel has been made, an accused "is not subject to further interrogation by the authorities until counsel has been made available to him, unless the accused himself initiates further communication, exchanges, or conversations with the police" and validly waives his rights to counsel and silence (*Edwards v. Arizona* 484–485, 486 n.9 [1981]). Police are not, however, required to honor (or even to clarify) vague comments about having a lawyer; "the suspect must unambiguously request counsel" and questioning can continue until he or she does (*Davis v. United States* 459 [1994]).

Unlike a request for the provision of counsel, there is no obvious point at which a request not to be interrogated has been fully honored, and the *Miranda* decision did not address the permissibility of a resumption of questioning after the right to silence has been asserted but counsel has not been requested. In considering the case of Richard Bert Mosley, the Court rejected the polar extremes that the suspect may never again be interrogated and that interrogation may resume after a momentary pause. The test, the Court concluded, requires a judgment about police behavior, for "the admissibility of statements obtained after the person in custody has decided to remain silent depends under *Miranda* on whether his 'right to cut off questioning' was 'scrupulously honored'" (*Michigan v. Mosley* 104 [1975]). Mosley, in custody for robbery, had declined to answer questions and interrogation had ceased. Two hours later, a different officer had again given him *Miranda* warnings and asked about an unrelated murder; this time Mosley had not asserted his rights and had incriminated himself.

The Court held that under the circumstances—full compliance with *Miranda* procedures in both instances and a significant lapse of time between them—Mosley's right to halt interrogation had been fully honored and his incriminating statements were therefore admissible against him.

When a suspect under interrogation without a lawyer does make incriminating statements, their admissibility is contingent on the state's ability to meet its burden of establishing a valid waiver of *Miranda* rights. For this purpose, an explicit oral or written statement of waiver by the suspect is usually but not necessarily sufficient; mere silence is never sufficient but a course of action indicating understanding of rights and willingness to forgo them may be. At bottom, "[t]he question is not one of form, but rather whether the defendant in fact knowingly and voluntarily waived the rights delineated in the *Miranda* case. . . . The courts must presume that a defendant did not waive his rights; the prosecution's burden is great; but in at least some cases waiver can be clearly inferred from the actions and words of the person interrogated" (*North Carolina v. Butler* 373 [1979]). William Thomas Butler, accused of kidnapping, armed robbery, and felonious assault, was advised of his rights and stated that he understood them; on the other hand, he refused to sign a waiver of rights and did not respond when advised of his right to an attorney. Because he never requested an attorney and freely answered questions, the Court found a valid implicit waiver of the right to counsel.

Noting Butler's contradictory behavior and disagreements about the timing of warnings and about Butler's literacy, Justice William J. Brennan in dissent objected to a formula "allowing courts to construct inferences from ambiguous words and gestures" (*North Carolina v. Butler* 377 [1979] [dissenting opinion]) and argued for a requirement of an explicit waiver of rights.

In the *Edwards* case, the Court found that the circumstances did not justify the inference that the suspect had waived his right to counsel. Robert Edwards, in custody on charges of burglary, robbery, and murder, asserted his right to counsel and interrogation ceased. The following day, still without counsel and over his objections, he was required to meet again with police and, after fresh warnings, made incriminating responses to their questions. The Court held that the state's ability to show that Edwards had spoken voluntarily did not meet its burden of also establishing that he had knowingly and intelligently waived the right to counsel, and it imposed the requirement (quoted above) that interrogation must cease until counsel has been provided.

A variation on this theme occurred when William Barrett refused to make a written statement about his participation in a sexual assault until his attorney was present but freely declared his willingness to discuss the matter orally in the meantime. The Wallingford, Connecticut, police did not (and could not) take and use a written statement at that point, but they did obtain and use an oral statement. The Supreme Court held that because Barrett's request for counsel had pertained only to a written statement and he had validly waived his right to silence otherwise, his oral statement was properly admissible at trial (*Connecticut v. Barrett* [1987]).

The Court subsequently reinforced *Miranda's* emphasis on the value of counsel at interrogation by concluding that a waiver of counsel in the *Edwards* circumstances could never be valid. Once counsel has been requested, it held, police may not reinitiate interrogation in the absence of counsel, even if the suspect has had an opportunity to consult with counsel in the meantime (*Minnick v. Mississippi* [1990]). By the same token, once counsel has been requested for one offense, police may not initiate questioning about any other offense in the absence of counsel, even if *Miranda* warnings have been given again (*Arizona v. Roberson* [1988]). Statements gained in violation of these rules are inadmissible.

On the other hand, the police have no obligation to facilitate the assistance of counsel when it has not been requested, and to some extent they may inhibit it. Brian Burbine was arrested for breaking and entering in Cranston, Rhode Island, but police soon learned that he might also have committed a murder in Providence and invited police there to come and question him. In the meantime, Burbine's sister had arranged for a public defender to represent him on the charge of breaking and entering; the attorney informed the Cranston police that she wished to consult with her client before questioning and was told that he would not be questioned until the next day. The police did not inform her of the murder investigation or of the pending interrogation by Providence police, which took place that evening. The police also failed to inform Burbine that he had a lawyer who wished to see him before he answered any questions, and after receiving proper warnings he signed a waiver of his rights and confessed to the murder. When Burbine challenged the use of the confession to obtain his conviction, the Court held that proper *Miranda* warnings, fully understood, provide all the information a suspect requires to exercise or waive his rights and are "sufficient to dispel whatever coercion is inherent in the interrogation process." Because Burbine had never requested an attorney and his waiver had been uncoerced, it was valid in spite of the police's withholding of other information from him and his attorney and their deception of the attorney. "No doubt the additional information would have been useful to respondent," wrote Justice Sandra Day O'Connor; "perhaps even it might have affected his decision to confess. But we have never read the Constitution to require that the police supply a suspect with a flow of information to help him calibrate his self-interest in deciding whether to speak or stand by his rights" (*Moran v. Burbine* 427, 422 [1986]). (The Court also held that the Sixth Amendment right to counsel had not been violated because it had not yet attached, and that the police misconduct was not so shocking as to constitute a violation of due process.)

Justice John Paul Stevens and two other dissenters found the majority's protection of "lawyer-free, incommunicado custodial interrogation" to be inconsistent with the rationale of *Miranda* and agreed with the many state courts that had held that an attorney's communication with a client has such "a direct 'bearing' on the knowing and intelligent waiver of constitutional rights" that police interference with that communication should invalidate any subsequent waiver (*Moran v. Burbine* 437, 456 [1986] [dissenting opinion]. The police do not have to fully inform a suspect with respect to the right to silence, either, for the Court has held that a waiver of the privilege against self-incrimination is not invalid simply because the police fail to advise a suspect under arrest for one crime that they intend to interrogate him about another crime as well (*Colorado v. Spring* [1987]).

Interrogation

Interrogation clearly occurs when police ask a suspect about his or her activities, but not when they ask routine "booking" questions about his or her name, address, age, etc. (*Pennsylvania v. Muniz* [1990]). Because the *Miranda* rules apply only to custodial interrogation initiated by the police or other agents of law enforcement, however, questions have arisen over just what actions—beyond direct questioning—constitute interrogation. The Court addressed this problem when it considered the case of Thomas J. Innis, who was arrested in Providence, Rhode Island, for the shotgun murder of one taxi driver and the armed robbery of another. After receiving three sets of *Miranda* warnings, Innis, who was unarmed when arrested, indicated his desire to consult counsel and was not questioned. During the ride to the police station, however, two officers discussed their concern that the shotgun might be found by a student in a nearby school for handicapped children, and that a terrible accident might occur. Innis thereupon stated that he wished to show them where the shotgun was hidden and, after receiving yet another set of *Miranda* warnings, did so. Over Innis's objections, the shotgun and the statements he had made about it were admitted as evidence at trial, and he was convicted of kidnapping, robbery, and murder. The Supreme Court took Innis's case "to address for the first time the meaning of 'interrogation' under *Miranda v. Arizona*" (*Rhode Island v. Innis* 297 [1980]).

Emphasizing that *Miranda* had discussed the need to protect suspects subjected to various police practices and psychological ploys designed to elicit information, as well as to direct questioning, Justice Potter Stewart for the majority held "that the *Miranda* safeguards come into play whenever a person in custody is subjected to either express questioning or its functional equivalent. That is to say, the term 'interrogation' under *Miranda* refers not only to express questioning, but also to any words or actions on the part of the police (other than those normally attendant to arrest and custody) that the police should know are reasonably likely to elicit an incriminating response from the suspect. The latter portion of this definition focuses primarily upon the perceptions of the suspect, rather than the intent of the police." The Court thus characterized interrogation broadly in the spirit of *Miranda,* which, as we have seen, requires that suspects who, like Innis, have requested a lawyer not be interrogated until counsel is present. To the dismay of three dissenters, however, Stewart then ruled that Innis had not been subjected to the functional equivalent of direct questioning and that his incriminating statements and the shotgun had therefore been properly admitted into evidence. "[T]he entire conversation appears to have consisted of no more than a few offhand remarks," Stewart noted, and "[i]t cannot be said . . . that Patrolmen Gleckman and McKenna should have known that their conversation was reasonably likely to elicit an incriminating response from the respondent. There is nothing in the record to suggest that the officers were aware that the respondent was peculiarly susceptible to an appeal to his conscience concerning the safety of handicapped children. Nor is there anything in the record to suggest that the police knew that the respondent was unusually disoriented or upset at the time of his arrest" (*Rhode Island v. Innis* 300–303 passim [1980]).

That conclusion made no sense, Justice Thurgood Marshall countered, for "[o]ne can scarcely imagine a stronger appeal to the conscience of a suspect—*any* suspect—than the assertion that if the weapon is not found an innocent person will be hurt or killed. And not just any innocent person, but an innocent child—a little girl—a helpless, handicapped little girl on her way to school. The notion that such an appeal could not be expected to have any effect unless the suspect were known to have some special interest in handicapped children verges on the ludicrous" (*Rhode Island v. Innis* 306 [1980] [dissenting opinion; emphasis in the original]). Going further, Justice Stevens argued that even if the officers had not anticipated the effect of their conversation, "*Miranda* protects a suspect in Innis's position not simply from interrogation that is likely to be successful, but from any interrogation at all." For that protection to be fully effective, "the definition of 'interrogation' must include any police statement or conduct that has the same purpose or effect as a direct question" (*Rhode Island v. Innis* 309 n.5, 311 [1980] [dissenting opinion]).

Justices Marshall and Stevens were also among the dissenters when the Court held that no interrogation had occurred when the police allowed a murder suspect to speak with his wife only in the presence of an officer who asked no questions but was obviously tape recording the conversation (*Arizona v. Mauro* [1987]). The Court was all but unanimous, however, in holding that when a psychiatrist testified for the prosecution, his court-ordered, custodial psychiatric examination of the defendant was an interrogation for which warnings were required (*Estelle v. Smith* [1981]).

Exceptions and Limitations

The sanction enforcing the *Miranda* rules is the exclusionary rule: statements obtained in violation of *Miranda* rights are not admissible as evidence against the person whose rights were violated. The Court has, however, created certain exceptions to this general standard. When Viven Harris was arrested for selling heroin to an undercover agent, he was questioned without having been warned of his right to counsel. The prosecution made no attempt to use his answers against him at trial, but when Harris told a contradictory story while testifying in his own defense, the judge allowed the prosecutor to question Harris about his inconsistent prior statements, instructing the jury to consider them solely for determination of Harris's credibility as a witness and not as evidence of guilt. When Harris appealed his conviction on the grounds that the unwarned statements should have been excluded, a closely divided Court decided that the statements (which Harris did not claim were coerced or involuntary) were admissible for purposes of impeaching his credibility. "The shield provided by *Miranda*," wrote Chief Justice Warren Burger, "cannot be perverted into a license to use perjury by way of a defense, free from the risk of confrontation with prior inconsistent utterances" (*Harris v. New York* 226 [1971]). The *Miranda* rules exist to deter police misconduct, he reasoned, and that purpose is sufficiently achieved by exclusion of incriminating statements from the case in chief.

In dissent, Justice Brennan argued that "[w]e settled this proposition in *Miranda* where we said: 'The privilege against self-incrimination protects the individual from being compelled to incriminate himself in *any* manner. . . . Statements merely intended to be exculpatory by the defendant are often *used to impeach his testimony at trial. . . . These statements are incriminating in any meaningful sense of the word and may not be used without the full warnings and effective waiver required for any other statement*' . . . (emphasis added)" (*Harris v. New York* 230–231 [1971] [dissenting opinion, citing *Miranda v. Arizona* 476–477 [1966]). "The objective of deterring improper police conduct is only part of the larger objective of safeguarding the integrity of our adversary system," Brennan argued, but this decision undermines that goal as well, for the "Court today tells the police that they may freely interrogate an accused incommunicado and without counsel and know that . . . any statement they obtain in violation of *Miranda* . . . may be introduced if the defendant has the temerity to testify in his own defense" (*Harris v. New York* 231, 232 [1971] [dissenting opinion]).

Four years later the Court went a step further, upholding the use, for purposes of impeachment, of statements made by a suspected bicycle thief who had received proper warnings but whose request for counsel had not yet been honored. In dissent, Justice Brennan argued that even after *Harris,* police had an incentive to follow *Miranda* in hopes of gaining statements that could be used in the case in chief. But once a suspect requested counsel, who would undoubtedly advise silence, police had every incentive not to honor the obligation to cease questioning until counsel was present if statements they gained could still be used for impeachment. Thus, Brennan concluded, this decision "goes beyond *Harris* in undermining *Miranda*" (*Oregon v. Hass* 725 [1975] [dissenting opinion]).

These decisions did not undermine the Fifth Amendment, however, for three years later the Court held that "*any* criminal trial use against a defendant of his *involuntary* statement is a denial of due process of law" (*Mincey v. Arizona* 398 [1978] [emphasis in the original]).

The Court's decision in *New York v. Quarles* (1984) created an exception of a different sort. A police officer had pursued a rape suspect, believed to be armed, into a supermarket and, upon taking him into custody, had found him to be wearing an empty shoulder holster. The officer asked where the gun was, Quarles told him, and only then did the officer read the suspect his *Miranda* rights. Quarles was prosecuted on a weapons charge, but the New York courts held that the gun and his statement about its location were inadmissible because he had not yet been warned, and that his postwarning statements about the gun were also inadmissible as fruits of the original violation. In reversing those rulings on suppression of evidence, the Court noted that here again, the privilege against self-incrimination itself had not been violated and held that "on these facts there is a 'public safety' exception to the requirement that *Miranda* warnings be given before a suspect's answers may be admitted into evidence." Warnings may deter suspects from responding, Justice Rehnquist argued. The *Miranda* decision was based on the judgment that the protection of rights was worth a consequent cost of loss of evidence and hence fewer convictions, but here the cost would be a threat to public safety as well. Police officers should not be required to strike that balance on the spot, Rehnquist concluded, so the Court struck it for them as a matter of principle: "the need for answers to questions in a situation posing a threat to the public safety outweighs the need for the prophylactic rule protecting the Fifth Amendment's privilege against self-incrimination" (*New York v. Quarles* 655, 657 [1984]).

Concurring in part and dissenting in part, Justice O'Connor argued that "since there is nothing about an exigency that makes custodial interrogation any less compelling, a principled application of *Miranda* requires that respondent's statement be suppressed" (*New York v. Quarles* 665 [1984] [dissenting opinion]), but that the gun should be admissible as nontestimonial evidence (see the discussion of testimonial evidence in the section on the testimonial privilege in Chapter 4). Justice Marshall and two other dissenters agreed with the New York courts that on the facts—a suspect in custody in an all but deserted supermarket in the middle of the night—no threat to public safety existed, and they decried "a chimerical quest for public safety" in which "the majority has abandoned the rule that brought 18 years of doctrinal tranquility to the field of custodial interrogations." Most fundamentally, however, they asserted that *Miranda* was not about striking a balance between the rights of suspects and the needs of society, but about improving the implementation of a clear constitutional command that compelled statements (defined as those made in the absence of warnings) not be used as evidence against the accused. The majority's argument, they concluded, conceded that the "'public-safety' exception is efficacious precisely because it permits police officers to coerce criminal defendants into making involuntary statements" (*New York v. Quarles* 679, 685 [1984] [dissenting opinion]).

The Court considered a related issue in the case of Thomas Wayne Tucker, who was appealing a conviction for rape. After defective warnings, Tucker had supplied police with the name of an alibi witness who turned out to be unfavorable to him and testified for the prosecution at trial. Tucker's statements were not used against him; the issue was rather the use of the testimony of the witness whose identity had been derived from them. The Court found it significant that the "police conduct at issue here did not abridge respondent's constitutional privilege against compulsory self-incrimination, but departed only from the prophylactic standards later laid down by this Court in *Miranda* to safeguard that privilege" (*Michigan v. Tucker* 446 [1974]), and that the error had involved no willful misconduct or even negligence, as the interrogation had taken place before *Miranda* was decided. (*Miranda* applied because the trial came after that decision.) As in *Harris*, the Court concluded that any slight deterrent effect on police misbehavior that exclusion might achieve was far outweighed by the value of the material for the truth-seeking process.

This line of reasoning also prevailed by a 6–3 vote in *Oregon v. Elstad* (1985). When asked about a burglary for which he was being arrested, Elstad stated that he had been there; only later was he read his *Miranda* rights, which he waived, and he then made a full confession. Elstad's initial, unwarned statement was not used to gain his conviction, but his appeal argued that the subsequent confession should not have been admitted as evidence, either. His claim was that because he had not known, and his *Miranda* warnings had not informed him, that his initial statement could not be used against him, he had confessed because he thought his fate was already sealed; thus the confession was the product of the *Miranda* violation. Writing for the majority, Justice O'Connor rejected this argument. "This Court has never held that the psychological impact of voluntary disclosure of a guilty secret qualifies as state compulsion or compromises the voluntariness of a subsequent informed waiver," she wrote, and the standard *Miranda* warnings Elstad had received negated his argument that the waiver had not been fully informed, for "[t]his Court has never embraced the theory that a defendant's ignorance of the full consequences of his decisions vitiates their voluntariness" (*Oregon v. Elstad* 312, 316 [1985]).

Writing in dissent, Justice Brennan found no justification for the majority's rejection of what he characterized as the standard presumption that in such circumstances the second confession is indeed the product of the initial constitutional violation, because the suspect mistakenly believes he has let the cat out of the bag. The contrast between the majority and minority views of law enforcement is evident in Justice O'Connor's conclusion that a requirement that the officer inform the suspect of the inadmissibility of the unwarned statements is "neither practicable nor constitutionally necessary" (*Oregon v. Elstad* 316 [1985]) and Justice Brennan's assertion that "[t]he experience of lower courts demonstrates that the police frequently have refused to comply with *Miranda* precisely in order to obtain incriminating statements that will undermine the voluntariness of the accused's decision to speak again once he has received the usual warnings; in such circumstances, subsequent confessions often follow on a 'silver platter'" (*Oregon v. Elstad* 356–357 [1985] [dissenting opinion]). Because police employ this tactic to induce suspects to waive their *Miranda* rights, Brennan argued, the prosecution should bear the burden of proving that the second confession is not tainted by the first, and that burden is not met simply by showing that intervening *Miranda* warnings were given.

Underlying this difference was a more fundamental disagreement over the premise on which the majority conclusion was based, which drew a distinction between the constitutional privilege against self-incrimination and the "prophylactic" *Miranda* rules established by the Court to protect it. Justice O'Connor maintained that "[t]he *Miranda* exclusionary rule . . . sweeps more broadly than the Fifth Amendment itself. It may be triggered even in the absence of a Fifth Amendment violation. The Fifth Amendment prohibits use by the prosecution in its case in chief only of *compelled* testimony. Failure to administer *Miranda* warnings creates a presumption of compulsion. Consequently, unwarned statements that are otherwise voluntary within the meaning of the Fifth Amendment must nevertheless be excluded from evidence under *Miranda.*" However, "a simple failure to administer *Miranda* warnings is not in itself a violation of the Fifth Amendment." In consequence, O'Connor then argued,

> [i]f errors are made by law enforcement officers in administering the prophylactic *Miranda* procedures, they should not breed the same irremediable consequences as police infringement of the Fifth Amendment itself. It is an unwarranted extension of *Miranda* to hold that a simple failure to administer the warnings, unaccompanied by any actual coercion or other circumstances calculated to undermine the suspect's ability to exercise his free will, so taints the investigatory process that a subsequent voluntary and informed waiver is ineffective for some indeterminate period. . . . In these circumstances, a careful and thorough administration of *Miranda* warnings serves to cure the condition that rendered the unwarned statement inadmissible. The warning conveys the relevant information and thereafter the suspect's choice whether to exercise his privilege to remain silent should ordinarily be viewed as an "act of free will." (*Oregon v. Elstad* 306–307 and n.1, 309–311 [1985] [emphasis in the original])

Far from seeing an unwarranted extension of *Miranda,* however, Justice Stevens maintained that

> [i]f we are faithful to the holding in *Miranda* itself, when we are considering the admissibility of evidence in the prosecutor's case in chief, we should not try to fashion a distinction between police misconduct that warrants a finding of actual coercion and police misconduct that establishes an irrebuttable presumption of coercion. . . . This Court's power to require state courts to exclude probative self-incriminatory statements rests entirely on the premise that the use of such evidence violates the Federal Constitution. The same constitutional analysis applies whether the custodial interrogation is actually coercive or irrebuttably presumed to be coercive. . . . If the Court accepts the proposition that respondent's [initial] self-incriminatory statement was inadmissible, it must also acknowledge that the *Federal Constitution* protected him from custodial police interrogation without first being advised of his right to remain silent. (*Oregon v. Elstad* 369–371 [1985] [dissenting opinion; emphasis supplied])

Therefore, the dissenters concluded, a violation of the *Miranda* rules *is* a violation of the Fifth Amendment and should have exactly the same consequences as a violation in the form of actual coercion; that is, "the prosecution must demonstrate that the second confession 'was an act independent of the [earlier] confession.' . . . The most effective means to ensure the voluntariness of an accused's subsequent confession is to advise the accused that his earlier admissions may not be admissible and therefore that he need not speak solely out of a belief that 'the cat is out of the bag'" (*Oregon v. Elstad* 325, 338 [1985] [dissenting opinion]). The majority's ruling upholding the admissibility of Elstad's subsequent statements would stand, but the argument over the constitutional status of *Miranda* rights was not over, and the *Elstad* ruling would later be challenged (see the discussion of *Dickerson v. United States* below and the discussion of the issue of prophylactic rules in Chapter 6).

Many supporters of the *Miranda* decision believe that these Burger Court (and some Rehnquist Court) exceptions to and limitations of its applicability seriously compromised the Warren Court's intent to erect clear constitutional protections for the rights of suspects. We will consider that issue further in Chapter 6.

The Sixth Amendment Right to Counsel after *Miranda*

Although it first appeared that *Escobedo v. Illinois* had signaled an expansion of the Sixth Amendment right to counsel by establishing the right during police interrogation, when it had not yet attached under the standard subsequently announced in *Kirby v. Illinois* (see the discussion of the right to counsel in pretrial proceedings in Chapter 3), the Court in *Miranda* made clear that in such circumstances the right to counsel is rather protected by the Fifth Amendment, as a means of safeguarding the privilege against self-incrimination. The *Escobedo* decision thus did not have significant consequences for the Sixth Amendment, but *Massiah v. United States,* also decided two years before *Miranda,* did signal a parallel elaboration of the Sixth Amendment right to counsel.

The Functional Equivalent of Interrogation

United States v. Henry (1980) was one of a series of cases in which the Court considered undercover police tactics similar to those employed in *Massiah.* Although Billy Gale Henry, who was under indictment for bank robbery, was incarcerated while awaiting trial, a federal agent arranged with a fellow inmate (and government informant) to report on any statements Henry might make but instructed him not to initiate conversation with Henry or ask him questions about the robbery. The informant, who had conversations with Henry, testified about incriminating statements he had heard and Henry was convicted. Despite the agent's specific instructions, the Court concluded, he must have known that an informant who was paid only if he produced useful information would deliberately elicit it, one way or another, as the court of appeals had found that he had. Thus, "[b]y intentionally creating a situation likely to induce Henry to make incriminating statements without the assistance of counsel, the Government violated Henry's Sixth Amendment right to counsel" (*United States v. Henry* 274 [1980]) and the informant's testimony should not have been admitted at trial.

In dissent, Justice Harry Blackmun argued that the decision stretched *Massiah's* "deliberately elicited" test out of all proportion and Justice Rehnquist, rejecting *Massiah* as well, argued that what the Sixth Amendment protects is the assistance of counsel in preparation for trial and that "there is no constitutional or historical support for concluding that an accused has a right to have his attorney serve as a sort of guru who must be present whenever an accused has an inclination to reveal incriminating information to anyone who acts to elicit such information at the behest of the prosecution" (*United States v. Henry* 295–296 [1980] [dissenting opinion]). Both dissenters also maintained that the decision denigrated the importance of undercover police work and deprived the state of reliable evidence with no correspondingly important benefit.

The state's violation was more clear-cut in *Maine v. Moulton* (1985), in which it employed evidence gained by a codefendant who had worn a recording device while discussing defense strategy with Moulton and who had actively induced him to speak of his crimes. It did not matter that Moulton rather than the police had set up the meeting or that the police were also legitimately investigating Moulton's threats to kill a witness (which the dissenters characterized as *the* purpose of the undercover operation), for "[b]y concealing the fact that [the codefendant] was an agent of the State, the police denied Moulton the opportunity to consult with counsel and thus denied him the assistance of counsel guaranteed by the Sixth Amendment" (*Maine v. Moulton* 177 [1985]). To avoid undue restriction of ongoing investigations, however, the decision did make clear that information gained about other crimes (such as the murder scheme) for which the right to counsel had not attached could be used against defendants in Moulton's position.

Henry and *Moulton* illustrate what *Innis* had termed the functional equivalent of interrogation, but neither case addressed the question of an undercover agent who remained genuinely passive, taking no action to solicit admissions and merely listening to the suspect. When confronted with that situation one year later, however, the Court held that "a defendant does not make out a violation of [the right to counsel] simply by showing that an informant, either through prior arrangement or voluntarily, reported his incriminating statements to the police. Rather, the defendant must demonstrate that the police and their informant took some action, beyond merely listening, that was designed deliberately to elicit incriminating remarks" (*Kuhlmann v. Wilson* 459 [1986]). They had not, and so Wilson's incriminating statements, reported by the informant who shared his jail cell, were admissible against him, even though obtained in the absence of counsel after that right had attached.

The Court considered more overt police tactics, and demonstrated its resolve to uphold the right to counsel, in the poignant circumstances of *Brewer v. Williams* (1977). On Christmas Eve in Des Moines, Iowa, Robert Anthony Williams, an escaped mental patient, kidnapped and, police subsequently learned, murdered a ten-year-old girl; in the meantime he was identified and an arrest warrant was issued on the abduction charge. Two days later, Williams surrendered to police in Davenport, having consulted by telephone with an attorney in Des Moines who notified police there. Williams was given *Miranda* warnings and arraigned in Davenport; his right to counsel had attached and he was counseled by an attorney there. Under an agreement between the attorneys and the police, officers from Des Moines would transport Williams back to that city but would not interrogate him until he had seen his lawyer there. Both lawyers advised him not to answer any questions in the meantime, and he stated that he would tell the whole story after he had seen his attorney in Des Moines. On the trip, however (on which the attorney in Davenport was not permitted to accompany his client), Detective Cleatus Leaming, who knew of Williams's mental illness and deep religious convictions, suggested that he should show him the location of the girl's body before it was hidden in the snow, so that her parents could give her a Christian burial. Williams did so, and both his statements and the circumstances of discovery of the body were admitted as evidence at his trial, the judge ruling that he had waived his right to counsel. (Although the Supreme Court accepted the facts as recounted here, at trial Detective Leaming maintained that there had been no agreement not to question Williams during the ride to Des Moines, and that the lawyer in Davenport had not been denied permission to accompany Williams on that ride [McInnis 2001, 7].)

When the Court reviewed Williams's conviction, a narrow majority found it unnecessary to rule on his claims that his *Miranda* rights had been violated or that his confession had been involuntary because the violation of his right to counsel was clear. Because Detective Leaming had "purposely sought during Williams's isolation from his lawyers to obtain as much incriminating information as possible . . . [t]he circumstances of this case are . . . constitutionally indistinguishable from those presented in *Massiah v. United States* . . ., the clear rule of [which] is that once adversary proceedings have commenced against an individual, he has a right to legal representation when the government interrogates him." In view of Williams's consistent acts and statements in reliance on counsel, the state had in no way met its burden of demonstrating a valid waiver of the right, and the conviction had to be overturned. Although "[t]he crime of which Williams was convicted was senseless and brutal, calling for swift and energetic action by the police . . ., so clear a violation of the Sixth and Fourteenth Amendments as here occurred cannot be condoned" (*Brewer v. Williams* 399–406 passim [1977]).

Four dissenters, on the other hand, thought that what could not be condoned was an unwarranted application of the right to counsel that required the invalidation of the conviction of someone incontestably guilty of a brutal murder. Detective Leaming's appeals to Williams's conscience did not constitute an interrogation, they concluded, and even if they did, Williams had, by his statements and actions if not expressly, made a knowing, intelligent, and voluntary waiver of his right to counsel. The dissenters deplored an application of the exclusionary rule that in their judgment made retrial and conviction all but impossible, but on this score they were mistaken. At a second trial, Williams's statements and the fact that he had led police to the body were not presented to the jury, but evidence concerning the body was, because the state was able to prove that the search that had been instituted would inevitably have discovered it in essentially the same condition, anyway. Williams's conviction and life sentence were upheld by the Supreme Court on the basis of the inevitable discovery exception to the exclusionary rule (*Nix v. Williams* [1984]).

Assertion and Waiver of the Right to Counsel

The question of whether the right to counsel pertains at a given point in proceedings against a suspect is a factual one that is reasonably easy to resolve. The Fifth Amendment protection arises when a suspect in custody requests counsel; the Sixth Amendment right attaches as soon as formal judicial proceedings against a suspect have been initiated. As the *Brewer* case illustrates, however, the question of whether or not a suspect has waived—or can waive—the right to counsel is more difficult. In *Edwards v. Arizona* (see the discussion of assertion and waiver of rights in the section on implementation of *Miranda* above), the Court ruled that when a suspect invokes his or her *Miranda* right to counsel, police may not initiate further interrogation until counsel has been made available, and that a waiver of the right to counsel is not established by the mere fact that the suspect subsequently voluntarily answered questions without benefit of counsel. Statements made under such circumstances are therefore inadmissible. The same rule was applied to the Sixth Amendment right to counsel in *Michigan v. Jackson* (1986). At his arraignment, at which point his Sixth Amendment right had attached, Jackson had asked the judge to appoint counsel, but before he saw the lawyer, he was given his *Miranda* rights again, signed a waiver, and gave incriminating responses to police questions. Because "the reasons for prohibiting the interrogation of an uncounseled prisoner who has asked for the help of a lawyer are even stronger after he has been formally charged with an offense than before," the Court held that "if police initiate interrogation after a defendant's assertion, at an arraignment or similar proceeding, of his right to counsel, any waiver of the defendant's right to counsel for that police-initiated interrogation is invalid" (*Michigan v. Jackson* 631, 636 [1986] and statements made under those circumstances are therefore inadmissible.

In his *Jackson* dissent, Justice Rehnquist noted the inconsistency of making the decision hinge on the defendant's request for counsel, even though the attachment of the Sixth Amendment right (unlike the *Miranda* protection buttressed in *Edwards*) is not contingent on such a request. The result, he argued, was "to extend the *Edwards* rule to the Sixth Amendment, yet limit that rule to those defendants foresighted enough, or just plain lucky enough, to have made an explicit request for counsel which we have always understood to be completely unnecessary for Sixth Amendment purposes" (*Michigan v. Jackson* 642 [1986] [dissenting opinion]. Two years later, the Court remained consistent to that result in the case of a suspect whose Sixth Amendment right had attached but who had *not* made any request for counsel. That suspect's waiver of *Miranda* rights was—in this setting of police interrogation, but not necessarily in all settings—also a valid waiver of the Sixth Amendment right to counsel, the Court held, and police were therefore free to initiate interrogation and use the results at trial, even though the defendant had not been advised by an attorney (*Patterson v. Illinois* [1988]).

The dissenters did not think *Miranda* warnings—given by an adversary—provided the basis of informed consent for a waiver of the Sixth Amendment right, even if only in the context of police interrogation. They further noted that although the Court had emphasized the significance of the initiation of judicial proceedings to justify the *denial* of counsel before such proceedings commenced (see the discussion of *Kirby v. Illinois* in the section on the right to counsel in pretrial proceedings in Chapter 3), "[t]oday . . . in reaching a decision similarly favorable to the interest in law enforcement unfettered by process concerns, the Court backs away from the significance previously attributed to the initiation of formal proceedings." They argued that "an evenhanded interpretation of the Amendment would support the view that additional protection should automatically attach the moment the formal proceedings begin" (*Patterson v. Illinois* 305, 303–304 [1988] [dissenting opinion]). Now chief justice and pleased with the result in *Patterson,* Rehnquist chose simply to join the majority and not contend that the dissenters' argument did not square with their rationale in the *Jackson* ruling. Taken together, the decisions in *Jackson* and *Patterson* provide a good illustration of the Court's difficulty in resolving the competing claims of the value of doctrinal consistency and the need for reasonable safeguards for the rights of suspects confronting the realities of police interrogation.

Another issue related to *Jackson* arose in the case of Tyris Lemont Harvey, an accused rapist. Under interrogation, Harvey had made statements that were inadmissible under the *Jackson* rule, but the trial judge allowed the prosecutor to use those statements to impeach the credibility of Harvey's testimony. Reasoning that "*Jackson* simply superimposed the Fifth Amendment analysis of *Edwards* onto the Sixth Amendment," the Supreme Court concluded that the doctrine of *Harris v. New York* and *Oregon v. Hass* should also be applied to the Sixth Amendment and held that the statements were admissible for purposes of impeachment (*Michigan v. Harvey* 350 [1990]). Four dissenters maintained that the Sixth Amendment more broadly protects a defendant's right to deal with the state through counsel and that the state should not be able to make any use of information that it obtains from confrontations that violate that right.

The Supreme Court continued the process of charting the overlapping but differing parameters of the Fifth and Sixth Amendment rights to counsel in *McNeil v. Wisconsin* (1991). *Patterson* had held that in some circumstances a waiver of the *Miranda* right is also a waiver of the Sixth Amendment right; *McNeil* held that the attachment of the Sixth Amendment right is not in and of itself an assertion of the *Miranda* right. When he was arrested for armed robbery, Paul McNeil asserted his *Miranda* right to silence but not to counsel. He was represented by a public defender at a bail hearing because the Sixth Amendment right had attached; after more *Miranda* warnings he was interrogated about a murder and other crimes unrelated to the robbery, and he confessed to those offenses and was convicted of them. McNeil appealed on the grounds that his confession should not have been used against him, but the Supreme Court disagreed, ruling on two important points.

First, following *Maine v. Moulton*, Justice Antonin Scalia's majority opinion held that the interrogation had not violated McNeil's Sixth Amendment right because that had attached as to the armed robbery but not as to the crimes about which he was questioned, as no formal proceedings against him had begun in those matters. Because the Sixth Amendment right is offense-specific, the Court held, the *Jackson* rule invalidating waivers of counsel in police-initiated interrogations did not apply in McNeil's circumstances.

Second, Scalia rejected McNeil's argument that, although he had waived his *Miranda* right to counsel, his invocation of the Sixth Amendment right was nevertheless an assertion of the *Miranda* right. Because the *Edwards* rule, as extended by *Arizona v. Roberson* (see the discussion of assertion and waiver of rights in the section on implementation of *Miranda* above), holds that once a suspect has invoked his or her *Miranda* right to counsel, police may not question him or her about *any* offense in the absence of counsel, and that if they do the fact that he or she answers does not constitute a waiver of the right, police interrogation of McNeil would have violated his *Miranda* rights if his argument was valid. It was not valid, however, for Justice Scalia distinguished between the *Miranda* right, which must be asserted in the context of a request for assistance in dealing with custodial interrogation, and the Sixth Amendment right, which attaches at the point at which the accused needs assistance in a confrontation with the legal expertise of the government in an adversarial proceeding. The police had been free to approach McNeil about crimes for which his Sixth Amendment right had not attached, his *Miranda* right had not been triggered by attachment of his Sixth Amendment right for a different crime, and he had not asserted his *Miranda* right when the police sought to interrogate him; therefore, his confession was admissible. In sum, *McNeil* declined to extend the *Jackson* rule in the way that *Roberson* had extended the *Edwards* rule, and it declined to hold that the *Edwards* rule had been triggered. The majority thought an opposite result would unduly inhibit police work; dissenters were sure that typical suspects relying on a lawyer for one charge also intend and expect to have such assistance for other charges but conceded they could achieve that result by asserting their *Miranda* rights. Ten years later, the Court affirmed that "our decision in *McNeil v. Wisconsin* . . . meant what it said, and that the Sixth Amendment right is 'offense specific,'" by disregarding the approach of most lower courts and applying the *McNeil* limitation of the *Jackson* rule even when the separate offenses were "closely related factually"—in this case, murders committed during the course of a burglary (*Texas v. Cobb* 164 [2001]).

Police and suspects have always played cat-and-mouse (if not more brutal) games, prosecuting and defense attorneys have always sparred by means of ingenious legal arguments, and judges and justices have always sought to render decisions that make good law and good policy. In the aftermath of *Miranda* and *Massiah,* the games have continued, the sparring has encompassed a whole new range of arguments, and judicial decisions balancing the claims of effective law enforcement against the claims of the right to counsel and the privilege against self-incrimination have spun out a vast new set of rules and doctrines. Those evolving rules and doctrines are not entirely consistent—that is the nature of the law—but as the twentieth century drew to a close, the large picture seemed reasonably clear. One major uncertainty, however, remained to be addressed.

MIRANDA CHALLENGED AND REAFFIRMED: *DICKERSON V. UNITED STATES*

Over the objection of Justice William O. Douglas, the majority in *Michigan v. Tucker* had asserted that "[t]he Court [in *Miranda*] recognized that these procedural safeguards were not themselves rights protected by the Constitution but were instead measures to insure that the right against compulsory self-incrimination was protected" (*Michigan v. Tucker* 444 [1974]); five years earlier, however, the Court had held that "the use of . . . admissions obtained in the absence of the required warnings was a flat violation of the Self-Incrimination Clause of the Fifth Amendment as construed in *Miranda*" (*Orozco v. Texas* 326 [1969]). The Court repeated the *Tucker* interpretation in *New York v. Quarles* and retreated only slightly in *Oregon v. Elstad,* conceding that "[f]ailure to administer *Miranda* warnings creates a presumption of compulsion," which is what the Fifth Amendment forbids, yet nevertheless rejecting the contention that "a failure to administer *Miranda* warnings necessarily breeds the same consequences as police infringement of a constitutional right" (*Oregon v. Elstad* 307, 304 [1985]).

These cases, and other limiting decisions like *Harris v. New York* and *Oregon v. Hass,* did not directly challenge *Miranda's* core prohibition of the use of unwarned statements against a defendant because they rather permitted the use of such statements under special circumstances (impeachment of credibility, public safety) or the use of evidence derived (or arguably derived) from such statements. The repeated characterization of the *Miranda* requirements as prophylactic rules rather than constitutional standards, however, raised the possibility that an increasingly conservative Supreme Court could reconsider the central issue and overturn *Miranda.* The basis for such an action had lain dormant since 1968, just two years after *Miranda* was decided.

In that year, when violence broke out in Chicago at the Democratic National Convention and in many cities after the assassination of Martin Luther King, Jr. and "law and order" became a major issue in the presidential campaign, Congress enacted the Omnibus Crime Control and Safe Streets Act of 1968, Title II of which provided that confessions that met the pre-*Miranda* voluntariness test (Massachusetts variant; see the discussion of competing claims of voluntariness and truthfulness in the section on the parallel track of coerced confession cases in Chapter 4) were admissible in federal court, and that the issues covered by *Miranda* warnings were merely factors to be considered in a determination of voluntariness on the basis of the totality of the circumstances (18 U.S.C. §3501 [2000]; hereinafter §3501). Although federal prosecutors occasionally tried to employ this statute, the Department of Justice consistently prohibited reliance on it in criminal prosecutions, regarding it as unconstitutional, and federal defendants of course had no occasion or motivation to invoke it. The federal statute did not have any effect on the admissibility of confessions in state courts (a companion measure to accomplish that had been defeated; U.S. Senate 2000, 1332 n.13), and therefore it remained in limbo until 1999, when in the case of an accused bank robber a three-judge panel of the U.S. Court of Appeals for the Fourth Circuit—generally regarded as the most conservative of the federal appeals courts—seized the initiative by allowing the Washington Legal Foundation and the Safe Streets Coalition as *amici curiae* (friends of the court) to make the argument that the government would not, that a confession that was technically in violation of *Miranda* but met the statute's standard of voluntariness should be admitted into evidence. The appeals court then held that the requirements for *Miranda* warnings were not constitutional rights but prophylactic, judicially created rules of procedure and evidence, that it was therefore within the legislative power of Congress to overrule and supersede them, that Congress had intended to do precisely that, and that §3501 rather than the *Miranda* rules was therefore the standard of admissibility of confessions in federal courts (*United States v. Dickerson* [4th Cir. 1999]).

The Department of Justice appealed this decision, taking the risk that if it lost in the Supreme Court, *Miranda* would be displaced not just in the Fourth Circuit but throughout the United States. The issue was clear. If the *Miranda* decision established constitutional rights, then Congress had no power to overturn it, for the Supreme Court is the ultimate interpreter of the Constitution and its interpretations can be overturned only by constitutional amendment. If, on the other hand, *Miranda* merely announced judicially created rules of evidence, then Congress could revise those rules for the federal courts, and the *Miranda* rules would not bind the states, either, for the Supreme Court has no supervisory administrative authority over the rules and procedures of state courts. Whatever the Supreme Court majority in 1966 may have intended on this point, if the appeals court had correctly gauged the sentiments of the current majority—and many hoped or feared that it had—then *Miranda* was in serious jeopardy.

When Chief Justice Rehnquist announced the decision of the Court, however, it became clear that *Miranda* rested on firmer ground than had appeared fifteen years earlier in *Elstad.* Of the three justices who had rejected the characterization of *Miranda* rules as merely prophylactic in that case, only Justice Stevens remained, but four of six new justices agreed that *Miranda* stated a constitutional rule and, more surprisingly, the Chief Justice (author of *Tucker* and *Quarles*) and Justice O'Connor (author of *Elstad*) now supported that position as well, providing a majority of seven to overrule the court of appeals. Having flirted with a new approach, the Court now returned to what it affirmed had been the clear understanding of the *Miranda* Court:

> We disagree with the Court of Appeals' conclusion, although we concede that there is language in some of our opinions that supports the view taken by that court. But first and foremost of the factors on the other side—that *Miranda* is a constitutional decision—is that both *Miranda* and two of its companion cases applied the rule to proceedings in state courts. . . . Since that time, we have consistently applied *Miranda*'s rule to prosecutions arising in state courts. . . . It is beyond dispute that we do not hold a supervisory power over the courts of the several States. . . . With respect to proceedings in state courts, our "authority is limited to enforcing the commands of the United States Constitution. . . .
>
> The *Miranda* opinion itself begins by stating that the Court granted certiorari "to explore some facets of the problems . . . of applying the privilege against self-incrimination to in-custody interrogation, *and to give concrete constitutional guidelines for law enforcement agencies and courts to follow.*" . . . In fact, the majority opinion is replete with statements indicating that the majority thought it was announcing a constitutional rule. Indeed, the Court's ultimate conclusion was that

the unwarned confessions obtained in the four cases before the Court in *Miranda* "were obtained from the defendant under circumstances that did not meet constitutional standards for protection of the privilege." (*Dickerson v. United States* 438–441 [2000] [emphasis in the original])

In *Miranda*, the Court had said that the warnings it stipulated were required unless Congress or the states could devise equally effective procedures for ensuring that suspects understood and were free to exercise the right to silence. To the contention that the statute satisfied that requirement, the Court responded that because §3501 did not require warnings, it was inadequate for that purpose. Furthermore, *Miranda* had determined that the totality-of-the-circumstances test posed an unacceptable risk of the admission of involuntary confessions; §3501 reinstated that test and "therefore cannot be sustained if *Miranda* is to remain the law" (*Dickerson v. United States* 443 [2000]).

Although Congress had no power to prevent *Miranda* from remaining the law, the Court remained free to overrule that decision but declined to do so. "Whether or not we would agree with *Miranda*'s reasoning and its resulting rule, were we addressing the issue in the first instance," declared the chief justice,

> the principles of *stare decisis* [adherence to precedent] weigh heavily against overruling it now. . . .
>
> *Miranda* has become embedded in routine police practice to the point where the warnings have become part of our national culture. . . . While we have overruled our precedents when subsequent cases have undermined their doctrinal underpinnings, . . . we do not believe that this has happened to the *Miranda* decision. If anything, our subsequent cases have reduced the impact of the *Miranda* rule on legitimate law enforcement while reaffirming the decision's core ruling that unwarned statements may not be used as evidence in the prosecution's case in chief.

> ... [E]xperience suggests that the totality-of-the-circumstances test which §3501 seeks to revive is more difficult than *Miranda* for law enforcement officers to conform to, and for courts to apply in a consistent manner.... The requirement that *Miranda* warnings be given does not, of course, dispense with the voluntariness inquiry. But as we said in *Berkemer v. McCarty* ..., "cases in which a defendant can make a colorable argument that a self-incriminating statement was 'compelled' despite the fact that the law enforcement authorities adhered to the dictates of *Miranda* are rare." (*Dickerson v. United States* 443–444 [2000])

Chief Justice Rehnquist's opinion left no doubt about the basic result, but by not repudiating the Court's prior pronouncements about prophylactic rules it left them in legal limbo (a topic to which we shall return in Chapter 6). Its defensive tone, moreover, reflected less than enthusiastic conviction on the part of at least some of the members of the majority. The opinion of the two dissenters, however, exhibited no such restraint. In one of his characteristically colorful and biting dissents, Justice Scalia (joined by Justice Clarence Thomas) disagreed with every aspect of the decision. "It was once possible," Scalia wrote, "to characterize the so-called *Miranda* rule as resting (however implausibly) upon the proposition that what the statute here before us permits—the admission at trial of un-*Mirandized* confessions—violates the Constitution. That is the fairest reading of the *Miranda* case itself.... So understood, *Miranda* was objectionable for innumerable reasons" (some of which Scalia discussed), but that interpretation would justify a declaration that §3501 was unconstitutional. The *Dickerson* opinion failed to make such an explicit declaration, however (saying rather that §3501 could not be sustained), principally because "[j]ustices whose votes are needed to compose today's majority [Kennedy, Rehnquist, and O'Connor] are on record as believing that a violation of *Miranda* is *not* a violation of the Constitution.... As the Court today acknowledges, since *Miranda* we have explicitly, and repeatedly, interpreted that decision as having announced . . . only 'prophylactic' rules that go beyond the right against compelled self-incrimination. . . . In light of these cases [*Tucker, Hass, Quarles,* and *Elstad*], and our statements to the same effect in others, . . . it is simply no longer possible for the Court to conclude, even if it wanted to, that a violation of *Miranda*'s rules is a violation of the Constitution. But . . . that is what is required before the Court may disregard a law of Congress governing the admissibility of evidence in federal court" (*Dickerson v. United States* 445–454 passim [2000] [dissenting opinion; emphasis in the original]).

The majority's explanation for this failure simply was not persuasive, Scalia maintained:

> The Court seeks to avoid this conclusion in two ways: First, by misdescribing these post-*Miranda* cases as mere dicta [statements by a court expressing an opinion but not a ruling]. The Court concedes only "that there is language in some of our opinions that supports the view" that *Miranda's* protections are not "constitutionally required." . . . It is not a matter of *language;* it is a matter of *holdings.* The proposition that failure to comply with *Miranda*'s rules does not establish a constitutional violation was central to the *holdings* of *Tucker, Hass, Quarles,* and *Elstad.*
>
> The second way the Court seeks to avoid the impact of these cases is simply to disclaim responsibility for reasoned decisionmaking. . . . [I]f confessions procured in violation of *Miranda* are confessions "compelled" in violation of the Constitution, the post-*Miranda* decisions I have discussed do not make sense. The only reasoned basis for their outcome was that a violation of *Miranda* is *not* a violation of the Constitution. (*Dickerson v. United States* 454–455 [2000] [dissenting opinion; emphasis in the original]).

Finally, neither the virtues of *stare decisis* nor the argument that *Miranda* must be a constitutional decision because it applies to the states was at all convincing to Justice Scalia:

> [T]he Court asserts that *Miranda* must be a "constitutional decision" announcing a "constitutional rule," and thus immune to congressional modification, because we have since its inception applied it to the States. If this argument is meant as an invocation of *stare decisis,* it fails because, though it is true that our cases applying *Miranda* against the States must be reconsidered if *Miranda* is not required by the Constitution, it is likewise true that our cases (discussed above) based on the principle that *Miranda* is *not* required by the Constitution will have to be reconsidered if it *is.* So the *stare decisis* argument is a wash. If, on the other hand, the argument is meant as an appeal to logic rather than *stare decisis,* it is a classic example of begging the question: Congress's attempt to set aside *Miranda,* since it represents an assertion that violation of *Miranda* is not a violation of the Constitution, *also* represents an assertion that the Court has no power to impose *Miranda* on the States. To answer this assertion—not by showing why violation of *Miranda is* a violation of the Constitution—but by asserting that *Miranda does* apply against the States, is to assume precisely the point at issue. In my view, our continued application of the *Miranda* code to the States despite our consistent statements that running afoul of its dictates does not necessarily—or even usually—result in an actual constitutional violation, represents not the source of *Miranda's* salvation but rather evidence of its ultimate illegitimacy. (*Dickerson v. United States* 456 [2000] [dissenting opinion; emphasis in the original])

The Court's failure to deal unambiguously with the constitutional status of *Miranda's* so-called prophylactic rules meant that *Dickerson* would not be the last word on the subject. Seven justices, however, apparently concluded that the requirement for *Miranda* warnings had successfully addressed a deficiency in the protection of constitutional rights, had been fine-tuned to achieve an acceptable balance between individual rights and law enforcement needs, and had become a routine part of police practice. Although the court of appeals had expressed its displeasure at the refusal of the Department of Justice to defend the constitutionality of §3501, ascribing that position to considerations of politics rather than law, the Supreme Court may well have drawn a different conclusion from the fact that the department responsible for overseeing all federal prosecutions had consistently supported *Miranda* ever since it was decided. In any event, in reaffirming *Miranda* seven justices applied the proverbial wisdom: if it ain't broke, don't fix it. For two other justices, however, *Miranda* remained broken beyond repair.

CONCLUSION

In the final third of the twentieth century, the Court launched and modified a new approach to protecting the privilege against self-incrimination by applying it to pretrial interrogation and imposing a new set of rules for police behavior. With the *Dickerson* decision, the *Miranda* approach appears finally to have gained the same assured constitutional status that the *Gideon* approach to safeguarding the right to counsel rapidly assumed (although serious doctrinal inconsistencies remain). *Miranda* accomplished its goal by creating a Fifth Amendment right to counsel that is distinct from, but closely interconnected with, the Sixth Amendment right to counsel. Both rights have continued to evolve through the normal processes of judicial interpretation, though not always in perfect harmony with each other. Apart from *Miranda,* the more traditional law of the Fifth Amendment's protection against compulsory self-incrimination continues to evolve as well. In the next chapter we consider some of the continuing and emerging jurisprudential issues and practical problems that seem likely to be prominent in the years ahead.

REFERENCES

Bowles, Keri L. 2002. "Thirty-first Annual Review of Criminal Procedure: II. Preliminary Proceedings: Grand Jury." *Georgetown Law Journal* 90:1305–1334.

Dripps, Donald A. 2001. "Constitutional Theory for Criminal Procedure: *Dickerson, Miranda,* and the Continuing Quest for Broad-but-shallow." *William and Mary Law Review* 43:1–77.

Kamisar, Yale, Wayne R. LaFave, Jerold H. Israel, and Nancy J. King. 2002. *Basic Criminal Procedure: Cases, Comments and Questions.* St Paul, MN: West Group.

McInnis, Thomas N. 2001. *The Christian Burial Case.* Westport, CT: Praeger.

U.S. Senate. 1992. *The Constitution of the United States of America: Analysis and Interpretation.* 103d Cong., 1st sess. S. Doc. 103–6. Washington, DC: Government Printing Office.

U.S. Senate. 2000. *The Constitution of the United States of America: Analysis and Interpretation, 2000 Supplement.* 106th Cong., 2d sess. S. Doc. 106–27. Washington, DC: Government Printing Office.

Warren, Earl. 1997. *The Memoirs of Earl Warren.* Garden City, NY: Doubleday.

6

The Twenty-First Century: Legal and Policy Issues

The continuing problems and controversies of the past, and new ones in the future, combine to ensure that the Supreme Court will continue to face important issues of counsel and confession. In this chapter we identify some of those issues that now seem most apparent, and look briefly at some of the policy problems they entail.

Miranda Warnings as a Cure for Previous Violations

In the early 2000s the Court strongly reaffirmed the principle that *Miranda* warnings by themselves do not render a confession admissible if it was the product of an unconstitutional arrest (*Kaupp v. Texas* [2003]), but the question of whether *Miranda* warnings cure other violations remains open.

Sixth Amendment Violations

The intertwining of issues of right to counsel, privilege against self-incrimination, and *Miranda* rights is well illustrated by the case of *Fellers v. United States* (2004). Police came to the home of John J. Fellers and initiated a conversation about his involvement in the distribution of drugs; they told him that he had been indicted and that they had a warrant for his arrest, but they did not read him his *Miranda* rights. Fellers talked freely about his activities, after which police took him to jail and read him his rights under *Miranda v. Arizona* and *Patterson v. Illinois* (see the discussion of assertion and waiver of the right to counsel in the section on the Sixth Amendment right to counsel after *Miranda* in Chapter 5). Fellers then waived his rights to silence and to counsel, was interrogated, and voluntarily made further incriminating statements. Finding a *Miranda* violation at Fellers's home, a magistrate judge recommended the suppression of his statements there and of those jailhouse statements that were the fruits thereof; the trial judge suppressed the former but admitted the latter, and Fellers was convicted.

On appeal, he argued that his Sixth Amendment right to counsel, which had attached because of his indictment, had been violated at his home, and that his jailhouse statements should have been suppressed as the fruits of that violation. The appeals court, however, found no violation because it determined that Fellers had not been interrogated at home; thus the only question was a Fifth Amendment one: whether the jailhouse statements had been knowingly and voluntarily made. Finding *Oregon v. Elstad* to be directly relevant (see the discussion of exceptions and limitations to the implementation of *Miranda* in Chapter 5), the appeals court ruled that the jailhouse statements were not the fruits of the prior *Miranda* violation because of the intervening valid waiver of *Miranda* rights, and that they had therefore been properly admitted. A concurring judge believed that a Sixth Amendment violation had occurred but that it had been cured by the subsequent warning and waiver (*United States v. Fellers* [8th Cir. 2002]).

Finding a Sixth Amendment violation and declining to assume that it had been cured by *Miranda* warnings, a unanimous Supreme Court reversed and remanded the case for further proceedings. Following *Massiah v. United States* and subsequent cases (see the discussion of *Massiah* in the section on the prelude to *Miranda,* and the discussion of the functional equivalent of interrogation in the section on the Sixth Amendment right to counsel after *Miranda,* in Chapter 5), the Court found a clear instance of the deliberate elicitation of incriminating information from Fellers at his home, in the absence of counsel and without waiver of that right. *Elstad* had held that a *Miranda* violation can be cured by a subsequent valid waiver of rights, as voluntary incriminating statements made thereafter are not the fruits of the violation and are therefore admissible, but Justice Sandra Day O'Connor's opinion pointedly noted that the Court had never had occasion to decide whether the logic of *Elstad* also applies to a prior Sixth Amendment violation. The Court therefore instructed the court of appeals to decide a Sixth Amendment question: when police violate the deliberate-elicitation standard of the right to counsel but then obtain a valid waiver of that right, must incriminating statements made thereafter be suppressed as fruits of the original violation? Whatever the response of the court of appeals, this question is likely to return to the Supreme Court for final determination.

Miranda *Violations*

Skeptics of police behavior (including Justice William J. Brennan dissenting in *Elstad*), worry that in situations like that in *Fellers,* police purposely omit *Miranda* warnings in the initial questioning, knowing that the results will be inadmissible but hoping that suspects, having already incriminated themselves, will, after warnings, be more likely to confess than they would have been otherwise. The constitutionality of that practice came before the Court with respect to the confession of Patrice Seibert and her conviction for second-degree murder. (She was an accessory in a sordid scheme that involved the intentional death of a mentally ill teenager in a fire set to destroy the body of another child who had died, in order to cover up evidence of Seibert's neglect.) Police arrested her at 3:00 A.M. and questioned her without giving the *Miranda* warnings, eliciting many damaging statements. After a twenty-minute break they read Seibert her rights (which she waived) and questioned her again, making reference to her previous admissions and gaining incriminating statements that were used at trial. The arresting officer candidly testified that he had consciously violated the *Miranda* requirements during the first interrogation to facilitate a subsequent confession, and that this technique was an integral part of his police training and practice. The Missouri Supreme Court overturned the conviction on the grounds that the second confession was clearly the product of the initial violation, and the state appealed.

The *Miranda* violation in *Oregon v. Elstad* had been inadvertent but the one here was intentional, and various federal courts of appeals had reached different conclusions on the question of whether a confession should be admissible under those circumstances. Writing for a plurality of four, Justice David Souter announced that the answer was no. The key point, he said, was that when the warned segment of the interrogation is essentially a continuation of the unwarned segment, it is unreasonable to believe that the warnings could effectively satisfy the *Miranda* requirement of enabling suspects to make a real and informed choice about the exercise of rights, which would entail a refusal to repeat admissions they have just made. The facts of the case "by any objective measure reveal a police strategy adapted to undermine the *Miranda* warnings"—in sharp contrast to the "arguably innocent neglect of *Miranda*" (*Missouri v. Seibert* slip opinion 14, 13 [2004] [plurality opinion]) in *Elstad,* where the second interrogation had also been distinct from the first. The crucial fifth vote concurring in the result came from Justice Anthony Kennedy, who would have imposed a more permissive rule. Intentional two-stage interrogations, he agreed, should result in the suppression of warned statements relating to unwarned ones unless curative measures were employed (perhaps a distinct break in the process, or a warning about the inadmissibility of the first statements). For unintentional violations, however, Kennedy would employ the *Elstad* approach, in which warnings cure the violation unless the goals of deterring police misconduct or ensuring the trustworthiness of evidence would be compromised (see the discussion of exceptions and limitations to the implementation of *Miranda* in Chapter 5).

Writing for four dissenters, Justice O'Connor complained that the plurality's reasoning "devours" *Elstad*—which she wrote (*Missouri v. Seibert* slip opinion 1 [2004] [dissenting opinion]). The plurality's rationale, she argued, was indistinguishable from the approach rejected in *Elstad*—that the warnings were inefficacious because the suspect believed she had let the cat out of the bag, which might well be true but had little to do with protection against *compelled* self-incrimination. The dissenters would thus not have decided the case but would have remanded it to the Missouri courts for a determination governed by *Elstad:* had intervening events attenuated the taint of the initial violation on the second interrogation and, that issue aside, were the second admissions voluntary in light of the circumstances of the second interrogation—including explicit police reference to admissions made during the first interrogation.

For the plurality of four, Justice Kennedy's distinction between intentional and unintentional two-stage interrogations was irrelevant because the warnings are inefficacious either way (although Justice Breyer noted separately that he would not automatically suppress the fruits of a good-faith failure to warn). For the four dissenters, Kennedy's distinction was undesirable because constitutional analysis should not be based on a determination of the subjective intent of interrogating officers. Justice Kennedy would join the dissenters, however, in following *Elstad* in all but intentional violations, which he termed "infrequent" (*Missouri v. Seibert* slip opinion 4 [2004] [concurring opinion]). Skeptics believe that it is only *admitted* intentional violations that are infrequent and worry that police will find a way to camouflage this tactic. If they do, there could be five (or possibly six) votes on this Court to follow *Elstad* (or, in Breyer's case, the approach of fruit of the poisonous tree, developed in Fourth Amendment cases) and uphold the admissibility of a second-stage confession. The split of the Court in *Seibert* thus resembles that in *Miranda,* with one group wanting a bright-line rule requiring suppression of incriminating statements if it is violated and another group preferring a case-by-case assessment of the totality of the circumstances of the interrogation. The difference is that in *Seibert* there is one justice holding the balance of power who could resurrect the latter approach in an appropriate case.

The Issue of Prophylactic Rules

In *Oregon v. Elstad* and other cases (see the discussion of exceptions and limitations to the implementation of *Miranda* in Chapter 5), the Court characterized the *Miranda* requirements as prophylactic rules of evidence rather than constitutional standards, and it therefore declined to apply the exclusionary rule to evidence that had not been compelled but was rather derived (or arguably derived) from statements gained in violation of *Miranda* (although the statements themselves were inadmissible). The doctrine of exclusion of the fruit of the poisonous tree, developed in search and seizure cases, applies only when the evidence is the fruit of a constitutional violation (such as an arrest or search without probable cause), the Court maintained, and the failure to give *Miranda* warnings is not a constitutional violation (although actual compulsion to confess is). In *Dickerson v. United States,* however, the Court affirmed that *Miranda* had stated a constitutional rule, without either repudiating or reaffirming the *Elstad* approach. The question remained, therefore, whether *Miranda* violations now necessarily required application of the exclusionary rule.

An opportunity to address the disparity between *Elstad* and *Dickerson,* and to reconsider the characterization of *Miranda* requirements as merely prophylactic rules, arose in the case of Samuel Francis Patane. Police in Colorado Springs arrested Patane but committed a *Miranda* violation by not fully reading him his rights when he announced that he already knew them. From subsequent questioning they learned the location of and seized Patane's gun, which was introduced as evidence at a federal trial in which he was found guilty of possession of a firearm by a convicted felon. The court of appeals overturned the conviction on the grounds that *Dickerson* required exclusion of the gun as evidence, but since *Dickerson* other federal appeals courts had reached the opposite conclusion with respect to the physical fruits of *Miranda* violations, and the Supreme Court took the case.

By a 5–4 vote, a fractured majority of the Court upheld the admissibility of the gun without persuasively clarifying the status of the concept of *Miranda* requirements as prophylactic rules. Announcing the judgment and joined by Chief Justice Rehnquist and Justice Scalia, Justice Thomas echoed *Elstad* in arguing that since the prophylactic *Miranda* rules "necessarily sweep beyond the actual protections of the Self-Incrimination Clause, . . . any further extension of these rules must be justified by its necessity for the protection of the actual right against compelled self-incrimination. . . . Introduction of the nontestimonial fruit of a voluntary statement . . . does not implicate the Self-Incrimination Clause. The admission of such fruit presents no risk that a defendant's coerced statements (however defined) will be used against him at a criminal trial. . . . There is simply no need to extend (and therefore no justification for extending) the prophylactic rule of *Miranda* to this context," Thomas concluded (*United States v. Patane* slip opinion 2, 11 [2004] [plurality opinion]), adding that nothing in *Dickerson* contradicted that interpretation.

Expressing a view that would surely have shocked Earl Warren and the rest of the *Miranda* majority, Thomas further asserted that "[t]he *Miranda* rule is not a code of police conduct, and police do not violate the Constitution (or even the *Miranda* rule, for that matter) by mere failures to warn"; only use of unwarned statements as evidence would do that, as the Court had recently held in *Chavez v. Martinez* (*United States v. Patane* slip opinion 4 [2004] [plurality opinion]. See the discussion of *Chavez* in the section below on the Fifth Amendment, due process, and protection against abuse by police). Therefore, he concluded, as long as such statements are not used there is no justification for applying the exclusionary rule because there is no police misconduct to deter. Justices Kennedy and O'Connor declined to endorse these more radical sentiments but did agree that use of physical evidence derived from a voluntary statement taken in violation of *Miranda* does not risk a violation of the self-incrimination clause and is therefore acceptable, thus providing the votes for a majority.

The plurality asserted that "statements taken without sufficient *Miranda* warnings are presumed to have been coerced only for certain purposes and then only when necessary to protect the privilege against self-incrimination" (*United States v. Patane* slip opinion 12 [2004] [plurality opinion]). Dissenting Justices Souter, Stevens, and Ginsburg made no such distinction, however, arguing that "in the absence of a very good reason, the logic of *Miranda* should be followed: a *Miranda* violation raises a presumption of coercion . . . and the Fifth Amendment privilege against compelled self-incrimination extends to the exclusion of derivative evidence. . . . That should be the end of this case" (*United States v. Patane* slip opinion 2 [2004] [dissenting opinion]). Contrary precedents were irrelevant, they argued: Patane was not attempting to shield perjury behind *Miranda* (*Harris v. New York*); his gun created no public emergency (*New York v. Quarles*); this was not a case where belated warnings could remove the taint from subsequently gained evidence (*Oregon v. Elstad*) because Patane's gun had been seized at the time of the violation; *Michigan v. Tucker* rested on different grounds. What the dissenters found most unfortunate about the decision, however, was its likely consequence: "[t]here is no way to read this case except as an unjustifiable invitation to law enforcement officers to flout *Miranda* when there may be physical evidence to be gained. The incentive is an odd one, coming from the Court on the same day it decides *Missouri v. Seibert* (*United States v. Patane* slip opinion 3 [2004] [dissenting opinion]). The final dissenter, Justice Breyer, generally agreed but wrote separately to endorse the same approach he advocated in *Seibert:* that the evidence should be suppressed unless the *Miranda* violation had been committed in good faith.

In their joint dissent in *Dickerson v. United States* (see the section on *Miranda* challenged and reaffirmed in Chapter 5), Scalia and Thomas emphasized a logical contradiction between the idea that the exclusionary rule does not necessarily apply to *Miranda* violations because they are violations of prophylactic rules rather than of the self-incrimination clause of the Constitution, and the idea that the *Miranda* rules can be enforced against the states (or that Congress cannot supersede them). Their conclusion that the evidence in *Patane* need not be excluded is consistent with their view that *Dickerson* was wrongly decided, but that cannot be the rationale for the decision of the Court because *Dickerson* was not overruled. Moreover, Rehnquist—author of *Dickerson*—joined them in saying that *Dickerson* did not contradict *Patane,* and Kennedy and O'Connor, also in the *Dickerson* majority, concurred without any indication that they thought otherwise. Since (1) *Miranda* rested on the theory that a violation of its rules was a constitutional violation, (2) *Dickerson* affirmed *Miranda,* and (3) *Patane* rests on the theory that a *Miranda* violation violates only prophylactic rules, the assertion that "nothing in *Dickerson,* including its characterization of *Miranda* as announcing a constitutional rule, . . . changes" the *Elstad* conception of prophylactic rules (*United States v. Patane* slip opinion 8 [2004] [plurality opinion]) seems plausible only in the unsatisfactory sense that *Dickerson* merely obfuscated the conception of prophylactic rules (or of a constitutional rule, or both). Since that was the point of their *Dickerson* dissent, Thomas and Scalia's espousal of the assertion just quoted seems disingenuous.

Since Rehnquist, O'Connor, and Kennedy were the only justices in the majority in both *Dickerson* and *Patane,* however, and the ones whose position on prophylactic rules in previous cases was called inconsistent with their position in *Dickerson* by Scalia and Thomas, dissenting in that case, the burden of explanation falls primarily on them. They did not assume that burden in *Patane,* or agree on a common position. A somewhat more useful version of their approach in *Patane* (which is Thomas and Scalia's approach as well) is the plurality's assertion that "nothing in *Dickerson* calls into question our continued insistence that the closest possible fit be maintained between the Self-Incrimination Clause and any rule designed to protect it" (*United States v. Patane* slip opinion 8–9 [2004] [plurality opinion]). The essence of the argument is that in order to ensure that the Constitution is not violated, it is sometimes necessary to provide more protection than the Constitution requires. That is their view of *Miranda* (whether they agree with that decision or not): in order to ensure that no involuntary statements are admitted into evidence, all unwarned statements are *presumed* to have been involuntary, even if they actually were not. That is all the largesse that is justified, however, for the admission of evidence that was not itself compelled but merely derived from unwarned statements runs no risk of the admission of those statements themselves (and no risk of the admission of statements shown to have actually been compelled, or of evidence derived therefrom), and that is all the Fifth Amendment requires.

What that interpretation fails to explain in doctrinal terms, however, is how rules that the *Miranda* majority considered to be of constitutional stature came to be prophylactic rules of evidence instead—an enigma that has now persisted for three decades. It is also unlikely that Scalia and Thomas believe that their *Dickerson* dissent has been successfully rebutted, and that Rehnquist, O'Connor, and Kennedy's positions are now internally consistent (points about which the *Dickerson* dissenters apparently held their counsel in the interest of forming a majority in *Patane*). The majority of the justices clearly weigh the rights of the accused against the interests of law enforcement and appear to have accepted doctrinal contradiction as the price of what they regard as desirable policy outcomes. One can only hope that the Court will attempt a more candid clarification of these matters in future cases.

The Continuing Policy Debate over *Miranda*

Controversy over the nature and desirability of *Miranda's* policy impact also persists. Some argue that *Miranda* continues to impose an unreasonable restriction on the ability of law enforcement officials to gain confessions and convict the guilty, while others maintain that *Miranda* as interpreted and applied in practice has in fact been an advantage to police and has failed to provide its intended protection for hapless suspects. Although studies in the first few years after its implementation consistently concluded that *Miranda* did not significantly hamper police work (see Leo 1996a for a summary of these studies), two decades later the issue flared up again with disagreements about both the validity of the earlier studies and the contemporary situation.

The most persistent conservative critic of *Miranda* has been Paul G. Cassell, a professor of law at the University of Utah and unsuccessful prime mover in the *Dickerson* litigation (whose role was changed by his appointment as a federal district judge in 2002). Cassell's critique resides in a series of law review articles in which he argues, for example, that the early studies actually show that *Miranda* causes the loss of well over 100,000 convictions annually for serious crimes of violence and property crimes—3.8 percent of such crimes (Cassell 1996, excerpted in Leo and Thomas 1998)—and, contrary to widespread belief, is responsible for a significant decline in the clearance rate (the percentage of known crimes that police are able to solve) (Cassell and Fowles 1998). Another prominent legal scholar, however, Stephen J. Schulhofer of the University of Chicago, examined the same data and counters that the percentage of lost convictions attributable to *Miranda* in the early data is at most 0.78 percent. Further, he argues, the situation is much better today than it was immediately after the decision, because police have adapted to its requirements and increased their professionalism (Schulhofer 1996b, excerpted in Leo and Thomas 1998). Nor do the data establish that *Miranda* caused the decline in the clearance rate, Schulhofer argues; the far more likely explanation is that police resources were increasing only modestly while the crime rate was soaring (Schulhofer 1996a). Cassell contends that his own study shows that in the 1990s *Miranda* was still extracting significant costs in terms of lost confessions and convictions (Cassell and Hayman 1996, excerpted in Leo and Thomas 1998); fellow legal scholar George C. Thomas III of Rutgers University counters that Cassell's data and data from a few other recent studies show no *Miranda* effect on the overall confession rate (Thomas 1996, excerpted in Leo and Thomas 1998). These contending scholars typically find fault with the methodology of those who disagree with them; they generally agree that more research is required.

Liberal analysts, meanwhile, have a very different criticism of *Miranda.* Far from impeding the police, they argue, it has actually worked to their advantage while failing to provide effective protection for the rights of suspects. For one thing, implementing decisions such as *Harris v. New York, Oregon v. Hass, Michigan v. Tucker, New York v. Quarles,* and *Oregon v. Elstad* (see the discussion of exceptions and limitations to the implementation of *Miranda* in Chapter 5) have limited the kind of evidence that must be excluded because of *Miranda* violations (and *United States v. Patane* may now be added to that list). Moreover, police have learned to pressure or cajole suspects into waiving their rights and then to interrogate them aggressively using deception and manipulative psychological techniques, and the courts now tend to presume the voluntariness of confessions when the formalities of warning and waiver have been observed. The consequence, these critics suggest, is that in some respects suspects under interrogation today have less protection than they had previously under the due process standard alone. It is no wonder that police now generally support *Miranda,* they assert, and the justices who had formerly criticized *Miranda* but voted to uphold it in *Dickerson* may well have done so because they were satisfied that it had been effectively neutralized and even turned to advantage (Garcia 2002; White 2001).

After the reaffirmation of *Miranda* in *Dickerson* one might well argue, as Schulhofer did earlier (Schulhofer 1997), that the impact of *Miranda* on law enforcement is beside the point because the provision of *Miranda* rights is constitutionally required. Commentators who take this position affirm that the framers of the Fifth Amendment intended to make law enforcement more difficult in order to protect fundamental rights. Debate properly continues, however, about whether or not *Miranda* has actually achieved that goal, and there is increasing support among both defense lawyers and law enforcement officials for the routine videotaping of interrogations to document what actually occurs (Liptak 2004, 35). Ironically, it was the inability of trial judges to ascertain the nature of interrogations that prompted the *Miranda* decision in the first place.

Opponents in the *Miranda* debate agree that about 80 percent of suspects waive their rights and submit to police questioning (White 2001, 76; Cassell and Hayman 1996, 859)—a result that surely neither the majority nor the dissenting justices in *Miranda* expected. We simply do not know to what extent that figure results from police intimidation or deception, from factors of personality and social adjustment, or from a calculation of self-interest, but the statistic should give pause to both those who defend *Miranda* as an essential bulwark of constitutional rights and those who see it as a significant impediment to effective police work (especially since the minority who do invoke their rights includes those who would be savvy enough to do so even in the absence of warnings). The statistic does lend some support—but scant comfort—to those who see *Miranda* as a failed initiative. Those who stand back from the fray point out that *Miranda* embodied a significant compromise: it sought to shield suspects from the necessity of facing questioning without benefit of counsel in the inherently coercive atmosphere of the police station, but it allowed police to secure waivers of their rights under precisely those conditions (Arenella 1997, 383–384). The Court, they note, rejected proposals to require the presence of defense counsel for all custodial interrogations (a logical next step if the Court had chosen to build on *Escobedo*). For all the controversy about *Miranda*, the fundamental questions, both before and after waiver, thus continue to be the same ones that vexed the Court prior to 1966: what sorts of pressure on suspects are tolerable, how much pressure on suspects is too much pressure, and how are police to be held to the standards we adopt?

It is generally agreed that the era of the third degree—using physical coercion of suspects to gain confessions—is essentially over, but the increasingly sophisticated and effective use of techniques of deception, falsehood, and psychological manipulation is well documented. David Simon's pungent journalistic description of police interrogation in Baltimore provides graphic evidence of the reality of the stationhouse (Simon 1991, excerpted in Leo and Thomas 1998), and scholars have documented and analyzed the same reality (White 2001, chapters 3, 7; Leo 1996b; Leo 1992, excerpted in Leo and Thomas 1998). The shift from regarding untrustworthiness as the sole basis for excluding confessions to excluding them on the basis of involuntariness (even if trustworthy) was one of the liberalizing reforms of the mid-twentieth century (see the discussion of *Lisenba v. California* in the section on the coerced confession cases, and the section on competing claims of voluntariness and truthfulness, in Chapter 4). Now, however, scholars are reexamining the linkage between those two concepts as concern rises about the incidence of false confessions resulting at least in part from modern psychological techniques of interrogation and often contributing to wrongful convictions (White 2001, Chapters 11, 12; Leo 2001; Leo 1998). The *Miranda* approach has largely transcended the voluntariness test by presuming that confessions after warnings are voluntary, but Welsh White concludes his influential book by calling for the *Miranda* approach to be supplemented by a renewed emphasis on the voluntariness test to preclude the admissibility of statements gained as the result of techniques of interrogation that are likely to engender false confessions (White 2001, Chapter 14). Paul Cassell has characteristically adopted a different perspective, arguing that false confessions—which do not always lead to conviction of an innocent person—are a far less serious *Miranda* problem than lost confessions, which lead to harm to those innocent persons who either are future victims of unconvicted criminals or are wrongly convicted in their stead (Cassell 1998). Both sides agree that reliable data on the magnitude of the false-confession problem are lacking, and the need for further study is clear. As other scholars argue, however (for example, Alschuler 1997), the most fundamental issue transcends this problem. It is—as it was in the era of the third degree—the issue of defining and enforcing acceptable forms of police behavior as we strike the balance between the liberty of the individual and the security of the society. That quest continues in the post-*Dickerson* era.

THE FIFTH AMENDMENT, DUE PROCESS, AND PROTECTION AGAINST ABUSE BY POLICE

As we have seen, *Miranda* issues and issues of the privilege against self-incrimination are not separable, and the relationship between the warnings and the privilege has been an object of continuing legal controversy. A further illustration is the case of *Chavez v. Martinez* (2003), in which a suspect sought civil damages from the police officer who had interrogated him. Without giving *Miranda* warnings, Sergeant Ben Chavez questioned Oliverio Martinez while he was in custody and undergoing emergency medical treatment. In great pain and in fear of dying from five police-inflicted gunshot wounds that would leave him blind and paralyzed, Martinez pleaded for him to stop; Chavez persisted and obtained incriminating statements. Martinez later sued Chavez for damages on the grounds that the unwarned and coercive interrogation had violated both his privilege against self-incrimination and his right to due process of law. Because Chavez was immune from liability for civil damages unless he had violated Martinez's constitutional rights, the issue for the Court was the scope of the rights in question. A fractured majority determined that because Martinez had not been prosecuted and his statements had not been used against him, his Fifth Amendment rights had not been violated even if the interrogation was coercive, because he had not been compelled to be a witness against himself in a criminal case. (The Court did, however, allow Martinez to pursue his suit on the basis of the due process clause.) In a strong dissent, Justice Anthony Kennedy and two others argued that "[o]ur cases and our legal tradition establish that the Self-Incrimination Clause is a substantive constraint on the conduct of the government, not merely an evidentiary rule governing the work of the courts. . . . The conclusion that the Self-

Incrimination Clause is not violated until the government seeks to use a statement in some later criminal proceeding strips the Clause of an essential part of its force and meaning. . . . In my view the Self-Incrimination Clause is applicable at the time and place police use compulsion to extract a statement from a suspect. The Clause forbids that conduct" (*Chavez v. Martinez* 791–795, passim [2003] [dissenting opinion]).

Critics of police behavior have always worried about the use of abusive methods of interrogation when there is no intent to use the fruits in a prosecution and the exclusionary rule is thus irrelevant, and that concern has new saliency in the period after 11 September 2001, when the primary goal of an interrogation may not be prosecution but rather the elicitation of intelligence about terrorist activities. Justice Kennedy did concede that "a ruling on substantive due process in this case could provide much of the essential protection the Self-Incrimination Clause secures" (*Chavez v. Martinez* 799 [2003] [dissenting opinion]), and the issue for the immediate future, in both federal and state jurisdictions, is the degree to which courts will employ the due process clause to provide protection against, or to allow compensation for, coercive interrogations per se. Ironically, due process was the standard for the admissibility of confessions in state courts until the reform accomplished by the incorporation of the self-incrimination clause in *Malloy v. Hogan* (1964).

Effective Assistance of Counsel

In Chapter 3 we noted that the Court's decision in *Williams v. Taylor* might have signaled that lower courts had allowed the standard of adequate performance of defense counsel to sink too low. That uncertainty persists, and tension has arisen between the standards of *United States v. Cronic* and *Strickland v. Washington* (see the discussion of effective assistance of counsel in the section on counsel and client in Chapter 3). On the one hand, in 2002 the

Court refused a request by the state of Texas to review a U.S. court of appeals decision upholding a claim of ineffective assistance in a notorious case in which the defense attorney slept repeatedly during the course of a murder trial (certiorari denied in *Cockrell v. Burdine* [2002]). Relying on *United States v. Cronic,* the Court of Appeals for the Fifth Circuit had held that Burdine had been denied counsel during a critical phase of the proceedings against him, and that he was therefore entitled to the presumption that his defense had been prejudiced (*Burdine v. Johnson* [5th Cir. 2001]). On the other hand, in *Bell v. Cone* [2002], the Supreme Court rejected a claim based on a defense attorney's failure to call witnesses and to make a closing statement during the sentencing phase of a capital case. The Court of Appeals for the Sixth Circuit had also relied on *United States v. Cronic,* finding that the attorney's omissions essentially denied Cone counsel during a critical phase of his trial, that the prosecution's position had therefore not been subjected to meaningful adversarial testing, and that prejudice could therefore be presumed. The Supreme Court, however, made clear that the *Cronic* standard applies when an attorney has *entirely* failed to subject the prosecution case to meaningful adversarial testing, but that the *Strickland* standard applies when the claim is only that counsel failed at specific points. Cone would therefore have to demonstrate both inadequate performance and a prejudicial effect on the outcome. Because the Court found valid strategic reasons for the attorney's decisions, his performance was not inadequate and Cone's claim failed at that point.

In 2003, however, the Court upheld a similar claim on the basis of *Strickland. Wiggins v. Smith* (2003) concerned the failure of counsel for convicted murderer Kevin Wiggins to offer, at the sentencing phase of his trial, abundant evidence of the gruesome sexual and physical abuse the marginally retarded defendant had suffered as a child and young adult. Appeals courts in Maryland and the federal Fourth Circuit had found that counsel made a rational decision to rely instead on an argument that Wiggins was not directly responsible for the victim's death, but the Supreme Court framed the issue differently. The question, wrote Justice Sandra Day O'Connor, was not the reasonableness of the strategic decision not to present mitigating evidence, but rather the reasonableness of the investigative effort on which that strategy was based. Counsel's failure to commission a social history of the defendant, which would have revealed the powerful case for mitigation that later emerged, fell well below prevailing professional standards, the Court found, and thus the deficiency prong of the *Strickland* test was satisfied. The prejudice prong was satisfied as well, O'Connor continued, because there was a reasonable probability that a jury hearing the case for mitigation would not have sentenced Wiggins to death. The similar case of *Williams v. Taylor* in 2000 was the first occasion on which the Court upheld a claim of ineffective assistance under the *Strickland* test of 1984. In *Wiggins* the Court took pains to reinforce *Williams* and to emphasize what it said *Strickland* had always meant with respect to claims of ineffective assistance of counsel based on strategic decisions that proved unsuccessful: the validity of the claim depends on whether those decisions were grounded in a thorough investigation of the law and the facts. Here, Wiggins's two lawyers had made no such investigation, and the Court criticized the Maryland courts' reliance on the justification of strategic decision as "more a *post-hoc* rationalization of counsel's conduct than an accurate description of their deliberations prior to sentencing" (*Wiggins v. Smith* 526–527 [2003]).

These cases raise the interrelated problems of the assessment of defense counsel's performance in hindsight and of the applicable legal standard by which that performance is to be judged. In *Bell v. Cone*, one position was that Cone had satisfied the *Cronic* standard of inadequate performance (failure to subject the prosecution's case to meaningful adversarial testing) and therefore did not have to demonstrate prejudice; the other position was that Cone was required to satisfy the *Strickland* standard of inadequate performance (representation falling below an objective standard of reasonableness under prevailing professional norms) and to demonstrate prejudice by showing a reasonable probability that the outcome would otherwise have been different. As we noted in Chapter 3, the *Strickland* standard has made it very difficult for claims of ineffective assistance to succeed. The *Cronic* standard has clearly been easier to meet, and most successful claims of ineffective assistance in lower courts have come in cases in which the court found *Cronic* to be the appropriate standard (Geimer 1995, 148).

To this point, the Court has considered *Cronic* to be limited to a narrow range of factual circumstances and *Strickland* to be the basic standard for claims of ineffective assistance, and its refusal to extend *Cronic* in *Cone* may well be more significant than its passive endorsement of reliance on *Cronic* in the egregious circumstances of *Burdine.* If lower courts continue to employ the *Cronic* standard more broadly, however, the Supreme Court will have to resolve the tension between that case and *Strickland.* There is already a considerable body of adverse commentary condemning *Strickland* for, in the blunt words of one critic, "fostering tolerance of abysmal lawyering" (Geimer 1995, 94), and in its *Williams* and *Wiggins* decisions the Court may be trying to correct that situation. At the same time, however, other commentators warn that "[e]rroneous overturning of judgments on bogus ineffective assistance claims, particularly in capital cases, is a major problem." (Oliphant 2002, 10).

A further aspect of the problem is the disagreement about whether to focus on process or result—the dispute between those who argue that, trivial matters aside, defective performance by a defense attorney should by itself suffice to entitle a defendant to a new trial, and those who maintain that a new trial is warranted only when the result of the first one was erroneous. The majority in *Strickland* asserted that "the purpose of the effective assistance guarantee of the Sixth Amendment is not to improve the quality of legal representation [but] simply to ensure that criminal defendants receive a fair trial" (*Strickland v. Washington* 689 [1984]), and supporters contend that it is both fair and efficient to refuse to relitigate questions that have already been correctly decided. Opponents, however, doubt that the issues of competent performance and reliable result are separable, for "[t]he majority opinion in *Strickland* overlooks the simple fact that the prosecutor's evidence will always appear unassailable when counsel for the accused neglects to conduct an investigation or fails to challenge the state's version of the case" (Bernhard 2001, 233). Nor is a reliable result the only constitutional requirement, Justice Thurgood Marshall argued in dissent, for the guarantee of effective assistance "also functions to ensure that convictions are obtained only through fundamentally fair procedures. The majority contends that the Sixth Amendment is not violated when a manifestly guilty defendant is convicted after a trial in which he was represented by a manifestly ineffective attorney. I cannot agree. Every defendant is entitled to a trial in which his interests are vigorously and conscientiously advocated by an able lawyer. A proceeding in which the defendant does not receive meaningful assistance in meeting the forces of the State does not, in my opinion, constitute due process" (*Strickland v. Washington* 711 [1984] [dissenting opinion]).

The challenge of achieving standards that ensure that defendants have the right not just to the presence of a licensed attorney but to competent representation is thus a moral and legal issue that the Court must continue to address. In the years to come we may expect the Court to clarify the applicability of the *Cronic* and *Strickland* standards, and we should watch to see if the rebuke of the Maryland courts in *Wiggins* presages a more demanding standard of reasonable professional performance. The full significance of the *Gideon* decision of 1963 thus remains an issue for the twenty-first century.

The Reality of Counsel for the Indigent

The issue of ineffective assistance of counsel will not go away because the reality of poor representation for indigent defendants is apparent. *Gideon* affirmed the right of all defendants to be represented but did not identify the quality or elements of representation to which they are entitled; *Strickland* posited only a general standard of reasonable performance and announced that "more specific guidelines are not appropriate" (*Strickland v. Washington* 688 [1984]). State and county governments typically share administration and funding of defense programs, in varying proportions (DeFrances 2001, 1). In that context, it is inevitable that the quality of appointed counsel varies considerably among jurisdictions, depending on the standards imposed by their courts and the resources their political systems are willing to commit.

Governments employ one or more of three basic mechanisms to meet their obligation to provide counsel for indigent defendants. The most fully institutionalized is the public defender office, an agency of government analogous to the office of prosecutor. A second system is for courts to appoint and compensate attorneys for indigent defendants; in some places the process is organized, with standards and training for attorneys, and in others it is informal and casual. A third alternative is for government to contract with private law firms or solo practitioners to provide legal services, sometimes for a lump sum to cover all cases in a stated period of time; a variant is provided by contracts with not-for-profit local legal aid societies, which often receive both public and private funding and also solicit attorneys to do *pro bono* work. Public defender offices are often underfunded and have high caseloads, and some states are now charging indigents modest fees for this service on the grounds that it would have to be cut back otherwise. (This practice is now under challenge in Minnesota. The Supreme Court passed on a related issue in *Fuller v. Oregon* [1974], holding that a statute allowing states to recoup costs of defense from convicted indigents who subsequently become able to pay without hardship does not violate either equal protection or the right to counsel.) Judges in appointive systems may be lax in their standards and, as compensation is often minimal, appointees may be unqualified or inexperienced; legal services companies or individual appointees not working on a fee-for-service basis have an incentive to minimize the time and resources spent on each case. A series of studies by the American Bar Association reveals equally serious deficiencies in the provision of the right to counsel in state juvenile justice systems. Across the board, there is need for more realistic levels of funding, effective training in the intricacies of relevant law and procedure (especially in capital cases), and clear and enforceable standards of professional competence (Bernhard 2001, 225–233; Pierre 2003, A1; American Bar Association 2003).

It is widely recognized that legal services for indigent defendants are seriously deficient, and around the turn of the twenty-first century critical evaluations and efforts at reform were seriously under way in the federal system and more than a dozen states. Indiana had achieved significant progress (Lefstein 1996), but especially close national scrutiny focused on Texas because its governor, George W. Bush, was running for president in 2000. A withering barrage of criticism and the embarrassment of the sleeping lawyer case, in which the Texas Court of Criminal Appeals had ruled that Calvin Burdine was not denied the effective assistance of counsel in his murder trial, were catalysts for passage of the Texas Fair Defense Act in 2001 and spurred efforts elsewhere as well (Butterfield 2001, 14; Goldman 2002, 1).

Much remains to be done, however, and the stakes are high. In October 2003 two nonprofit advocacy groups, the Equal Justice Center and the Texas Defender Service, released a report concluding that most Texas counties had thus far fallen seriously short of compliance with the requirements of the new Texas statute (Equal Justice Center and Texas Defender Service 2003). In felony cases nationwide, public defenders or assigned counsel represent 66 percent of defendants in federal trials and 82 percent in state trials in large counties (Harlow 2000, 1). Appeals in capital cases reveal the magnitude of deficiencies at the trial level. A study commissioned by the U.S. Senate Committee on the Judiciary revealed that in 4,578 appeals of death sentences in the years 1973–1995, 68 percent were overturned; most of those persons were subsequently found to deserve lesser sentences and some were exonerated altogether. The study found the principal causes of this alarming statistic to be "egregiously incompetent defense lawyers" and police and prosecutorial misconduct, chiefly the suppression of exculpatory evidence (Liebman, Fagan, and West 2000, ii). Two Supreme Court justices have expressed concern about the adequacy of representation in capital cases. In off-the-bench comments in 2001, Justice Ruth Bader Ginsburg bluntly stated that "I have yet to see a death case among the dozens coming to the Supreme Court on eve-of-execution stay applications in which the defendant was well represented at trial," (cited in Gearan 2001, A18), and Justice Sandra Day O'Connor suggested that "[p]erhaps it's time to look at minimum standards for appointed counsel in death cases and adequate compensation for appointed counsel when they are used" (cited in Baca 2001, 1A).

For several years Congress has considered a proposed Innocence Protection Act, which would create a national commission to develop standards of representation of indigents in capital cases and establish a system of grants to help states implement the standards and otherwise improve their systems of appointed counsel. As of July 2004, the House of Representatives had passed and the Senate Judiciary Committee was actively considering a bill on DNA testing that does not create a commission but does incorporate a provision for federal grants to states to improve the provision of defense services in capital cases (and adds a provision for comparable grants to facilitate prosecution) (H.R. 3214, S. 1700, 108th Cong., 1st sess.). Those grants would apply to services for both trial and appeal, which might alleviate an acute problem for convicts appealing a sentence of death, especially those who have exhausted their right to appointed counsel and are dependent on volunteer efforts; many of them go for long periods with minimal representation or none at all (Hines 2001, A1). For governments at all levels and for law firms providing services *pro bono,* the financial burden of providing appointed counsel is severe. For the constitutional right to counsel, it is not just the fate of indigent defendants that is at stake; it is also the integrity of the criminal justice system.

Constitutional Rights and the War on Terror

The terrorist attacks on New York and Washington on 11 September 2001, and the unprecedented American response both at home and abroad, have created an entirely new perspective on the question of the constitutional rights—if any—of some categories of the accused. Persons accused of committing or plotting acts of terror, persons merely suspected of terrorism, persons designated as enemy combatants, and persons accused or guilty of immigration violations have all found themselves in the custody of the federal government. Their cases raise troubling questions of probable cause for detention, length and conditions of detention, the secrecy of proceedings, and access to the courts, as well as the questions of right to counsel and privilege against self-incrimination that concern us here.

Some of the persons in detention are American citizens and some are not; some were apprehended in the United States and some abroad; some are held in the United States and some are held by the United States on foreign soil; some were fighting against the United States in Afghanistan and some are allegedly agents of international terrorist organizations. The most fundamental policy dilemma in these cases seems to be the overlapping claims of the civilian justice system, the military justice system, and the military intelligence-gathering process.

Issues of the Right to Counsel

In the period following 9/11, many foreign nationals in the United States were apprehended and detained until it could be determined whether or not they posed a threat or were eligible for deportation. Such persons needed counsel but were often ill-equipped to secure it, and in some places the government placed significant obstacles in their way. For example, a report by the Inspector General of the Department of Justice found that at the Metropolitan Detention Center in Brooklyn, New York, prison officials failed to provide accurate lists of attorneys willing to take cases *pro bono,* severely restricted the privilege of making telephone calls to attorneys, and hindered the ability of attorneys to visit their clients (U.S. Department of Justice 2003a, chap. 7 sec. V).

The inspector general also found illegal violations of attorney-client confidentiality at the same facility, in the form of widespread videotaping of detainees' meetings with counsel. The government has long had the power to monitor such conversations if it can obtain a warrant by establishing probable cause that the two parties are furthering a crime, but that requirement was disregarded at the Metropolitan Detention Center, and some of the lawyers filed damage suits against prison officials (U.S. Department of Justice 2003b, sec. III B; Cole and Dempsey 2002, 173–174; Bernstein 2004, B1). Shortly after 9/11 (and long before the inspector general's report) the government lowered the bar for such surveillance by adopting a federal regulation allowing the attorney general to order the monitoring of attorney-client conversations if the head of a federal law enforcement or intelligence agency has determined that there is reasonable suspicion to believe that a particular inmate might use such communications to further terrorism. No warrant from a judge is required but privileged information is not to be revealed to prosecutors (28 C.F.R. 501.3[d] [2003]).

A major issue of entitlement to the right to counsel concerned enemy combatants and arose as part of a more fundamental component of due process: the right to a hearing in one's case. An enemy combatant is someone the United States government has designated as acting on behalf of the enemy in a time of war—a so-called unlawful combatant, as distinct from a prisoner of war, a status that entails the protections of the Geneva Convention (Brill 2003, 393). (The war, of course, is the amorphous and open-ended war on terror.) It was the position of the U.S. government that enemy combatants could be held indefinitely without charges and had no right to consult a lawyer or contest their detention in court. Most of the persons so designated were among the 650 or so foreign citizens captured abroad (chiefly as a result of the war in Afghanistan) and detained at the American naval base at Guantánamo, Cuba. The two most prominent, however, were American citizens held in the United States.

Yaser Esam Hamdi, born in Louisiana, was captured as a Taliban soldier in Afghanistan; he was sent to the detention center at the naval base at Guantánamo and then transferred to the naval brig at Norfolk, Virginia, when officials learned of his American citizenship. José Padilla (also known as Abdullah al-Muhajir), a former Chicago gang member and habitual criminal who was suspected of plotting with Al Qaeda to detonate a radioactive bomb in the United States, was arrested by the FBI at O'Hare International Airport in Chicago as he returned from Pakistan. He was held as a material witness in New York for a grand jury investigating the 9/11 attacks, as the law allows the detention of persons who have information but would be likely to flee if served with a subpoena. Judge Michael B. Mukasey appointed an attorney for Padilla and she challenged his detention, but two days before the hearing on that issue he was reclassified as an enemy combatant, perhaps because he would have claimed the privilege against self-incrimination and demanded immunity before the grand jury, and could not have been criminally indicted and prosecuted because the government either lacked sufficient information against him or was unwilling to produce Al Qaeda informants, held abroad, who could supply it (Brill 2003, 574; Wedgwood 2003, A27; A. Lewis 2003, 52–54). Both Padilla and Hamdi were denied access to counsel, but lawyers acting on behalf of both filed habeas corpus petitions in federal court to challenge their designations as enemy combatants and their continued detention. Although Padilla had been transferred to the naval brig at Charleston, South Carolina, his attorney filed her case in New York, where the court had already been considering his status; Hamdi's attorney filed in Virginia.

Although the government initially maintained that the executive branch had sole discretion to classify persons as enemy combatants, both federal district judges in these cases ruled that the plaintiffs had a limited right to challenge that designation in court, and that they had a due process right to consult with counsel about information to be submitted on their behalf. In the Padilla case Judge Mukasey ruled that the attorney-client meetings could be monitored by the government; in the *Hamdi* case Judge Robert G. Doumar, who had also appointed a public defender, ruled that they could not. The differing approaches of the two judges were also illustrated by the fact that Mukasey ruled that the government had to meet only the minimal standard of presenting some evidence that Padilla was involved in a mission against the United States on behalf of an enemy with whom it was at war, while Doumar ordered the government to provide extensive records of Hamdi's interrogation by intelligence agents.

The Court of Appeals for the Fourth Circuit reversed Judge Doumar's order giving Hamdi access to counsel, while on the issue of evidence the government relented slightly, submitting a brief affadavit stating the grounds for classification as an enemy combatant (in effect acknowledging Judge Mukasey's "some evidence" standard in the *Padilla* case). Judge Doumar rejected that submission as inadequate but the court of appeals, emphasizing the need for great deference to the government in a time of war, upheld it as sufficient and directed that Hamdi's habeas corpus petition be dismissed without further factual inquiry. He was not entitled to due process, it held, because he had not been charged with a crime (Shenon 2002, A8; Liptak, Lewis, and Weiser 2002, 20; Seelye 2002c, A22; Seelye 2002b, A19; Weiser 2002b, A24; *Hamdi v. Rumsfeld* [4th Cir. 2003]). The appeals court thus denied Hamdi the right to meet with an attorney or to present evidence contesting his classification.

The appeals court limited its ruling to the circumstances of Hamdi's capture among the Taliban fighters in Afghanistan, noting that a different analysis might be required of the courts hearing the case of José Padilla, who was apprehended in Chicago. In that case, the government submitted a classified rationale for its enemy-combatant designation to the judge, but not to the defense, and released an unclassified version that it said was sufficient to resolve the matter. Judge Mukasey declined to follow the lead of the *Hamdi* decision and persisted in his order that Padilla be allowed to consult with attorneys about presentation of evidence, on terms acceptable to the attorneys on both sides. When the government refused to enter into such an arrangement, Mukasey certified several questions to the Court of Appeals for the Second Circuit, including the authority of the president to designate as an enemy combatant and detain a U.S. citizen captured on U.S. soil, the right of the detainee to present evidence to support his habeas corpus petition, and the authority of the judge to order that he be given access to counsel for that purpose.

Relying on the Non-Detention Act, which stipulates that "[n]o citizen shall be imprisoned or otherwise detained by the United States except pursuant to an Act of Congress" (18 U.S.C. §4001[a] [2000]), the appeals court in mid-December 2003 ruled that Congress had taken no such action with respect to enemy combatants and that under such circumstances the president as commander in chief had no constitutional authority to order the detention of a U.S. citizen in the United States and outside a combat zone (*Padilla v. Rumsfeld* [2d Cir. 2003]). (The appeals court in *Hamdi* had concluded that the president had such authority in the circumstances of that case.) Although only two of the judges agreed on this result, all three agreed that Padilla was entitled to contest his detention in a federal court and to have the assistance of counsel in doing so.

Just as the Court of Appeals for the Fourth Circuit had explicitly not addressed the case of a U.S. citizen arrested in the United States when it decided the *Hamdi* case, the Court of Appeals for the Second Circuit explicitly did not address the case of a U.S. citizen apprehended in the combat zone of Afghanistan. The two situations are distinct but clearly related, and the issues of access to courts and right to counsel are common to both. The government's position on the issue of right to counsel, expressed in filings in the *Padilla* case, was that access to counsel "would jeopardize the two core purposes of detaining enemy combatants—gathering intelligence about the enemy, and preventing the detainee from aiding in any further attacks against America" (cited in Weiser 2002a, A17), as a lawyer could unwittingly serve to pass on information detrimental to national security. In particular, the government also claimed, military personnel had been interrogating Padilla for several months and allowing him to see a lawyer "would threaten permanently to undermine the military's efforts to develop a relationship of trust and dependency that is essential to effective interrogation" (cited in Weiser 2003, A11). The Sixth Amendment confers the right to counsel "in all criminal cases" but, the government argued, Padilla's "detention as an enemy combatant is in no sense 'criminal,' and it has no penal consequences whatever" (cited in Weiser 2002a, A17).

Civil libertarians, on the other hand, agreed with Judge Doumar's lament that "[t]his [*Hamdi*] case appears to be the first in American jurisprudence where an American citizen has been held incommunicado and subjected to an indefinite detention in the continental United States without charges, without any findings by a military tribunal, and without access to a lawyer" (*Hamdi v. Rumsfeld* 528 [2002]). What happened to José Padilla was even worse, they believed, because he was apprehended as a material witness in the United States by civil authorities, allowed the services of counsel, and then stripped of his rights by being designated as an enemy combatant and turned over to the military. "This is the model we all should fear," commented Frank W. Dunham Jr., chief federal public defender for the eastern district of Virginia and the man Judge Doumar appointed as counsel for Yaser Esam Hamdi. "The executive branch can arrest an American citizen here and then declare him an enemy combatant and put him outside the reach of the courts. They can keep him indefinitely without charging him or giving him access to a lawyer or presenting any evidence" (cited in Liptak, Lewis, and Weiser 2002, 20). What particularly galled critics of the government was the argument that it could deny detainees the basic protections of the criminal justice process simply by not charging them with any crime—or by dropping charges already filed, as it did when it reclassified a Qatari student, Ali Saleh Kahlah al-Marri, as an enemy combatant, allowing further interrogation for intelligence purposes but also implicitly threatening other uncooperative terrorist suspects facing criminal charges (Lichtblau 2003a, Lichtblau 2003c). But even if detainees are not technically entitled to the Sixth Amendment right to counsel and may be interrogated for intelligence purposes without counsel, critics contended, they are entitled to due process of law, which includes the right to contest their detention and to have the assistance of counsel in doing so. To the contrary, argued William J. Haynes II, general counsel of the Department of Defense, "[t]here is no due process or any other legal basis, under either domestic or international law, that entitles enemy combatants to legal counsel" (cited in Seelye 2002a, A13).

Late in 2003 the government, which had apparently completed its interrogation of Yaser Esam Hamdi for intelligence purposes, relented to the extent of agreeing to allow him to consult with his attorney—as a matter of policy and discretion, not as a precedent. The government still maintained that enemy combatants had no constitutional right to counsel or to access to the courts, and its move was widely interpreted as part of its effort to persuade the Supreme Court not to hear Hamdi's case (N. Lewis 2003b, A1, A36). That effort was unsuccessful, however, and when José Padilla prevailed in the Court of Appeals for the Second Circuit, it was the government's turn to ask the Supreme Court to take the case and to hear it in conjunction with *Hamdi,* which it agreed to do. Padilla was then allowed to consult with his attorneys; his meetings and Hamdi's were monitored and videotaped by the government (Sontag 2004, 1; Schoenberg 2004, 4).

In the Supreme Court, José Padilla's quest for due process was delayed by a 5–4 ruling on a jurisdictional issue (*Rumsfeld v. Padilla* [2004]). The Court held that, because he had just been transferred to the naval brig at Charleston, his petition for habeas corpus should have been filed with the federal district court in South Carolina rather than New York, so the litigation shifted to that venue—where it would be influenced by a major substantive ruling in favor of Yaser Esam Hamdi.

In that case, although the other eight justices split three ways, only Clarence Thomas agreed with the government's position that as long as it presented some evidence supporting its designation of enemy combatants, it was entitled to detain them indefinitely without access to counsel or opportunity to challenge their detention in court. The polar opposite position was taken by the unlikely pair of Antonin Scalia and John Paul Stevens, who argued that "Hamdi is entitled to a habeas decree requiring his release unless (1) criminal proceedings are promptly brought [presumably for treason], or (2) Congress has suspended the writ of habeas corpus" (*Hamdi v. Rumsfeld* slip opinion 21[2004] [dissenting opinion]). Justices David Souter and Ruth Bader Ginsburg reached essentially the same decision as the court of appeals in the *Padilla* case, arguing that the Authorization to Use Military Force (115 Stat. 224 [2001], a congressional resolution in the wake of 9/11 authorizing the president to use force against all those who participated in the terrorist attacks or aided the perpetrators) did not authorize the president to hold enemy combatants and that "[i]f the Government raises nothing further than the record now shows, the Non-Detention Act entitles Hamdi to be released" (*Hamdi v. Rumsfeld* slip opinion 3[2004] [dissenting opinion]).

The controlling opinion, written by Sandra Day O'Connor and joined by William Rehnquist, Anthony Kennedy, and Stephen Breyer, found that the resolution on force did authorize Hamdi's detention, a holding for which Justice Thomas provided the fifth (majority) vote. (The Court limited this result to enemy combatants who, like Hamdi, had been part of hostile forces engaged in armed conflict against the United States, so the ruling on this point in Padilla's case could be different.) On the other hand, however, the plurality announced that "a citizen-detainee seeking to challenge his classification as an enemy combatant must receive notice of the factual basis for his classification, and a fair opportunity to rebut the Government's factual assertions before a neutral decisionmaker" (*Hamdi v. Rumsfeld* slip opinion 26 [2004] [plurality opinion]). Justices Souter and Ginsburg, who considered Hamdi's detention illegal, concurred with that point to create a majority, so the statement of Hamdi's right to a hearing was also a holding of the Court. What the Court explicitly did not decide, however, was exactly what facets of due process would be required in a detention hearing, and whether a military tribunal rather than a civilian court could be a constitutionally acceptable forum. In any event, the decision did not set Hamdi free; it merely granted him the right to a hearing on the validity of his continued detention.

The plurality declined Hamdi's request to overrule the court of appeals' ruling denying him access to an attorney because the government had subsequently allowed it, but it stated that "[h]e unquestionably has the right to access to counsel in connection with the proceedings on remand" of the case to the lower courts (*Hamdi v. Rumsfeld* slip opinion 32 [2004] [plurality opinion]). Justices Souter and Ginsburg echoed that view and Justice Thomas conceded that if the plurality approach prevailed, enemy combatants would sometimes be entitled to counsel—but not when that would interfere with the gathering of intelligence. Justices Scalia and Stevens believed Hamdi was subject only to criminal prosecution, where the right would pertain without question. Although they did not join two colleagues in reluctantly concurring in a judgment they all deemed too restrictive of liberty, it may be inferred that they, too, supported Hamdi's right to counsel in habeas corpus proceedings.

With nothing like a consensus among its members, the Court made no definitive statement of the scope of the right to counsel for citizen enemy combatants. Hamdi had counsel, so "[n]o further consideration of this issue is necessary at this stage of the case" (*Hamdi v. Rumsfeld* slip opinion 32 [2004] [plurality opinion]). The clear implication was that further issues of counsel would arise, however, and one likely candidate was the matter of the confidentiality of attorney-client meetings. The plurality noted that the government had eventually allowed Hamdi to have unmonitored meetings with his counsel, but as of early July 2004 it had not accorded the same privilege to José Padilla (personal communication from the office of Donna R. Newman, Esq.).

Similar issues arose with respect to foreign enemy combatants detained at Guantánamo Bay, Cuba. In cases brought by persons allowed to act on behalf of various groups of detainees (British, Australian, and Kuwaiti citizens), federal district judge Colleen Kollar-Kotelly ruled in favor of the government, and the U.S. Court of Appeals for the District of Columbia upheld that position, ruling that Guantánamo was not under the sovereignty of the United States, that aliens therefore could not claim constitutional rights there, and thus that no U.S. court had jurisdiction to entertain their claims (*Al Odah v. United States* [DC Cir. 2003]). By the time another federal appeals court had reached the opposite result (*Gherebi v. Bush* [9th Cir. 2003]), the Supreme Court had agreed to decide the issue.

The sole question addressed by the Court was whether or not federal district courts have jurisdiction to hear habeas corpus petitions filed by foreign nationals captured abroad and detained at Guantánamo. In ruling that they do not, the court of appeals in *Al Odah* had relied on *Johnson v. Eisentrager* (1950), a World War II decision that German enemy aliens captured, interrogated, tried by military commission, and imprisoned abroad had no constitutional right to habeas corpus. Now, however, five justices found the *Eisentrager* precedent inapplicable because subsequent legislation had created a statutory right to habeas corpus to which the Guantánamo detainees were entitled (and a sixth concurred in the result on different grounds). The majority thus upheld the jurisdiction of district courts to hear the petitions, while three dissenters vigorously disagreed and feared the opening of the floodgates to petitions from captured enemies around the world. The Court offered no guidance to judges who would weigh enemy combatants' claims of liberty against the government's claims of security and stated that "[w]hether and what further proceedings may become necessary after respondents make their response to the merits of petitioners' claims are matters that we need not address now" (*Rasul v. Bush* slip opinion 17 [2004]).

The decision acknowledged the issue of counsel only to the extent of a footnote affirming that "[p]etitioners' allegations—that, although they have engaged neither in combat nor in acts of terrorism against the United States, they have been held in Executive detention for more than two years in territory subject to the long-term, exclusive jurisdiction and control of the United States, without access to counsel and without being charged with any wrongdoing—unquestionably describe 'custody in violation of the Constitution or laws or treaties of the United States'" (*Rasul v.*

Bush slip opinion 15 n.15 [2004]). In response, the government allowed attorneys to visit Guantánamo clients as a matter of dicretion but filed a brief arguing that detainees were still not entitled to constitutional rights, so that in the aftermath of *Rasul* that issue has not been settled. (N. Lewis 2004c, A18; N. Lewis 2004d, A16).

At the same time, the government also commenced an attempt to minimize the number of federal court hearings. Existing plans to assess the danger and intelligence value of detainees, to determine which could be released, were revised to create Combatant Status Review Tribunals, composed of three military officers, to hear challenges to classification as an enemy combatant and authorize the release of persons found not to merit that designation. Several aspects of the new procedures were subject to legal challenge, particularly a provision for personal representatives—but not legal counsel—to assist detainees in their presentations (Marquis 2004, A11). As in *Hamdi* and *Padilla,* the Court in *Rasul* had taken only the first steps into a new legal realm. The arena of judicial decisionmaking shifted back to the federal district courts, and many important questions had yet to be addressed.

Although the main goal of the U.S. government was to interrogate the Guantánamo prisoners in order to gather intelligence about terrorist activities, it also moved to prosecute some of them for war crimes in military tribunals. On 3 July 2003, President Bush designated six enemy combatants as eligible for that process, and as of July of 2004 nine more had been designated and four had been formally charged. They had military lawyers for such proceedings and could retain private counsel, which the Pentagon tried to help recruit. The National Association of Criminal Defense Lawyers, which had been considering the recruitment of a corps of volunteers to donate their services, instead advised its members that it would be unethical to serve—and thus lend legitimacy to the proceedings—for several reasons: restrictions on the gathering of information; the right of the military to monitor conversations with clients (though only for security purposes and not for use by the prosecution); a requirement to inform military authorities about any indication of future crimes; a requirement to inform the prosecution of all defense evidence a week before trial; and a requirement to pay up to $2,800 for a security clearance, in addition to travel expenses to Guantánamo. (The government subsequently agreed to inform attorneys when conversations with clients were to be monitored.) The American Bar Association similarly criticized the restrictions on civilian counsel, citing also the lack of a requirement that exculpatory evidence be turned over to them and restrictions on external consultation (Seelye 2003, A16; N. Lewis 2003a, 1, 20; Glater 2003, A18; Mintz 2004b, A11; Marquis 2004, A11; Zagaris 2004).

As of July 2004, no tribunal had yet commenced, principally because military defense counsel had taken several legal actions aggressively challenging the fairness of procedures, especially the lack of any review by civilian courts. With those claims pending, the government was clearly trying to balance the goals of having the proceedings seem fair in the eyes of the world and preserving its ability to gather intelligence about terrorism (for surely, the threat of trial before a military tribunal that may impose the death penalty is an inducement to cooperate with interrogators seeking intelligence). As these issues were framed, the debates were as much about security policy as about legal rights.

Issues of Self-Incrimination

The war on terror has thus far entailed fewer consequences for the privilege against self-incrimination, principally because that right does not even come into play unless the government seeks to use the products of coercive interrogation in a criminal trial. (Recall that in the *Chavez* case, discussed earlier in this chapter, the Supreme Court ruled that the Fifth Amendment offers no protection against coercion when a person has not been compelled to be a witness against himself or herself. Due process may offer some protection, but even if enemy combatants manage to challenge techniques of interrogation in military tribunals or civilian courts, the extent of their due process rights is not clear.) When the focus of investigation is not punishment but prevention—that is, when interrogation is designed not to obtain a confession but to elicit intelligence about terrorist activities—then the fundamental question becomes political rather than constitutional: how much and what sort of coercion are we willing to tolerate in order to gain information that may help prevent future terrorist attacks?

Initially, there was very little public knowledge—or curiosity—about the methods being employed to interrogate American citizens Yaser Esam Hamdi and José Padilla and the non-Americans held at Guantánamo and other foreign locations. With respect to the latter, by early 2003 it had been reported that the rules of the game appeared to allow all methods short of outright torture to disorient prisoners and break their will. Techniques of physical and psychological pressure include subjection to uncomfortable positions, nudity, constant light or darkness, temperature extremes, sleep deprivation, and irregular meals and medical attention, in some cases over a period of months (Schmitt 2002; Lichtblau and Liptak 2003; Van Natta 2003).

A year later, this issue came dramatically to the forefront with widespread reports of sexual humiliation, hooding, beating of prisoners, and use of dogs at Abu Ghraib prison and other installations in Iraq and Afghanistan, ostensibly for the purpose of facilitating interrogation. Further revelations concerned the treatment of high-level Al Qaeda prisoners at undisclosed locations, where CIA tactics of interrogation included measures to induce a realistic fear of being drowned, hanged, or shot (Johnston 2004, A8). It was apparently concern about those operations that led U.S. Department of Justice lawyers to draft several memoranda arguing that Al Qaeda and Taliban prisoners were not entitled to the protection of international treaties against torture, defining the concept of torture very narrowly, devising arguments to immunize U.S. agents from a federal statute making torture by a U.S. citizen a crime anywhere in the world, and asserting that the president as commander in chief was not bound by either the treaties or the statute (Lewis and Schmitt 2004, A1; N. Lewis 2004b, A8). When the memoranda became public, the Bush administration disavowed much of their contents, terming the arguments theoretical and denying that they had become the basis of policy (N. Lewis 2004a, A8; Jehl 2004, A7).

As of July 2004, with multiple investigations in progress, it was not at all clear how much of this coercive activity was attributable to low-level malfeasance, how much to inadequate training and supervision, and how much to high-level policy. Only a few low-ranking soldiers had been court-martialed, one CIA civilian contractor had been indicted for assault that resulted in death, and some victims of abuse at Abu Ghraib had filed suit against the prison's civilian contractors under the Alien Tort Claims Act. Many of the techniques of interrogation employed abroad by the military and the CIA would render a confession inadmissible in a normal criminal trial in a civilian court, but whether or not they constitute torture is a different issue, and the extent to which that issue will be adjudicated by civilian courts is unclear. What is clear is that the practical and ethical dilemmas of balancing the claims of security and human rights in the war on terror will confront the political and legal system for years to come.

The rules of procedure for the military tribunals to be held at Guantánamo provide that defendants may decline to testify and stipulate that no adverse inferences may be drawn from that decision. Prior statements made by the accused are admissible, however, and there is no rule requiring suppression of coerced statements. Military attorneys representing those initially charged have not alleged that their clients have been subjected to abusive interrogation, but they have voiced the suspicion that prosecution witnesses may have been so treated. These issues of the admissibility of the products of interrogation are left to the discretion of tribunal judges (U.S. Department of Defense 2002, secs. 5(F), 6(D); Mintz 2004a, A2).

A modest number of criminal prosecutions for terrorism have come before federal courts, and issues of self-incrimination are slowly emerging. Although the Supreme Court has not explicitly ruled on the matter, it seems clear that the privilege applies to aliens who are interrogated and prosecuted in the United States. The *Eisentrager* precedent of 1950 has stood for the general proposition that aliens subjected to detention and trial by military commission abroad may not assert U.S. constitutional rights, such as the privilege against self-incrimination, in federal courts. Since *Rasul* was decided on statutory rather than constitutional grounds, that may well continue to be the case, although the concurrence in *Rasul* argued, and the majority opinion hinted, that access to rights could depend on the circumstances of the detention. This issue goes to the heart of the current controversy over whether Guantánamo defendants will be entitled to civilian court review of convictions. Location may also matter, as Guantánamo has been found within the jurisdiction of federal courts but other foreign locales may not be. Aliens tried by military tribunal abroad could also be given some form of statutory protection against self-incrimination, and Department of Defense regulations customarily accord some rights to the alien accused, such as the partial privilege accorded Guantánamo defendants.

The question of the privilege against self-incrimination for aliens interrogated by American agents abroad but prosecuted in the United States is of much more recent vintage. In the first ruling on this issue—with respect to two persons accused of involvement in the bombings of American embassies in Kenya and Tanzania in 1998—federal district judge Leonard B. Sand held that the privilege does apply in those circumstances (*United States v. Bin Laden* [2001]). Judge Sand reasoned that a constitutional violation occurs at the point at which compelled statements are introduced at trial in the United States, and that the Fifth Amendment states that "no person" shall be subject to such compulsion. Because the Fifth Amendment does apply, the judge continued, aliens interrogated by American agents abroad are also entitled to *Miranda* warnings. This ruling was not appealed, but it is not binding on other courts, so the issue awaits definitive resolution.

The privilege against self-incrimination and *Miranda* rights apply to U.S. citizens interrogated by U.S. agents abroad and tried in the United States, but the kinds of problems that can arise are illustrated by the inconclusive case of John Walker Lindh, the young American who was captured among the Taliban soldiers in Afghanistan. Lindh was questioned first by army interrogators who were seeking intelligence and did not inform him of his rights, and then by an FBI agent seeking information for a criminal prosecution. In the meantime he was bound naked to a stretcher, kept cold and hungry in a windowless shipping container, and denied medical care for a bullet wound. The FBI agent informed him of his rights but made clear that no lawyers were available in Afghanistan, a point he repeated when Lindh asked to consult one. He did not inform Lindh that his father had retained an attorney who was trying to see him, or pass along his father's message, which had been sent to the Red Cross at his location. The Justice Department's Professional Responsibility Advisory Office, which advises departmental attorneys on ethical issues, had concluded that the FBI could not interrogate Lindh in the absence of a defense attorney, but the department apparently relied on *Moran v. Burbine,* in which the Supreme Court had ruled that interrogators do not have to inform a suspect that a lawyer has been retained on his behalf, and that a waiver of *Miranda* rights may be valid even if the suspect is unaware of that information (see the discussion of assertion and waiver of rights in the section on implementation of *Miranda* in Chapter 5).

Under these circumstances, Lindh waived his rights and made incriminating statements, apparently to avoid being returned to the conditions of physical privation in which he had been kept.

Before his lawyer was able to see him, the government indicted Lindh on multiple charges of aiding and supporting the Taliban and Al Qaeda and of conspiring to kill Americans overseas. The charges carried a possible penalty of life in prison, and Attorney General John Ashcroft, who announced the indictment in a press conference, indicated the possibility of an additional charge of treason that would carry the death penalty (Brill 2003, passim; Lichtblau 2003b, A15).

Defense attorneys were prepared to move for suppression of Lindh's statements—on which the indictment had been based—on the grounds that his *Edwards* right not to be questioned further after requesting a lawyer had been violated, his waiver was not intelligent and voluntary, and his confession had been coerced (Darmer 2002, 242, 244 n.20. See the discussion of assertion and waiver of rights in the section on implementation of *Miranda* in Chapter 5.). The possibility of judicial rulings on the admissibility of Lindh's statements was foreclosed, however, when the case was resolved by a plea bargain in which Lindh pleaded guilty to lesser offenses carrying a maximum sentence of twenty years. The government apparently concluded that Lindh could not be portrayed as a major terrorist and may have been worried about issues of admissibility (and also about the credibility of the FBI agent's reports of his interrogation). Lindh avoided the possibility of a life sentence, and his lawyer sensed antagonism on the part of the trial judge and had to be concerned also about the conservative appeals court in the Fourth Circuit—the same court that would decide the *Hamdi* case (Brill 2003, passim; N. Lewis 2002, A1). Many questions thus went unanswered, including the point at which Lindh was entitled to *Miranda* rights and to a lawyer, and the effect of the context of the war against terror on the judicial assessment of the voluntariness of waivers and confessions.

The government interrogated Lindh in order to gain information both to combat terrorism and to support a criminal prosecution. The compatibility of those goals, and the extent to which the government will attempt to pursue them simultaneously, remain issues. The courts have barely begun to grapple with these problems, and the legal rights of various categories of the accused, in either civilian courts or military tribunals, are not yet clear. As with other questions we have explored, answers will be developed through a gradual process in which discrete issues are decided, patterns become apparent, and—one hopes—coherent doctrine ultimately emerges.

The Long View

Our story began in an era in England and on the European continent when the accused were not permitted the assistance of counsel in serious cases and could be required to answer any questions put to them. In the United States several centuries later, the right to counsel and privilege against self-incrimination are entrenched as constitutional rights and disagreements relate only to their scope and limitations—though such disagreements can be intense.

Under the U.S. Constitution, the right to counsel has always been honored in principle; defendants have an unchallenged right to retain an attorney. The real issues have concerned honoring the right in practice for those who cannot afford an attorney or face other impediments. *Powell v. Alabama* brought that problem into stark relief and effectively guaranteed counsel in capital cases, and the Supreme Court took a cautious step further in *Betts v. Brady* with a guarantee of representation for defendants with "special circumstances." The *Gideon* and *Argersinger* decisions, mandating provision of counsel to all indigent defendants charged with nonpetty offenses and applying that Sixth Amendment right against the states, were a pivotal development in which the Court acted on the growing consensus that there is no fundamental conflict between the interests of society and the interests of the individual with respect to the competent representation of the accused at trial. Our continuing twin challenges are to find the means to provide adequate criminal defense services and to enforce standards of professional competence that ensure the effective assistance of counsel. The issue of counsel at pretrial proceedings, especially police interrogation, has been more contentious, principally because at this stage the role of counsel may be seen to impede rather than further the administration of justice. The right to counsel at this point is, however, one means to forestall police abuse. In fact, the typical defendant waives counsel during interrogation, receives counsel thereafter, and eventually negotiates a plea of guilty. There is a rough balance here.

There is considerably less consensus about the very concept of the privilege against self-incrimination. Earlier in our history, the privilege related to legal compulsion imposed in court or a similar forum, as, for example, testimony required upon pain of contempt, while the problem of inculpatory statements coerced by police interrogation raised issues of the right to due process of law. In *Bram v. United States* the Supreme Court declared the privilege applicable to issues of confession in federal cases, but the due process approach in fact continued to hold sway and was the only standard available for state cases. The Court applied that standard to the states for the first time in *Brown v. Mississippi* and gradually narrowed the range of acceptable coercion in cases such as *Chambers, Ashcraft,* and *Spano.* It applied the self-incrimination clause against the states in *Malloy v. Hogan,* a case involving traditional legal compulsion, and then in *Miranda v. Arizona* integrated the law of confessions (developed as a matter of due process) into the law of self-incrimination. Issues related to interrogation arouse the most public controversy and engender the most political and scholarly debate.

We have come a long way since *Brown v. Mississippi,* and the use of brute force to extract confessions is emphatically rejected by commentators on all sides of the issue. Beyond that point, however, opinions begin to diverge, and none of the rationales for the privilege adequately explains it in practice (see the discussion of the privilege in Chapter 1). It appeared at the time of the *Boyd* decision in 1886 that the Court considered the core of the privilege to be the protection of privacy, but the exceptions that have been carved out since—corporate records, required records, nontestimonial evidence, private papers—belie that notion, as does compulsion with less than transactional immunity. As one critic has recently observed,

> to the extent that the Court has chipped away at its own broad self-incrimination doctrines, it has articulated few guiding principles capable of explaining the law of self-incrimination. Thus, the ad hoc limitations on self-incrimination clause jurisprudence [yield a] self-incrimination doctrine . . . characterized by an inconsistent combination of difficult-to-justify broad rules and a hodgepodge of miscellaneous exceptions. Consider, for example, that physical evidence is compellable regardless of any claims of constitutional privilege [*Schmerber v. California*]. Except when it is the fruit of privileged testimony [*Kastigar v. United States*]. Unless that testimony took place in the station house rather than the court room [*Oregon v. Elstad*]. Records a person is required by the government to keep are not protected by the privilege [*Shapiro v. United States*]. Unless the government's records requirement is aimed at precisely those activities that are least defensible [*Marchetti v. United States*]. Suspects are told they have a right to stop police questioning [*Miranda v. Arizona*]. Yet the very rules that require such a warning give police a strong incentive to violate that usually remedy-less "right" [either because they seek information that will be useful even if inadmissible, or because they can take advantage of exceptions to the application of the exclusionary rule—*Harris v. New York, Oregon v. Hass, Michigan v. Tucker, Oregon v. Elstad, New York v. Quarles, United States v. Patane*]. (Witt 1999, 908–909)

The consensus against the use of force reflects consensus on a rationale of the protection of persons against abuses of power by police and other officials, but there is wide disagreement on what procedures, rules, and tactics short of force constitute abuse or basic unfairness, particularly when weighed against other values—most fundamentally, the search for the truth in criminal investigations. Eliciting confessions from suspects is still widely viewed as one of the most effective ways to ferret out the truth and gain convictions of the guilty, a reality well illustrated by police adaptation of the techniques of interrogation in the wake of *Miranda.* The arguments are essentially about the extent to which police falsehood and deception are permissible, and the extent to which incriminating statements should be inadmissible when police break the rules. That situation bespeaks great progress beyond an era in which police commonly employed brute force and were not effectively controlled by rules at all.

Fundamental agreement on the proper scope of the privilege against self-incrimination, however, continues to elude us. For example, Akhil Reed Amar, a leading scholar who views the ensuring of the reliability of evidence as the core principle of the privilege, would narrow it (and more fully integrate the process of interrogation into the traditional concept of legal compulsion) by instituting pretrial interrogations performed by a magistrate. Suspects would be required to answer all questions on pain of contempt; nothing they said could be used against them, but fruits of their statements, such as physical evidence or third-party testimony derived from their admissions, could be. Unlike a statement itself, such fruits of a statement could not be rendered untrustworthy by the means used to obtain them. The result, Amar argues, would be to reduce police abuses while enhancing the acquisition and use of reliable evidence (Amar 1997, 47–48, 70, 76, 87).

Amar's proposal builds on the Supreme Court's interpretation of the term "to be a witness" as limited to the process of giving testimony, and on its progressive denigration of *Boyd v. United States* and its rationale of the protection of privacy. Justices Clarence Thomas and Antonin Scalia, however, as we noted in discussing *United States v. Hubbell* in Chapter 4, argue that the eighteenth-century understanding of the concept of being a witness was broader: giving or furnishing evidence. They are prepared to reinstate *Boyd's* protection of private papers—physical evidence—and their approach would also provide an opening to question the Court's refusal in *Schmerber v. California* to extend the protection of the privilege to nontestimonial evidence—a refusal that Amar cites as being consistent with his proposal. In short, Amar relies on a rationale of ensuring reliability to advocate narrowing the privilege and further restricting its applicability to physical evidence, while Thomas and Scalia rely on a rationale of protection of privacy to advocate restoring prior breadth to the privilege and increasing its applicability to physical evidence. We may expect these sorts of basic disagreement to persist, for we have yet to achieve a settled interpretation of the history and philosophy of the privilege against self-incrimination.

In the final analysis, of course, virtually nothing in American constitutional law is ever finally settled. The conditions and problems of society change, as do the perceptions and values of those who observe and respond. The Supreme Court is by no means the only significant shaper of the law in practice—as the experience with *Miranda* certainly illustrates. The Court has, however, played the leading role in shaping far-reaching change in the right to counsel and privilege against self-incrimination over more than two centuries. We may confidently expect that process to continue.

References

Alschuler, Albert W. 1997. "Constraint and Confession." *Denver University Law Review.* 74:957–978.

Amar, Akhil Reed. 1997. *The Constitution and Criminal Procedure: First Principles.* New Haven, CT: Yale University Press.

American Bar Association. 2003. *Justice Cut Short: New Reports Show That "Conveyor Belt Justice" Hurts Children.* News release and state reports available online at <http://www.manningmedia.net/Clients/ABA/ABA274/index.htm>.

Arenella, Peter. 1997. "*Miranda* Stories." *Harvard Journal of Law and Public Policy* 20:375–387.

Baca, Maria Elena. 2001. "O'Connor Critical of Death Penalty." *Minneapolis Star Tribune* (3 July, 1A, Metro edition).

Bernhard, Adele. 2001. Effective Assistance of Counsel. Chap. 11 in *Wrongly Convicted: Perspectives on Failed Justice,* edited by Saundra D. Westervelt and John A. Humphrey. New Brunswick, NJ: Rutgers University Press.

Bernstein, Nina. 2004. "Lawyers Sue over Secret Jail Recordings." *New York Times* (2 July, B1, late edition).

Brill, Steven. 2003. *After: How America Confronted the September 12 Era.* New York: Simon and Schuster.

Butterfield, Fox. 2001. "Texas Nears Creation of State Public Defender System." *New York Times* (6 April, A14, late edition).

Cassell, Paul G. 1996. "*Miranda's* Social Costs: An Empirical Reassessment." *Northwestern University Law Review* 90:387–499.

———. 1998. "Protecting the Innocent from False Confessions and Lost Confessions—and from *Miranda.*" *Journal of Criminal Law and Criminology* 88:497–556.

Cassell, Paul G., and Bret S. Hayman. 1996. "Police Interrogation in the 1990s: An Empirical Study of the Effects of *Miranda.*" *UCLA Law Review* 43:839–931.

Cassell, Paul G., and Richard Fowles. 1998. "Handcuffing the Cops? A Thirty-Year Perspective on *Miranda's* Harmful Effects on Law Enforcement." *Stanford Law Review* 50:1055–1145.

Cole, David, and James X. Dempsey. 2002. *Terrorism and the Constitution: Sacrificing Civil Liberties in the Name of National Security.* New York: The New Press.

Darmer, M. K. B. 2002. "Lessons From the *Lindh* Case: Public Safety and the Fifth Amendment." *Brooklyn Law Review* 68:241–287.

DeFrances, Carol J. 2001. *State-Funded Indigent Defense Services, 1999.* A U.S. Department of Justice Bureau of Justice Statistics Special Report, available online at <http://www.ojp.usdoj.gov/bjs/abstract/sfids99.htm>.

Equal Justice Center and Texas Defender Service. 2003. *Texas Death Penalty Practices: Quality of Regional Standards and County Plans Governing Indigent Defense in Capital Cases,* 2d ed. Available online at <http://equaljusticecenter.org>.

Garcia, Alfredo. 2002. *The Fifth Amendment: A Comprehensive Approach.* Westport, CT: Greenwood Press.

Gearan, Anne. 2001. "Supreme Court Justice Backs Proposed Death Penalty Freeze." *The Record* (Bergen County, NJ, 10 April, A18).

Geimer, William S. 1995. "A Decade of *Strickland's* Tin Horn: Doctrinal and Practical Undermining of the Right to Counsel." *William and Mary Bill of Rights Journal* 4:91–178.

Glater, Jonathan D. 2003. "A.B.A. Urges Wider Rights in Cases Tried By Tribunals." *New York Times* (13 August, A18, late edition).

Goldman, Erica Lehrer. 2002. "Judge's Ruling on Representation in *Burdine* Strikes Some as Ironic." *Texas Lawyer* (22 July, 1).

Harlow, Caroline Wolf. 2000. *Defense Counsel in Criminal Cases.* A U.S. Department of Justice Bureau of Justice Statistics Special Report, available online at <http://www.ojp.usdoj.gov/bjs/id.htm>.

Hines, Crystal Nix. 2001. "Lack of Lawyers Hinders Appeals in Capital Cases." *New York Times* (5 July, A1, late edition).

Jehl, Douglas. 2004. "U.S. Rules on Prisoners Seen as a Back and Forth of Mixed Messages to G.I.s." *New York Times* (22 June, A7, late edition).

Johnston, David. 2004. "Uncertainty about Interrogation Rules Seen as Slowing the Hunt for Information on Terrorists." *New York Times* (28 June, A8, late edition).

Lefstein, Norman. 1996. "Reform of Defense Representation in Capital Cases: The Indiana Experience and Its Implications for the Nation." *Indiana Law Review* 29:495–533.

Leo, Richard A. 1992. "From Coercion to Deception: The Changing Nature of Police Interrogation in America." *Crime, Law and Social Change* 18:35–59.

———. 1996a. "The Impact of *Miranda* Revisited." *Journal of Criminal Law and Criminology* 86:621–692.

———. 1996b. "*Miranda's* Revenge: Police Interrogation as a Confidence Game." *Law and Society Review* 30:259–288.

———. 1998. *Miranda* and the Problem of False Confessions. Chap. 20 in *The* Miranda *Debate: Law, Justice, and Policing,* edited by Richard A. Leo and George C. Thomas III. Boston: Northeastern University Press.

———. 2001. False Confessions: Causes, Consequences, and Solutions. Chap. 2 in *Wrongly Convicted,* edited by Saundra D. Westervelt and John A. Humphrey. New Brunswick, NJ: Rutgers University Press.

Leo, Richard A., and George C. Thomas III, eds. 1998. *The* Miranda *Debate: Law, Justice, and Policing.* Boston: Northeastern University Press.

Leone, Richard C., and Greg Anrig Jr., eds. 2003. *The War on Our Freedoms: Civil Liberties in an Age of Terrorism.* New York: The Century Foundation.

Lewis, Anthony. 2003. Security and Liberty: Preserving the Values of Freedom. Chap. 2 in *The War on Our Freedoms: Civil Liberties in an Age of Terrorism,* edited by Richard C. Leone and Greg Anrig Jr. New York: The Century Foundation.

Lewis, Neil A. 2002. "Traces of Terror: The Captive." *New York Times* (16 July, A1, late edition).

———. 2003a. "Rules for Terror Tribunals May Deter Lawyers." *New York Times* (13 July, 1, early edition).

———. 2003b. "Sudden Shift on Detainee." *New York Times* (4 December, A1, late edition).

———. 2004a. "Ashcroft Says the White House Never Authorized Tactics Breaking Laws on Torture." *New York Times* (9 June, A8, late edition).

———. 2004b. "Documents Build a Case for Working Outside the Laws in Interrogations." *New York Times* (9 June, A8, late edition).

———. 2004c. "New Fight on Guantánamo Rights." *New York Times* (31 July, A18, late edition).

———. 2004d. "U.S. Allows Lawyers to Meet Detainees." *New York Times* (3 July, A16, late edition).

Lewis, Neil A., and Eric Schmitt. 2004. "Lawyers Decided Bans on Torture Didn't Bind Bush." *New York Times* (8 June, A1, late edition).

Lichtblau, Eric. 2003a. "Bush Declares Student an Enemy Combatant." *New York Times* (24 June, A15, late edition).

———. 2003b. "Dispute over Legal Advice Costs a Job and Complicates a Nomination." *New York Times* (22 May, A15, late edition).

———. 2003c. "Enemy Combatant Decision Marks Change, Officials Say." *New York Times* (25 June, A14, late edition).

Lichtblau, Eric, and Adam Liptak. 2003. "Questioning of Accused Expected to be Humane, Legal and Aggressive." *New York Times* (4 March, A13, late edition).

Liebman, James, Jeffrey Fagan, and Valerie West. 2000. "A Broken System: Error Rates in Capital Cases, 1973–1995." A study commissioned by the U.S. Senate Judiciary Committee, available online at <http://justice.policy.net/proactive/newsroom/release.vtml?id=18200>.

Liptak, Adam. 2004. "Taping of Interrogations Is Praised by Police." *New York Times* (13 June, 35, early edition).

Liptak, Adam, Neil A. Lewis, and Benjamin Weiser. 2002. "After September 11, a Legal Battle on the Limits of Civil Liberty." *New York Times* (4 August, 1, early edition).

Marquis, Christopher. 2004. "Pentagon Will Permit Captives at Cuba Base to Appeal Status." *New York Times* (8 July, A1, late edition).

Mintz, John. 2004a. "Interrogations Are Criticized; Lawyers Fault Tactics Used on Witnesses against Detainees." *Washington Post* (9 June, A2, final edition).

———. 2004b. "Pentagon to Alter Military Tribunal Rules; U.S. to Tell Attorneys When Listening In on Talks with Guantánamo Clients." *Washington Post* (6 February, A11, final edition).

Oliphant, Jim. 2002. "How Bad Is Bad? The Justices on Trial Lawyers." *Legal Times* (1 July, 10).

Pierre, Robert E. 2003. "Right to an Attorney Comes at a Price; Minnesota Law Requiring Fees for Public Defenders Is Challenged." *Washington Post* (20 October, A1, final edition).

Schmitt, Eric. 2002. "There Are Ways to Make Them Talk." *New York Times* (16 June, sec. 4, p. 1, late edition).

Schoenberg, Tom. 2004. "A First for Everything." *Legal Times* (9 February, 4).

Schulhofer, Stephen J. 1996a. "*Miranda* and Clearance Rates." *Northwestern University Law Review* 91:278–294.

———. 1996b. "*Miranda's* Practical Effect: Substantial Benefits and Vanishingly Small Social Costs." *Northwestern University Law Review* 90:500–563.

———. 1997. "Bashing *Miranda* Is Unjustified—And Harmful." *Harvard Journal of Law and Public Policy* 20:347–373.

Seelye, Katharine Q. 2002a. "Court to Hear Arguments in Groundbreaking Case of U.S. Citizen Seized with Taliban." *New York Times* (28 October, A13, late edition).

———. 2002b. "Judge Questions Detention of American in War Case." *New York Times* (14 August, A19, late edition).

———. 2002c. "Judge Suspends Proceedings in Standoff on War Prisoner." *New York Times* (8 August, A22, late edition).

———. 2003. "U.S. Seeking Guantánamo Defense Staff." *New York Times* (23 May, A16, late edition).

Shenon, Philip. 2002. "Appeals Court Keeps Detainee and His Lawyer Apart." *New York Times* (13 July, A8, late edition).

Simon, David. 1991. *Homicide: A Year on the Killing Streets.* Boston: Houghton Mifflin.

Sontag, Deborah. 2004. "Terror Suspect's Path from Streets to Brig." *New York Times* 25 April, 1, early edition).

Thomas, George C., III. 1996. "Plain Talk About the *Miranda* Empirical Debate: A 'Steady-State' Theory of Confessions." *UCLA Law Review* 33:933–959.

U.S. Department of Defense. 2002. *Military Commission Order No. 1.* Available online at <http://www.defenselink.mil/news/Mar2002/d20020321ord.pdf.>

U.S. Department of Justice, Office of the Inspector General. 2003a. *The September 11 Detainees: A Review of the Treatment of Aliens Held on Immigration Charges in Connection with the Investigation of the September 11 Attacks.* June. A Special Report available online at <http://www.usdoj.gov:80/oig/special/0306/index.htm>.

———. 2003b. *Supplemental Report on September 11 Detainees' Allegations of Abuse at the Metropolitan Detention Center in Brooklyn, New York.* December. A Special Report available online at <http://www.usdoj.gov:80/oig/special/0312/index.htm>.

Van Natta, Don, Jr. 2003. "Questioning Terror Suspects in a Dark and Surreal World." *New York Times* (9 March, 1, early edition).

Wedgwood, Ruth. 2003. "The Rule of Law and the War on Terror." *New York Times* (23 December, A27, late edition).

Weiser, Benjamin. 2002a. "'Enemy Combatant' Fights to Obtain Counsel." *New York Times* (30 October, A17, late edition).

———. 2002b. "Judge Says Man Can Meet with Lawyer to Challenge Detention as Enemy Plotter." *New York Times* (5 December, A24, late edition).

———. 2003. "U.S. Asks Judge to Deny Terror Suspect Access to Lawyer, Saying It Could Harm Interrogation." *New York Times* (10 January, A11, late edition).

Westervelt, Saundra D., and John A. Humphrey, eds. 2001. *Wrongly Convicted: Perspectives on Failed Justice.* New Brunswick, NJ: Rutgers University Press.

White, Welsh S. 2001. Miranda's *Waning Protections.* Ann Arbor: University of Michigan Press.

Witt, John Fabian. 1999. "Making the Fifth: The Constitutionalization of American Self-Incrimination Doctrine, 1791–1903." *Texas Law Review* 77: 825–922.

Zagaris, Bruce. 2004. "U.S. Names More Guantánamo Detainees for Trial, Changes Rules, and Allows First Attorney Meeting for Hamdi." *International Enforcement Law Reporter* 20, No. 4: unpaginated.

7

Key People, Cases, and Events

Adams v. Maryland (1954)

Held that in order to compel self-incriminating testimony, Congress may grant immunity that applies in state as well as federal courts.

Adams v. United States ex rel. McCann (1942)

Affirmed that a defendant has the right to waive his or her constitutional right to the assistance of counsel.

Adamson v. California (1947)

Held that the Fifth Amendment privilege against self-incrimination did not apply to the states. Overruled by *Malloy v. Hogan.*

Al Odah v. United States (2003)

Court of appeals decision holding that enemy combatants held at Guantánamo, Cuba, could not contest their detention in any American court. Overruled by *Rasul v. Bush.*

Alabama v. Shelton **(2002)**

Held that a state cannot impose a suspended sentence of imprisonment unless the defendant was represented by counsel at trial or waived the right to counsel.

Albertson v. Subversive Activities Control Board **(1965)**

Held that an order, pursuant to a federal statute, requiring members of the Communist Party and other communist organizations to register as such and submit a form providing other information violated the privilege against self-incrimination.

Allen v. Illinois **(1986)**

Held that compelled statements may be used in a civil proceeding for involuntary commitment, because the privilege against self-incrimination may be asserted only to prevent use of information in criminal proceedings.

Andresen v. Maryland **(1976)**

Held that the privilege against self-incrimination does not prevent the government from acquiring a person's business records by lawful search and seizure and using them against him.

Apprendi v. New Jersey **(2000)**

Held that due process requires that factors that could extend a sentence beyond the statutory maximum must be charged in the indictment and proved beyond a reasonable doubt.

Argersinger v. Hamlin **(1972)**

Held that no person may be imprisoned for any offense, however petty, unless he or she was represented by counsel at trial or waived the right to counsel.

Arizona v. Fulminante (1991)

Held that admission of an involuntary confession into evidence may be harmless error.

Arizona v. Mauro (1987)

Held that after a suspect had been given *Miranda* warnings and had declined to answer questions, police could openly monitor his conversation with his wife and use his incriminating statements against him.

Arizona v. Roberson (1988)

Held that once the *Miranda* right to counsel has been invoked, police may not initiate interrogation in the absence of counsel for any offense.

Ashcraft v. Tennessee (1944)

Characterized intensive interrogation for thirty-six hours as inherently coercive and held that use of a confession gained thereby violated due process of law.

Baldwin v. New York (1970)

Held that the right to trial by jury applies only in cases in which the offense carries a prison sentence of more than six months.

Baltimore City Department of Social Services v. Bouknight (1990)

Held that a court order to a mother to produce a child thought to be the victim of abuse did not violate her privilege against self-incrimination because it was in furtherance of a compelling regulatory purpose, and because she was under the obligations of a legal custodian.

***Barron v. Baltimore* (1833)**

Held that the provisions of the Bill of Rights were not applicable to the states. Superseded by a series of incorporation cases under the Fourteenth Amendment.

***Baxter v. Palmigiano* (1976)**

Held that inmates do not have a right to retained or appointed counsel in prison disciplinary proceedings, even when the conduct charged could also be prosecuted as a crime, and that prison officials may draw adverse inferences from inmates' decisions not to testify on their own behalf in such proceedings.

***Beckwith v. United States* (1976)**

Held that a suspect who is the focus of an investigation but is questioned in his or her home and office is not in custody and therefore not entitled to *Miranda* warnings prior to interrogation.

***Bell v. Cone* (2002)**

Held that, in claims of ineffective assistance of counsel, the standard of *United States v. Cronic* applies when an attorney has *entirely* failed to subject the prosecution case to meaningful adversarial testing, but that the standard of *Strickland v. Washington* applies when the claim is only that counsel failed at specific points.

***Bellis v. United States* (1974)**

Held that a small business partnership has no privilege against self-incrimination, and that the custodian of partnership records may be compelled to produce them even if they incriminate him or her personally.

Berkemer v. McCarty (1984)

Held that *Miranda v. Arizona* applies to misdemeanors as well as to felonies but that warnings are not required for traffic stops prior to the point at which the suspect is formally taken into custody.

Berry v. City of Cincinnati (1973)

Made the decision in *Argersinger v. Hamlin* retroactive.

Betts v. Brady (1942)

Held that a state court's failure to appoint counsel for an indigent defendant was a violation of due process only if it resulted in a trial that was, under the circumstances, fundamentally unfair. Overruled by *Gideon v. Wainwright.*

Black, Hugo L. (1886–1971)

A U.S. senator and important supporter of the New Deal, and associate justice of the Supreme Court, 1937–1971. Black's ascension to the Court was marred by a furor over his brief membership in the Ku Klux Klan, but he became one of the most influential civil libertarians ever to serve on the high court. He was the author of important decisions on right to counsel in *Johnson v. Zerbst* and *Gideon v. Wainwright,* and on coerced confession in *Chambers v. Florida* and *Ashcraft v. Tennessee.* Black was also a staunch supporter of First Amendment and other freedoms, as long as he could find clear support for them in constitutional text.

Blau v. United States (1950)

Held that the privilege against self-incrimination protects a grand jury witness from answering questions about associations with the Communist Party because of the threat of prosecution under the Smith Act.

***Bounds v. Smith* (1977)**

Held that state prison authorities must provide prisoners with adequate law libraries or adequate assistance from persons trained in the law to help them file legal papers.

***Boyd v. United States* (1886)**

Held that both the self-incrimination clause of the Fifth Amendment and the search and seizure clause of the Fourth Amendment prohibited the government from requiring an individual to produce private papers to be used as evidence against him. Superseded by a series of cases.

***Brady v. United States* (1970)**

Held that the inducements to plead guilty inherent in plea bargaining do not constitute compulsion in violation of the privilege against self-incrimination.

***Bram v. United States* (1897)**

Held that in federal trials the standard for admissibility of pretrial confessions claimed to have been involuntary is the self-incrimination clause of the Fifth Amendment (but this approach was not immediately followed).

***Braswell v. United States* (1988)**

Applied the rule that the custodian of organizational records may be compelled to produce them even if they incriminate him or her personally and he or she is the president and sole shareholder of the corporation.

Brennan, William J. (1906–1997)

A pragmatic liberal associate justice of the Supreme Court, 1956–1990, Brennan wrote the decisions in *Malloy v. Hogan* but also *Schmerber v. California;* he wrote strong dissents in *Harris v. New York* and *Oregon v. Elstad.* Brennan also wrote important decisions for the Court in the areas of legislative apportionment, freedom of expression, and equality for women and the poor.

***Brewer v. Williams* (1977)**

Overturned a murder conviction based on evidence that was inadmissible because police had obtained it from the defendant by interrogating him in the absence of counsel, when that right had attached and not been waived. See also *Nix v. Williams.*

***Brown v. Allen* (1953)**

Held that state use of a confession made during an interrogation in the absence of counsel did not necessarily violate due process, even if the accused would be entitled to an attorney at trial under the rule of *Betts v. Brady.* Superseded by *Miranda v. Arizona.*

***Brown v. Illinois* (1975)**

Held that a confession that is inadmissible as the product of an illegal arrest is not saved by the fact that *Miranda* warnings were given.

***Brown v. Mississippi* (1936)**

Held that even though the privilege against self-incrimination did not (at that time) apply to the states, a conviction based on confessions extorted by torture was a denial of due process of law.

***Brown v. United States* (1958)**

Affirmed that a witness who testifies voluntarily may not invoke the privilege against self-incrimination on cross-examination, but that a witness who testifies under compulsion may invoke the privilege at any point that presents a risk of incrimination.

***Brown v. Walker* (1896)**

Held that a witness could be compelled to incriminate himself or herself in return for a grant of transactional immunity.

***Bruno v. United States* (1939)**

Held that the federal statute providing that a defendant's failure to testify shall not create a presumption against him or her creates a right, upon request, to have the judge instruct the jury to that effect.

***Burdine v. Johnson* (2001)**

Court of appeals decision upholding a claim of ineffective assistance of counsel when the defense attorney had slept repeatedly during a murder trial; in *Cockrell v. Burdine* the Supreme Court declined to review.

***Burgett v. Texas* (1967)**

Made clear that the decision in *Gideon v. Wainwright* applied retroactively.

***California v. Beheler* (1983)**

Held that the question of whether a suspect is entitled to *Miranda* warnings depends not on the location of the detention but on whether the suspect is under formal arrest or a comparable restraint.

California v. Byers (1971)

Ruled that a requirement that drivers involved in accidents stop and provide their names and addresses furthered a civil regulatory purpose of ensuring financial responsibility for damages and did not violate the privilege against self-incrimination.

California v. Prysock (1981)

Held that *Miranda* warnings do not have to take the precise form spelled out in that case as long as they fully inform suspects of their rights.

Carnley v. Cochran (1962)

Held that the attachment of the Sixth Amendment right to counsel is not dependent upon a request by the defendant.

Carter v. Kentucky (1981)

Held that the privilege against self-incrimination creates a right of a defendant, upon request, to have the judge instruct the jury not to draw adverse inferences from his or her exercise of the right not to testify.

Chambers v. Florida (1940)

Held that the use at state trial of confessions based on marathon interrogation under intimidating circumstances violated the right to due process.

Chandler v. Fretag (1954)

Held that due process of law requires that a defendant be given a reasonable opportunity to retain and consult with counsel.

Chapman v. California (1967)

Held that the constitutional standard of harmless error is that the error was harmless beyond a reasonable doubt.

Chavez v. Martinez (2003)

Held that a coercive interrogation does not violate the self-incrimination clause unless the compelled statements are used against the defendant in a criminal prosecution (but that there may be a violation of the due process clause).

Cockrell v. Burdine (2002)

Refused to review a court of appeals decision in *Burdine v. Johnson,* upholding a claim of ineffective assistance of counsel when the defense attorney had slept repeatedly during a murder trial.

Coleman v. Alabama (1970)

Held that when proceedings may materially affect the conduct of the trial, a preliminary hearing is a critical stage of the prosecution at which an accused person has a right to counsel.

Colorado v. Connelly (1986)

Held that a confession is involuntary only when the compulsion to confess is the product of police coercion, and not some other factor such as mental illness.

Colorado v. Spring (1987)

Held that a waiver of the privilege against self-incrimination is not invalid simply because the police fail to advise a suspect under arrest for one crime that they intend to interrogate him about another crime as well.

Connecticut v. Barrett (1987)

Held that when a suspect who has been given *Miranda* warnings declines to make a written statement until counsel is present but freely agrees to make an oral statement in the meantime, such oral statement is admissible at trial.

Couch v. United States (1973)

Held that an accused person's privilege against self-incrimination is not violated by enforcement of a summons requiring her accountant to produce material that would potentially incriminate her, because the privilege protects against being compelled to incriminate oneself, not against the revelation of incriminating information.

Counselman v. Hitchcock (1892)

Held that the privilege against self-incrimination could be claimed in a grand jury hearing and could be overcome only by a grant of transactional immunity. Superseded in the latter respect by *Kastigar v. United States.*

Crooker v. California (1958)

Held that state use of a confession made during an interrogation in which a suspect was denied a request to consult his own attorney did not necessarily violate due process. Overruled by *Escobedo v. Illinois* and *Miranda v. Arizona.*

Curcio v. United States (1957)

Held that although the custodian of organizational records may be compelled to produce them even if they incriminate him or her, he or she may not be compelled to answer questions about them.

Cuyler v. Sullivan (1980)

Made clear that a claim of ineffective assistance of counsel can be made with respect to a retained as well as an appointed attorney.

Davis v. United States (1994)

Held that during a custodial interrogation, police are not required to honor a request for counsel unless it is unambiguous.

Dickerson v. United States (2000)

Reaffirmed that *Miranda* warnings are constitutional rights and held that a federal statute could not replace them as the standard of admissibility for confessions in federal courts.

Doe v. United States (1988)

Held that the privilege against self-incrimination does not prohibit the government from compelling a person to sign a document authorizing disclosure of records of foreign bank accounts, when the document does not acknowledge the identity of, control over, or even existence of any such accounts, because the signature does not communicate any information to the government.

Douglas v. California (1963)

Held that the right to counsel entitles indigent defendants to appointed counsel in appeals of right in state courts.

Doyle v. Ohio (1976)

Held that once suspects have been arrested and assured of their right to silence through *Miranda* warnings, use of their subsequent silence to impeach their testimony at trial violates due process of law.

Duckworth v. Eagan (1989)

Held that the requirement for *Miranda* warnings was satisfied when the suspect was told that he had a right to appointed counsel prior to and during interrogation, but also told that the police could not provide a lawyer but that one would be appointed if and when he went to court.

Edwards v. Arizona (1981)

Held that once a suspect asserts his or her *Miranda* right to counsel, police may not initiate further interrogation until counsel has been made available, and that a waiver of the right to counsel is not established by the mere fact that the suspect subsequently voluntarily answered questions without benefit of counsel.

Escobedo v. Illinois (1964)

Held that when an investigation becomes accusatory, focusing upon a specific suspect with the purpose of eliciting a confession, the accused (even if unindicted) must be permitted to consult his attorney, and that if he is not, his statements are inadmissible at trial.

Estelle v. Smith (1981)

Held that information derived from a court-ordered, custodial psychiatric examination cannot be used against a defendant in a capital sentencing hearing unless he or she was given *Miranda* warnings at the time of the examination, because the privilege against self-incrimination applies to a sentencing hearing.

Evitts v. Lucey (1985)

Held that the right to counsel includes the right to the effective assistance of counsel on an appeal of right.

***Fahy v. Connecticut* (1963)**

Made clear that a confession that is the product of an unlawful search and seizure is inadmissible.

***Faretta v. California* (1975)**

Held that the Sixth Amendment protects the defendant's right to self-representation at trial.

***Feldman v. United States* (1944)**

Held that self-incriminating testimony compelled by state officials under a state grant of immunity could be used against the witness in a federal prosecution. Overruled by *Murphy v. Waterfront Commission.*

***Fellers v. United States* (2004)**

Remanded to a court of appeals the question of whether incriminating statements that are the fruits of a violation of the Sixth Amendment right to counsel must be suppressed if there has been an intervening waiver of that right.

***Fikes v. Alabama* (1957)**

Held that state use of a confession made during an illegal detention did not necessarily violate due process.

***Fisher v. United States* (1976)**

Held that the attorney-client privilege does not protect an attorney from being compelled to produce his client's papers if the privilege against self-incrimination would not protect the client from being compelled to produce them, and that the privilege against self-incrimination does not protect a person from being compelled to produce voluntarily prepared business records unless the act of production itself would in some way amount to testimonial self-incrimination.

Fletcher v. Weir (1982)

Held that the prosecution's use of a defendant's silence after arrest but prior to *Miranda* warnings to impeach the credibility of his or her testimony at trial does not violate due process of law.

Fortas, Abe (1910–1982)

A prominent attorney and former government official, Fortas was asked by the Supreme Court to represent Clarence Earl Gideon. His argument that the Sixth Amendment right to counsel should be applied to the states and that indigent defendants in state trials were thereby entitled to appointed counsel prevailed in *Gideon v. Wainwright.* Fortas was appointed as associate justice of the Supreme Court in 1965 and nominated to succeed Earl Warren as chief justice in 1968 but was not confirmed. He resigned from the Court the following year when it became known that he had accepted an annual retainer from a person under investigation for violation of federal securities laws.

Foster v. California (1969)

Held that lineup procedures that were highly suggestive of a desired outcome were a denial of due process of law.

Frank v. Mangum (1915)

Made clear that federal courts would not normally review the substance of claims of denial of due process by states when the form of procedural review was available in state courts. Modified by *Moore v. Dempsey.*

***Fuller v. Oregon* (1974)**

Held that a statute allowing states to recoup costs of defense counsel from convicted indigents who subsequently become able to pay without hardship does not violate either equal protection or the right to counsel, even when a sentence of probation is contingent upon such an arrangement.

***Gagnon v. Scarpelli* (1973)**

Held that the right to counsel at parole and probation revocation hearings is not guaranteed by the Sixth Amendment but is to be determined case by case on the basis of the due process standard of fundamental fairness. Modified by *Mempa v. Rhay.*

***Gallegos v. Nebraska* (1951)**

Held that a confession gained during an illegal detention is not necessarily inadmissible in state court.

***Gardner v. Broderick* (1968)**

Held that public employees may not be fired for asserting the privilege against self-incrimination and refusing to sign a waiver of immunity.

***Garner v. United States* (1976)**

Held that incriminating information on a tax return could be used against the taxpayer on the grounds that, because he had failed to assert the privilege against self-incrimination on the return, the information had not been compelled.

***Garrity v. New Jersey* (1967)**

Held that incriminating statements made by a public official who would have been fired for asserting the privilege against self-incrimination were compelled and thus inadmissible as evidence against him.

Geders v. United States (1976)

Held that a trial judge's refusal to allow an attorney to consult with his client during an overnight recess violated the defendant's right to counsel.

Gherebi v. Bush (2003)

Court of appeals decision holding that federal courts have jurisdiction to adjudicate claims of enemy combatants being detained at the Guantánamo Naval Base in Cuba.

Gideon, Clarence Earl (1910–1972)

An indigent drifter and occasional burglar who was denied appointed counsel in his trial for breaking into a pool hall in Panama City, Florida. Vigorously asserting his innocence and stubbornly insisting on what he thought were his rights, Gideon requested Supreme Court review of his case in a petition written in pencil on prison stationery. The result was the landmark decision in *Gideon v. Wainwright.* Granted a new trial, Gideon was acquitted with the aid of an able attorney, W. Fred Turner.

Gideon v. Wainwright (1963)

Incorporated the Sixth Amendment right to counsel into the due process clause of the Fourteenth Amendment, thereby applying it to the states and requiring them to appoint trial counsel for indigent defendants in serious cases.

Gilbert v. California (1967)

Held that there is no right to counsel for the taking of handwriting exemplars, and that being compelled to provide a handwriting exemplar does not violate the privilege against self-incrimination.

Glover v. United States (2001)

Held that imposition of increased prison time satisfies the prejudice prong of the *Strickland* test for ineffective assistance of counsel when the court made a classification error against which the attorney raised no argument.

Griffin v. California (1965)

Held that the self-incrimination clause of the Fifth Amendment prohibits federal and state prosecutors and judges from making adverse comments about a defendant's exercise of his or her right not to testify at trial.

Griffin v. Illinois (1956)

Held that both the due process and equal protection clauses prevent a state from denying an appeal to a defendant solely because he or she is unable to afford a trial transcript.

Grosso v. United States (1968)

Held that a gambler may not be prosecuted for failing to comply with a statutory requirement to register and pay an excise tax, because the requirement violates the privilege against self-incrimination.

Grunewald v. United States (1957)

Held that a defendant who had asserted the privilege against self-incrimination as to questions before a grand jury but had answered those questions at trial could not be cross-examined on his actions before the grand jury when his exculpatory testimony at trial was not inconsistent with his earlier assertion of the privilege.

***Hale v. Henkel* (1906)**

Held that a corporation has no privilege against self-incrimination.

***Hamdi v. Rumsfeld* (2002)**

A federal district judge's order to the government (subsequently overruled) to turn over documents supporting its designation of Yaser Esam Hamdi as an enemy combatant.

***Hamdi v. Rumsfeld* (2003)**

Court of appeals decision holding that a brief evidentiary submission was sufficient to justify the government's classification of a detainee as an enemy combatant, and that the detainee was not entitled to have the assistance of counsel or present evidence in opposition. Overruled by *Hamdi v. Rumsfeld* (2004).

***Hamdi v. Rumsfeld* (2004)**

Held that U.S. citizens engaged in armed conflict against the United States abroad can be classified as enemy combatants and detained by presidential authority, but are entitled to a hearing on their status before a neutral decisionmaker, and to the assistance of counsel for that purpose.

***Hamilton v. Alabama* (1961)**

Held that an arraignment is a critical stage of the prosecution at which an accused person has a right to counsel if rights may be sacrificed or lost at the proceeding.

Harlan, John Marshall II (1899–1971)

Supreme Court justice 1955–1971, and grandson of another justice of the same name. A master judicial craftsman, Harlan is known for his principled dissents in *Malloy v. Hogan* and, especially, *Miranda v. Arizona.*

***Harris v. New York* (1971)**

Held that statements made in the absence of *Miranda* warnings may be used to impeach that defendant's testimony at trial.

***Haynes v. United States* (1968)**

Held that a statutory requirement to register a firearm that it is illegal to possess violated the privilege against self-incrimination.

***Haynes v. Washington* (1963)**

Characterized intermittent questioning over sixteen hours of incommunicado detention as an inherently coercive context and therefore held the resulting confession to have been involuntary.

***Heike v. United States* (1913)**

Announced that the standard language of federal statutory immunity provisions would be interpreted as essentially coterminous with the scope of the privilege against self-incrimination.

***Hill v. Lockhart* (1985)**

Held that the *Strickland* test for ineffective assistance of counsel applies in cases that are decided by a plea bargain.

***Hoffman v. United States* (1951)**

Provides guidelines for the degree of risk a witness must establish in order to claim the privilege against self-incrimination.

Holt v. United States (1910)

Held that the privilege against self-incrimination in court is a privilege against compelled testimony, not against use of the accused's body as evidence.

Hopt v. Utah Territory (1884)

Case in which the Supreme Court for the first time invoked the rule against the admission of involuntary confessions, on the basis of the common law rather than the Fifth Amendment.

Hughes, Charles Evans (1862–1948)

Chief justice of the United States from 1930 to 1941 and author of the opinion in *Brown v. Mississippi,* overturning on grounds of due process the convictions of three young black men against whom the only evidence had been confessions obtained by savage beatings. After being governor of New York, Hughes had also served as an associate justice of the Supreme Court from 1910 to 1916, when he resigned to become the unsuccessful Republican candidate for president. Before rejoining the Supreme Court, Hughes also served as secretary of state and as a member of the Permanent Court of International Justice. As chief justice, Hughes was best known as the architect of the Supreme Court's strategic retreat from its opposition to the New Deal programs of President Franklin D. Roosevelt.

Hurtado v. California (1884)

Rejected the argument that the provisions of the Bill of Rights could be made applicable to the states through incorporation into the due process clause of the Fourteenth Amendment. Superseded by a series of subsequent cases.

Illinois v. Allen **(1970)**

Held that an unruly defendant, even if representing himself, may be removed from the courtroom.

Illinois v. Perkins **(1990)**

Held that *Miranda* warnings are not required when an undercover agent posing as a prison inmate elicits information from a fellow prisoner.

In re Gault **(1967)**

Held that various components of due process of law, including the right to counsel and the privilege against self-incrimination, apply in juvenile delinquency proceedings.

Jackson v. Denno **(1964)**

Held that a procedure in which the same jury that determines guilt or innocence also determines the voluntariness of a confession violates due process of law.

Jenkins v. Anderson **(1980)**

Held that the prosecution's use of a defendant's prearrest silence to impeach the credibility of his or her testimony at trial does not violate the privilege against self-incrimination or due process of law.

Johnson v. Eisentrager **(1950)**

World War II case in which the Supreme Court denied the right to petition for habeas corpus to enemy aliens interrogated and tried abroad by military commission, on the grounds that the Fifth Amendment and other constitutional guarantees do not apply to such persons.

***Johnson v. New Jersey* (1966)**

Held that the decisions in *Miranda v. Arizona* and *Escobedo v. Illinois* did not apply retroactively.

***Johnson v. Zerbst* (1938)**

Held that the Sixth Amendment prohibits federal trials of defendants without counsel unless that right has been waived.

***Kastigar v. United States* (1972)**

Held that use and derivative use immunity is coextensive with the privilege against self-incrimination and that self-incriminating testimony may therefore be compelled when such immunity is granted; transactional immunity is not required. Superseded *Counselman v. Hitchcock* in this respect.

***Kaupp v. Texas* (2003)**

Reaffirmed the principle that *Miranda* warnings by themselves do not render a confession admissible if that confession was the product of an unconstitutional arrest.

***Kirby v. Illinois* (1972)**

Held that the Sixth Amendment right to counsel does not attach until the point at which adversary judicial proceedings have been initiated against the defendant.

***Kitchens v. Smith* (1971)**

Made clear that the decision in *Gideon v. Wainwright* applied retroactively.

Knapp v. Schweitzer (1958)

Held that the privilege against self-incrimination did not entitle a witness who had received immunity from state prosecution to refuse to testify in a state forum because he feared federal prosecution. Overruled by *Murphy v. Waterfront Commission.*

Kuhlmann v. Wilson (1986)

Upheld the admissibility of statements made to an undercover government agent in the absence of counsel when the statements were voluntarily made and the agent took no action to elicit them but merely listened.

Lakeside v. Oregon (1978)

Held that a trial judge may instruct the jury not to draw adverse inferences from the defendant's exercise of the right not to testify, even if the defendant objects.

Lefkowitz v. Cunningham (1977)

Held that a person may not be removed from political party office and temporarily barred from holding any party or public office for asserting the privilege against self-incrimination before a grand jury or refusing to waive immunity from prosecution.

Lefkowitz v. Turley (1973)

Held that a person's privilege of entering into business contracts with the government may not be suspended for asserting the privilege against self-incrimination rather than answering questions about such business before a grand jury, unless immunity has been granted.

Lewis v. United States (1955)

Held that a prospective requirement that gamblers register and pay occupational and excise taxes did not violate the privilege against self-incrimination. Effectively overruled by *Marchetti v. United States* and *Grosso v. United States.*

Lisenba v. California (1941)

Announced that the due process standard for the admissibility of confessions was voluntariness (irrespective of the truth or falsehood of the confession), and that methods of interrogation did not have to be revolting to violate that standard, only destructive of free choice in answering.

Madison, James (1751–1836)

The most influential member of the Constitutional Convention of 1787 and author of about one-third of the *Federalist Papers,* including the classic number ten, which is perhaps the single most important essay ever written about the American constitutional system. As a member of the House of Representatives in the first Congress, Madison proposed amendments to the Constitution that became the Bill of Rights in 1791. He later served as secretary of state under Thomas Jefferson and succeeded Jefferson as president.

Maine v. Moulton (1985)

Held a suspect's incriminating statements inadmissible because the government had exploited an opportunity to confront him in the absence of counsel by concealing the fact that the person to whom he was speaking was an agent of the state, in violation of the Sixth Amendment.

***Malinski v. New York* (1945)**

Held that use of an involuntary confession at trial required that a conviction be overturned, even if other evidence might have been sufficient to establish guilt.

***Mallory v. United States* (1957)**

Reaffirmed the federal rule of evidence that bars use of a confession made during a detention rendered illegal by failure to take the suspect before a judicial officer, as required by Rule 5(a) of the Federal Rules of Criminal Procedure.

***Malloy v. Hogan* (1964)**

Incorporated the self-incrimination clause of the Fifth Amendment into the due process clause of the Fourteenth Amendment, thereby applying it to the states, and held that the same standards apply in federal and state proceedings.

***Marchetti v. United States* (1968)**

Held that a gambler may not be prosecuted for failing to comply with a statutory requirement to register and pay an occupational tax, because the requirement violates the privilege against self-incrimination.

***Martinez v. Court of Appeal* (2000)**

Held that there is no right to self-representation on appeal.

Mason, George (1725–1792)

A prominent Virginia statesman who was an activist in the cause of American independence. His draft of the Virginia Declaration of Rights had great influence on other states, and he was an influential delegate at the Constitutional Convention in Philadelphia.

Mason nevertheless sharply criticized the new Constitution because it lacked a bill of rights, and his ideas had great impact upon the amendments that remedied that defect in 1791.

Massiah v. United States (1964)

Held that incriminating statements made by an indicted defendant to a confederate secretly functioning as a government agent could not be used against him because, once the right to counsel has attached, a suspect may not be interrogated in the absence of counsel unless the right has been waived.

Mathis v. United States 1968)

Held that a suspect already in prison for another offense is in custody and therefore entitled to *Miranda* warnings prior to interrogation.

McCarthy v. Arndstein (1924)

Reaffirmed that the privilege against self-incrimination can be invoked in any proceeding, civil or criminal, in which testimony can be compelled.

McKaskle v. Wiggins (1984)

Held that, over the objection of a defendant representing himself or herself, a trial judge may appoint standby counsel to assist with matters of courtroom procedure and protocol.

McKune v. Lile (2002)

Held that imposition of more restrictive terms of confinement on a prisoner who refused to confess to crimes as part of a sexual offender treatment program did not amount to compulsion and therefore did not violate the privilege against self-incrimination.

McLeod v. Ohio (1965)

Applied the holding in *Massiah v. United States* to the states.

McMann v. Richardson (1970)

Stated definitively that the right to counsel includes the right to the effective assistance of counsel at trial.

McNabb v. United States (1943)

Established a federal rule of evidence that bars use of a confession made during a detention rendered illegal by failure to take the suspect before a judicial officer, as required by statute.

McNeil v. Wisconsin (1991)

Held that the Sixth Amendment right to counsel is offense-specific and does not apply with respect to other offenses for which the right has not attached, and that an assertion of the Sixth Amendment right to counsel outside the context of custodial interrogation is not an assertion of the *Miranda* right to counsel with respect to subsequent interrogation about offenses for which the Sixth Amendment right has not attached.

Mempa v. Rhay (1967)

Made it clear that a sentencing hearing is a critical stage of a prosecution at which a defendant has a right to counsel, and held that the right applies at a probation revocation hearing if sentencing has been deferred to that point.

Michigan v. Harvey (1990)

Held that statements that are otherwise inadmissible as evidence because obtained in violation of the Sixth Amendment right to counsel are admissible for the purpose of impeaching the credibility of that defendant's testimony at trial.

Michigan v. Jackson (1986)

Held that if police initiate an interrogation with a suspect who has validly asserted his or her Sixth Amendment right to counsel but has not seen a lawyer, any waiver of counsel for that interrogation is invalid and statements made under those circumstances are therefore inadmissible.

Michigan v. Mosley (1975)

Held that the admissibility of statements elicited from a suspect after invocation of the *Miranda* right to silence depends on whether the suspect's right to cut off questioning was scrupulously honored.

Michigan v. Tucker (1974)

Allowed the use of testimony for the prosecution from a witness whose identity had been revealed by statements made by the defendant in the absence of valid *Miranda* warnings.

Mincey v. Arizona (1978)

Held that a defendant's involuntary statements may not be used against him or her at trial for any purpose, including impeachment of his or her testimony.

Minnesota v. Murphy (1984)

Held that a probationer undergoing a required interview with his supervising agent is not in custody for *Miranda* purposes, and made clear that the privilege against self-incrimination may not be asserted to prevent use of information in a proceeding for revocation of probation, as that involves no additional criminal liability.

Minnick v. Mississippi (1990)

Held that once the *Miranda* right to counsel has been invoked, police may not reinitiate interrogation in the absence of counsel, even if the suspect has had an opportunity to consult with counsel in the meantime.

Miranda, Ernesto (1941–1976)

A young Mexican American high school dropout who suffered from sexual fantasies and had been imprisoned several times prior to his arrest for the rape of an eighteen-year-old woman in Phoenix, Arizona, in 1963. His conviction for that offense was overturned by the Supreme Court when it ruled in the landmark case of *Miranda v. Arizona* that his confession should not have been used against him because he had not been informed of his rights. Upon retrial, however, Miranda was convicted again on the basis of other evidence, and he served a prison term. A few years later he was stabbed to death in a barroom brawl; when police arrested a suspect they immediately read him his *Miranda* rights.

Miranda v. Arizona (1966)

Held that statements made by a suspect under interrogation while in custody are inadmissible at trial unless the suspect has been given prior warnings about his rights to counsel and privilege against self-incrimination and has exercised or validly waived the former right and validly waived the latter right.

Missouri v. Seibert (2004)

Applied the exclusionary rule to warned statements gained from the second stage of an interrogation because police had deliberately failed to give *Miranda* warnings during the first stage.

Mitchell v. United States **(1999)**

Held that the privilege against self-incrimination applies at the sentencing phase of a noncapital case, even if the defendant has pleaded guilty, and that adverse inferences may not be drawn from his or her failure to testify at a sentencing hearing.

Mooney v. Holohan **(1935)**

Held that the prosecution's knowing use of perjured testimony was a denial of due process of law.

Moore v. Dempsey **(1923)**

Signaled that the Supreme Court would examine not just the forms but the substance of state criminal processes, an initiative that developed into the fair-trial rule of due process.

Moran v. Burbine **(1986)**

Held that even though police had failed to inform a suspect that an attorney wished to see him, and had deceived the attorney about an imminent interrogation, the suspect's waiver of his rights was valid because proper *Miranda* warnings provide all the information necessary for informed choice.

Morris v. Slappy **(1983)**

Held that a defendant is not entitled to his or her preferred public defender if that attorney is incapacitated and a qualified substitute is prepared to proceed.

Murphy v. Waterfront Commission **(1964)**

Held that the privilege against self-incrimination protects both federal and state witnesses from compelled self-incrimination under the laws of either jurisdiction, and that the federal government may not use testimony or fruits thereof, compelled in a state forum, against that witness.

Murray v. Giarratano (1989)
Held that there is no right to counsel for state postconviction proceedings (other than appeals of right) in capital cases.

New Jersey v. Portash (1979)
Held that a defendant's prior immunized testimony may not be used to impeach his or her testimony at trial.

New York v. Quarles (1984)
Created a public safety exception to the rule that incriminating statements made in the absence of *Miranda* warnings are inadmissible at trial.

Nix v. Williams (1984)
Upheld the use of evidence, otherwise inadmissible because obtained in violation of the right to counsel, because the state proved that it would inevitably have been discovered in essentially the same condition.

Norris v. Alabama (1935)
Overturned a conviction of one of the Scottsboro defendants on the grounds of the exclusion of blacks from jury service.

North Carolina v. Butler (1979)
Held that an explicit waiver of *Miranda* rights is not necessarily required for an incriminating statement to be admissible, as a knowing and voluntary waiver can sometimes be inferred from a suspect's words and actions.

Ohio v. Reiner (2001)

Affirmed that the privilege against self-incrimination may be claimed by witnesses who assert their innocence, as long as they have a reasonable fear that their answers could be used in a criminal prosecution against them.

Oregon v. Elstad (1985)

Held that when a suspect has made an unwarned but uncoerced incriminating statement, the administration of *Miranda* warnings is ordinarily sufficient to render a second confession admissible, even though it is made because of a mistaken belief that the first statement is admissible.

Oregon v. Hass (1975)

Held that statements made after *Miranda* warnings have been given but before a request for counsel has been honored may be used to impeach that defendant's testimony at trial.

Oregon v. Mathiason (1977)

Held that a suspect who is in a police station voluntarily, not under arrest, and free to leave is not in custody and therefore not entitled to *Miranda* warnings prior to interrogation.

Orozco v. Texas (1969)

Held that a suspect who is under arrest in his or her home is in custody and therefore entitled to *Miranda* warnings prior to interrogation.

Padilla v. Rumsfeld (2003)

Court of appeals decision holding that the president cannot classify as enemy combatants and detain American citizens captured in the United States, away from a combat zone, without authorization from Congress, and that such detainees are entitled to challenge their detention in federal court and to have the assistance of counsel in doing so.

***Palko v. Connecticut* (1937)**

Case in which the Supreme Court adopted the theory of selective incorporation of provisions of the Bill of Rights into the due process clause of the Fourteenth Amendment, thereby applying them to the states.

***Patterson v. Alabama* (1935)**

Overturned a conviction of one of the Scottsboro defendants on the grounds of the exclusion of blacks from jury service.

***Patterson v. Illinois* (1988)**

Held that if police initiate an interrogation with a suspect whose Sixth Amendment right to counsel has attached but who has not asserted it, a waiver of *Miranda* rights is also a waiver of the Sixth Amendment right and statements made are admissible.

***Pennsylvania v. Finley* (1987)**

Held that there is no right to counsel for state postconviction proceedings (other than appeals of right).

***Pennsylvania v. Muniz* (1990)**

Held that a videotaped presentation of a defendant's slurred speech and lack of muscular coordination did not violate the privilege against self-incrimination because the incriminating elements were nontestimonial, and that routine "booking" questions do not constitute interrogation for *Miranda* purposes.

People ex rel. Hackley v. Kelly (1861)

State case holding that the privilege against self-incrimination could be claimed only at one's own criminal trial to prevent use of one's own words as evidence.

Perry v. Leeke (1989)

Made clear that when government action prevents the assistance of counsel altogether, a defendant claiming ineffective assistance of counsel is not required to establish prejudice (but upheld a prohibition of consultation with counsel during a trial recess of only fifteen minutes).

Pickelsimer v. Wainwright (1963)

Overturned convictions of defendants who had lacked counsel and remanded their cases to the Supreme Court of Florida, with the implication that the decision in *Gideon v. Wainwright* should be applied retroactively. See *Burgett v. Texas* and *Kitchens v. Smith.*

Powell v. Alabama (1932)

Held that in a capital case in which defendants clearly required the assistance of counsel, both the judge's failure to provide defendants an opportunity to retain counsel and his failure to make an effective appointment of counsel for them were denials of due process of law.

Rasul v. Bush (2004)

Held that foreign nationals detained by the United States as enemy combatants at Guantánamo, Cuba, have the right to file habeas corpus petitions in federal court.

Rehnquist, William H. (1924–)

Associate justice of the Supreme Court 1972–1986 and chief justice thereafter, Rehnquist has consistently voted for governmental powers of law enforcement against claims of the rights of the accused, and he wrote the decision in *New York v. Quarles.* Although hostile to the *Miranda* revolution, he wrote *Dickerson v. United States,* reaffirming *Miranda* in an opinion that satisfied legal commentators on neither side of the issue. Rehnquist has also been an active opponent of abortion and affirmative action, and he presided over the impeachment trial of President Bill Clinton.

***Rhode Island v. Innis* (1980)**

Held that *Miranda* rights with respect to interrogation apply not only to express questioning but also to its functional equivalent, but that, in this case, a conversation between officers that elicited incriminating information from a suspect was not an interrogation.

***Rock v. Arkansas* (1987)**

Held that the right to testify in one's own defense is a fundamental aspect of due process and of the Sixth Amendment rights to conduct a personal defense and summon witnesses in one's own behalf, and is a necessary corollary of the Fifth Amendment right not to be compelled to testify.

***Rogers v. Richmond* (1961)**

Held that the determination of the voluntariness of a confession must not be affected by considerations of the truthfulness of the confession.

***Rogers v. United States* (1951)**

Reaffirmed the rule that once witnesses have incriminated themselves, they have no privilege not to answer additional questions on the same topic that do not present a risk of further incrimination.

Ross v. Moffitt (1974)
Held that states are not required to provide indigent defendants with appointed counsel for discretionary appeals or petitions for certiorari to the U.S. Supreme Court.

Rumsfeld v. Padilla (2004)
Held that the habeas corpus petition of enemy combatant José Padilla had been filed in a federal court lacking jurisdiction and would have to be refiled in the proper court in order to be heard.

Scalia, Antonin (1936–)
An associate justice of the Supreme Court since 1986, Scalia has consistently taken conservative positions in the areas of criminal justice, abortion, establishment of religion, affirmative action, and state sovereignty, but has been more moderate in the area of freedom of expression and would restore Fifth Amendment protection to private papers. He is known for powerful and scathing dissents, as in *Dickerson v. United States.*

Schmerber v. California (1966)
Upheld the admissibility of evidence derived from a blood sample that the defendant had been compelled to provide, elaborating the rationale for the distinction between testimonial or communicative evidence, which is protected by the privilege against self-incrimination, and physical evidence from the body, which is not.

Scott v. Illinois (1979)

Held that the constitutional standard for determining whether indigent defendants must be provided with counsel in petty cases is actual imprisonment, not authorized imprisonment.

Scottsboro Boys

Nine black, largely illiterate youths—Clarence Norris, Charley Weems, Haywood Patterson, Ozie Powell, Willie Roberson, Andy Wright, Eugene Williams, Olen Montgomery, and Roy Wright—who were falsely accused and convicted of rape near Scottsboro, Alabama, in 1931. Their convictions were overturned by the United States Supreme Court on grounds of denial of right to counsel in the landmark case of *Powell v. Alabama,* but they were retried, convicted again, and served various amounts of prison time. Their fate is a classic example of miscarriage of justice, largely the product of racial bias.

Selective Service System v. Minnesota Public Interest Research Group (1984)

Held that a requirement that young men who have failed to register for the draft must do so late in order to qualify for federal financial aid for college attendance, thereby revealing their violation of the law to the Selective Service System, does not violate their privilege against self-incrimination.

Shapiro v. United States (1948)

Reaffirmed the interpretation that records required to be kept by law are not protected by the privilege against self-incrimination, and held that such records are therefore not covered by the standard federal statutory grant of immunity, either.

Slochower v. Board of Higher Education (1956)

Held that the discharge, without notice or hearing, of a municipal employee who had claimed the privilege against self-incrimination in testifying before a congressional committee was a violation of due process.

Snyder v. Massachusetts (1934)

Discussed the scope of state discretion to regulate criminal procedure under the due process standard prior to incorporation of relevant provisions of the Bill of Rights, including the ability to force criminal defendants to testify at their trials.

South Dakota v. Neville (1983)

Allowed the introduction into evidence of a suspect's refusal to take a blood-alcohol test, holding that the refusal was not coerced but the product of free choice, even though the results of the test could have been used against him and the refusal resulted in the automatic forfeiture of his driver's license.

Spano v. New York (1959)

Overturned a conviction based on a confession gained as the result of prolonged, late-night interrogation and false statements designed to play on the suspect's sympathy.

Spevack v. Klein (1967)

Held that a lawyer may not be disbarred for asserting the privilege against self-incrimination in a disciplinary hearing.

Spies v. Illinois (1887)

Held that a petitioner could not claim federal constitutional protection against alleged state denial of the privilege against self-incrimination.

Stein v. New York (1953)

Upheld a conviction when it could not be determined whether the jury had determined a confession to be voluntary and relied on it or determined it to be involuntary, disregarded it, and convicted on the basis of other evidence. Overruled by *Jackson v. Denno.*

Stovall v. Denno (1967)

Provides guidance for the adjudication of claims of denial of due process of law in criminal cases.

Strickland v. Washington (1984)

Articulated the basic standard for ineffective assistance of counsel by holding that to prevail on such a claim under most circumstances, a defendant must show that counsel's performance was deficient and that the deficient performance prejudiced the defense.

Sutherland, George (1862–1941)

Congressman, senator, and Supreme Court justice, 1922–1938, and author of the Court's landmark opinion in *Powell v. Alabama,* overturning an egregious miscarriage of justice by holding that the state had denied the defendant Scottsboro Boys due process of law by depriving them of the right to counsel. Sutherland was, however, much better known as a defender of states' rights and economic conservatism and as the leader of the bloc of justices known as the Four Horsemen for their opposition to President Franklin Roosevelt's New Deal programs.

Swidler and Berlin v. United States (1998)

Held that the attorney-client privilege continues after the death of the client in a criminal investigation.

Texas v. Cobb (2001)

Reaffirmed *McNeil v. Wisconsin's* holding that the Sixth Amendment right to counsel applies only to offenses for which the right has attached by holding that the right does not apply to other offenses that are closely related factually.

Townsend v. Burke (1948)

Held that the lack of counsel at a sentencing hearing, in circumstances in which prejudice to the defendant results, violates due process of law.

Twining v. New Jersey (1908)

Held that the Fifth Amendment privilege against self-incrimination does not apply to the states. Overruled by *Malloy v. Hogan.*

Ullmann v. United States (1956)

Reaffirmed *Brown v. Walker* in ruling that the privilege against self-incrimination protects only against the danger of criminal prosecution and that self-incriminating testimony can be compelled under a grant of immunity.

United States v. Apfelbaum (1980)

Held that neither the federal immunity statute nor the Fifth Amendment prohibits the use of both true and false testimony given under a grant of use immunity in a prosecution of the witness for perjury while testifying under immunity.

United States v. Ash (1973)

Held that there is no right to counsel for photographic displays of suspects to witnesses and redefined critical stages of a prosecution at which the right to counsel pertains as events involving an adversarial confrontation between the prosecution and the accused.

***United States v. Balsys* (1998)**

Held that a witness may not assert the privilege against self-incrimination for fear of prosecution in a foreign court.

***United States v. Bin Laden* (2001)**

District court ruling that aliens interrogated abroad by American agents and tried in the United States are protected by the privilege against self-incrimination and are entitled to *Miranda* rights.

***United States v. Cronic* (1984)**

Held that some circumstances may warrant a presumption of the ineffective assistance of counsel, but that under most circumstances, a defendant making that claim must identify specific acts or omissions of counsel and meet the standard of *Strickland v. Washington.*

***United States v. Dickerson* (1999)**

Court of appeals decision holding that the *Miranda* warnings were not constitutional rights and that a federal statute had replaced them as the standard of admissibility for confessions in federal courts. Overruled by *Dickerson v. United States.*

***United States v. Dionisio* (1973)**

Held that being compelled to provide a voice exemplar does not violate the privilege against self-incrimination.

***United States v. Doe* (1984)**

Held that the privilege against self-incrimination does not protect the contents of voluntarily prepared business records but does protect their production to the government when that act in itself would be incriminating. Production can be compelled only when the accused is granted use immunity as to the act of production (but not as to the contents of the material produced).

United States v. Fellers (2002)

Court of appeals decision concerning issues of right to counsel and admissibility of evidence that were returned to the court for further consideration by *Fellers v. United States.*

United States v. Hale (1975)

Held that once suspects have been arrested and assured of their right to silence through *Miranda* warnings, their subsequent silence may not be used to impeach their testimony at a federal trial (case decided on the basis of supervisory power over federal courts rather than on the basis of the Constitution).

United States v. Henry (1980)

Held a suspect's incriminating statements inadmissible because the government had deliberately created a situation in which he was likely to make them in the absence of counsel, in violation of the Sixth Amendment.

United States v. Hubbell (2000)

Enforced the requirement that the government may not make derivative use of the testimonial aspects of a compelled act of production of evidence under a grant of immunity.

United States v. Kahriger (1953)

Held that a prospective requirement that gamblers register and pay occupational and excise taxes did not violate the privilege against self-incrimination. Effectively overruled by *Marchetti v. United States* and *Grosso v. United States.*

***United States v. Monia* (1943)**

Affirmed that a witness must claim the privilege against self-incrimination or else his or her testimony will not be considered to have been compelled.

***United States v. Murdock* (1931)**

Held that the immunity required to displace the privilege against self-incrimination need apply only to the jurisdiction compelling the testimony. Overruled on this point by *Murphy v. Waterfront Commission.*

***United States v. Patane* (2004)**

Upheld the admissibility of physical evidence derived from a voluntary statement taken in violation of the *Miranda* rules.

***United States v. Robinson* (1988)**

Held that a defendant's privilege against self-incrimination had not been violated when a defense attorney whose client had not testified complained in a closing statement that the government had denied the accused a chance to explain his actions, and the judge, while cautioning the jury not to draw any inferences from the defendant's failure to testify, had allowed the prosecutor to tell the jury that the defendant could have taken the stand to explain anything he wished.

***United States v. Sullivan* (1927)**

Held that one may not refuse to file an income tax return on grounds of self-incrimination but noted that one may assert the privilege on the return with respect to specific requests for information.

United States v. Van Duzee (1891)

Stated that the federal government was obligated to allow defendants to retain counsel but not to appoint counsel for them. Superseded by *Johnson v. Zerbst.*

United States v. Wade (1967)

Held that the Sixth Amendment right to counsel applies at all critical stages of a prosecution—here, at a pretrial lineup. Modified by *Kirby v. Illinois* and *United States v. Ash.* Held also that being compelled to appear in a lineup and speak words spoken by the perpetrator does not violate the privilege against self-incrimination.

United States v. White (1944)

Held that an unincorporated labor union has no privilege against self-incrimination, and that the custodian of union records may be compelled to produce them even if they incriminate him or her personally.

Upshaw v. United States (1948)

Held that failure to afford a suspect in custody a timely appearance before a magistrate was not just a factor to be considered but rather an error rendering a resulting confession inadmissible in federal court.

Uveges v. Pennsylvania (1948)

Candidly acknowledged and described the split among justices of the Supreme Court over the scope of the right to counsel in the years after *Betts v. Brady.*

Wainwright v. Torna **(1982)**

Held that claims of ineffective assistance of counsel cannot be made with respect to situations in which the constitutional right to counsel does not apply—here, a discretionary appeal.

Wan v. United States **(1924)**

Held that, in addition to threats or promises, lengthy and arduous detention and interrogation could also constitute compulsion that violated the privilege against self-incrimination.

Warren, Earl (1891–1974)

Attorney general and governor of California and chief justice of the United States, 1953–1969. Warren wrote the decisions in *Chandler v. Fretag, Spano v. New York,* and *Miranda v. Arizona.* He also wrote the opinion in *Brown v. Board of Education* and, besides criminal justice and racial equality, the Court under his leadership also made major civil liberties decisions respecting freedom of expression, separation of church and state, privacy, and legislative apportionment. Warren also chaired the commission that investigated the assassination of President John F. Kennedy.

Watkins v. United States **(1957)**

Reaffirmed that witnesses may assert the privilege against self-incrimination before a congressional investigating committee.

Watts v. Indiana **(1949)**

Overturned a conviction based on a confession obtained by relentless interrogation, deprivation of food and sleep, and denial of legal rights.

***Wheat v. United States* (1988)**

Held that a defendant is not entitled to the attorney of his or her choice if that attorney's representation of codefendants would create a conflict of interest.

White, Byron (1917–2002)

Associate justice of the Supreme Court 1962–1993, a Kennedy appointee who was more conservative than expected. He wrote forceful dissents in *Massiah v. United States, Escobedo v. Illinois,* and *Miranda v. Arizona,* as well as in the abortion decision *Roe v. Wade.*

***White v. Maryland* (1963)**

Held that a preliminary hearing is a critical stage of the prosecution at which an accused person has a right to counsel when such assistance is clearly needed—as, here, in pleading to a capital offense.

***Wiggins v. Smith* (2003)**

Upheld a claim of ineffective assistance of counsel under the *Strickland* test because counsel had failed to conduct a thorough investigation of Wiggins's background in preparation for his sentencing hearing in a capital case. See *Strickland v. Washington.*

***Williams v. Taylor* (2000)**

The first Supreme Court case in which a defendant was held to have satisfied both prongs of the *Strickland* test for the ineffective assistance of counsel, who had failed to conduct a thorough investigation of Williams's background in preparation for his sentencing hearing in a capital case. See *Strickland v. Washington.*

Wilson v. United States (1893)
Upheld the statutory right of a defendant in a federal trial not to have the prosecutor create a presumption against him by commenting adversely on his decision not to testify in his own behalf.

Wilson v. United States (1911)
Held that the custodian of corporate records may be compelled to produce them even if they incriminate him or her personally, and announced that records of public offices and records required to be kept by law are not protected by the privilege against self-incrimination.

Wolff v. McDonnell (1974)
Held that inmates do not have a right to retained or appointed counsel in prison disciplinary proceedings.

Wong Sun v. United States (1963)
Held that a confession that is the product of an illegal arrest is inadmissible.

8

DOCUMENTS

Excerpted below are the majority opinions in the four seminal counsel and self-incrimination cases. Internal citations and footnotes have been deleted without indication.

POWELL V. ALABAMA, 287 U.S. 45 (1932)

Justice SUTHERLAND delivered the opinion of the Court.

. . . It is hardly necessary to say that, the right to counsel being conceded, a defendant should be afforded a fair opportunity to secure counsel of his own choice. Not only was that not done here, but such designation of counsel as was attempted was either so indefinite or so close upon the trial as to amount to a denial of effective and substantial aid in that regard. . . .

It is not enough to assume that counsel thus precipitated into the case thought there was no defense, and exercised their best judgment in proceeding to trial without preparation. Neither they nor the court could say what a prompt and thoroughgoing investigation might disclose as to the facts. No attempt was made to investigate. No opportunity to do so was given. Defendants were immediately hurried to trial. Chief Justice Anderson, after disclaiming any intention to criticize harshly counsel who attempted to represent defendants at the trials, said: " . . . the record indicates that the appearance was rather pro forma than zealous and active . . ." Under the circumstances disclosed, we hold that defendants were not accorded the right of counsel in any substantial sense. To decide otherwise, would simply be to ignore actualities. . . .

. . . The prompt disposition of criminal cases is to be commended and encouraged. But in reaching that result a defendant, charged with a serious crime, must not be stripped of his right to have sufficient time to advise with counsel and prepare his defense. To do that is not to proceed promptly in the calm spirit of regulated justice but to go forward with the haste of the mob.

. . . The question . . . which it is our duty . . . to decide, is whether the denial of the assistance of counsel contravenes the due process clause of the Fourteenth Amendment to the federal Constitution. . . .

One test which has been applied to determine whether due process of law has been accorded in given instances is to ascertain what were the settled usages and modes of proceeding under the common and statute law of England before the Declaration of Independence, subject, however, to the qualification that they be shown not to have been unsuited to the civil and political conditions of our ancestors by having been followed in this country after it became a nation. Plainly . . . this test, as thus qualified, has not been met in the present case.

We do not overlook the case of *Hurtado v. California*. . . .

. . . In the face of the reasoning of the *Hurtado* case, if it stood alone, it would be difficult to justify the conclusion that the right to counsel, being . . . specifically granted by the Sixth Amendment, was also within the intendment of the due process of law clause. But the *Hurtado* case does not stand alone. . . .

. . . [L]ater cases establish that notwithstanding the sweeping character of the language in the *Hurtado* case, the rule laid down is not without exceptions. The rule is an aid to construction, and in some instances may be conclusive; but it must yield to more compelling considerations whenever such considerations exist. The fact that the right involved is of such a character that it cannot be denied without violating those "fundamental principles of liberty and justice which lie at the base of all our civil and political institutions" is obviously one of those compelling considerations which must prevail in determining whether it is embraced within the due process clause of the Fourteenth Amendment, although it be specifically dealt with in another part of the federal Constitution. . . . While the question has never been categorically determined by this court, a consideration of the nature of the right and a review of the expressions of this and other courts, makes it clear that the right to the aid of counsel is of this fundamental character.

It never has been doubted by this court, or any other so far as we know, that notice and hearing are preliminary steps essential to the passing of an enforceable judgment, and that they, together with a legally competent tribunal having jurisdiction of the case, constitute basic elements of the constitutional requirement of due process of law. . . .

What, then, does a hearing include? Historically and in practice, in our own country at least, it has always included the right to the aid of counsel when desired and provided by the party asserting the right. The right to be heard would be, in many cases, of little avail if it did not comprehend the right to be heard by counsel. Even the intelligent and educated layman has small and sometimes no skill in the science of law. If charged with crime, he is incapable, generally, of determining for himself whether the indictment is good or bad. He is unfamiliar with the rules of evidence. Left without the aid of counsel he may be put on trial without a proper charge, and convicted upon incompetent evidence, or evidence irrelevant to the issue or otherwise inadmissible. He lacks both the skill and knowledge adequately to prepare his defense, even though he had a perfect one. He requires the guiding hand of counsel at every step in the proceedings against him. Without it, though he be not guilty, he faces the danger of conviction because he does not know how to establish his innocence. If that be true of men of intelligence, how much more true is it of the ignorant and illiterate, or those of feeble intellect. If in any case, civil or criminal, a state or federal court were arbitrarily to refuse to hear a party by counsel, employed by and appearing for him, it reasonably may not be doubted that such a refusal would be a denial of a hearing, and, therefore, of due process in the constitutional sense. . . .

In the light of the facts outlined in the forepart of this opinion—the ignorance and illiteracy of the defendants, their youth, the circumstances of public hostility, the imprisonment and the close surveillance of the defendants by the military forces, the fact that their friends and families were all in other states and communication with them necessarily difficult, and above all that they stood in deadly peril of their lives—we think the failure of the trial court to give them reasonable time and opportunity to secure counsel was a clear denial of due process.

But passing that, and assuming their inability, even if opportunity had been given, to employ counsel, as the trial court evidently did assume, we are of opinion that, under the circumstances just stated, the necessity of counsel was so vital and imperative that the failure of the trial court to make an effective appointment of counsel was likewise a denial of due process within the meaning of the Fourteenth Amendment. Whether this would be so in other criminal prosecutions, or under other circumstances, we need not determine. All that it is necessary now to decide, as we do decide, is that in a capital case, where the defendant is unable to employ counsel, and is incapable adequately of making his own defense because of ignorance, feeble mindedness, illiteracy, or the like, it is the duty of the court, whether requested or not, to assign counsel for him as a necessary requisite of due process of law; and that duty is not discharged by an assignment at such a time or under such circumstances as to preclude the giving of effective aid in the preparation and trial of the case. To hold otherwise would be to ignore the fundamental postulate, already adverted to, "that there are certain immutable principles of justice which inhere in the very idea of free government which no member of the Union may disregard." In a case such as this, whatever may be the rule in other cases, the right to have counsel appointed, when necessary, is a logical corollary from the constitutional right to be heard by counsel. . . .

The United States by statute and every state in the Union by express provision of law, or by the determination of its courts, make it the duty of the trial judge, where the accused is unable to employ counsel, to appoint counsel for him. In most states the rule applies broadly to all criminal prosecutions, in others it is limited to the more serious crimes, and in a very limited number, to capital cases. A rule adopted with such unanimous accord reflects, if it does not establish, the inherent right to have counsel appointed, at least in cases like the present, and lends convincing support to the conclusion we have reached as to the fundamental nature of that right.

The judgments must be reversed. . . .

BROWN V. MISSISSIPPI, 297 U.S. 278 (1936)

Chief Justice HUGHES delivered the opinion of the Court.

The question in this case is whether convictions, which rest solely upon confessions shown to have been extorted by officers of the State by brutality and violence, are consistent with the due process of law required by the Fourteenth Amendment of the Constitution of the United States. . . .

Aside from the confessions, there was no evidence sufficient to warrant the submission of the case to the jury. After a preliminary inquiry, testimony as to the confessions was received over the objection of defendants' counsel. Defendants then testified that the confessions were false and had been procured by physical torture. The case went to the jury with instructions, upon the request of defendants' counsel, that if the jury had reasonable doubt as to the confessions having resulted from coercion, and that they were not true, they were not to be considered as evidence. . . .

1. The State stresses the statement in *Twining v. New Jersey* that "exemption from compulsory self-incrimination in the courts of the States is not secured by any part of the Federal Constitution," and the statement in *Snyder v. Massachusetts* that "the privilege against self-incrimination may be withdrawn and the accused put upon the stand as a witness for the State." But the question of the right of the State to withdraw the privilege against self-incrimination is not here involved. The compulsion to which the quoted statements refer is that of the processes of justice by which the accused may be called as a witness and required to testify. Compulsion by torture to extort a confession is a different matter.

The State is free to regulate the procedure of its courts in accordance with its own conceptions of policy, unless in so doing it "offends some principle of justice so rooted in the traditions and conscience of our people as to be ranked as fundamental." . . . But the freedom of the State in establishing its policy is the freedom of constitutional government and is limited by the requirement of due process of law. Because a State may dispense with a jury trial, it does not follow that it may substitute trial by ordeal. The rack and torture chamber may not be substituted for the witness stand. The . . . trial . . . is a mere pretense where the state authorities have contrived a conviction resting solely upon confessions obtained by violence. The due process clause requires "that state action, whether through one agency or another, shall be consistent with the fundamental principles of liberty and justice which lie at the base of all our civil and political institutions." It would be difficult to conceive of methods more revolting to the sense of justice than those taken to procure the confessions of these petitioners, and the use of the confessions thus obtained as the basis for conviction and sentence was a clear denial of due process.

2. . . . [T]he further contention of the State . . . rests upon the failure of counsel for the accused, who had objected to the admissibility of the confessions, to move for their exclusion after they had been introduced and the fact of coercion had been proved. It is a contention which proceeds upon a misconception of the nature of petitioners' complaint. That complaint is not of the commission of mere error, but of a wrong so fundamental that it made the whole proceeding a mere pretense of a trial and rendered the conviction and sentence wholly void. We are not concerned with a mere question of state practice, or whether counsel assigned to petitioners were competent or mistakenly assumed that their first objections were sufficient. . . .

In the instant case, the trial court was fully advised by the undisputed evidence of the way in which the confessions had been procured. The trial court knew that there was no other evidence upon which conviction and sentence could be based. Yet it proceeded to permit conviction and to pronounce sentence. The conviction and sentence were void for want of the essential elements of due process, and the proceeding thus vitiated could be challenged in any appropriate manner. It was challenged before the Supreme Court of the State by the express invocation of the Fourteenth Amendment. That court entertained the challenge, considered the federal question thus presented, but declined to enforce petitioners' constitutional right. The court thus denied a federal right fully established and specially set up and claimed and the judgment must be

Reversed.

GIDEON V. WAINWRIGHT, 372 U.S. 335 (1963)

Justice BLACK delivered the opinion of the Court.

Petitioner was charged in a Florida state court with having broken and entered a poolroom with intent to commit a misdemeanor. This offense is a felony under Florida law. Appearing in court without funds and without a lawyer, petitioner asked the court to appoint counsel for him, whereupon the following colloquy took place:

"The COURT: Mr. Gideon, I am sorry, but I cannot appoint Counsel to represent you in this case. Under the laws of the State of Florida, the only time the Court can appoint Counsel to represent a Defendant is when that person is charged with a capital offense. I am sorry, but I will have to deny your request to appoint Counsel to defend you in this case.

"The DEFENDANT: The United States Supreme Court says I am entitled to be represented by Counsel."

Put to trial before a jury, Gideon conducted his defense about as well as could be expected from a layman. He made an opening statement to the jury, cross-examined the State's witnesses, presented witnesses in his own defense, declined to testify himself, and made a short argument "emphasizing his innocence to the charge contained in the Information filed in this case." The jury returned a verdict of guilty, and petitioner was sentenced to serve five years in the state prison. . . . Since 1942, when *Betts v. Brady* was decided by a divided Court, the problem of a defendant's federal constitutional right to counsel in a state court has been a continuing source of controversy and litigation in both state and federal courts. To give this problem another review here, we granted certiorari. Since Gideon was proceeding in forma pauperis, we appointed counsel to represent him and requested both sides to discuss in their briefs and oral arguments the following: "Should this Court's holding in *Betts v. Brady* be reconsidered?"

I.

The facts upon which Betts claimed that he had been unconstitutionally denied the right to have counsel appointed to assist him are strikingly like the facts upon which Gideon here bases his federal constitutional claim. . . . Betts was denied any relief, and on review this Court affirmed. It was held that a refusal to appoint counsel for an indigent defendant charged with a felony did not necessarily violate the Due Process Clause of the Fourteenth Amendment, which for reasons given the Court deemed to be the only applicable federal constitutional provision. The Court said:

"Asserted denial [of due process] is to be tested by an appraisal of the totality of facts in a given case. That which may, in one setting, constitute a denial of fundamental fairness, shocking to the universal sense of justice, may, in other circumstances, and in the light of other considerations, fall short of such denial."

Treating due process as "a concept less rigid and more fluid than those envisaged in other specific and particular provisions of the Bill of Rights," the Court held that refusal to appoint counsel under the particular facts and circumstances in the *Betts* case was not so "offensive to the common and fundamental ideas of fairness" as to amount to a denial of due process. Since the facts and circumstances of the two cases are so nearly indistinguishable, we think the *Betts v. Brady* holding if left standing would require us to reject Gideon's claim that the Constitution guarantees him the assistance of counsel. Upon full reconsideration we conclude that *Betts v. Brady* should be overruled.

II.

The Sixth Amendment provides, "In all criminal prosecutions, the accused shall enjoy the right . . . to have the Assistance of Counsel for his defence." We have construed this to mean that in federal courts counsel must be provided for defendants unable to employ counsel unless the right is competently and intelligently waived. Betts argued that this right is extended to indigent defendants in state courts by the Fourteenth Amendment. In response the Court stated that, while the Sixth Amendment laid down "no rule for the conduct of the States, the question recurs whether the constraint laid by the Amendment upon the national courts expresses a rule so fundamental and essential to a fair trial, and so, to due process of law, that it is made obligatory upon the States by the Fourteenth Amendment." In order to decide whether the Sixth Amendment's guarantee of counsel is of this fundamental nature, the Court in Betts set out and considered "relevant data on the subject . . . afforded by constitutional and statutory provisions subsisting in the colonies and the States prior to the inclusion of the Bill of Rights in the national Constitution, and in the constitutional, legislative, and judicial history of the States to the present date." On the basis of this historical data the Court concluded that "appointment of counsel is not a fundamental right, essential to a fair trial." It was for this reason the Betts Court refused to accept the contention that the Sixth Amendment's guarantee of counsel for indigent federal defendants was extended to or, in the words of that Court, "made obligatory upon the States by the Fourteenth Amendment." Plainly, had the Court concluded that appointment of counsel for an indigent criminal defendant was "a fundamental right, essential to a fair trial," it would have held that the Fourteenth Amendment requires appointment of counsel in a state court, just as the Sixth Amendment requires in a federal court.

We think the Court in *Betts* had ample precedent for acknowledging that those guarantees of the Bill of Rights which are fundamental safeguards of liberty immune from federal abridgment are equally protected against state invasion by the Due Process Clause of the Fourteenth Amendment. This same principle was recognized, explained, and applied in *Powell v. Alabama,* a case upholding the right of counsel, where the Court held that despite sweeping language to the contrary in *Hurtado v. California,* the Fourteenth Amendment "embraced" those "'fundamental principles of liberty and justice which lie at the base of all our civil and political institutions,'" even though they had been "specifically dealt with in another part of the federal Constitution." In many cases other than *Powell* and *Betts,* this Court has looked to the fundamental nature of original Bill of Rights guarantees to decide whether the Fourteenth Amendment makes them obligatory on the States. . . . [I]n *Palko v. Connecticut* . . . the Court . . . was careful to emphasize that "immunities that are valid as against the federal government by force of the specific pledges of particular amendments have been found to be implicit in the concept of ordered liberty, and thus, through the Fourteenth Amendment, become valid as against the states" and that guarantees "in their origin . . . effective against the federal government alone" had by prior cases "been taken over from the earlier articles of the federal bill of rights and brought within the Fourteenth Amendment by a process of absorption."

We accept *Betts v. Brady's* assumption, based as it was on our prior cases, that a provision of the Bill of Rights which is "fundamental and essential to a fair trial" is made obligatory upon the States by the Fourteenth Amendment. We think the Court in *Betts* was wrong, however, in concluding that the Sixth Amendment's guarantee of counsel is not one of these fundamental rights. Ten years before *Betts v. Brady,* this Court, after full consideration of all the historical data examined in *Betts,* had unequivocally declared that "the right to the aid of counsel is of this fundamental character." *Powell v. Alabama.* While the Court at the close of its *Powell* opinion did by its language, as this Court frequently does, limit its holding to the particular facts and circumstances of that case, its conclusions about the fundamental nature of the right to counsel are unmistakable. . . .

In light of . . . many . . . prior decisions of this Court, it is not surprising that the *Betts* Court, when faced with the contention that "one charged with crime, who is unable to obtain counsel, must be furnished counsel by the State," conceded that "expressions in the opinions of this court lend color to the argument. . . ." The fact is that in deciding as it did—that "appointment of counsel is not a fundamental right, essential to a fair trial"—the Court in *Betts v. Brady* made an abrupt break with its own well-considered precedents. In returning to these old precedents, sounder we believe than the new, we but restore constitutional principles established to achieve a fair system of justice. Not only these precedents but also reason and reflection require us to recognize that in our adversary system of criminal justice, any person haled into court, who is too poor to hire a lawyer, cannot be assured a fair trial unless counsel is provided for him. This seems to us to be an obvious truth. Governments, both state and federal, quite properly spend vast sums of money to establish machinery to try defendants accused of crime. Lawyers to prosecute are everywhere deemed essential to protect the public's interest in an orderly society. Similarly, there are few defendants charged with crime, few indeed, who fail to hire the best lawyers they can get to prepare and present their defenses. That government hires lawyers to prosecute and defendants who have the money hire lawyers to defend are the strongest indications of the widespread belief that lawyers in criminal courts are necessities, not luxuries. The right of one charged with crime to counsel may not be deemed fundamental and essential to fair trials in some countries, but it is in ours. From the very beginning, our state and national constitutions and laws have laid great emphasis on procedural and substantive safeguards designed to assure fair trials before impartial tribunals in which every defendant stands equal before the law. This noble ideal cannot be realized if the poor man charged with crime has to face his accusers without a lawyer to assist him. A defendant's need for a lawyer is nowhere better stated than in the moving words of Mr. Justice Sutherland in *Powell v. Alabama*. . . . The Court in *Betts v. Brady* departed from the sound wisdom upon which the Court's holding in *Powell v. Alabama* rested. Florida, supported by two other States, has asked that *Betts v. Brady* be left intact. Twenty-two States, as friends of the Court, argue that Betts was "an anachronism when handed down" and that it should now be overruled. We agree.

MIRANDA V. ARIZONA, 384 U.S. 436 (1966)

Chief Justice WARREN delivered the opinion of the Court.

The cases before us raise questions which go to the roots of our concepts of American criminal jurisprudence: the restraints society must observe consistent with the Federal Constitution in prosecuting individuals for crime. More specifically, we deal with the admissibility of statements obtained from an individual who is subjected to custodial police interrogation and the necessity for procedures which assure that the individual is accorded his privilege under the Fifth Amendment to the Constitution not to be compelled to incriminate himself.

We dealt with certain phases of this problem recently in *Escobedo v. Illinois.* . . .

This case has been the subject of judicial interpretation and spirited legal debate since it was decided two years ago. . . . We granted certiorari in these cases in order further to explore some facets of the problems, thus exposed, of applying the privilege against self-incrimination to in-custody interrogation, and to give concrete constitutional guidelines for law enforcement agencies and courts to follow.

We start here, as we did in *Escobedo,* with the premise that our holding is not an innovation in our jurisprudence, but is an application of principles long recognized and applied in other settings. We have undertaken a thorough re-examination of the *Escobedo* decision and the principles it announced, and we reaffirm it. That case was but an explication of basic rights that are enshrined in our Constitution—that "No person . . . shall be compelled in any criminal case to be a witness against himself," and that "the accused shall . . . have the Assistance of Counsel"—rights which were put in jeopardy in that case through official overbearing. These precious rights were fixed in our Constitution only after centuries of persecution and struggle. And in the words of Chief Justice Marshall, they were secured "for ages to come, and . . . designed to approach immortality as nearly as human institutions can approach it."

Over 70 years ago, our predecessors on this Court eloquently stated:

"The maxim *nemo tenetur seipsum accusare* had its origin in a protest against the inquisitorial and manifestly unjust methods of interrogating accused persons, which [have] long obtained in the continental system, and, until the expulsion of the Stuarts from the British throne in 1688, and the erection of additional barriers for the protection of the people against the exercise of arbitrary power, [were] not uncommon even in England. While the admissions or confessions of the prisoner, when voluntarily and freely made, have always ranked high in the scale of incriminating evidence, if an accused person be asked to explain his apparent connection with a crime under investigation, the ease with which the questions put to him may assume an inquisitorial character, the temptation to press the witness unduly, to browbeat him if he be timid or reluctant, to push him into a corner, and to entrap him into fatal contradictions, which is so painfully evident in many of the earlier state trials, . . . made the system so odious as to give rise to a demand for its total abolition. . . . So deeply did the iniquities of the ancient system impress themselves upon the minds of the American colonists that the States, with one accord, made a denial of the right to question an accused person a part of their fundamental law, so that a maxim, which in England was a mere rule of evidence, became clothed in this country with the impregnability of a constitutional enactment.

. . . The meaning and vitality of the Constitution have developed against narrow and restrictive construction."

This was the spirit in which we delineated, in meaningful language, the manner in which the constitutional rights of the individual could be enforced against overzealous police practices. It was necessary in *Escobedo,* as here, to insure that what was proclaimed in the Constitution had not become but a "form of words" in the hands of government officials. And it is in this spirit, consistent with our role as judges, that we adhere to the principles of *Escobedo* today.

Our holding will be spelled out with some specificity in the pages which follow but briefly stated it is this: the prosecution may not use statements, whether exculpatory or inculpatory, stemming from custodial interrogation of the defendant unless it demonstrates the use of procedural safeguards effective to secure the privilege against self-incrimination. By custodial interrogation, we mean questioning initiated by law enforcement officers after a person has been taken into custody or otherwise deprived of his freedom of action in any significant way. As for the procedural safeguards to be employed, unless other fully effective means are devised to inform accused persons of their right of silence and to assure a continuous opportunity to exercise it, the following measures are required. Prior to any questioning, the person must be warned that he has a right to remain silent, that any statement he does make may be used as evidence against him, and that he has a right to the presence of an attorney, either retained or appointed. The defendant may waive effectuation of these rights, provided the waiver is made voluntarily, knowingly and intelligently. If, however, he indicates in any manner and at any stage of the process that he wishes to consult with an attorney before speaking there can be no questioning. Likewise, if the individual is alone and indicates in any manner that he does not wish to be interrogated, the police may not question him. The mere fact that he may have answered some questions or volunteered some statements on his own does not deprive him of the right to refrain from answering any further inquiries until he has consulted with an attorney and thereafter consents to be questioned.

I.

The constitutional issue we decide in each of these cases is the admissibility of statements obtained from a defendant questioned while in custody or otherwise deprived of his freedom of action in any significant way. In each, the defendant was questioned by police officers, detectives, or a prosecuting attorney in a room in which he was cut off from the outside world. In none of these cases was the defendant given a full and effective warning of his rights at the outset of the interrogation process. In all the cases, the questioning elicited oral admissions, and in three of them, signed statements as well which were admitted at their trials. They all thus share salient features—incommunicado interrogation of individuals in a police-dominated atmosphere, resulting in self-incriminating statements without full warnings of constitutional rights.

An understanding of the nature and setting of this in-custody interrogation is essential to our decisions today. The difficulty in depicting what transpires at such interrogations stems from the fact that in this country they have largely taken place incommunicado. From extensive factual studies undertaken in the early 1930's, including the famous Wickersham Report to Congress by a Presidential Commission, it is clear that police violence and the "third degree" flourished at that time. In a series of cases decided by this Court long after these studies, the police resorted to physical brutality—beating, hanging, whipping—and to sustained and protracted questioning incommunicado in order to extort confessions. The Commission on Civil Rights in 1961 found much evidence to indicate that "some policemen still resort to physical force to obtain confessions." The use of physical brutality and violence is not, unfortunately, relegated to the past or to any part of the country. . . .

The examples given above are undoubtedly the exception now, but they are sufficiently widespread to be the object of concern. Unless a proper limitation upon custodial interrogation is achieved—such as these decisions will advance—there can be no assurance that practices of this nature will be eradicated in the foreseeable future. . . .

. . . [W]e stress that the modern practice of in-custody interrogation is psychologically rather than physically oriented. As we have stated before, "Since *Chambers v. Florida* this Court has recognized that coercion can be mental as well as physical, and that the blood of the accused is not the only hallmark of an unconstitutional inquisition." Interrogation still takes place in privacy. Privacy results in secrecy and this in turn results in a gap in our knowledge as to what in fact goes on in the interrogation rooms. A valuable source of information about present police practices, however, may be found in various police manuals and texts which document procedures employed with success in the past, and which recommend various other effective tactics. These texts are used by law enforcement agencies themselves as guides. It should be noted that these texts professedly present the most enlightened and effective means presently used to obtain statements through custodial interrogation. By considering these texts and other data, it is possible to describe procedures observed and noted around the country. . . .

From these representative samples of interrogation techniques, the setting prescribed by the manuals and observed in practice becomes clear. In essence, it is this: To be alone with the subject is essential to prevent distraction and to deprive him of any outside support. The aura of confidence in his guilt undermines his will to resist. He merely confirms the preconceived story the police seek to have him describe. Patience and persistence, at times relentless questioning, are employed. To obtain a confession, the interrogator must "patiently maneuver himself or his quarry into a position from which the desired objective may be attained." When normal procedures fail to produce the needed result, the police may resort to deceptive stratagems such as giving false legal advice. It is important to keep the subject off balance, for example, by trading on his insecurity about himself or his surroundings. The police then persuade, trick, or cajole him out of exercising his constitutional rights.

Even without employing brutality, the "third degree" or the specific stratagems described above, the very fact of custodial interrogation exacts a heavy toll on individual liberty and trades on the weakness of individuals. . . .

In the cases before us today, . . . we might not find the defendants' statements to have been involuntary in traditional terms. Our concern for adequate safeguards to protect precious Fifth Amendment rights is, of course, not lessened in the slightest. In each of the cases, the defendant was thrust into an unfamiliar atmosphere and run through menacing police interrogation procedures. . . . To be sure, the records do not evince overt physical coercion or patent psychological ploys. The fact remains that in none of these cases did the officers undertake to afford appropriate safeguards at the outset of the interrogation to insure that the statements were truly the product of free choice.

It is obvious that such an interrogation environment is created for no purpose other than to subjugate the individual to the will of his examiner. This atmosphere carries its own badge of intimidation. To be sure, this is not physical intimidation, but it is equally destructive of human dignity. The current practice of incommunicado interrogation is at odds with one of our Nation's most cherished principles—that the individual may not be compelled to incriminate himself. Unless adequate protective devices are employed to dispel the compulsion inherent in custodial surroundings, no statement obtained from the defendant can truly be the product of his free choice.

From the foregoing, we can readily perceive an intimate connection between the privilege against self-incrimination and police custodial questioning. It is fitting to turn to history and precedent underlying the Self-Incrimination Clause to determine its applicability in this situation.

II.

. . . Those who framed our Constitution and the Bill of Rights were ever aware of subtle encroachments on individual liberty. They knew that "illegitimate and unconstitutional practices get their first footing . . . by silent approaches and slight deviations from legal modes of procedure." The privilege was elevated to constitutional status and has always been "as broad as the mischief against which it seeks to guard." We cannot depart from this noble heritage.

Thus we may view the historical development of the privilege as one which groped for the proper scope of governmental power over the citizen. . . . [O]ur accusatory system of criminal justice demands that the government seeking to punish an individual produce the evidence against him by its own independent labors, rather than by the cruel, simple expedient of compelling it from his own mouth. In sum, the privilege is fulfilled only when the person is guaranteed the right "to remain silent unless he chooses to speak in the unfettered exercise of his own will."

The question in these cases is whether the privilege is fully applicable during a period of custodial interrogation. . . . We are satisfied that all the principles embodied in the privilege apply to informal compulsion exerted by law-enforcement officers during in-custody questioning. An individual swept from familiar surroundings into police custody, surrounded by antagonistic forces, and subjected to the techniques of persuasion described above cannot be otherwise than under compulsion to speak. As a practical matter, the compulsion to speak in the isolated setting of the police station may well be greater than in courts or other official investigations, where there are often impartial observers to guard against intimidation or trickery. . . .

Our decision in *Malloy v. Hogan* necessitates an examination of the scope of the privilege in state cases. . . . In *Malloy,* we squarely held the privilege applicable to the States, and held that the substantive standards underlying the privilege applied with full force to state court proceedings. . . . [T]he reasoning in *Malloy* made clear what had already become apparent—that the substantive and procedural safeguards surrounding admissibility of confessions in state cases had become exceedingly exacting, reflecting all the policies embedded in the privilege. The voluntariness doctrine in the state cases, as *Malloy* indicates, encompasses all interrogation practices which are likely to exert such pressure upon an individual as to disable him from making a free and rational choice. . . .

. . . The presence of counsel, in all the cases before us today, would be the adequate protective device necessary to make the process of police interrogation conform to the dictates of the privilege. His presence would insure that statements made in the government-established atmosphere are not the product of compulsion.

. . . That counsel is present when statements are taken from an individual during interrogation obviously enhances the integrity of the fact-finding processes in court. The presence of an attorney, and the warnings delivered to the individual, enable the defendant under otherwise compelling circumstances to tell his story without fear, effectively, and in a way that eliminates the evils in the interrogation process. Without the protections flowing from adequate warnings and the rights of counsel, "all the careful safeguards erected around the giving of testimony, whether by an accused or any other witness, would become empty formalities in a procedure where the most compelling possible evidence of guilt, a confession, would have already been obtained at the unsupervised pleasure of the police."

Today, then, there can be no doubt that the Fifth Amendment privilege is available outside of criminal court proceedings and serves to protect persons in all settings in which their freedom of action is curtailed in any significant way from being compelled to incriminate themselves. We have concluded that without proper safeguards the process of in-custody interrogation of persons suspected or accused of crime contains inherently compelling pressures which work to undermine the individual's will to resist and to compel him to speak where he would not otherwise do so freely. In order to combat these pressures and to permit a full opportunity to exercise the privilege against self-incrimination, the accused must be adequately and effectively apprised of his rights and the exercise of those rights must be fully honored.

. . . [U]nless we are shown other procedures which are at least as effective in apprising accused persons of their right of silence and in assuring a continuous opportunity to exercise it, the following safeguards must be observed.

At the outset, if a person in custody is to be subjected to interrogation, he must first be informed in clear and unequivocal terms that he has the right to remain silent. . . .

The Fifth Amendment privilege is so fundamental to our system of constitutional rule and the expedient of giving an adequate warning as to the availability of the privilege so simple, we will not pause to inquire in individual cases whether the defendant was aware of his rights without a warning being given. . . .

The warning of the right to remain silent must be accompanied by the explanation that anything said can and will be used against the individual in court. . . .

The circumstances surrounding in-custody interrogation can operate very quickly to overbear the will of one merely made aware of his privilege by his interrogators. Therefore, the right to have counsel present at the interrogation is indispensable to the protection of the Fifth Amendment privilege under the system we delineate today. . . . [T]he need for counsel to protect the Fifth Amendment privilege comprehends not merely a right to consult with counsel prior to questioning, but also to have counsel present during any questioning if the defendant so desires.

The presence of counsel at the interrogation may serve several significant subsidiary functions as well. If the accused decides to talk to his interrogators, the assistance of counsel can mitigate the dangers of untrustworthiness. With a lawyer present the likelihood that the police will practice coercion is reduced, and if coercion is nevertheless exercised the lawyer can testify to it in court. The presence of a lawyer can also help to guarantee that the accused gives a fully accurate statement to the police and that the statement is rightly reported by the prosecution at trial.

An individual need not make a pre-interrogation request for a lawyer. While such request affirmatively secures his right to have one, his failure to ask for a lawyer does not constitute a waiver. No effective waiver of the right to counsel during interrogation can be recognized unless specifically made after the warnings we here delineate have been given. . . .

Accordingly we hold that an individual held for interrogation must be clearly informed that he has the right to consult with a lawyer and to have the lawyer with him during interrogation under the system for protecting the privilege we delineate today. As with the warnings of the right to remain silent and that anything stated can be used in evidence against him, this warning is an absolute prerequisite to interrogation. . . .

If an individual indicates that he wishes the assistance of counsel before any interrogation occurs, the authorities cannot rationally ignore or deny his request on the basis that the individual does not have or cannot afford a retained attorney. The financial ability of the individual has no relationship to the scope of the rights involved here. . . .

In order fully to apprise a person interrogated of the extent of his rights under this system then, it is necessary to warn him not only that he has the right to consult with an attorney, but also that if he is indigent a lawyer will be appointed to represent him. . . .

Once warnings have been given, the subsequent procedure is clear. If the individual indicates in any manner, at any time prior to or during questioning, that he wishes to remain silent, the interrogation must cease. . . . If the individual states that he wants an attorney, the interrogation must cease until an attorney is present. At that time, the individual must have an opportunity to confer with the attorney and to have him present during any subsequent questioning. If the individual cannot obtain an attorney and he indicates that he wants one before speaking to police, they must respect his decision to remain silent. . . .

If the interrogation continues without the presence of an attorney and a statement is taken, a heavy burden rests on the government to demonstrate that the defendant knowingly and intelligently waived his privilege against self-incrimination and his right to retained or appointed counsel. . . .

The warnings required and the waiver necessary in accordance with our opinion today are, in the absence of a fully effective equivalent, prerequisites to the admissibility of any statement made by a defendant. . . .

IV.

. . . In announcing these principles, we are not unmindful of the burdens which law enforcement officials must bear, often under trying circumstances. We also fully recognize the obligation of all citizens to aid in enforcing the criminal laws. This Court, while protecting individual rights, has always given ample latitude to law enforcement agencies in the legitimate exercise of their duties. The limits we have placed on the interrogation process should not constitute an undue interference with a proper system of law enforcement. As we have noted, our decision does not in any way preclude police from carrying out their traditional investigatory functions. Although confessions may play an important role in some convictions, the cases before us present graphic examples of the overstatement of the "need" for confessions. In each case authorities conducted interrogations ranging up to five days in duration despite the presence, through standard investigating practices, of considerable evidence against each defendant. . . .

Over the years the Federal Bureau of Investigation has compiled an exemplary record of effective law enforcement while advising any suspect or arrested person, at the outset of an interview, that he is not required to make a statement, that any statement may be used against him in court, that the individual may obtain the services of an attorney of his own choice and, more recently, that he has a right to free counsel if he is unable to pay. A letter received from the Solicitor General in response to a question from the Bench makes it clear that the present pattern of warnings and respect for the rights of the individual followed as a practice by the FBI is consistent with the procedure which we delineate today. . . .

The practice of the FBI can readily be emulated by state and local enforcement agencies. The argument that the FBI deals with different crimes than are dealt with by state authorities does not mitigate the significance of the FBI experience. . . .

V.

Because of the nature of the problem and because of its recurrent significance in numerous cases, we have to this point discussed the relationship of the Fifth Amendment privilege to police interrogation without specific concentration on the facts of the cases before us. We turn now to these facts to consider the application to these cases of the constitutional principles discussed above. In each instance, we have concluded that statements were obtained from the defendant under circumstances that did not meet constitutional standards for protection of the privilege.

Chronology

1641 The Courts of High Commission and Star Chamber and the oath *ex officio* are eliminated in England.

1791 The Bill of Rights is added to the U.S. Constitution.

1833 *Barron v. Baltimore* holds that the Bill of Rights does not apply to the states.

1884 *Hurtado v. California* holds that the Bill of Rights cannot be applied to the states through the due process clause of the Fourteenth Amendment.

Hopt v. Utah Territory invokes a common-law rule against the admission of involuntary confessions in federal cases.

1886 *Boyd v. United States* holds that the privilege against self-incrimination protects against the compelled production of private papers.

1892 *Counselman v. Hitchcock* applies the privilege against self-incrimination to grand jury hearings and requires transactional immunity to overcome it.

1896 *Brown v. Walker* holds that a witness can be compelled to incriminate himself in return for a grant of transactional immunity.

1897 *Bram v. United States* holds that the federal standard for admissibility of confessions is the self-incrimination clause.

1906 *Hale v. Henkel holds* that a corporation has no privilege against self-incrimination.

1908 *Twining v. New Jersey* holds that the privilege against self-incrimination does not apply to the states.

1910 *Holt v. United States* holds that the privilege against self-incrimination does not protect against use of the accused's body as evidence.

1924 *Wan v. United States* holds that lengthy and arduous detention and interrogation may violate the privilege against self-incrimination.

McCarthy v. Arndstein affirms that the privilege against self-incrimination can be invoked in any proceeding in which testimony can be compelled.

1932 *Powell v. Alabama* overturns the conviction of the Scottsboro Boys because of the judge's failure to ensure the effective retention or appointment of counsel.

1936 *Brown v. Mississippi* holds that a conviction based on confessions extorted by torture is a denial of due process of law.

1937 *Palko v. Connecticut* allows the selective application of provisions of the Bill of Rights to the states.

1938 *Johnson v. Zerbst* holds that the Sixth Amendment prohibits federal trials of defendants without counsel unless that right has been waived.

1940 *Chambers v. Florida* overturns a state conviction based on the use of confessions gained from marathon interrogation under intimidating circumstances.

1941 *Lisenba v. California* announces that the due process standard for the admissibility of confessions is voluntariness, not truth.

1942 *Betts v. Brady* holds that states are required to appoint counsel for indigent defendants only when failure to do so would be fundamentally unfair.

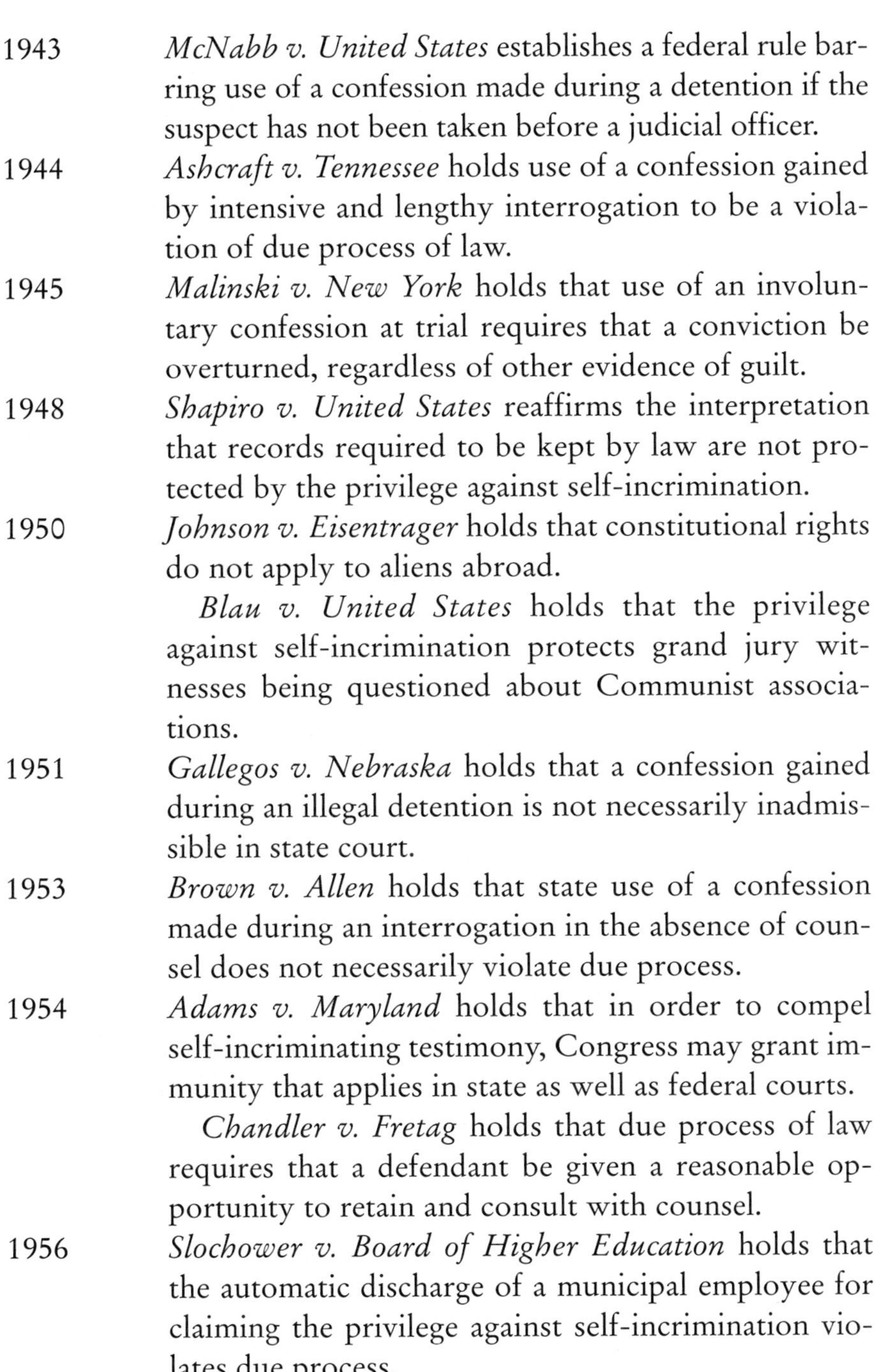

1943 *McNabb v. United States* establishes a federal rule barring use of a confession made during a detention if the suspect has not been taken before a judicial officer.

1944 *Ashcraft v. Tennessee* holds use of a confession gained by intensive and lengthy interrogation to be a violation of due process of law.

1945 *Malinski v. New York* holds that use of an involuntary confession at trial requires that a conviction be overturned, regardless of other evidence of guilt.

1948 *Shapiro v. United States* reaffirms the interpretation that records required to be kept by law are not protected by the privilege against self-incrimination.

1950 *Johnson v. Eisentrager* holds that constitutional rights do not apply to aliens abroad.

Blau v. United States holds that the privilege against self-incrimination protects grand jury witnesses being questioned about Communist associations.

1951 *Gallegos v. Nebraska* holds that a confession gained during an illegal detention is not necessarily inadmissible in state court.

1953 *Brown v. Allen* holds that state use of a confession made during an interrogation in the absence of counsel does not necessarily violate due process.

1954 *Adams v. Maryland* holds that in order to compel self-incriminating testimony, Congress may grant immunity that applies in state as well as federal courts.

Chandler v. Fretag holds that due process of law requires that a defendant be given a reasonable opportunity to retain and consult with counsel.

1956 *Slochower v. Board of Higher Education* holds that the automatic discharge of a municipal employee for claiming the privilege against self-incrimination violates due process.

1957 *Mallory v. United States* reaffirms the federal rule barring use of a custodial confession if the suspect has not been taken before a judicial officer.

1959 *Spano v. New York* overturns a conviction based on a confession gained as the result of prolonged, late-night interrogation and false statements to the suspect.

1961 *Rogers v. Richmond* holds that the determination of the voluntariness of a confession must not be affected by considerations of its truthfulness.

Hamilton v. Alabama holds that an accused person has a right to counsel at arraignment if rights may be sacrificed or lost at the proceeding.

1963 *Wong Sun v. United States* holds that a confession that is the product of an illegal arrest is inadmissible.

Gideon v. Wainwright applies the right to counsel to the states and requires them to appoint trial counsel for indigent defendants in felony cases.

Douglas v. California requires the states to appoint counsel for indigent defendants in appeals of right.

White v. Maryland holds that an accused person has a right to counsel at a preliminary hearing where such assistance is clearly needed.

Fahy v. Connecticut makes clear that a confession that is the product of an unlawful search and seizure is inadmissible.

1964 *Massiah v. United States* holds that use of incriminating statements gained by an undercover interrogation of an indicted defendant violates the right to counsel.

Malloy v. Hogan applies the privilege against self-incrimination to the states and holds that the same standards apply in federal and state proceedings.

Murphy v. Waterfront Commission holds that incriminating testimony compelled in one jurisdiction may not be used in another jurisdiction.

Jackson v. Denno holds that the same jury may not determine both the voluntariness of a confession and the guilt or innocence of the defendant.

Escobedo v. Illinois holds that a suspect upon whom an investigation has focused has a right to consult an attorney during interrogation.

1965 *Griffin v. California* holds that federal and state prosecutors and judges may not make adverse comments about a defendant's decision not to testify at trial.

Albertson v. Subversive Activities Control Board holds that the government may not require registration of members of the Communist Party.

1966 *Miranda v. Arizona* requires police to warn suspects about their right to counsel and privilege against self-incrimination prior to custodial interrogation.

Schmerber v. California holds that testimonial or communicative evidence, not physical evidence, is protected by the privilege against self-incrimination.

1967 *In re Gault* holds that the right to counsel and privilege against self-incrimination apply in juvenile delinquency proceedings.

United States v. Wade holds that the right to counsel applies at all critical stages of a prosecution, including lineups, and that being compelled to appear in a lineup and speak words spoken by the perpetrator does not violate the privilege against self-incrimination.

Mempa v. Rhay makes clear that a sentencing hearing is a critical stage of a prosecution at which a defendant has a right to counsel.

1968 *Marchetti v. United States* and *Grosso v. United States* hold that a requirement that gamblers register violates the privilege against self-incrimination.

Gardner v. Broderick holds that public employees may not be fired for asserting the privilege against self-incrimination and refusing to sign a waiver of immunity.

1970 *McMann v. Richardson* states definitively that the right to counsel includes the right to the effective assistance of counsel at trial.

Coleman v. Alabama holds that the right to counsel applies to a preliminary hearing at which proceedings may materially affect the conduct of the trial.

1971 *Harris v. New York* holds that uncoerced statements made in the absence of *Miranda* warnings may be used to impeach that defendant's testimony at trial.

California v. Byers holds that a requirement that drivers involved in accidents stop and provide their names and addresses does not violate the privilege against self-incrimination.

1972 *Kastigar v. United States* holds that use and derivative use immunity are sufficient to overcome the privilege against self-incrimination.

Kirby v. Illinois holds that the right to counsel does not attach until the point at which adversary judicial proceedings have been initiated against the defendant.

Argersinger v. Hamlin holds that a state must provide counsel to indigents, even for petty offenses, if it wishes to impose a sentence of imprisonment.

1973 *United States v. Ash* redefines critical stages of a prosecution, when the right to counsel pertains, as events involving an adversarial confrontation between the prosecution and the accused.

1974 *Michigan v. Tucker* allows the use of testimony from a witness whose identity was revealed as a result of *Miranda* violations.

Ross v. Moffitt holds that states are not required to provide indigent defendants with appointed counsel for discretionary appeals.

1975 *Faretta v. California* holds that the Sixth Amendment protects the defendant's right to self-representation at trial.

1976 *Fisher v. United States* holds that the privilege against self-incrimination does not protect voluntarily prepared business records unless the act of production itself would in some way amount to testimonial self-incrimination.

Andresen v. Maryland holds that the privilege against self-incrimination does not protect business records from lawful search and seizure.

1977 *Brewer v. Williams* overturns a murder conviction based on statements and evidence gained by interrogation in violation of the right to counsel.

1978 *Mincey v. Arizona* holds that a defendant's involuntary statements may not be used against him or her at trial for any purpose.

1980 *Rhode Island v. Innis* holds that *Miranda* rights with respect to interrogation apply not only to express questioning but also to its functional equivalent.

1981 *Estelle v. Smith* holds that *Miranda* rules apply to a court-ordered, custodial psychiatric examination and that the privilege against self-incrimination applies to a sentencing hearing.

Edwards v. Arizona holds that once a suspect asserts his or her *Miranda* right to counsel, police may not initiate further interrogation until counsel has been made available.

1984 *United States v. Doe* holds that the privilege against self-incrimination does not protect the contents of voluntarily prepared business records but does protect their production when that act in itself would be incriminating.

Strickland v. Washington holds that under most circumstances a claim of ineffective assistance of counsel must show that counsel's performance was deficient and that the deficient performance prejudiced the defense.

New York v. Quarles creates a public safety exception to the rule that statements made in the absence of *Miranda* warnings are inadmissible at trial.

Berkemer v. McCarty holds that *Miranda* rules apply to misdemeanors as well as felonies but that traffic stops are not initially custodial.

1985 *Evitts v. Lucey* holds that the right to counsel includes the right to the effective assistance of counsel on an appeal of right.

Oregon v. Elstad holds that administration of *Miranda* warnings is ordinarily sufficient to overcome a prior *Miranda* violation.

1986 *Moran v. Burbine* upholds a waiver of *Miranda* rights even though police had failed to inform the suspect that an attorney wished to see him and had deceived the attorney about an imminent interrogation.

Michigan v. Jackson holds that if police initiate an interrogation after an assertion of the Sixth Amendment right to counsel, any waiver of counsel for that interrogation is invalid.

Colorado v. Connelly holds that a confession is involuntary only when the compulsion to confess is the product of governmental coercion.

1987 *Rock v. Arkansas* upholds the right to testify in one's own defense.

1988 *Arizona v. Roberson* holds that once the *Miranda* right to counsel has been invoked, police may not initiate interrogation in the absence of counsel for any offense.

1990 *Michigan v. Harvey* holds that statements that are otherwise inadmissible because obtained in violation of the Sixth Amendment right to counsel are admissible for the purpose of impeaching the credibility of that defendant's testimony at trial.

Illinois v. Perkins holds that *Miranda* warnings are not required when an undercover agent posing as a prisoner elicits information from a fellow prisoner.

Minnick v. Mississippi holds that once the *Miranda* right to counsel has been invoked, police may not reinitiate interrogation in the absence of counsel, even if counsel has been consulted in the meantime.

1991 *McNeil v. Wisconsin* holds that the Sixth Amendment right to counsel is offense-specific and does not apply with respect to other offenses for which the right has not attached.

1999 *Mitchell v. United States* holds that the privilege against self-incrimination applies at a noncapital sentencing hearing, even if the defendant has pleaded guilty, and that adverse inferences may not be drawn from failure to testify.

2000 *Martinez v. Court of Appeal* holds that there is no right to self-representation on appeal.

Dickerson v. United States reaffirms that *Miranda* warnings are constitutional rights.

2001 *Ohio v. Reiner* affirms that the privilege against self-incrimination may be claimed by witnesses who assert their innocence.

2003 *Chavez v. Martinez* holds that a coercive interrogation does not violate the self-incrimination clause unless the compelled statements are used against the defendant in a criminal prosecution.

Wiggins v. Smith upholds a claim of ineffective assistance of counsel because the attorney's strategy was based on inadequate investigation of relevant material.

2004 *Rasul v. Bush* allows foreign enemy combatants held at Guantánamo Bay, Cuba, to challenge detention in court.

Hamdi v. Rumsfeld grants a U.S. enemy combatant a hearing before a neutral decisionmaker.

Missouri v. Seibert excludes post-warning statements from two-stage interrogations involving a deliberate violation of *Miranda* rights.

United States v. Patane allows admission of physical evidence derived from *Miranda* violations.

Table of Cases

Adams v. Maryland, 347 U.S. 179 (1954)
Adams v. United States ex rel. McCann, 317 U.S. 269 (1942)
Adamson v. California, 332 U.S. 46 (1947)
Al Odah v. United States, 321 F. 3d 1134 (DC Cir. 2003)
Alabama v. Shelton, 535 U.S. 654 (2002)
Albertson v. Subversive Activities Control Board, 382 U.S. 70 (1965)
Allen v. Illinois, 478 U.S. 364 (1986)
Andresen v. Maryland, 427 U.S. 463 (1976)
Apprendi v. New Jersey, 530 U.S. 466 (2000)
Argersinger v. Hamlin, 407 U.S. 25 (1972)
Arizona v. Fulminante, 499 U.S. 279 (1991)
Arizona v. Mauro, 481 U.S. 520 (1987)
Arizona v. Roberson, 486 U.S. 675 (1988)
Ashcraft v. Tennessee, 322 U.S. 143 (1944)
Baldwin v. New York, 399 U.S. 66 (1970)
Baltimore City Department of Social Services v. Bouknight, 493 U.S. 549 (1990)
Barron v. Baltimore, 32 U.S. (7 Pet.) 243 (1833)
Baxter v. Palmigiano, 425 U.S. 308 (1976)
Beckwith v. United States, 425 U.S. 341 (1976)
Bell v. Cone, 535 U.S. 685 (2002)
Bellis v. United States, 417 U.S. 85 (1974)
Berkemer v. McCarty, 468 U.S. 420 (1984)

Berry v. City of Cincinnati, 414 U.S. 29 (1973)
Betts v. Brady, 316 U.S. 455 (1942)
Blau v. United States, 340 U.S. 159 (1950)
Bounds v. Smith, 430 U.S. 817 (1977)
Boyd v. United States, 116 U.S. 616 (1886)
Brady v. United States, 397 U.S. 742 (1970)
Bram v. United States, 168 U.S. 532 (1897)
Braswell v. United States, 487 U.S. 99 (1988)
Brewer v. Williams, 430 U.S. 387 (1977)
Brown v. Allen, 344 U.S. 443 (1953)
Brown v. Illinois, 422 U.S. 590 (1975)
Brown v. Mississippi, 297 U.S. 278 (1936)
Brown v. United States, 356 U.S. 148 (1958)
Brown v. Walker, 161 U.S. 591 (1896)
Bruno v. United States, 308 U.S. 287 (1939)
Burdine v. Johnson, 262 F.3d 336 (5th Cir. 2001)
Burgett v. Texas, 389 U.S. 109 (1967)
California v. Beheler, 463 U.S. 1121 (1983)
California v. Byers, 402 U.S. 424 (1971)
California v. Prysock, 453 U.S. 355 (1981)
Carnley v. Cochran, 369 U.S. 506 (1962)
Carter v. Kentucky, 450 U.S. 288 (1981)
Chambers v. Florida, 309 U.S. 227 (1940)
Chandler v. Fretag, 348 U.S. 3 (1954)
Chapman v. California, 386 U.S. 18 (1967)
Chavez v. Martinez, 538 U.S. 760 (2003)
Cockrell v. Burdine, 535 U.S. 1120 (2002)
Coleman v. Alabama, 399 U.S. 1 (1970)
Colorado v. Connelly, 479 U.S. 157 (1986)
Colorado v. Spring, 479 U.S. 564 (1987)
Connecticut v. Barrett, 479 U.S. 523 (1987)
Couch v. United States, 409 U.S. 322 (1973)
Counselman v. Hitchcock, 142 U.S. 547 (1892)
Crooker v. California, 357 U.S. 433 (1958)

Curcio v. United States, 354 U.S. 118 (1957)
Cuyler v. Sullivan, 446 U.S. 335 (1980)
Davis v. United States, 512 U.S. 452 (1994)
Dickerson v. United States, 530 U.S. 428 (2000)
Doe v. United States, 487 U.S. 201 (1988)
Douglas v. California, 372 U.S. 353 (1963)
Doyle v. Ohio, 426 U.S. 610 (1976)
Duckworth v. Eagan, 492 U.S. 195 (1989)
Edwards v. Arizona, 451 U.S. 477 (1981)
Escobedo v. Illinois, 378 U.S. 478 (1964)
Estelle v. Smith, 451 U.S. 454 (1981)
Evitts v. Lucey, 469 U.S. 387 (1985)
Fahy v. Connecticut, 375 U.S. 85 (1963)
Faretta v. California, 422 U.S. 806 (1975)
Feldman v. United States, 322 U.S. 487 (1944)
Fellers v. United States, 540 U.S. ___, 124 S. Ct. 1019, 157 L. Ed. 2d 1016 (2004). Slip opinions are available online at <http://www.supremecourtus.gov/opinions/opinions.html>.
Fikes v. Alabama, 352 U.S. 191 (1957)
Fisher v. United States, 425 U.S. 391 (1976)
Fletcher v. Weir, 455 U.S. 603 (1982)
Foster v. California, 394 U.S. 440 (1969)
Frank v. Mangum, 237 U.S. 309 (1915)
Fuller v. Oregon, 417 U.S. 40 (1974)
Gagnon v. Scarpelli, 411 U.S. 778 (1973)
Gallegos v. Nebraska, 342 U.S. 55 (1951)
Gardner v. Broderick, 392 U.S. 273 (1968)
Garner v. United States, 424 U.S. 648 (1976)
Garrity v. New Jersey, 385 U.S. 493 (1967)
Geders v. United States, 425 U.S. 80 (1976)
Gherebi v. Bush, 352 F. 3d 1278 (9th Cir. 2003)
Gideon v. Wainwright, 372 U.S. 335 (1963)
Gilbert v. California, 388 U.S. 263 (1967)
Glover v. United States, 531 U.S. 198 (2001)

Griffin v. California, 380 U.S. 606 (1965)
Griffin v. Illinois, 351 U.S. 12 (1956)
Grosso v. United States, 390 U.S. 62 (1968)
Grunewald v. United States, 353 U.S. 391 (1957)
Hale v. Henkel, 201 U.S. 43 (1906)
Hamdi v. Rumsfeld, 243 F. Supp. 2d 527 (2002)
Hamdi v. Rumsfeld, 316 F. 3d 450 (4th Cir. 2003)
Hamdi v. Rumsfeld, 542 U.S. ___, 124 S. Ct. 2633, 159 L. Ed. 2d 578 (2004). Slip opinions are available online at <http://www.supremecourtus.gov/opinions/opinions.html>.
Hamilton v. Alabama, 368 U.S. 52 (1961)
Harris v. New York, 401 U.S. 222 (1971)
Haynes v. United States, 390 U.S. 85 (1968)
Haynes v. Washington, 373 U.S. 503 (1963)
Heike v. United States, 227 U.S. 131 (1913)
Hill v. Lockhart, 474 U.S. 52 (1985)
Hoffman v. United States, 341 U.S. 479 (1951)
Holt v. United States, 218 U.S. 245 (1910)
Hopt v. Utah Territory, 110 U.S. 574 (1884)
Hurtado v. California, 110 U.S. 516 (1884)
Illinois v. Allen, 397 U.S. 337 (1970)
Illinois v. Perkins, 496 U.S. 292 (1990)
In re Gault, 387 U.S. 1 (1967)
Jackson v. Denno, 378 U.S. 368 (1964)
Jenkins v. Anderson, 447 U.S. 231 (1980)
Johnson v. Eisentrager, 339 U.S. 763 (1950)
Johnson v. New Jersey, 384 U.S. 719 (1966)
Johnson v. Zerbst, 304 U.S. 458 (1938)
Kastigar v. United States, 406 U.S. 441 (1972)
Kaupp v. Texas, 538 U.S. 626 (2003)
Kirby v. Illinois, 406 U.S. 682 (1972)
Kitchens v. Smith, 401 U.S. 847 (1971)
Knapp v. Schweitzer, 357 U.S. 371 (1958)
Kuhlmann v. Wilson, 477 U.S. 436 (1986)

Lakeside v. Oregon, 435 U.S. 333 (1978)
Lefkowitz v. Cunningham, 431 U.S. 801 (1977)
Lefkowitz v. Turley, 414 U.S. 70 (1973)
Lewis v. United States, 348 U.S. 419 (1955)
Lisenba v. California, 314 U.S. 219 (1941)
Maine v. Moulton, 474 U.S. 159 (1985)
Malinski v. New York, 324 U.S. 401 (1945)
Mallory v. United States, 354 U.S. 449 (1957)
Malloy v. Hogan, 378 U.S. 1 (1964)
Marchetti v. United States 390 U.S. 39 (1968)
Martinez v. Court of Appeal, 528 U.S. 152 (2000)
Massiah v. United States, 377 U.S. 201 (1964)
Mathis v. United States, 391 U.S. 1 (1968)
McCarthy v. Arndstein, 266 U.S. 34 (1924)
McKaskle v. Wiggins, 465 U.S. 168 (1984)
McKune v. Lile, 536 U.S. 24 (2002)
McLeod v. Ohio, 381 U.S. 356 (1965)
McMann v. Richardson, 397 U.S. 759 (1970)
McNabb v. United States, 318 U.S. 332 (1943)
McNeil v. Wisconsin, 501 U.S. 171 (1991)
Mempa v. Rhay, 389 U.S. 128 (1967)
Mincey v. Arizona, 437 U.S. 385 (1978)
Michigan v. Harvey, 494 U.S. 344 (1990)
Michigan v. Jackson, 475 U.S. 625 (1986)
Michigan v. Mosley, 423 U.S. 96 (1975)
Michigan v. Tucker, 417 U.S. 433 (1974)
Minnesota v. Murphy, 465 U.S. 420 (1984)
Minnick v. Mississippi, 498 U.S. 146 (1990)
Miranda v. Arizona, 384 U.S. 436 (1966)
Missouri v. Seibert, 542 U.S. ___, 124 S. Ct. 2601, 159 L. Ed. 2d 643 (2004). Slip opinions are available online at <http://www.supremecourtus.gov/opinions/opinions.html>.
Mitchell v. United States, 526 U.S. 314 (1999)
Mooney v. Holohan, 294 U.S. 103 (1935)

Moore v. Dempsey, 261 U.S. 86 (1923)
Moran v. Burbine, 475 U.S. 412 (1986)
Morris v. Slappy, 461 U.S. 1 (1983)
Murphy v. Waterfront Commission, 378 U.S. 52 (1964)
Murray v. Giarratano, 492 U.S. 1 (1989)
New Jersey v. Portash, 440 U.S. 450 (1979)
New York v. Quarles, 467 U.S. 649 (1984)
Nix v. Williams, 467 U.S. 431 (1984)
Norris v. Alabama, 294 U.S. 587 (1935)
North Carolina v. Butler, 441 U.S. 369 (1979)
Ohio v. Reiner, 532 U.S. 17 (2001)
Oregon v. Elstad, 470 U.S. 298 (1985)
Oregon v. Hass, 420 U.S. 714 (1975)
Oregon v. Mathiason, 429 U.S. 492 (1977)
Orozco v. Texas, 394 U.S. 324 (1969)
Padilla v. Rumsfeld, 352 F. 3d 695 (2d Cir. 2003)
Palko v. Connecticut, 302 U.S. 319 (1937)
Patterson v. Alabama, 294 U.S. 600 (1935)
Patterson v. Illinois, 487 U.S. 285 (1988)
Pennsylvania v. Finley, 481 U.S. 551 (1987)
Pennsylvania v. Muniz, 496 U.S. 582 (1990)
People ex rel. Hackley v. Kelly, 24 N.Y. 74 (1861)
Perry v. Leeke, 488 U.S. 272 (1989)
Pickelsimer v. Wainwright, 375 U.S. 2 (1963)
Powell v. Alabama, 287 U.S. 45 (1932)
Rasul v. Bush, 542 U.S. ___, 124 S. Ct. 2686, 159 L. Ed. 2d 548 (2004). Slip opinions are available online at <http://www.supremecourtus.gov/opinions/opinions.html>.
Rhode Island v. Innis, 446 U.S. 291 (1980)
Rock v. Arkansas, 483 U.S. 44 (1987)
Rogers v. Richmond, 365 U.S. 534 (1961)
Rogers v. United States, 340 U.S. 367 (1951)
Ross v. Moffitt, 417 U.S. 600 (1974)

Rumsfeld v. Padilla, 542 U.S. ___, 124 S. Ct. 2711, 159 L. Ed. 2d 513 (2004). Slip opinions are available online at <http://www.supremecourtus.gov/opinions/opinions.html>.
Schmerber v. California, 384 U.S. 757 (1966)
Scott v. Illinois, 440 U.S. 367 (1979)
Selective Service System v. Minnesota Public Interest Research Group, 468 U.S. 841 (1984)
Shapiro v. United States, 335 U.S. 1 (1948)
Slochower v. Board of Higher Education, 350 U.S. 551 (1956)
Snyder v. Massachusetts, 291 U.S. 97 (1934)
South Dakota v. Neville, 459 U.S. 553 (1983)
Spano v. New York, 360 U.S. 315 (1959)
Spevack v. Klein, 385 U.S. 511 (1967)
Spies v. Illinois, 123 U.S. 131 (1887)
Stein v. New York, 346 U.S. 156 (1953)
Stovall v. Denno, 388 U.S. 293 (1967)
Strickland v. Washington, 466 U.S. 668 (1984)
Swidler and Berlin v. United States, 524 U.S. 399 (1998)
Texas v. Cobb, 532 U.S. 162 (2001)
Townsend v. Burke, 334 U.S. 736 (1948)
Twining v. New Jersey, 211 U.S. 78 (1908)
Ullmann v. United States, 350 U.S. 422 (1956)
United States v. Apfelbaum, 445 U.S. 115 (1980)
United States v. Ash, 413 U.S. 300 (1973)
United States v. Balsys, 524 U.S. 666 (1998)
United States v. Bin Laden, 132 F. Supp. 2d 168 (2001)
United States v. Cronic, 466 U.S. 648 (1984)
United States v. Dickerson, 166 F. 3d 667 (4th Cir. 1999)
United States v. Dionisio, 410 U.S. 1 (1973)
United States v. Doe, 465 U.S. 605 (1984)
United States v. Fellers, 285 F. 3d 721 (8th Cir. 2002)
United States v. Hale, 422 U.S. 171 (1975)
United States v. Henry, 447 U.S. 264 (1980)
United States v. Hubbell, 530 U.S. 27 (2000)

United States v. Kahriger, 345 U.S. 22 (1953)
United States v. Monia, 317 U.S. 424 (1943)
United States v. Murdock, 284 U.S. 141 (1931)
United States v. Patane, 542 U.S. ___, 124 S. Ct. 2620, 159 L. Ed. 2d 667 (2004). Slip opinions are available online at <http://www.supremecourtus.gov/opinions/opinions.html>.
United States v. Robinson, 485 U.S. 25 (1988)
United States v. Sullivan, 274 U.S. 259 (1927)
United States v. Van Duzee, 140 U.S. 169 (1891)
United States v. Wade, 388 U.S. 218 (1967)
United States v. White, 322 U.S. 694 (1944)
Upshaw v. United States, 335 U.S. 410 (1948)
Uveges v. Pennsylvania, 335 U.S. 437 (1948)
Wainwright v. Torna, 455 U.S. 586 (1982)
Wan v. United States, 266 U.S. 1 (1924)
Watkins v. United States, 354 U.S. 178 (1957)
Watts v. Indiana, 338 U.S. 49 (1949)
Wheat v. United States, 486 U.S. 153 (1988)
White v. Maryland, 373 U.S. 59 (1963)
Wiggins v. Smith, 539 U.S. 510 (2003)
Williams v. Taylor, 529 U.S. 362 (2000)
Wilson v. United States, 149 U.S. 60 (1893)
Wilson v. United States, 221 U.S. 361 (1911)
Wolff v. McDonnell, 418 U.S. 539 (1974)
Wong Sun v. United States, 371 U.S. 471 (1963)

Annotated Bibliography

General Works

Two good general introductions to the American criminal justice system are George F. Cole and Christopher E. Smith, 2004, *The American System of Criminal Justice,* 10th ed. (Belmont, CA: Wadsworth); and Larry J. Siegel and Joseph J. Senna 2004, *Introduction to Criminal Justice,* 10th ed. (Belmont, CA: Wadsworth).

A frequently updated anthology of important readings is George F. Cole, Marc G. Gertz, and Amy Bunger, 2004, *The Criminal Justice System: Politics and Policies,* 9th ed. (Belmont, CA: Wadsworth).

Jerold H. Israel, Yale Kamisar, and Wayne R. LaFave's annually published *Criminal Procedure and the Constitution: Leading Supreme Court Cases and Introductory Text* (St. Paul, MN: West Publishing Company) provides excerpted Supreme Court opinions set in context; and Yale Kamisar, Wayne R. LaFave, Jerold H. Israel, and Nancy J. King, 2002, *Basic Criminal Procedure: Cases, Comments, and Questions,* 10th ed. (St. Paul, MN: West Publishing Company), is a definitive law school textbook that incorporates both cases and expert commentary.

In its May issue each year, the *Georgetown Law Journal* publishes a comprehensive review of federal criminal procedure, covering developments in the U.S. Supreme Court and federal courts of appeals.

An authoritative analysis of how each provision of the Constitution has been interpreted over time by the Supreme Court is provided by U.S. Senate, 1992, *The Constitution of the United States of America: Analysis and Interpretation,* 103d Cong., 1st sess. S. Doc. 103–6, available in federal government depository libraries and online at <http://www.access.gpo.gov/

congress/senate/constitution/toc.html#92ed>, and in periodic supplements, most recently the *2000 Supplement:* 106th Cong., 2d sess. S. Doc. 106–27, available in the same libraries and online at <http://www.access.gpo.gov/congress/senate/constitution/toc.html#00supp>.

The general process of application of provisions of the Bill of Rights to the states through their incorporation into the due process clause of the Fourteenth Amendment is analyzed in Richard C. Cortner, 1981, *The Supreme Court and the Second Bill of Rights: The Fourteenth Amendment and the Nationalization of Civil Liberties* (Madison: University of Wisconsin Press), and Roald Y. Mykkeltvedt, 1983, *The Nationalization of the Bill of Rights: Fourteenth Amendment Due Process and Procedural Rights* (Port Washington, NY: Associated Faculty Press).

The Criminal Law Reporter's 1978 volume *The Criminal Law Revolution and Its Aftermath: 1960–1977* (Washington: Bureau of National Affairs) provides a term-by-term survey of cases during a critical era in which the Supreme Court strengthened many rights of the accused and applied them against the states. Significant commentaries from that era include David Fellman, 1976, *The Defendant's Rights Today* (Madison: University of Wisconsin Press), and Fred P. Graham, 1970, *The Due Process Revolution: The Warren Court's Impact on Criminal Law* (Rochelle Park, NJ: Hayden Book Company, Inc., originally published in 1970 as *The Self-Inflicted Wound* [New York: Macmillan]).

A strong critique of the post–Warren Court decisions of the Supreme Court limiting the rights of the accused is John F. Decker, 1992, *Revolution to the Right: Criminal Procedure Jurisprudence During the Burger-Rehnquist Court Era* (New York: Garland Publishing, Inc.). A work that argues that in some respects the Court has gone too far in the other direction is Akhil Reed Amar, 1997, *The Constitution and Criminal Procedure: First Principles* (New Haven, CT: Yale University Press). A more fundamental critique of the Court's whole approach to criminal procedure, claiming that it has led to a dysfunctional criminal justice system, may be found in Donald A. Dripps, 2003, *About Guilt and Innocence: The Origins, Development, and Future of Constitutional Criminal Procedure* (Westport, CT: Praeger).

Right to Counsel

Competent reviews of the English and colonial background of the right to counsel and its development in American courts through the mid-twentieth century are provided by William M. Beaney, 1955, *The Right to Counsel in American Courts* (Ann Arbor: University of Michigan Press), and Francis Heller, 1969, *The Sixth Amendment to the Constitution of the United States* (New York: Greenwood Press, originally published in 1951 [Lawrence: University of Kansas Press]).

A thorough and judicious exposition of the nature, scope, content, and rationale of the contemporary right to counsel may be found in James J. Tomkovicz, 2002, *The Right to the Assistance of Counsel: A Reference Guide to the United States Constitution* (Westport, CT: Greenwood Press). Alfredo Garcia, 1992, *The Sixth Amendment in Modern American Jurisprudence: A Critical Perspective* (New York: Greenwood Press), contains a critique of the Burger and Rehnquist Court decisions restricting the right to counsel.

William F. McDonald, ed., 1983, *The Defense Counsel* (Beverly Hills, CA: Sage Publications), is an older but still useful study of defense counsel that focuses on the problem of defense of the indigent and carefully examines various systems of delivery of defense services.

Robert L. Spangenberg and Marea L. Beeman, 1995, "Indigent Defense Systems in the United States," *Law and Contemporary Problems* 58:31–49, provides a detailed survey of how states organize and fund their trial and appellate indigent defense systems, written as the reform movement was gathering steam. Three useful government reports on the same subject are Carol J. DeFrances, 2001, *State-Funded Indigent Defense Services, 1999,* a U.S. Department of Justice Bureau of Justice Statistics Special Report available online at <http://www.ojp.usdoj.gov/bjs/abstract/sfids99.htm>; Carol J. DeFrances and Marika F. X. Litras, 2000, *Indigent Defense Services in Large Counties, 1999,* a U.S. Department of Justice Bureau of Justice Statistics Bulletin, available online at <http://www.ojp.usdoj.gov/bjs/abstract/idslc99.htm>; and Caroline Wolf Harlow, 2000, *Defense Counsel in Criminal Cases,* a U.S. Department of Justice Bureau of Justice Statistics Special Report, available online at <http://www.ojp.usdoj.gov/bjs/abstract/dccc.htm>.

Richard Klein and Robert L. Spangenberg, 1993, provide a critique in *The Indigent Defense Crisis* (Washington, DC: American Bar Association). Glaring deficiencies in the provision of indigent defense services in New York City were documented by Jane Fritsch and David Rohde in a three-part series in the *New York Times* in 2003: "Lawyers Often Fail New York's Poor," (8 April, 1, late edition); "For the Poor, a Lawyer with 1600 Clients" (9 April, A1, late edition); "For Poor, Appeals Are Luck of the Draw" (10

April, A1, late edition). A more generalized critique is presented by Adele Bernhard, 2001, Effective Assistance of Counsel, Chap. 11 in *Wrongly Convicted: Perspectives on Failed Justice,* edited by Saundra D. Westervelt and John A. Humphrey (New Brunswick, NJ: Rutgers University Press).

Stephen B. Bright, 1994, "Counsel for the Poor: The Death Sentence Not for the Worst Crime but for the Worst Lawyer," *Yale Law Journal* 103:1835–1883, is an impassioned critique of the pervasive inadequacy of legal representation of indigent defendants in capital cases. Evidence for that interpretation can be found in James Liebman, Jeffrey Fagan, and Valerie West, 2000, *A Broken System: Error Rates in Capital Cases, 1973–1995,* a study commissioned by the U.S. Senate Judiciary Committee, available online at <http://justice.policy.net/proactive/newsroom/release.vtml?id=18200>, that documents the alarming rate of errors in capital trials and places much of the blame on incompetent defense counsel.

The acute shortage of counsel in death penalty appeals and the reasons why major law firms are increasingly unwilling to take on such cases as *pro bono* work are examined by Crystal Nix Hines, 2001, "Lack of Lawyers Hinders Appeals in Capital Cases," *New York Times* (5 July, A1, late edition).

The perspective of the federal court system on the problem of containing costs while providing effective appointed counsel in death-penalty cases was articulated by the Committee on Defender Services of the Judicial Conference of the United States, Subcommittee on Federal Death Penalty Cases, in a 1998 study, *Federal Death Penalty Cases: Recommendations Concerning the Cost and Quality of Defense Representation* (Washington, DC: Administrative Office of the U.S. Courts, Defender Services Division), available online at <http://www.uscourts.gov/dpenalty/1COVER.htm>.

A successful reform at the state level is discussed by Norman Lefstein, 1996, "Reform of Defense Representation in Capital Cases: The Indiana Experience and its Implications for the Nation," *Indiana Law Review* 29:495–533. On the other hand, serious failure of compliance with the Texas Fair Defense Act of 2001 is documented by the Equal Justice Center and the Texas Defender Service, 2003, in *Texas Death Penalty Practices: Quality of Regional Standards and County Plans Governing Indigent Defense in Capital Cases,* 2d ed., available online at <http://equaljusticecenter.org/new_page_47.htm>.

Deficiencies in the provision of defense services for indigents raise the more general problem of enforcement of standards of performance for attorneys. Michelle Craven and Michael Pitman, 2001, "To the Best of One's Ability: A Guide to Effective Lawyering," *Georgetown Journal of Legal Ethics* 14:983–999, examines the Model Rules of Professional Conduct and various methods of ensuring the competence of attorneys.

William S. Geimer, 1995, "A Decade of *Strickland's* Tin Horn: Doctrinal and Practical Undermining of the Right to Counsel," *William and Mary Bill of Rights Journal* 4:91–178, argues that the standard for determining claims of ineffective assistance of counsel enunciated in *Strickland v. Washington* has "deincorporated" the Sixth Amendment and tolerates unacceptably bad performance by defense attorneys. The notion of *Strickland's* tin horn is an ironic reference to Anthony Lewis's concept of *Gideon's* trumpet.

A survey of the law and practice of provision of counsel in juvenile proceedings is available in Tory J. Caeti, Craig Hemmens, and Velmer S. Burton Jr., 1996, "Juvenile Right to Counsel: A National Comparison of State Legal Codes," *American Journal of Criminal Law* 23:611–632. In 2003 the American Bar Association published a series of reports documenting serious inadequacies in the provision of counsel in juvenile justice systems, covering twelve states so far: *Justice Cut Short: New Reports Show That "Conveyor Belt Justice" Hurts Children,* news release and state reports available online at <http://www.manningmedia.net/Clients/ABA/ABA274/index.htm>.

For right-to-counsel cases, see the classic study of the circumstances of *Powell v. Alabama* in Dan T. Carter, 1969 (rev. ed. 1979), *Scottsboro: A Tragedy of the American South* (Baton Rouge: Louisiana State University Press), a fine analysis of the social milieu, litigation, and political machinations in the Scottsboro affair. Gilbert Geis and Leigh B. Bienen, 1998, *Crimes of the Century* (Boston: Northeastern University Press), includes a chapter that presents a concise and sometimes provocative account of the Scottsboro cases but contains some factual errors. A rich and fascinating tapestry of essays exploring the character and perspective of all the important participants in the infinitely complex saga of the Scottsboro affair is presented in James Goodman, 1995, *Stories of Scottsboro* (New York: Vintage Books, originally published in 1994 by New York: Pantheon Books).

Anthony Lewis, 1964, *Gideon's Trumpet* (New York: Random House), became an instant classic as a well-written and informative case study that recounts the story of the landmark right-to-counsel decision in *Gideon v. Wainwright,* while more generally providing a good introduction to the operating procedures of the Supreme Court. Jerold H. Israel, 1963, "*Gideon v. Wainwright:* The 'Art' of Overruling," *Supreme Court Review*

1963:211–272, uses the same case to analyze the need for persuasive reasons to justify the overruling of a precedent of constitutional dimension.

Thomas N. McInnis, 2001, *The Christian Burial Case* (Westport, CT: Praeger), is an introductory textbook on the operation of the criminal justice process, organized around the case of *Brewer v. Williams.*

Privilege against Self-Incrimination

For many years the standard work on the history of this topic was Leonard W. Levy, 1968, *Origins of the Fifth Amendment: The Right Against Self-Incrimination* (New York: Oxford University Press). Levy provides an exhaustive study of the English and colonial background of the Fifth Amendment that is still valuable but in some respects has been challenged by more recent research. The foremost authority now is R. H. Helmholz, Charles M. Gray, John H. Langbein, Eben Moglen, Henry E. Smith, and Albert W. Alschuler, 1997, *The Privilege against Self-Incrimination: Its Origins and Development* (Chicago: University of Chicago Press), a careful treatment of the evolution of the privilege from the Middle Ages to contemporary controversy.

Erwin N. Griswold's 1955 volume *The Fifth Amendment Today* (Cambridge, MA: Harvard University Press) is a traditional defense of the privilege, written by an eminent legal scholar during its disparagement in the McCarthy era; Sidney Hook, 1957, *Common Sense and the Fifth Amendment* (New York: Criterion Books), is a partial rebuttal by a controversial philosopher.

More legally sophisticated critiques from the time the privilege was being liberalized by the Supreme Court include Lewis Mayers, 1959, *Shall We Amend the Fifth Amendment?* (New York: Harper), and, especially influential, Henry J. Friendly, 1968, "The Fifth Amendment Tomorrow: The Case for Constitutional Change," *University of Cincinnati Law Review* 37:671–726. Friendly, an eminent jurist, applauded Griswold's stand against McCarthyism but, in his title as well as his text, suggested that in a new era the Warren Court had engaged in unwarranted extensions of the privilege. The challenge posed by McCarthyism is not forgotten, however, as evidenced by Haig A. Bosmajian, 1999, *The Freedom Not to Speak* (New York: New York University Press), a critique of compelled revelations of political beliefs and associations that raises issues under both the First and Fifth Amendments.

Mark Berger, 1980, *Taking the Fifth: The Supreme Court and the Privilege against Self-Incrimination* (Lexington, MA: Lexington Books), is a careful study of the history, philosophy, and legal evolution of the privilege through the 1970s. Stephen A. Saltzburg, 1986, "The Required Records Doctrine: Its Lessons for the Privilege against Self-Incrimination," *University of Chicago Law Review* 53:6–44, analyzes the doctrinal problems and practical considerations regarding the privilege as revealed in relationships among major self-incrimination decisions regarding required records, reporting and disclosure, and corporate entities.

John Fabian Witt, 1999, "Making the Fifth: The Constitutionalization of American Self-Incrimination Doctrine, 1791–1903," *Texas Law Review* 77:825–922, presents an analysis of the nineteenth-century transformation of the privilege in state and federal law from a common-law doctrine to bar self-serving testimony to a constitutional right of the individual based on privacy—and of the doctrinal confusion resulting from the twentieth-century abandonment of that rationale. A leading defender of the privilege as a protector of privacy is Robert S. Gerstein, 1970, "Privacy and Self-Incrimination," *Ethics,* 80:87–101.

Other commentators, however, find no coherent rationale for the privilege, whatever its practical benefits. One of those is Donald A. Dripps, 1988, "Against Police Interrogation—And the Privilege against Self-Incrimination," *Journal of Criminal Law and Criminology* 78:699–734, and another is David Dolinko, 1986, "Is There a Rationale for the Privilege against Self-Incrimination?" *U.C.L.A. Law Review* 33:1063–1148. Dolinko argues that the privilege cannot be supported as furthering either the goals of the criminal justice system or individual rights and therefore "can be explained by specific historical developments, but cannot be justified either functionally or conceptually" (1147).

In a 1988 article, "Self-Incrimination and Excuse," *Columbia Law Review* 88:1227–1296, William J. Stuntz adopts a pragmatic view of the privilege as best explained as a policy choice that is preferable to rampant perjury or a doctrine of excusable self-protective perjury.

In contrast to the critics of the Warren Court jurisprudence, some commentators think the Court has unduly narrowed the privilege. For example, Richard A. Nagareda, 1999, "Compulsion 'To Be a Witness' and the Resurrection of *Boyd,*" *New York University Law Review* 74:1575–1659, argues that in allowing the compelled production of incriminating documents the

Court has significantly and erroneously reduced the protections available prior to the twentieth century.

Stark descriptions of the brutal "third degree" tactics of police interrogation that were common in an earlier era are contained in Emanuel H. Levine, 1930, *The "Third Degree": A Detailed and Appalling Exposé of Police Brutality* (New York: Vanguard Press); Ernest J. Hopkins, 1931, *Our Lawless Police* (New York: Viking); and the National Commission on Law Observance and Enforcement, 1931, *Report on Lawlessness in Law Enforcement*—the Wickersham Commission Report (Washington: U.S. Government Printing Office).

The transition to a new style of interrogation is shown by Richard A. Leo, 1992, "From Coercion to Deception: The Changing Nature of Police Interrogation in America," *Crime, Law and Social Change* 18:35–59. David Simon, 1991, *Homicide: A Year on the Killing Streets* (Boston: Houghton Mifflin), is a riveting journalistic account of policing in Baltimore that includes a vivid description of deceptive and manipulative techniques of interrogation. Addressing these more sophisticated modern practices, Lawrence S. Wrightsman and Saul M. Kassin's 1993 book *Confessions in the Courtroom* (Newbury Park, CA: Sage Publications) analyzes the law and psychology of confession with attention to techniques of interrogation, motivation for true and false confession, the problem of determining voluntariness, and juror reactions to confessions.

Richard A. Leo, 2001, False Confessions: Causes, Consequences, and Solutions, Chap. 2 in In *Wrongly Convicted: Perspectives on Failed Justice,* edited by Saundra D. Westervelt and John A. Humphrey (New Brunswick, NJ: Rutgers University Press), is an analysis of how the psychological techniques of police interrogation can induce persons to confess to crimes they did not commit. Albert W. Alschuler, 1997, "Constraint and Confession," *Denver University Law Review* 74:957–978, discusses offensive police interrogation practices that should render confessions inadmissible.

Charles D. Weisselberg, 1998, "Saving *Miranda,*" *Cornell Law Review* 84:109–192, warns of the growing practice of police interrogation "outside *Miranda*"—that is, interrogation in deliberate violation of *Miranda* requirements. Jan Hoffman reports on many of these problems in two *New York Times* articles in 1998: "Police Tactics Chipping Away at Suspects' Rights" (29 March, 1, late edition), and "Police Refine Methods So Potent, Even the Innocent Have Confessed" (30 March, A1, late edition). Donald A. Dripps, 1988, "Against Police Interrogation—And the Privilege against Self-Incrimination," *Journal of Criminal Law and Criminology* 78:699–734, argues that a proper balance between the goals of gathering evidence of crime and preventing abusive police tactics can be achieved only by abolishing the privilege against self-incrimination, making all statements taken by police inadmissible, and having magistrates conduct the examination of suspects.

Roger W. Shuy, 1998, *The Language of Confession, Interrogation, and Deception* (Thousand Oaks, CA: Sage Publications), explores forensic linguistics, focusing on the elicitation and interpretation of criminal confessions as presented in case studies of actual police interrogations. Peter Brooks, 2000, *Troubling Confessions: Speaking Guilt in Law and Literature* (Chicago: University of Chicago Press), is an extended essay on the ambivalence of our cultural, religious, literary, psychological, and legal conceptions of the concept of confession.

Miranda v. Arizona

Otis H. Stephens, 1973, *The Supreme Court and Confessions of Guilt* (Knoxville: University of Tennessee Press), is a study of the evolution of the law of coerced confessions in the Supreme Court, written shortly after the *Miranda* decision. A journalist's detailed account of that case and the surrounding legal and political issues is Liva Baker's 1983 volume *Miranda: Crime, Law and Politics* (New York: Atheneum). Key law review articles by the leading defender of *Miranda* are collected in Yale Kamisar, 1980, *Police Interrogation and Confessions: Essays in Law and Policy* (Ann Arbor: University of Michigan Press).

A leading critic of *Miranda,* Joseph D. Grano, reworked his law review articles into book form and in 1993 published *Confessions, Truth, and the Law* (Ann Arbor: University of Michigan Press), the most systematic and sustained rebuttal of the law and policy of the *Miranda* decision, arguing that it downgrades the goal of discovering truth by unduly restricting police interrogation. Kamisar had already responded to Grano in 1990, "Remembering the 'Old World' of Criminal Procedure: A Reply to Professor Grano," *University of Michigan Journal of Law Reform* 23:537–589.

Surveying the first decade of implementation of *Miranda,* Geoffrey R. Stone in 1977 argued in "The *Miranda* Doctrine in the Burger Court," *Supreme Court Review* 1977:99–169, that a majority of justices basically hostile to the decision had refrained from overruling its core holding but consistently limited its application in ways that supported law enforcement.

John N. Ferdico's 2001 textbook for law enforcement officers, *Criminal Procedure for the Criminal Justice Professional,* 8th ed. (Belmont, CA: Wadsworth), has a detailed chapter on issues of compliance with *Miranda.* Police adaptation to the new requirements in order to gain waivers of rights and incriminating statements from suspects is shown by Richard A. Leo, 1996, "*Miranda's* Revenge: Police Interrogation as a Confidence Game," *Law and Society Review* 30:259–288, and by Leo and Welsh S. White, 1999, "Adapting to *Miranda:* Modern Interrogators' Strategies for Dealing with the Obstacles Posed by *Miranda,*" *Minnesota Law Review* 84:397–472. These developments have drawn serious criticism from Welsh S. White, 2001, *Miranda's Waning Protections* (Ann Arbor: University of Michigan Press), who concludes that, in practice, *Miranda* neither significantly handicaps police nor adequately protects suspects, and Alfredo Garcia, 2002, *The Fifth Amendment: A Comprehensive Approach* (Westport, CT: Greenwood Press), who offers a withering criticism of the emasculation of *Miranda.*

There has been a major debate over whether or not *Miranda* has had a deleterious effect on law enforcement. Richard A. Leo and George C. Thomas III, eds., 1998, *The Miranda Debate: Law, Justice, and Policing* (Boston: Northeastern University Press), is a balanced and carefully edited compilation of supportive and critical analyses of the legal, policy, and ethical dimensions of the *Miranda* decision and of its actual effect on police behavior. Readers wishing to explore the *Miranda* debate would do well to start here.

The most sustained and forceful criticism of *Miranda* appears in the works of Paul G. Cassell, who argues that the decision exacts a high cost in lost confessions and convictions. His major articles include, 1996, "Miranda's Social Costs: An Empirical Reassessment," *Northwestern University Law Review* 90:387–499; 1998, "Protecting the Innocent from False Confessions and Lost Confessions—and from Miranda," *Journal of Criminal Law and Criminology* 88:497–556; with Bret S. Hayman, 1996, "Police Interrogation in the 1990s: An Empirical Study of the Effects of *Miranda,*" *UCLA Law Review* 43:839–931; and with Richard Fowles, 1998, "Handcuffing the Cops? A Thirty-Year Perspective on *Miranda's* Harmful Effects on Law Enforcement," *Stanford Law Review* 50:1055–1145.

Stephen J. Schulhofer counters in two 1996 articles that the evidence reveals that *Miranda* imposes no such cost on law enforcement: "*Miranda's* Practical Effect: Substantial Benefits and Vanishingly Small Social Costs," *Northwestern University Law Review* 90:500–563, and "*Miranda* and

Clearance Rates," *Northwestern University Law Review* 91:278–294. George C. Thomas III, 1996, "Plain Talk About the *Miranda* Empirical Debate: A 'Steady-State' Theory of Confessions," *UCLA Law Review* 33:933–959, agrees that the data fail to demonstrate an adverse effect on the confession rate. In a third article, Schulhofer asserts that even if *Miranda* did burden law enforcement that would simply be a necessary cost of enforcing a constitutional requirement: 1997, "Bashing Miranda Is Unjustified—and Harmful," *Harvard Journal of Law and Public Policy* 20:347–373.

Balanced assessments of the policy debate may be found in several sources. Richard A. Leo, 1996, "The Impact of *Miranda* Revisited," *Journal of Criminal Law and Criminology* 86:621–692, concludes that the most important consequence of *Miranda* has been its civilizing and professionalizing effect on police behavior. George C. Thomas III and Richard A. Leo, 2002, "The Effects of *Miranda v. Arizona:* 'Embedded' in Our National Culture?" *Crime and Justice* 29:203–271, agree with Welsh White that *Miranda* has neither significantly helped suspects nor significantly hindered police. Peter Arenella provides a witty but serious critique of the excesses and weaknesses in the arguments of both Cassell and Schulhofer in his 1997 article "*Miranda* Stories," *Harvard Journal of Law and Public Policy* 20:375–387.

Other Self-Incrimination Cases

Richard C. Cortner, 1986, *A "Scottsboro" Case in Mississippi: The Supreme Court and* Brown v. Mississippi (Jackson: University Press of Mississippi), is a study of the first key case in which the Supreme Court held a state's use of coerced confessions to be a violation of due process of law.

There are innumerable law review articles on Supreme Court decisions, and the citations that follow bear on some of the issues discussed in this volume. John H. Mansfield, 1966, "The *Albertson* Case: Conflict Between the Privilege against Self-Incrimination and the Government's Need for Information," *Supreme Court Review* 1966, 103–166, is a contemporary analysis of *Albertson v. Subversive Activities Control Board,* interpreting it as a threshold attempt to achieve a better balance between the privilege against self-incrimination and the legitimate need of the government for extensive information. Bernard D. Meltzer, 1971, "Privilege against Self-Incrimination and the Hit-and-Run Opinions," *Supreme Court Review* 1971, 1–30, is an analysis of *California v. Byers* that concludes that neither the plurality nor the dissenting opinions succeeded in bringing doctrinal order to past reporting and required records decisions, and that Justice Harlan's concurring opinion made the most sense. Robert P. Mosteller, 2001, "Cowboy Prosecutors and Subpoenas for Incriminating Evidence: The Consequences and Correction of Excess," *Washington and Lee Law Review* 58:487–548, is a critique of *United States v. Hubbell,* arguing that a reckless strategy by the Office of Independent Counsel led to a decision that restricted the ability of prosecutors to make use of documents for which immunity has been granted as to the act of production. Mosteller judges the rebuke to prosecutors well deserved and the consequences for future cases unclear; H. Richard Uviller, 2001, "*Fisher* Goes On the Quintessential Fishing Expedition and Hubbell Is off the Hook," *Journal of Criminal Law and Criminology* 91:311–335, argues that the *Hubbell* decision threatens to cripple the investigation of complex cases of white-collar crime.

Alexa Young, 1999, Note: "When Is a Request a Request?: Inadequate Constitutional Protection for Women in Police Interrogations," *Florida Law Review* 51:143–160, is a feminist critique of *Davis v. United States,* arguing that the requirement of unambiguous requests for counsel under *Miranda* warnings discriminates against the less assertive and more indirect linguistic style of many women. *Dickerson v. United States,* the decision reaffirming *Miranda,* is examined by *Miranda's* leading defender in Yale Kamisar, 2001, "*Miranda* Thirty-five Years Later: A Close Look at the Majority and Dissenting Opinions in *Dickerson,*" *Arizona State Law Journal* 33:387–428, and by its leading critic in Paul Cassell, 2001, "The Paths Not Taken: The Supreme Court's Failures in *Dickerson,*" *Michigan Law Review* 99:898–940. Donald A. Dripps, 2001, "Constitutional Theory for Criminal Procedure: *Dickerson, Miranda,* and the Continuing Quest for Broad-but-shallow," *William and Mary Law Review* 43:1–77, defends the broad rule laid down in *Miranda* but uses *Dickerson* to explain why it is so difficult to sustain the justification of broad rules over time.

Constitutional Rights and the War on Terror

David Cole and James X. Dempsey, 2002, *Terrorism and the Constitution: Sacrificing Civil Liberties in the Name of National Security* (New York: The New Press), is a critique of the antiterror policies and activities of the U.S. government, with primary emphasis on the threat to First Amendment values. Cynthia Brown, ed., 2003, *Lost Liberties: Ashcroft and the Assault on Personal Freedom* (New York: The New Press), is a collection of powerful essays about the perceived loss of civil liberties under the second Bush administration. In his 2003 volume *Enemy Aliens: Double Standards and Constitutional Freedoms in the War on Terrorism* (New York: The New Press), David Cole makes the case for treating citizens and noncitizens equally under the law. Richard C. Leone and Greg Anrig Jr., 2003, *The War on Our Freedoms: Civil Liberties in an Age of Terrorism* (New York: The Century Foundation), a collection of essays by a panel of distinguished commentators, presents a more balanced position but is still highly critical of government policy. Philip B. Heymann, 2003, *Terrorism, Freedom, and Security: Winning Without War* (Cambridge, MA: MIT Press), concedes the need to deal with the threat of terrorism but finds current policies not worth the cost to democratic values.

In his 2003 book *After: How America Confronted the September 12 Era* (New York: Simon and Schuster), Steven Brill presents a day-by-day chronicle of the activities of the U.S. government and other important parties during the year following the terrorist attacks of 11 September 2001, with much information about the law enforcement policies and strategies of Attorney General John Ashcroft.

Adam Liptak, Neil A. Lewis, and Benjamin Weiser, 2002, "After September 11, a Legal Battle on the Limits of Civil Liberty," *New York Times* (4 August, 1, early edition), discusses various civil liberties issues that arose in connection with the detention of material witnesses, enemy combatants, and persons charged with immigration violations. Legal issues arising in the case of the "American Taliban" John Walker Lindh are analyzed in M. K. B. Darmer, 2002, "Lessons from the *Lindh* Case: Public Safety and the Fifth Amendment," *Brooklyn Law Review* 68:241–287.

A more general discussion of the applicability of the privilege against self-incrimination to persons interrogated by American agents overseas appears in Adam Shedd, 2003, Comment: "The Fifth Amendment Privilege against Self-Incrimination—Does It Exist Extraterritorially?" *Tulane Law Review* 77:767–787.

Internet Sources

Some specific sources available online have been cited above. More generally, useful sites include:

Bureau of Justice Statistics
<http://www.ojp.usdoj.gov/bjs/welcome.html>. Much statistically based information about the criminal justice system is available from the bureau, which is part of the U.S. Department of Justice. Indigent defense statistics are at <http://www.ojp.usdoj.gov/bjs/id.htm>.

Famous Trials
<http://www.law.umkc.edu/faculty/projects/ftrials/ftrials.htm>. This site provides vivid accounts of many famous trials in history, including the trial of the Scottsboro Boys, along with biographies of key participants.

Findlaw
<http://www.findlaw.com>. A comprehensive site with information for legal professionals, students, and the general public. Supreme Court decisions from 1893 to the present are accessible at <http://www.findlaw.com/casecode/supreme.html>.

Guide to Law Online
<http://www.loc.gov/law/guide>. A very helpful compilation of links to sites on a great many legal topics, prepared by the U.S. Law Library of Congress.

Lexis-Nexis Academic Universe
<http://web.lexis-nexis.com/universe>. Lexis-Nexis is a subscription database for general news and legal and business information. The Academic Universe is available without charge at most educational institutions and gives access to all federal court decisions, state appellate court decisions, federal and state laws, and law review articles.

U.S. Code
<http://www.gpoaccess.gov/uscode/index.html>. The official codification of all federal laws, in searchable form. The code may also be searched at
<http://uscode.house.gov/usc.htm>.

U.S. Courts
<http://www.uscourts.gov/links.html>. Provides links to the websites of all the federal courts of appeals and district courts, where their decisions are available.

U.S. Department of Justice

<http://www.usdoj.gov>. The perspective of the federal government on legal issues, particularly those relating to the war on terror, is available on this site, along with some official documents.

U.S. Supreme Court

<http://www.supremecourtus.gov>. Provides information about the Supreme Court for practicing attorneys and the general public, including briefs, transcripts of oral arguments, recent decisions, and information about the status of pending cases.

Index

About the Author

John B. Taylor is Louis L. Goldstein Professor of Public Affairs and chair of the department of political science at Washington College, Chestertown, Maryland, where he teaches courses on American criminal justice and civil liberties and advises pre-law students. He received his doctorate from Princeton University and also studied at the University of California, Santa Barbara, on a fellowship from the National Endowment for the Humanities. Professor Taylor specializes in American constitutional law and history and issues of civil liberties, and his publications include articles in the *Review of Politics* and the *Journal of Supreme Court History.*